A Popular Account of Dr. Livingstone's Expedition to the Zambesi and Its Tributaries

David Livingstone

Contents

NOTICE TO THIS WORK. 8
PREFACE. 9
THE ZAMBESI AND ITS TRIBUTARIES. 11
INTRODUCTION. 11
CHAPTER I. 16
CHAPTER II. 36
CHAPTER III. 55
CHAPTER IV. 72
CHAPTER V. 94
CHAPTER VI. 113
CHAPTER VII. 133
CHAPTER VIII. 154
CHAPTER IX. 174
CHAPTER X. 197
CHAPTER XI. 215
CHAPTER XII. 236
CHAPTER XIII. 257
CHAPTER XIV. 279
CHAPTER XV. 300
NOTES 311

A POPULAR ACCOUNT OF DR. LIVINGSTONE'S EXPEDITION TO THE ZAMBESI AND ITS TRIBUTARIES

BY
David Livingstone

TO THE RIGHT HON. LORD PALMERSTON, K.G., G.C.B.

My Lord,

I beg leave to dedicate this Volume to your Lordship, as a tribute justly due to the great Statesman who has ever had at heart the amelioration of the African race; and as a token of admiration of the beneficial effects of that policy which he has so long laboured to establish on the West Coast of Africa; and which, in improving that region, has most forcibly shown the need of some similar system on the opposite side of the Continent.

DAVID LIVINGSTONE.

NOTICE TO THIS WORK.

The name of the late Mr. Charles Livingstone takes a prominent place amongst those who acted under the leadership of Dr. Livingstone during the adventurous sojourn of the "Zambesi Expedition" in East Africa. In laying the result of their discoveries before the public, it was arranged that Mr. Charles Livingstone should place his voluminous notes at the disposal of his brother: they are incorporated in the present work, but in a necessarily abridged form.

PREFACE.

It has been my object in this work to give as clear an account as I was able of tracts of country previously unexplored, with their river systems, natural productions, and capabilities; and to bring before my countrymen, and all others interested in the cause of humanity, the misery entailed by the slave-trade in its inland phases; a subject on which I and my companions are the first who have had any opportunities of forming a judgment. The eight years spent in Africa, since my last work was published, have not, I fear, improved my power of writing English; but I hope that, whatever my descriptions want in clearness, or literary skill, may in a measure be compensated by the novelty of the scenes described, and the additional information afforded on that curse of Africa, and that shame, even now, in the 19th century, of an European nation,--the slave-trade.

I took the "Lady Nyassa" to Bombay for the express purpose of selling her, and might without any difficulty have done so; but with the thought of parting with her arose, more strongly than ever, the feeling of disinclination to abandon the East Coast of Africa to the Portuguese and slave-trading, and I determined to run home and consult my friends before I allowed the little vessel to pass from my hands. After, therefore, having put two Ajawa lads, Chuma and Wakatani, to school under the eminent missionary the Rev. Dr. Wilson, and having provided satisfactorily for the native crew, I started homewards with the three white sailors, and reached London July 20th, 1864. Mr. and Mrs. Webb, my much-loved friends, wrote to Bombay inviting me, in the event of my coming to England, to make Newstead Abbey my headquarters, and on my arrival renewed their invitation: and though, when I accepted it, I had no intention of remaining so long with my kind-hearted generous friends, I stayed with them until April, 1865, and under their roof transcribed from my own and my brother's journal the whole of this present book. It is with heartfelt gratitude I would record their unwearied kindness. My acquaintance with Mr. Webb began in Africa, where he was a daring and successful hunter, and his continued friendship is most valuable because he has seen missionary work, and he would not accord his respect and esteem to me had he not believed that I, and my brethren also, were to be looked on as honest men earnestly trying to do our duty.

The Government have supported the proposal of the Royal Geographical Society made by my friend Sir Roderick Murchison, and have united with that body to aid me in another attempt to open Africa to civilizing influences, and a valued private friend has given a thousand pounds for the same object. I propose to go inland, north of the territory which the Portuguese in Europe claim, and endeavour to commence that system on the East which has been so eminently successful on the West Coast; a system combining the repressive efforts of H.M. cruisers with lawful trade and Christian Missions--the moral and material results of which have been so gratifying. I hope to ascend the Rovuma, or some other river North of Cape Delgado, and, in addition to my other work, shall strive, by passing along the Northern end of Lake Nyassa and round the Southern end of Lake Tanganyika, to ascertain the watershed of that part of Africa. In so doing, I have no wish to unsettle what with so much toil and danger was accomplished by Speke and Grant, but rather to confirm their illustrious discoveries.

I have to acknowledge the obliging readiness of Lord Russell in lending me the drawings taken by the artist who was in the first instance attached to the Expedition. These sketches, with photographs by Charles Livingstone and Dr. Kirk, have materially assisted in the illustrations. I would also very sincerely thank my friends Professor Owen and Mr. Oswell for many valuable hints and other aid in the preparation of this volume.

Newstead Abbey,
April 16, 1865.

THE ZAMBESI AND ITS TRIBUTARIES.
INTRODUCTION.

Objects of the Expedition--Personal Interest shown by Naval Authorities--Members of the Zambesi Expedition.

When first I determined on publishing the narrative of my "Missionary Travels," I had a great misgiving as to whether the criticism my endeavours might provoke would be friendly or the reverse, more particularly as I felt that I had then been so long a sojourner in the wilderness, as to be quite a stranger to the British public. But I am now in this, my second essay at authorship, cheered by the conviction that very many readers, who are personally unknown to me, will receive this narrative with the kindly consideration and allowances of friends; and that many more, under the genial influences of an innate love of liberty, and of a desire to see the same social and religious blessings they themselves enjoy, disseminated throughout the world, will sympathize with me in the efforts by which I have striven, however imperfectly, to elevate the position and character of our fellow-men in Africa. This knowledge makes me doubly anxious to render my narrative acceptable to all my readers; but, in the absence of any excellence in literary composition, the natural consequence of my pursuits, I have to offer only a simple account of a mission which, with respect to the objects proposed to be thereby accomplished, formed a noble contrast to some of the earlier expeditions to Eastern Africa. I believe that the information it will give, respecting the people visited and the countries traversed, will not be materially gainsaid by any future commonplace traveller like myself, who may be blest with fair health and a gleam of sunshine in his breast. This account is written in the earnest hope that it may contribute to that information which will yet cause the great and fertile continent of Africa to be no longer kept wantonly sealed, but made available as the scene of European enterprise, and will enable its people to take a place among the nations of the earth, thus securing the happiness and prosperity of tribes now sunk in barbarism or debased by slavery; and, above all, I cherish the hope that it may lead to the introduction of the blessings of the Gospel.

In order that the following narrative may be clearly understood, it is necessary to call to mind some things which took place previous to the Zambesi Expedition being sent out. Most geographers are aware that, before the discovery of Lake Ngami and the well-watered country in which the Makololo dwell, the idea prevailed that a large part of the interior of Africa consisted of sandy deserts, into which rivers ran and were lost. During my journey in 1852-6, from sea to sea, across the south intertropical part of the continent, it was found to be a well-watered country, with large tracts of fine fertile soil covered with forest, and beautiful grassy valleys, occupied by a considerable population; and one of the most wonderful waterfalls in the world was brought to light. The peculiar form of the continent was then ascertained to be an elevated plateau, somewhat depressed in the centre, and with fissures in the sides by which the rivers escaped to the sea; and this great fact in physical geography can never be referred to without calling to mind the remarkable hypothesis by which the distinguished President of the Royal Geographical Society (Sir Roderick I. Murchison) clearly indicated this peculiarity, before it was verified by actual observation of the altitudes of the country and by the courses of the rivers. New light was thrown on other portions of the continent by the famous travels of Dr. Barth, by the researches of the Church of England missionaries Krapf, Erkhardt, and Rebman, by the persevering efforts of Dr. Baikie, the last martyr to the climate and English enterprise, by the journey of Francis Galton, and by the most interesting discoveries of Lakes Tanganyika and Victoria Nyanza by Captain Burton, and by Captain Speke, whose untimely end we all so deeply deplore. Then followed the researches of Van der Decken, Thornton, and others; and last of all the grand discovery of the main source of the Nile, which every Englishman must feel an honest pride in knowing was accomplished by our gallant countrymen, Speke and Grant. The fabulous torrid zone, of parched and burning sand, was now proved to be a well-watered region resembling North America in its fresh-water lakes, and India in its hot humid lowlands, jungles, ghauts, and cool highland plains.

A Popular Account of Dr. Livingstone's Expedition to the Zambesi

The main object of this Zambesi Expedition, as our instructions from Her Majesty's Government explicitly stated, was to extend the knowledge already attained of the geography and mineral and agricultural resources of Eastern and Central Africa--to improve our acquaintance with the inhabitants, and to endeavour to engage them to apply themselves to industrial pursuits and to the cultivation of their lands, with a view to the production of raw material to be exported to England in return for British manufactures; and it was hoped that, by encouraging the natives to occupy themselves in the development of the resources of the country, a considerable advance might be made towards the extinction of the slave- trade, as they would not be long in discovering that the former would eventually be a more certain source of profit than the latter. The Expedition was sent in accordance with the settled policy of the English Government; and the Earl of Clarendon, being then at the head of the Foreign Office, the Mission was organized under his immediate care. When a change of Government ensued, we experienced the same generous countenance and sympathy from the Earl of Malmesbury, as we had previously received from Lord Clarendon; and, on the accession of Earl Russell to the high office he has so long filled, we were always favoured with equally ready attention and the same prompt assistance. Thus the conviction was produced that our work embodied the principles, not of any one party, but of the hearts of the statesmen and of the people of England generally. The Expedition owes great obligations to the Lords of the Admiralty for their unvarying readiness to render us every assistance in their power; and to the warm-hearted and ever-obliging hydrographer to the Admiralty, the late Admiral Washington, as a subordinate, but most effective agent, our heartfelt gratitude is also due; and we must ever thankfully acknowledge that our efficiency was mainly due to the kind services of Admirals Sir Frederick Grey, Sir Baldwin Walker, and all the naval officers serving under them on the East Coast. Nor must I omit to record our obligations to Mr. Skead, R.N. The Luawe was carefully sounded and surveyed by this officer, whose skilful and zealous labours, both on that river, and afterwards on the Lower Zambesi, were deserving of all praise.

In speaking of what has been done by the Expedition, it should always be understood that Dr. Kirk, Mr. Charles Livingstone, Mr. R. Thornton, and others composed it. In using the plural number they are meant, and I wish to bear testimony to the untiring zeal, energy, courage, and perseverance with which my companions laboured; undaunted by difficulties, dangers, or hard fare. It is my firm belief that, were their services required in any other capacity, they might be implicitly relied on to perform their duty like men. The reason why Dr. Kirk's name does not appear on the title-page of this narrative is, because it is hoped that he may give an account of the botany and natural history of the Expedition in a separate work from his own pen. He collected above four thousand species of plants, specimens of most of the valuable woods, of the different native manufactures, of the articles of food, and of the different kinds of cotton from every spot we visited, and a great variety of birds and insects; besides making meteorological observations, and affording, as our instructions required, medical assistance to the natives in every case where he could be of any use.

Charles Livingstone was also fully occupied in his duties in following out the general objects of our mission, in encouraging the culture of cotton, in making many magnetic and meteorological observations, in photographing so long as the materials would serve, and in collecting a large number of birds, insects, and other objects of interest. The collections, being Government property, have been forwarded to the British Museum, and to the Royal Botanic, Gardens at Kew; and should Dr. Kirk undertake their description, three or four years will be required for the purpose.

Though collections were made, it was always distinctly understood that, however desirable these and our explorations might be, "Her Majesty's Government attached more importance to the moral influence that might be exerted on the minds of the natives by a well-regulated and orderly household of Europeans setting an example of consistent moral conduct to all who might witness it; treating the people with kindness, and relieving their wants, teaching them to make experiments in agriculture, explaining to them the more simple arts, imparting to them religious instruction as far as they are capable of receiving it, and inculcating peace and good will to each other."

It would be tiresome to enumerate in detail all the little acts which were performed by us while following out our instructions. As a rule, whenever the steamer stopped to take in wood, or for any other purpose, Dr. Kirk and Charles Livingstone went ashore to their duties: one of our party, who it was intended should navigate the vessel and lay down the geographical positions, having failed to answer the expectations formed of him, these duties fell chiefly to my share. They involved a considerable amount of night work, in which I was always cheerfully aided by my companions, and the results were regularly communicated to our warm and ever-ready friend, Sir Thomas Maclear of the Royal Observatory, Cape of Good Hope. While this work was going through the press, we were favoured with the longitudes of several stations determined from observed occultations of stars by the moon, and from eclipses and reappearances of Jupiter's satellites, by Mr. Mann, the able Assistant to the Cape Astronomer Royal; the lunars are still in the hands of Mr. G. W. H. Maclear of the same Observatory. In addition to these, the altitudes, variations of the compass, latitudes and longitudes, as calculated on the spot, appear in the map by Mr. Arrowsmith, and it is hoped may not differ much from the results of the same data in abler hands. The office of "skipper," which, rather than let the Expedition come to a stand, I undertook, required no great ability in one "not too old to learn:" it saved a salary, and, what was much more valuable than gold, saved the Expedition from the drawback of any one thinking that he was indispensable to its further progress. The office required attention to the vessel both at rest and in motion. It also involved considerable exposure to the sun; and to my regret kept me from much anticipated intercourse with the natives, and the formation of full vocabularies of their dialects.

I may add that all wearisome repetitions are as much as possible avoided in the narrative; and, our movements and operations having previously been given in a series of despatches, the attempt is now made to give as fairly as possible just what would most strike any person of ordinary intelligence in passing through the country. For the sake of the freshness which usually attaches to first impressions, the Journal of Charles Livingstone has been incorporated in the narrative; and many remarks made by the natives, which ho put down at the moment of translation, will convey to others the same ideas as they did to ourselves. Some are no doubt trivial; but it is by the little acts and words of every-day life that character is truly and best known. And doubtless many will prefer to draw their own conclusions from them rather than to be schooled by us.

CHAPTER I.

Arrival at the Zambesi--Rebel Warfare--Wild Animals--Shupanga--Hippopotamus Hunters--The Makololo--Crocodiles.

The Expedition left England on the 10th of March, 1858, in Her Majesty's Colonial Steamer "Pearl," commanded by Captain Duncan; and, after enjoying the generous hospitality of our friends at Cape Town, with the obliging attentions of Sir George Grey, and receiving on board Mr. Francis Skead, R.N., as surveyor, we reached the East Coast in the following May.

Our first object was to explore the Zambesi, its mouths and tributaries, with a view to their being used as highways for commerce and Christianity to pass into the vast interior of Africa. When we came within five or six miles of the land, the yellowish-green tinge of the sea in soundings was suddenly succeeded by muddy water with wrack, as of a river in flood. The two colours did not intermingle, but the line of contact was as sharply defined as when the ocean meets the land. It was observed that under the wrack--consisting of reeds, sticks, and leaves,--and even under floating cuttlefish bones and Portuguese "men-of-war" (Physalia), numbers of small fish screen themselves from the eyes of birds of prey, and from the rays of the torrid sun.

We entered the river Luawe first, because its entrance is so smooth and deep, that the "Pearl," drawing 9 feet 7 inches, went in without a boat sounding ahead. A small steam launch having been brought out from England in three sections on the deck of the "Pearl" was hoisted out and screwed together at the anchorage, and with her aid the exploration was commenced. She was called the "Ma Robert," after Mrs. Livingstone, to whom the natives, according to their custom, gave the name Ma (mother) of her eldest son. The harbour is deep, but shut in by mangrove swamps; and though the water a few miles up is fresh, it is only a tidal river; for, after ascending some seventy miles, it was found to end in marshes blocked up with reeds and succulent aquatic plants. As the Luawe had been called "West Luabo," it was supposed to be a branch of the Zambesi, the main stream of which is called "Luabo," or "East Luabo." The "Ma Robert" and "Pearl" then went to what proved to be a real mouth of the river we sought.

The Zambesi pours its waters into the ocean by four mouths, namely, the Milambe, which is the most westerly, the Kongone, the Luabo, and the Timbwe (or Muselo). When the river is in flood, a natural canal running parallel with the coast, and winding very much among the swamps, forms a secret way for conveying slaves from Quillimane to the bays Massangano and Nameara, or to the Zambesi itself. The Kwakwa, or river of Quillimane, some sixty miles distant from the mouth of the Zambesi, has long been represented as the principal entrance to the Zambesi, in order, as the Portuguese now maintain, that the English cruisers might be induced to watch the false mouth, while slaves were quietly shipped from the true one; and, strange to say, this error has lately been propagated by a map issued by the colonial minister of Portugal.

After the examination of three branches by the able and energetic surveyor, Francis Skead, R.N., the Kongone was found to be the best entrance. The immense amount of sand brought down by the Zambesi has in the course of ages formed a sort of promontory, against which the long swell of the Indian Ocean, beating during the prevailing winds, has formed bars, which, acting against the waters of the delta, may have led to their exit sideways. The Kongone is one of those lateral branches, and the safest; inasmuch as the bar has nearly two fathoms on it at low water, and the rise at spring tides is from twelve to fourteen feet. The bar is narrow, the passage nearly straight, and, were it buoyed and a beacon placed on Pearl Island, would always be safe to a steamer. When the wind is from the east or north, the bar is smooth; if from the south and south-east, it has a heavy break on it, and is not to be attempted in boats. A strong current setting to the east when the tide is flowing, and to the west when ebbing, may drag a boat or ship into the breakers. If one is doubtful of his longitude and runs east, he will soon see the land at Timbwe disappear away to the north; and coming west again, he can easily make out East Luabo from its great size; and Kongone follows several miles west. East Luabo has a good but long bar, and not to be attempted unless the wind be north-east or east. It has sometimes been called "Barra Catrina," and was used in the embarkations of slaves. This may have been the "River of Good Signs," of Vasco da Gama, as the mouth is more easily seen from the seaward than any other; but the absence of the pillar dedicated by that navigator to "St. Raphael," leaves the matter in doubt. No Portuguese live within eighty miles of any mouth of the Zambesi.

The Kongone is five miles east of the Milambe, or western branch, and seven miles west from East Luabo, which again is five miles from the Timbwe. We saw but few natives, and these, by escaping from their canoes into the mangrove thickets the moment they caught sight of us, gave unmistakeable indications that they had no very favourable opinion of white men. They were probably fugitives from Portuguese slavery. In the grassy glades buffaloes, wart-hogs, and three kinds of antelope were abundant, and the latter easily obtained. A few hours' hunting usually provided venison enough for a score of men for several days.

On proceeding up the Kongone branch it was found that, by keeping well in the bends, which the current had worn deep, shoals were easily avoided. The first twenty miles are straight and deep; then a small and rather tortuous natural canal leads off to the right, and, after about five miles, during which the paddles almost touch the floating grass of the sides, ends in the broad Zambesi. The rest of the Kongone branch comes out of the main stream considerably higher up as the outgoing branch called Doto.

The first twenty miles of the Kongone are enclosed in mangrove jungle; some of the trees are ornamented with orchilla weed, which appears never to have been gathered. Huge ferns, palm bushes, and occasionally wild date-palms peer out in the forest, which consists of different species of mangroves; the bunches of bright yellow, though scarcely edible fruit, contrasting prettily with the graceful green leaves. In some spots the Milola, an umbrageous hibiscus, with large yellowish flowers, grows in masses along the bank. Its bark is made into cordage, and is especially valuable for the manufacture of ropes attached to harpoons for killing the hippopotamus. The Pandanus or screw-palm, from which sugar bags are made in the Mauritius, also appears, and on coming out of the canal into the Zambesi many are so tall as in the distance to remind us of the steeples of our native land, and make us relish the remark of an old sailor, "that but one thing was wanting to complete the picture, and that was a 'grog-shop near the church.'" We find also a few guava and lime- trees growing wild, but the natives claim the crops. The dark woods resound with the lively and exultant song of the kinghunter (***Halcyon striolata***), as he sits perched on high among the trees. As the steamer moves on through the winding channel, a pretty little heron or bright kingfisher darts out in alarm from the edge of the bank, flies on ahead a short distance, and settles quietly down to be again frightened off in a few seconds as we approach. The magnificent fishhawk (***Halietus vocifer***) sits on the top of a mangrove-tree, digesting his morning meal of fresh fish, and is clearly unwilling to stir until the imminence of the danger compels him at last to spread his great wings for flight. The glossy ibis, acute of ear to a remarkable degree, hears from afar the unwonted sound of the paddles, and, springing from the mud where his family has been quietly feasting, is off, screaming out his loud, harsh, and defiant Ha! ha! ha! long before the danger is near.

Several native huts now peep out from the bananas and cocoa-palms on the right bank; they stand on piles a few feet above the low damp ground, and their owners enter them by means of ladders. The soil is wonderfully rich, and the gardens are really excellent. Rice is cultivated largely; sweet potatoes, pumpkins, tomatoes, cabbages, onions (shalots), peas, a little cotton, and sugar-cane are also raised. It is said that English potatoes, when planted at Quillimane on soil resembling this, in the course of two years become in taste like sweet potatoes (***Convolvulus batatas***), and are like our potato frosted. The whole of the fertile region extending from the Kongone canal to beyond Mazaro, some eighty miles in length, and fifty in breadth, is admirably adapted for the growth of sugar-cane; and were it in the hands of our friends at the Cape, would supply all Europe with sugar. The remarkably few people seen appear to be tolerably well fed, but there was a dearth of clothing among them; all were blacks, and nearly all Portuguese "colonos" or serfs. They manifested no fear of white men, and stood in groups on the bank gazing in astonishment at the steamers, especially at the "Pearl," which accompanied us thus far up the river. One old man who came on board remarked that never before had he seen any vessel so large as the "Pearl," it was like a village, "Was it made out of one tree?" All were eager traders, and soon came off to the ship in light swift canoes with every kind of fruit and food they possessed; a few brought honey and beeswax, which are found in quantities in the mangrove forests. As the ships steamed off, many anxious sellers ran along the bank, holding up fowls, baskets of rice and meal, and shouting "Malonda, Malonda," "things for sale," while others followed in canoes, which they sent through the water with great velocity by means of short broad-bladed paddles.

Finding the "Pearl's" draught too great for that part of the river near the island of Simbo, where the branch called the Doto is given off to the Kongone on the right bank, and another named Chinde departs to the secret canal already mentioned on the left, the goods belonging to the expedition were taken out of her, and placed on one of the grassy islands about forty miles from the bar. The "Pearl" then left us, and we had to part with our good friends Duncan and Skead; the former for Ceylon, the latter to return to his duties as Government Surveyor at the Cape.

Of those who eventually did the work of the expedition the majority took a sober common-sense view of the enterprise in which we were engaged. Some remained on Expedition Island from the 18th June until the 13th August, while the launch and pinnace were carrying the goods up to Shupanga and Senna. The country was in a state of war, our luggage was in danger, and several of our party were exposed to disease from inactivity in the malaria of the delta. Here some had their first introduction to African life, and African fever. Those alone were safe who were actively employed with the vessels, and of course, remembering the perilous position of their fellows, they strained every nerve to finish the work and take them away.

Large columns of smoke rose daily from different points of the horizon, showing that the natives were burning off the immense crops of tall grass, here a nuisance, however valuable elsewhere. A white cloud was often observed to rest on the head of the column, as if a current of hot damp air was sent up by the heat of the flames and its moisture was condensed at the top. Rain did not follow, though theorists have imagined that in such cases it ought.

Large game, buffaloes, and zebras, were abundant abreast the island, but no men could be seen. On the mainland, over on the right bank of the river, we were amused by the eccentric gyrations and evolutions of flocks of small seed-eating birds, who in their flight wheeled into compact columns with such military precision as to give us the impression that they must be guided by a leader, and all directed by the same signal. Several other kinds of small birds now go in flocks, and among others the large Senegal swallow. The presence of this bird, being clearly in a state of migration from the north, while the common swallow of the country, and the brown kite are away beyond the equator, leads to the conjecture that there may be a double migration, namely, of birds from torrid climates to the more temperate, as this now is, as well as from severe winters to sunny regions; but this could not be verified by such birds of passage as ourselves.

On reaching Mazaro, the mouth of a narrow creek which in floods communicates with the Quillimane river, we found that the Portuguese were at war with a half-caste named Mariano *alias* Matakenya, from whom they had generally fled, and who, having built a stockade near the mouth of the Shire, owned all the country between that river and Mazaro. Mariano was best known by his native name Matakenya, which in their tongue means "trembling," or quivering as trees do in a storm. He was a keen slave-hunter, and kept a large number of men, well armed with muskets. It is an entire mistake to suppose that the slave trade is one of buying and selling alone; or that engagements can be made with labourers in Africa as they are in India; Mariano, like other Portuguese, had no labour to spare. He had been in the habit of sending out armed parties on slave-hunting forays among the helpless tribes to the north-east, and carrying down the kidnapped victims in chains to Quillimane, where they were sold by his brother-in-law Cruz Coimbra, and shipped as "Free emigrants" to the French island of Bourbon. So long as his robberies and murders were restricted to the natives at a distance, the authorities did not interfere; but his men, trained to deeds of violence and bloodshed in their slave forays, naturally began to practise on the people nearer at hand, though belonging to the Portuguese, and even in the village of Senna, under the guns of the fort. A gentleman of the highest standing told us that, while at dinner with his family, it was no uncommon event for a slave to rush into the room pursued by one of Mariano's men with spear in hand to murder him.

The atrocities of this villain, aptly termed by the late governor of Quillimane a "notorious robber and murderer," became at length intolerable. All the Portuguese spoke of him as a rare monster of inhumanity. It is unaccountable why half-castes, such as he, are so much more cruel than the Portuguese, but such is undoubtedly the case.

It was asserted that one of his favourite modes of creating an impression in the country, and making his name dreaded, was to spear his captives with his own hands. On one occasion he is reported to have thus killed forty poor wretches placed in a row before him. We did not at first credit these statements, and thought that they were merely exaggerations of the incensed Portuguese, who naturally enough were exasperated with him for stopping their trade, and harbouring their runaway slaves; but we learned afterwards from the natives, that the accounts given us by the Portuguese had not exceeded the truth; and that Mariano was quite as great a ruffian as they had described him. One expects slave-owners to treat their human chattels as well as men do other animals of value, but the slave-trade seems always to engender an unreasoning ferocity, if not blood-thirstiness.

War was declared against Mariano, and a force sent to take him; he resisted for a time; but seeing that he was likely to get the worst of it, and knowing that the Portuguese governors have small salaries, and are therefore "disposed to be reasonable," he went down to Quillimane to "arrange" with the Governor, as it is termed here; but Colonel da Silva put him in prison, and then sent him for trial to Mozambique. When we came into the country, his people were fighting under his brother Bonga. The war had lasted six months and stopped all trade on the river during that period. On the 15th June we first came into contact with the "rebels." They appeared as a crowd of well-armed and fantastically-dressed people under the trees at Mazaro. On explaining that we were English, some at once came on board and called to those on shore to lay aside their arms. On landing among them we saw that many had the branded marks of slaves on their chests, but they warmly approved our objects, and knew well the distinctive character of our nation on the slave question. The shout at our departure contrasted strongly with the suspicious questioning on our approach. Hence-forward we were recognized as friends by both parties.

At a later period we were taking in wood within a mile of the scene of action, but a dense fog prevented our hearing the noise of a battle at Mazaro; and on arriving there, immediately after, many natives and Portuguese appeared on the bank.

Dr. Livingstone, landing to salute some of his old friends among the latter, found himself in the sickening smell, and among the mutilated bodies of the slain; he was requested to take the Governor, who was very ill of fever, across to Shupanga, and just as he gave his assent, the rebels renewed the fight, and the balls began to whistle about in all directions. After trying in vain to get some one to assist the

Governor down to the steamer, and unwilling to leave him in such danger, as the officer sent to bring our Kroomen did not appear, he went into the hut, and dragged along his Excellency to the ship. He was a very tall man, and as he swayed hither and thither from weakness, weighing down Dr. Livingstone, it must have appeared like one drunken man helping another. Some of the Portuguese white soldiers stood fighting with great bravery against the enemy in front, while a few were coolly shooting at their own slaves for fleeing into the river behind. The rebels soon retired, and the Portuguese escaped to a sandbank in the Zambesi, and thence to an island opposite Shupanga, where they lay for some weeks, looking at the rebels on the mainland opposite. This state of inactivity on the part of the Portuguese could not well be helped, as they had expended all their ammunition and were waiting anxiously for supplies; hoping, no doubt sincerely, that the enemy might not hear that their powder had failed. Luckily their hopes were not disappointed; the rebels waited until a supply came, and were then repulsed after three-and-a-half hours' hard fighting. Two months afterwards Mariano's stockade was burned, the garrison having fled in a panic; and as Bonga declared that he did not wish to fight with this Governor, with whom he had no quarrel, the war soon came to an end. His Excellency meanwhile, being a disciple of Raspail, had taken nothing for the fever but a little camphor, and after he was taken to Shupanga became comatose. More potent remedies were administered to him, to his intense disgust, and he soon recovered. The Colonel in attendance, whom he never afterwards forgave, encouraged the treatment. "Give what is right; never mind him; he is very (***muito***) impertinent:" and all night long, with every draught of water the Colonel gave a quantity of quinine: the consequence was, next morning the patient was cinchonized and better.

For sixty or seventy miles before reaching Mazaro, the scenery is tame and uninteresting. On either hand is a dreary uninhabited expanse, of the same level grassy plains, with merely a few trees to relieve the painful monotony. The round green top of the stately palm-tree looks at a distance, when its grey trunk cannot be seen, as though hung in mid- air. Many flocks of busy sand-martins, which here, and as far south as the Orange River, do not migrate, have perforated the banks two or three feet horizontally, in order to place their nests at the ends, and are now chasing on restless wing the myriads of tropical insects. The broad river has many low islands, on which are seen various kinds of waterfowl, such as geese, spoonbills, herons, and flamingoes. Repulsive crocodiles, as with open jaws they sleep and bask in the sun on the low banks, soon catch the sound of the revolving paddles and glide quietly into the stream. The hippopotamus, having selected some still reach of the river to spend the day, rises out of the bottom, where he has been enjoying his morning bath after the labours of the night on shore, blows a puff of spray from his nostrils, shakes the water out of his ears, puts his enormous snout up straight and yawns, sounding a loud alarm to the rest of the herd, with notes as of a monster bassoon.

As we approach Mazaro the scenery improves. We see the well-wooded Shupanga ridge stretching to the left, and in front blue hills rise dimly far in the distance. There is no trade whatever on the Zambesi below Mazaro. All the merchandise of Senna and Tette is brought to that point in large canoes, and thence carried six miles across the country on men's heads to be reshipped on a small stream that flows into the Kwakwa, or Quillimane river, which is entirely distinct from the Zambesi. Only on rare occasions and during the highest floods can canoes pass from the Zambesi to the Quillimane river through the narrow natural canal **Mutu**. The natives of Maruru, or the country around Mazaro, the word Mazaro meaning the "mouth of the creek" Mutu, have a bad name among the Portuguese; they are said to be expert thieves, and the merchants sometimes suffer from their adroitness while the goods are in transit from one river to the other. In general they are trained canoe-men, and man many of the canoes that ply thence to Senna and Tette; their pay is small, and, not trusting the traders, they must always have it before they start. Africans being prone to assign plausible reasons for their conduct, like white men in more enlightened lands, it is possible they may be good-humouredly giving their reason for insisting on being invariably paid in advance in the words of their favourite canoe-song, "Uachingere, Uachingere Kale," "You cheated me of old;" or, "Thou art slippery slippery truly."

The Landeens or Zulus are lords of the right bank of the Zambesi; and the Portuguese, by paying this fighting tribe a pretty heavy annual tribute, practically admit this. Regularly every year come the Zulus in force to Senna and Shupanga for the accustomed tribute. The few wealthy merchants of Senna groan under the burden, for it falls chiefly on them. They submit to pay annually 200 pieces of cloth, of sixteen yards each, besides beads and brass wire, knowing that refusal involves war, which might end in the loss of all they possess. The Zulus appear to keep as sharp a look out on the Senna and Shupanga people as ever landlord did on tenant; the more they cultivate, the more tribute they have to pay. On asking some of them why they did not endeavour to raise certain highly profitable products, we were answered, "What's the use of our cultivating any more than we do? the Landeens would only come down on us for more tribute."

In the forests of Shupanga the Mokundu-kundu tree abounds; its bright yellow wood makes good boat-masts, and yields a strong bitter medicine for fever; the Gunda-tree attains to an immense size; its timber is hard, rather cross-grained, with masses of silica deposited in its substance; the large canoes, capable of carrying three or four tons, are made of its wood. For permission to cut these trees, a Portuguese gentleman of Quillimane was paying the Zulus, in 1858, two hundred dollars a year, and his successor now pays three hundred.

At Shupanga, a one-storied stone house stands on the prettiest site on the river. In front a sloping lawn, with a fine mango orchard at its southern end, leads down to the broad Zambesi, whose green islands repose on the sunny bosom of the tranquil waters. Beyond, northwards, lie vast fields and forests of palm and tropical trees, with the massive mountain of Morambala towering amidst the white clouds; and further away more distant hills appear in the blue horizon. This beautifully situated house possesses a melancholy interest from having been associated in a most mournful manner with the history of two English expeditions. Here, in 1826, poor Kirkpatrick, of Captain Owen's Surveying Expedition, died of fever; and here, in 1862, died, of the same fatal disease, the beloved wife of Dr. Livingstone. A hundred yards east of the house, under a large Baobab-tree, far from their native land, both are buried.

The Shupanga-house was the head-quarters of the Governor during the Mariano war. He told us that the province of Mosambique costs the Home Government between 5000*l*. and 6000*l*. annually, and East Africa yields no reward in return to the mother country. We met there several other influential Portuguese. All seemed friendly, and expressed their willingness to assist the expedition in every way in their power; and better still, Colonel Nunes and Major Sicard put their goodwill into action, by cutting wood for the steamer and sending men to help in unloading. It was observable that not one of them knew anything about the Kongone

Mouth; all thought that we had come in by the "Barra Catrina," or East Luabo. Dr. Kirk remained here a few weeks; and, besides exploring a small lake twenty miles to the south-west, had the sole medical care of the sick and wounded soldiers, for which valuable services he received the thanks of the Portuguese Government. We wooded up at this place with African ebony or black wood, and lignum vitae; the latter tree attains an immense size, sometimes as much as four feet in diameter; our engineer, knowing what ebony and lignum vitae cost at home, said it made his heart sore to burn wood so valuable. Though botanically different, they are extremely alike; the black wood as grown in some districts is superior, and the lignum vitae inferior in quality, to these timbers brought from other countries. Caoutchouc, or India-rubber, is found in abundance inland from Shupanga-house, and calumba-root is plentiful in the district; indigo, in quantities, propagates itself close to the banks of the Aver, and was probably at some time cultivated, for manufactured indigo was once exported. The India-rubber is made into balls for a game resembling "fives," and calumba-root is said to be used as a mordant for certain colours, but not as a dye itself.

We started for Tette on the 17th August, 1858; the navigation was rather difficult, the Zambesi from Shupanga to Senna being wide and full of islands; our black pilot, John Scisssors, a serf, sometimes took the wrong channel and ran us aground. Nothing abashed, he would exclaim in an aggrieved tone, "This is not the path, it is back yonder." "Then why didn't you go yonder at first?" growled out our Kroomen, who had the work of getting the vessel off. When they spoke roughly to poor Scissors, the weak cringing slave-spirit came forth in, "Those men scold me so, I am ready to run away." This mode of finishing up an engagement is not at all uncommon on the Zambesi; several cases occurred, when we were on the river, of hired crews decamping with most of the goods in their charge. If the trader cannot redress his own wrongs, he has to endure them. The Landeens will not surrender a fugitive slave, even to his master. One belonging to Mr. Azevedo fled, and was, as a great favour only, returned after a present of much more than his value.

We landed to wood at Shamoara, just below the confluence of the Shire. Its quartz hills are covered with trees and gigantic grasses; the buaze, a small forest-tree, grows abundantly; it is a species of polygala; its beautiful clusters of sweet-scented pinkish flowers perfume the air with a rich fragrance; its seeds produce a fine drying oil, and the bark of the smaller branches yields a fibre finer and stronger than flax; with which the natives make their nets for fishing. Bonga, the brother of the rebel Mariano, and now at the head of the revolted natives, with some of his principal men came to see us, and were perfectly friendly, though told of our having carried the sick Governor across to Shupanga, and of our having cured him of fever. On our acquainting Bonga with the object of the expedition, he remarked that we should suffer no hindrance from his people in our good work. He sent us a present of rice, two sheep, and a quantity of firewood. He never tried to make any use of us in the strife; the other side showed less confidence, by carefully cross-questioning our pilot whether we had sold any powder to the enemy. We managed, however, to keep on good terms with both rebels and Portuguese.

Senna is built on a low plain, on the right bank of the Zambesi, with some pretty detached hills in the background; it is surrounded by a stockade of living trees to protect its inhabitants from their troublesome and rebellious neighbours. It contains a few large houses, some ruins of others, and a weather-beaten cross, where once stood a church; a mound shows the site of an ancient monastery, and a mud fort by the river is so dilapidated, that cows were grazing peacefully over its prostrate walls.

The few Senna merchants, having little or no trade in the village, send parties of trusted slaves into the interior to hunt for and purchase ivory. It is a dull place, and very conducive to sleep. One is sure to take fever in Senna on the second day, if by chance one escapes it on the first day of a sojourn there; but no place is entirely bad. Senna has one redeeming feature: it is the native village of the large-hearted and hospitable Senhor H. A. Ferrao. The benevolence of this gentleman is unbounded. The poor black stranger passing through the town goes to him almost as a matter of course for food, and is never sent away hungry. In times of famine the starving natives are fed by his generosity; hundreds of his own people he never sees except on these occasions; and the only benefit derived from being their master is, that they lean on him as a patriarchal chief, and he has the satisfaction of settling their differences, and of saving their lives in seasons of drought and scarcity.

Senhor Ferrao received us with his usual kindness, and gave us a bountiful breakfast. During the day the principal men of the place called, and were unanimously of opinion that the free natives would willingly cultivate large quantities of cotton, could they find purchasers. They had in former times exported largely both cotton and cloth to Manica and even to Brazil. "On their own soil," they declared, "the natives are willing to labour and trade, provided only they can do so to advantage: when it is for their interest, blacks work very hard." We often remarked subsequently that this was the opinion of men of energy; and that all settlers of activity, enterprise, and sober habits had become rich, while those who were much addicted to lying on their backs smoking, invariably complained of the laziness of the negroes, and were poor, proud, and despicable.

Beyond Pita lies the little island Nyamotobsi, where we met a small fugitive tribe of hippopotamus hunters, who had been driven by war from their own island in front. All were busy at work; some were making gigantic baskets for grain, the men plaiting from the inside. With the civility so common among them the chief ordered a mat to be spread for us under a shed, and then showed us the weapon with which they kill the hippopotamus; it is a short iron harpoon inserted in the end of a long pole, but being intended to unship, it is made fast to a strong cord of milola, or hibiscus, bark, which is wound closely round the entire length of the shaft, and secured at its opposite end. Two men in a swift canoe steal quietly down on the sleeping animal. The bowman dashes the harpoon into the unconscious victim, while the quick steersman sweeps the light craft back with his broad paddle; the force of the blow separates the harpoon from its corded handle, which, appearing on the surface, sometimes with an inflated bladder attached, guides the hunters to where the wounded beast hides below until they despatch it.

These hippopotamus hunters form a separate people, called Akombwi, or Mapodzo, and rarely--the women it is said never--intermarry with any other tribe. The reason for their keeping aloof from certain of the natives on the Zambesi is obvious enough, some having as great an abhorrence of hippopotamus meat as Mahomedans have of swine's flesh. Our pilot, Scissors, was one of this class; he would not even cook his food in a pot which had contained hippopotamus meat, preferring to go hungry till he could find another; and yet he traded eagerly in the animal's tusks, and ate with great relish the flesh of the foul-feeding marabout. These hunters go out frequently on long expeditions, taking in their canoes their wives and children, cooking-pots, and sleeping-mats. When they reach a good game district, they erect temporary huts on the bank, and there dry the meat they have killed.

They are rather a comely-looking race, with very black smooth skins, and never disfigure themselves with the frightful ornaments of some of the other tribes. The chief declined to sell a harpoon, because they could not now get the milola bark from the coast on account of Mariano's war. He expressed some doubts about our being children of the same Almighty Father, remarking that "they could not become white, let them wash ever so much." We made him a present of a bit of cloth, and he very generously gave us in return some fine fresh fish and Indian corn.

The heat of the weather steadily increases during this month (August), and foggy mornings are now rare. A strong breeze ending in a gale blows up stream every night. It came in the afternoon a few weeks ago, then later, and at present its arrival is near midnight; it makes our frail cabin-doors fly open before it, but continues only for a short time, and is succeeded by a dead calm. Game becomes more abundant; near our wooding-places we see herds of zebras, both Burchell's and the mountain variety, pallahs (***Antelope melampus***), waterbuck, and wild hogs, with the spoor of buffaloes and elephants.

Shiramba Dembe, on the right bank, is deserted; a few old iron guns show where a rebel stockade once stood; near the river above this, stands a magnificent Baobab hollowed out into a good-sized hut, with bark inside as well as without. The old oaks in Sherwood Forest, when hollow, have the inside dead or rotten; but the Baobab, though stripped of its bark outside, and hollowed to a cavity inside, has the power of exuding new bark from its substance to both the outer and inner surfaces; so, a hut made like that in the oak called the "Forest Queen," in Sherwood, would soon all be lined with bark.

The portions of the river called Shigogo and Shipanga are bordered by a low level expanse of marshy country, with occasional clumps of palm-trees and a few thorny acacias. The river itself spreads out to a width of from three to four miles, with many islands, among which it is difficult to navigate, except when the river is in flood. In front, a range of high hills from the north-east crosses and compresses it into a deep narrow channel, called the Lupata Gorge. The Portuguese thought the steamer would not stem the current here; but as it was not more than about three knots, and as there was a strong breeze in our favour, steam and sails got her through with ease. Heavy-laden canoes take two days to go up this pass. A current sweeps round the little rocky promontories Chifura and Kangomba, forming whirlpools and eddies dangerous for the clumsy craft, which are dragged past with long ropes.

The paddlers place meal on these rocks as an offering to the turbulent deities, which they believe preside over spots fatal to many a large canoe. We were slily told that native Portuguese take off their hats to these river gods, and pass in solemn silence; when safely beyond the promontories, they fire muskets, and, as we ought to do, give the canoe- men grog. From the spoor of buffaloes and elephants it appears that these animals frequent Lupata in considerable numbers, and--we have often observed the association--the tsetse fly is common. A horse for the Governor of Tette was sent in a canoe from Quillimane; and, lest it should be wrecked on the Chifura and Kangomba rocks, it was put on shore and sent in the daytime through the pass. It was of course bitten by the tsetse, and died soon after; it was thought that the *air* of Tette had not agreed with it. The currents above Lupata are stronger than those below; the country becomes more picturesque and hilly, and there is a larger population.

The ship anchored in the stream, off Tette, on the 8th September, 1858, and Dr. Livingstone went ashore in the boat. No sooner did the Makololo recognize him, than they rushed to the water's edge, and manifested great joy at seeing him again. Some were hastening to embrace him, but others cried out, "Don't touch him, you will spoil his new clothes." The five headmen came on board and listened in quiet sadness to the story of poor Sekwebu, who died at the Mauritius on his way to England. "Men die in any country," they observed, and then told us that thirty of their own number had died of smallpox, having been bewitched by the people of Tette, who envied them because, during the first year, none of their party had died. Six of their young men, becoming tired of cutting firewood for a meagre pittance, proposed to go and dance for gain before some of the neighbouring chiefs. "Don't go," said the others, "we don't know the people of this country;" but the young men set out and visited an independent half-caste chief, a few miles to the north, named Chisaka, who some years ago burned all the Portuguese villas on the north bank of the river; afterwards the young men went to Bonga, son of another half- caste chief, who bade defiance to the Tette authorities, and had a stockade at the confluence of the Zambesi and Luenya, a few miles below that village. Asking the Makololo whence they came, Bonga rejoined, "Why do you come from my enemy to me?

You have brought witchcraft medicine to kill me." In vain they protested that they did not belong to the country; they were strangers, and had come from afar with an Englishman. The superstitious savage put them all to death. "We do not grieve," said their companions, "for the thirty victims of the smallpox, who were taken away by Morimo (God); but our hearts are sore for the six youths who were murdered by Bonga." Any hope of obtaining justice on the murderer was out of the question. Bonga once caught a captain of the Portuguese army, and forced him to perform the menial labour of pounding maize in a wooden mortar. No punishment followed on this outrage. The Government of Lisbon has since given Bonga the honorary title of Captain, by way of coaxing him to own their authority; but he still holds his stockade.

Tette stands on a succession of low sandstone ridges on the right bank of the Zambesi, which is here nearly a thousand yards wide (960 yards). Shallow ravines, running parallel with the river, form the streets, the houses being built on the ridges. The whole surface of the streets, except narrow footpaths, were overrun with self-sown indigo, and tons of it might have been collected. In fact indigo, senna, and stramonium, with a species of cassia, form the weeds of the place, which are annually hoed off and burned. A wall of stone and mud surrounds the village, and the native population live in huts outside. The fort and the church, near the river, are the strongholds; the natives having a salutary dread of the guns of the one, and a superstitious fear of the unknown power of the other. The number of white inhabitants is small, and rather select, many of them having been considerately sent out of Portugal "for their country's good." The military element preponderates in society; the convict and "incorrigible" class of soldiers, receiving very little pay, depend in great measure on the produce of the gardens of their black wives; the moral condition of the resulting population may be imagined.

Droughts are of frequent occurrence at Tette, and the crops suffer severely. This may arise partly from the position of the town between the ranges of hills north and south, which appear to have a strong attraction for the rain-clouds. It is often seen to rain on these hills when not a drop falls at Tette. Our first season was one of drought. Thrice had the women planted their gardens in vain, the seed, after just vegetating, was killed by the intense dry heat. A fourth planting shared the same hard fate, and then some of the knowing ones discovered the cause of the clouds being frightened away: our unlucky rain-gauge in the garden. We got a bad name through that same rain-gauge, and were regarded by many as a species of evil omen. The Makololo in turn blamed the people of Tette for drought: "A number of witches live here, who won't let it rain." Africans in general are sufficiently superstitious, but those of Tette are in this particular pre-eminent above their fellows. Coming from many different tribes, all the rays of the separate superstitions converge into a focus at Tette, and burn out common sense from the minds of the mixed breed. They believe that many evil spirits live in the air, the earth, and the water. These invisible malicious beings are thought to inflict much suffering on the human race; but, as they have a weakness for beer and a craving for food, they may be propitiated from time to time by offerings of meat and drink. The serpent is an object of worship, and hideous little images are hung in the huts of the sick and dying. The uncontaminated Africans believe that Morungo, the Great Spirit who formed all things, lives above the stars; but they never pray to him, and know nothing of their relation to him, or of his interest in them. The spirits of their departed ancestors are all good, according to their ideas, and on special occasions aid them in their enterprises. When a man has his hair cut, he is careful to burn it, or bury it secretly, lest, falling into the hands of one who has an evil eye, or is a witch, it should be used as a charm to afflict him with headache. They believe, too, that they will live after the death of the body, but do not know anything of the state of the Barimo (gods, or departed spirits).

    The mango-tree grows luxuriantly above Lupata, and furnishes a grateful shade. Its delicious fruit is superior to that on the coast. For weeks the natives who have charge of the mangoes live entirely on the fruit, and, as some trees bear in November and some in March, while the main crop comes between, fruit in abundance may easily be obtained during four months of the year; but no native can be induced to plant a mango. A wide-spread superstition has become riveted in the native mind, that if any one plants this tree he will soon die. The Makololo, like other natives, were very fond of the fruit; but when told to take up some mango- stones, on their return, and plant them in their own country--they too having become deeply imbued with the belief that it was a suicidal act to do so--replied "they did not wish to die too soon." There is also a superstition even among the native Portuguese of Tette, that if a man plants coffee he will never afterwards be happy: they drink it, however, and seem the happier for it.

The Portuguese of Tette have many slaves, with all the usual vices of their class, as theft, lying, and impurity. As a general rule the real Portuguese are tolerably humane masters and rarely treat a slave cruelly; this may be due as much to natural kindness of heart as to a fear of losing the slaves by their running away. When they purchase an adult slave they buy at the same time, if possible, all his relations along with him. They thus contrive to secure him to his new home by domestic ties. Running away then would be to forsake all who hold a place in his heart, for the mere chance of acquiring a freedom, which would probably be forfeited on his entrance into the first native village, for the chief might, without compunction, again sell him into slavery.

A rather singular case of voluntary slavery came to our knowledge: a free black, an intelligent active young fellow, called Chibanti, who had been our pilot on the river, told us that he had sold himself into slavery. On asking why he had done this, he replied that he was all alone in the world, had neither father nor mother, nor any one else to give him water when sick, or food when hungry; so he sold himself to Major Sicard, a notoriously kind master, whose slaves had little to do, and plenty to eat. "And how much did you get for yourself?" we asked. "Three thirty- yard pieces of cotton cloth," he replied; "and I forthwith bought a man, a woman, and child, who cost me two of the pieces, and I had one piece left." This, at all events, showed a cool and calculating spirit; he afterwards bought more slaves, and in two years owned a sufficient number to man one of the large canoes. His master subsequently employed him in carrying ivory to Quillimane, and gave him cloth to hire mariners for the voyage; he took his own slaves, of course, and thus drove a thriving business; and was fully convinced that he had made a good speculation by the sale of himself, for had he been sick his master must have supported him. Occasionally some of the free blacks become slaves voluntarily by going through the simple but significant ceremony of breaking a spear in the presence of their future master. A Portuguese officer, since dead, persuaded one of the Makololo to remain in Tette, instead of returning to his own country, and tried also to induce him to break a spear before him, and thus acknowledge himself his slave, but the man was too shrewd for this; he was a great elephant doctor, who accompanied the hunters, told them when to attack the huge beast, and gave them medicine to ensure success.

Unlike the real Portuguese, many of the half-castes are merciless slave-holders; their brutal treatment of the wretched slaves is notorious. What a humane native of Portugal once said of them is appropriate if not true: "God made white men, and God made black men, but the devil made half-castes."

The officers and merchants send parties of slaves under faithful headmen to hunt elephants and to trade in ivory, providing them with a certain quantity of cloth, beads, etc., and requiring so much ivory in return. These slaves think that they have made a good thing of it, when they kill an elephant near a village, as the natives give them beer and meal in exchange for some of the elephant's meat, and over every tusk that is brought there is expended a vast amount of time, talk, and beer. Most of the Africans are natural-born traders, they love trade more for the sake of trading than for what they make by it. An intelligent gentleman of Tette told us that native traders often come to him with a tusk for sale, consider the price he offers, demand more, talk over it, retire to consult about it, and at length go away without selling it; next day they try another merchant, talk, consider, get puzzled and go off as on the previous day, and continue this course daily until they have perhaps seen every merchant in the village, and then at last end by selling the precious tusk to some one for even less than the first merchant had offered. Their love of dawdling in the transaction arises from the self- importance conferred on them by their being the object of the wheedling and coaxing of eager merchants, a feeling to which even the love of gain is subordinate.

The native medical profession is reasonably well represented. In addition to the regular practitioners, who are a really useful class, and know something of their profession, and the nature and power of certain medicines, there are others who devote their talents to some speciality. The elephant doctor prepares a medicine which is considered indispensable to the hunters when attacking that noble and sagacious beast; no hunter is willing to venture out before investing in this precious nostrum. The crocodile doctor sells a charm which is believed to possess the singular virtue of protecting its owner from crocodiles. Unwittingly we offended the crocodile school of medicine while at Tette, by shooting one of these huge reptiles as it lay basking in the sun on a sandbank; the doctors came to the Makololo in wrath, clamouring to know why the white man had shot their crocodile.

A shark's hook was baited one evening with a dog, of which the crocodile is said to be particularly fond; but the doctors removed the bait, on the principle that the more crocodiles the more demand for medicine, or perhaps because they preferred to eat the dog themselves. Many of the natives of this quarter are known, as in the South Seas, to eat the dog without paying any attention to its feeding. The dice doctor or diviner is an important member of the community, being consulted by Portuguese and natives alike. Part of his business is that of a detective, it being his duty to discover thieves. When goods are stolen, he goes and looks at the place, casts his dice, and waits a few days, and then, for a consideration, tells who is the thief: he is generally correct, for he trusts not to his dice alone; he has confidential agents all over the village, by whose inquiries and information he is enabled to detect the culprit. Since the introduction of muskets, gun doctors have sprung up, and they sell the medicine which professes to make good marksmen; others are rain doctors, etc., etc. The various schools deal in little charms, which are hung round the purchaser's neck to avert evil: some of them contain the medicine, others increase its power.

Indigo, about three or four feet high, grows in great luxuriance in the streets of Tette, and so does the senna plant. The leaves are undistinguishable from those imported in England. A small amount of first-rate cotton is cultivated by the native population for the manufacture of a coarse cloth. A neighbouring tribe raises the sugar- cane, and makes a little sugar; but they use most primitive wooden rollers, and having no skill in mixing lime with the extracted juice, the product is of course of very inferior quality. Plenty of magnetic iron ore is found near Tette, and coal also to any amount; a single cliff-seam measuring twenty-five feet in thickness. It was found to burn well in the steamer on the first trial. Gold is washed for in the beds of rivers, within a couple of days of Tette. The natives are fully aware of its value, but seldom search for it, and never dig deeper than four or five feet. They dread lest the falling in of the sand of the river's bed should bury them. In former times, when traders went with hundreds of slaves to the washings, the produce was considerable. It is now insignificant. The gold-producing lands have always been in the hands of independent tribes. Deep cuttings near the sources of the gold-yielding streams seem never to have been tried here, as in California and Australia, nor has any machinery been used save common wooden basins for washing.

CHAPTER II.

Kebrabasa Rapids--Tette--African fever--Exploration of the Shire--Discovery of Lake Shirwa.

Our curiosity had been so much excited by the reports we had heard of the Kebrabasa rapids, that we resolved to make a short examination of them, and seized the opportunity of the Zambesi being unusually low, to endeavour to ascertain their character while uncovered by the water. We reached them on the 9th of November. The country between Tette and Panda Mokua, where navigation ends, is well wooded and hilly on both banks. Panda Mokua is a hill two miles below the rapids, capped with dolomite containing copper ore.

Conspicuous among the trees, for its gigantic size, and bark coloured exactly like Egyptian syenite, is the burly Baobab. It often makes the other trees of the forest look like mere bushes in comparison. A hollow one, already mentioned, is 74 feet in circumference, another was 84, and some have been found on the West Coast which measure 100 feet. The lofty range of Kebrabasa, consisting chiefly of conical hills, covered with scraggy trees, crosses the Zambesi, and confines it within a narrow, rough, and rocky dell of about a quarter of a mile in breadth; over this, which may be called the flood-bed of the river, large masses of rock are huddled in indescribable confusion. The drawing, for the use of which, and of others, our thanks are due to Lord Russell, conveys but a faint idea of the scene, inasmuch as the hills which confine the river do not appear in the sketch. The chief rock is syenite, some portions of which have a beautiful blue tinge like ***lapis lazuli*** diffused through them; others are grey. Blocks of granite also abound, of a pinkish tinge; and these with metamorphic rocks, contorted, twisted, and thrown into every conceivable position, afford a picture of dislocation or unconformability which would gladden a geological lecturer's heart; but at high flood this rough channel is all smoothed over, and it then conforms well with the river below it, which is half a mile wide. In the dry season the stream runs at the bottom of a narrow and deep groove, whose sides are polished and fluted by the boiling action of the water in flood, like the rims of ancient Eastern wells by the draw-ropes. The breadth of the groove is often not more than from forty to sixty yards, and it has some sharp turnings, double channels, and little cataracts in it. As we steamed up, the masts of the "Ma Robert," though some thirty feet high, did not reach the level of the flood-channel above, and the man in the chains sung out, "No bottom at ten fathoms." Huge pot-holes, as large as draw-wells, had been worn in the sides, and were so deep that in some instances, when protected from the sun by overhanging boulders, the water in them was quite cool. Some of these holes had been worn right through, and only the side next the rock remained; while the sides of the groove of the flood-channel were polished as smooth as if they had gone through the granite-mills of Aberdeen. The pressure of the water must be enormous to produce this polish. It had wedged round pebbles into chinks and crannies of the rocks so firmly that, though they looked quite loose, they could not be moved except with a hammer. The mighty power of the water here seen gave us an idea of what is going on in thousands of cataracts in the world. All the information we had been able to obtain from our Portuguese friends amounted to this, that some three or four detached rocks jutted out of the river in Kebrabasa, which, though dangerous to the cumbersome native canoes, could be easily passed by a steamer, and that if one or two of these obstructions were blasted away with gunpowder, no difficulty would hereafter be experienced. After we had painfully explored seven or eight miles of the rapid, we returned to the vessel satisfied that much greater labour was requisite for the mere examination of the cataracts than our friends supposed necessary to remove them; we therefore went down the river for fresh supplies, and made preparation for a more serious survey of this region.

The steamer having returned from the bar, we set out on the 22nd of November to examine the rapids of Kebrabasa. We reached the foot of the hills again, late in the afternoon of the 24th, and anchored in the stream. Canoe-men never sleep on the river, but always spend the night on shore. The natives on the right bank, in the country called Shidima, who are Banyai, and even at this short distance from Tette, independent, and accustomed to lord it over Portuguese traders, wondered what could be our object in remaining afloat, and were naturally suspicious at our departing from the universal custom.

They hailed us from the bank in the evening with "Why don't you come and sleep onshore like other people?"

The answer they received from our Makololo, who now felt as independent as the Banyai, was, "We are held to the bottom with iron; you may see we are not like your Bazungu."

This hint, a little amplified, saved us from the usual exactions. It is pleasant to give a present, but that pleasure the Banyai usually deny to strangers by making it a fine, and demanding it in such a supercilious way, that only a sorely cowed trader could bear it. They often refuse to touch what is offered--throw it down and leave it--sneer at the trader's slaves, and refuse a passage until the tribute is raised to the utmost extent of his means.

Leaving the steamer next morning, we proceeded on foot, accompanied by a native Portuguese and his men and a dozen Makololo, who carried our baggage. The morning was pleasant, the hills on our right furnished for a time a delightful shade; but before long the path grew frightfully rough, and the hills no longer shielded us from the blazing sun. Scarcely a vestige of a track was now visible; and, indeed, had not our guide assured us to the contrary, we should have been innocent of even the suspicion of a way along the patches of soft yielding sand, and on the great rocks over which we so painfully clambered. These rocks have a singular appearance, from being dislocated and twisted in every direction, and covered with a thin black glaze, as if highly polished and coated with lamp-black varnish. This seems to have been deposited while the river was in flood, for it covers only those rocks which lie between the highest water-mark and a line about four feet above the lowest. Travellers who have visited the rapids of the Orinoco and the Congo say that the rocks there have a similar appearance, and it is attributed to some deposit from the water, formed only when the current is strong. This may account for it in part here, as it prevails only where the narrow river is confined between masses of rock, backed by high hills, and where the current in floods is known to be the strongest; and it does not exist where the rocks are only on one side, with a sandy beach opposite, and a broad expanse of river between. The hot rocks burnt the thick soles of our men's feet, and sorely fatigued ourselves. Our first day's march did not exceed four miles in a straight line, and that we found more than enough to be pleasant.

The state of insecurity in which the Badema tribe live is indicated by the habit of hiding their provisions in the hills, and keeping only a small quantity in their huts; they strip a particular species of tree of its bitter bark, to which both mice and monkeys are known to have an antipathy, and, turning the bark inside out, sew it into cylindrical vessels for their grain, and bury them in holes and in crags on the wooded hill-sides. By this means, should a marauding party plunder their huts, they save a supply of corn. They "could give us no information, and they had no food; Chisaka's men had robbed them a few weeks before."

"Never mind," said our native Portuguese, "they will sell you plenty when you return, they are afraid of you now, as yet they do not know who you are." We slept under trees in the open air, and suffered no inconvenience from either mosquitoes or dew: and no prowling wild beast troubled us; though one evening, while we were here, a native sitting with some others on the opposite bank was killed by a leopard.

One of the Tette slaves, who wished to be considered a great traveller, gave us, as we sat by our evening fire, an interesting account of a strange race of men whom he had seen in the interior; they were only three feet high, and had horns growing out of their heads; they lived in a large town and had plenty of food. The Makololo pooh-poohed this story, and roundly told the narrator that he was telling a downright lie. " *We* come from the interior," cried out a tall fellow, measuring some six feet four, "are *we* dwarfs? have *we* horns on our heads?" and thus they laughed the fellow to scorn. But he still stoutly maintained that he had seen these little people, and had actually been in their town; thus making himself the hero of the traditional story, which before and since the time of Herodotus has, with curious persistency, clung to the native mind. The mere fact that such absurd notions are permanent, even in the entire absence of literature, invests the religious ideas of these people also with importance, as fragments of the wreck of the primitive faith floating down the stream of time.

We waded across the rapid Luia, which took us up to the waist, and was about forty yards wide. The water was discoloured at the time, and we were not without apprehension that a crocodile might chance to fancy a white man for dinner. Next day one of the men crawled over the black rocks to within ten yards of a sleeping hippopotamus, and shot him through the brain. The weather being warm, the body floated in a few hours, and some of us had our first trial of hippopotamus flesh. It is a cross-grained meat, something between pork and beef,--pretty good food when one is hungry and can get nothing better. When we reached the foot of the mountain named Chipereziwa, whose perpendicular rocky sides are clothed with many-coloured lichens, our Portuguese companion informed us there were no more obstructions to navigation, the river being all smooth above; he had hunted there and knew it well. Supposing that the object of our trip was accomplished we turned back; but two natives, who came to our camp at night, assured us that a cataract, called Morumbwa, did still exist in front. Drs. Livingstone and Kirk then decided to go forward with three Makololo and settle the question for themselves. It was as tough a bit of travel as they ever had in Africa, and after some painful marching the Badema guides refused to go further; "the Banyai," they said, "would be angry if they showed white men the country; and there was besides no practicable approach to the spot, neither elephant, nor hippopotamus, nor even a crocodile could reach the cataract." The slopes of the mountains on each side of the river, now not 300 yards wide, and without the flattish flood-channel and groove, were more than 3000 feet from the sky-line down, and were covered either with dense thornbush or huge black boulders; this deep trough-like shape caused the sun's rays to converge as into a focus, making the surface so hot that the soles of the feet of the Makololo became blistered. Around, and up and down, the party clambered among these heated blocks, at a pace not exceeding a mile an hour; the strain upon the muscles in jumping from crag to boulder, and wriggling round projections, took an enormous deal out of them, and they were often glad to cower in the shadow formed by one rock overhanging and resting on another; the shelter induced the peculiarly strong and overpowering inclination to sleep, which too much sun sometimes causes. This sleep is curative of what may be incipient sunstroke: in its first gentle touches, it caused the dream to flit over the boiling brain, that they had become lunatics and had been sworn in as members of the Alpine club; and then it became so heavy that it made them feel as if a portion of existence had been cut out from their lives. The sun is excessively hot, and feels sharp in Africa; but, probably from the greater dryness of the atmosphere, we never heard of a single case of sunstroke, so common in India. The Makololo told Dr. Livingstone they "always thought he had a heart, but now they believed he had none," and tried to persuade Dr. Kirk to return, on the ground that it must be evident that, in attempting to go where no living foot could tread, his leader had given unmistakeable signs of having gone mad. All their efforts of persuasion, however, were lost upon Dr. Kirk, as he had not yet learned their language, and his leader, knowing his companion to be equally anxious with himself to solve the problem of the navigableness of Kebrabasa, was not at pains to enlighten him. At one part a bare mountain spur barred the way, and had to be surmounted by a perilous and circuitous route, along which the crags were so hot that it was scarcely possible for the hand to hold on long enough to ensure safety in the passage; and had the foremost of the party lost his hold, he would have hurled all behind him into the river at the foot of the promontory; yet in this wild hot region, as they descended again to the river, they met a fisherman casting his hand-net into the boiling eddies, and he pointed out the cataract of Morumbwa; within an hour they were trying to measure it from an overhanging rock, at a height of about one hundred feet. When you stand facing the cataract, on the north bank, you see that it is situated in a sudden bend of the river, which is flowing in a short curve; the river above it is jammed between two mountains in a channel with perpendicular sides, and less than fifty yards wide; one or two masses of rock jut out, and then there is a sloping fall of perhaps twenty feet in a distance of thirty yards. It would stop all navigation, except during the highest floods; the rocks showed that the water then rises upwards of eighty feet perpendicularly.

Still keeping the position facing the cataract, on its right side rises Mount Morumbwa from 2000 to 3000 feet high, which gives the name to the spot. On the left of the cataract stands a noticeable mountain which may be called onion-shaped, for it is partly conical and a large concave flake has peeled off, as granite often does, and left a broad, smooth convex face as if it were an enormous bulb. These two mountains extend their bases northwards about half a mile, and the river in that distance, still very narrow, is smooth, with a few detached rocks standing out from its bed. They climbed as high up the base of Mount Morumbwa, which touches the cataract, as they required. The rocks were all water-worn and smooth, with huge potholes, even at 100 feet above low water. When at a later period they climbed up the north-western base of this same mountain, the familiar face of the onion-shaped one opposite was at once recognised; one point of view on the talus of Mount Morumbwa was not more than 700 or 800 yards distant from the other, and they then completed the survey of Kebrabasa from end to end.

They did not attempt to return by the way they came, but scaled the slope of the mountain on the north. It took them three hours' hard labour in cutting their way up through the dense thornbush which covered the ascent. The face of the slope was often about an angle of 70 degrees, yet their guide Shokumbenla, whose hard, horny soles, resembling those of elephants, showed that he was accustomed to this rough and hot work, carried a pot of water for them nearly all the way up. They slept that night at a well in a tufaceous rock on the N.W. of Chipereziwa, and never was sleep more sweet.

A band of native musicians came to our camp one evening, on our own way down, and treated us with their wild and not unpleasant music on the Marimba, an instrument formed of bars of hard wood of varying breadth and thickness, laid on different-sized hollow calabashes, and tuned to give the notes; a few pieces of cloth pleased them, and they passed on.

The rainy season of Tette differs a little from that of some of the other intertropical regions; the quantity of rain-fall being considerably less. It begins in November and ends in April. During our first season in that place, only a little over nineteen inches of rain fell. In an average year, and when the crops are good, the fall amounts to about thirty-five inches. On many days it does not rain at all, and rarely is it wet all day; some days have merely a passing shower, preceded and followed by hot sunshine; occasionally an interval of a week, or even a fortnight, passes without a drop of rain, and then the crops suffer from the sun. These partial droughts happen in December and January. The heat appears to increase to a certain point in the different latitudes so as to necessitate a change, by some law similar to that which regulates the intense cold in other countries. After several days of progressive heat here, on the hottest of which the thermometer probably reaches 103 degrees in the shade, a break occurs in the weather, and a thunderstorm cools the air for a time. At Kuruman, when the thermometer stood above 84 degrees, rain might be expected; at Kolobeng, the point at which we looked for a storm was 96 degrees. The Zambesi is in flood twice in the course of the year; the first flood, a partial one, attains its greatest height about the end of December or beginning of January; the second, and greatest, occurs after the river inundates the interior, in a manner similar to the overflow of the Nile, this rise not taking place at Tette until March. The Portuguese say that the greatest height which the March floods attain is thirty feet at Tette, and this happens only about every fourth year; their observations, however, have never been very accurate on anything but ivory, and they have in this case trusted to memory alone. The only fluviometer at Tette, or anywhere else on the river, was set up at our suggestion; and the first flood was at its greatest height of thirteen feet six inches on the 17th January, 1859, and then gradually fell a few feet, until succeeded by the greater flood of March. The river rises suddenly, the water is highly discoloured and impure, and there is a four-knot current in many places; but in a day or two after the first rush of waters is passed, the current becomes more equally spread over the whole bed of the river, and resumes its usual rate in the channel, although continuing in flood. The Zambesi water at other times is almost chemically pure, and the photographer would find that it is nearly as good as distilled water for the nitrate of silver bath.

A third visit to Kebrabasa was made for the purpose of ascertaining whether it might be navigable when the Zambesi was in flood, the chief point of interest being of course Morumbwa; it was found that the rapids observed in our first trip had disappeared, and that while they were smoothed over, in a few places the current had increased in strength. As the river fell rapidly while we were on the journey, the cataract of Morumbwa did not differ materially from what it was when discovered. Some fishermen assured us that it was not visible when the river was at its fullest, and that the current was then not very strong. On this occasion we travelled on the right bank, and found it, with the additional inconvenience of rain, as rough and fatiguing as the left had been. Our progress was impeded by the tall wet grass and dripping boughs, and consequent fever. During the earlier part of the journey we came upon a few deserted hamlets only; but at last in a pleasant valley we met some of the people of the country, who were miserably poor and hungry. The women were gathering wild fruits in the woods. A young man having consented for two yards of cotton cloth to show us a short path to the cataract led us up a steep hill to a village perched on the edge of one of its precipices; a thunderstorm coming on at the time, the headman invited us to take shelter in a hut until it had passed.

Our guide having informed him of what he knew and conceived to be our object, was favoured in return with a long reply in well-sounding blank verse; at the end of every line the guide, who listened with deep attention, responded with a grunt, which soon became so ludicrous that our men burst into a loud laugh. Neither the poet nor the responsive guide took the slightest notice of their rudeness, but kept on as energetically as ever to the end. The speech, or more probably our bad manners, made some impression on our guide, for he declined, although offered double pay, to go any further.

A great deal of fever comes in with March and April; in March, if considerable intervals take place between the rainy days, and in April always, for then large surfaces of mud and decaying vegetation are exposed to the hot sun. In general an attack does not continue long, but it pulls one down quickly; though when the fever is checked the strength is as quickly restored. It had long been observed that those who were stationed for any length of time in one spot, and lived sedentary lives, suffered more from fever than others who moved about and had both mind and body occupied; but we could not all go in the small vessel when she made her trips, during which the change of place and scenery proved so conducive to health; and some of us were obliged to remain in charge of the expedition's property, making occasional branch trips to examine objects of interest in the vicinity. Whatever may be the cause of the fever, we observed that all were often affected at the same time, as if from malaria. This was particularly the case during a north wind: it was at first commonly believed that a daily dose of quinine would prevent the attack. For a number of months all our men, except two, took quinine regularly every morning. The fever some times attacked the believers in quinine, while the unbelievers in its prophylactic powers escaped. Whether we took it daily, or omitted it altogether for months, made no difference; the fever was impartial, and seized us on the days of quinine as regularly and as severely as when it remained undisturbed in the medicine chest, and we finally abandoned the use of it as a prophylactic altogether. The best preventive against fever is plenty of interesting work to do, and abundance of wholesome food to eat. To a man well housed and clothed, who enjoys these advantages, the fever at Tette will not prove a more formidable enemy than a common cold; but let one of these be wanting--let him be indolent, or guilty of excesses in eating or drinking, or have poor, scanty fare,--and the fever will probably become a more serious matter. It is of a milder type at Tette than at Quillimane or on the low sea-coast; and, as in this part of Africa one is as liable to fever as to colds in England, it would be advisable for strangers always to hasten from the coast to the high lands, in order that when the seizure does take place, it may be of the mildest type. Although quinine was not found to be a preventive, except possibly in the way of acting as a tonic, and rendering the system more able to resist the influence of malaria, it was found invaluable in the cure of the complaint, as soon as pains in the back, sore bones, headache, yawning, quick and sometimes intermittent pulse, noticeable pulsations of the jugulars, with suffused eyes, hot skin, and foul tongue, began. {1}

Very curious are the effects of African fever on certain minds. Cheerfulness vanishes, and the whole mental horizon is overcast with black clouds of gloom and sadness. The liveliest joke cannot provoke even the semblance of a smile. The countenance is grave, the eyes suffused, and the few utterances are made in the piping voice of a wailing infant. An irritable temper is often the first symptom of approaching fever. At such times a man feels very much like a fool, if he does not act like one. Nothing is right, nothing pleases the fever-stricken victim. He is peevish, prone to find fault and to contradict, and think himself insulted, and is exactly what an Irish naval surgeon before a court-martial defined a drunken man to be: "a man unfit for society."

Finding that it was impossible to take our steamer of only ten-horse power through Kebrabasa, and convinced that, in order to force a passage when the river was in flood, much greater power was required, due information was forwarded to Her Majesty's Government, and application made for a more suitable vessel. Our attention was in the mean time turned to the exploration of the river Shire, a northern tributary of the Zambesi, which joins it about a hundred miles from the sea. We could learn nothing satisfactory from the Portuguese regarding this affluent; no one, they said, had ever been up it, nor could they tell whence it came. Years ago a Portuguese expedition is said, however, to have attempted the ascent, but to have abandoned it on account of the impenetrable duckweed (***Pistia stratiotes***.) We could not learn from any record that the Shire had ever been ascended by Europeans. As far, therefore, as we were concerned, the exploration was absolutely new. All the Portuguese believed the Manganja to be brave but bloodthirsty savages; and on our return we found that soon after our departure a report was widely spread that our temerity had been followed by fatal results, Dr. Livingstone having been shot, and Dr. Kirk mortally wounded by poisoned arrows.

Our first trip to the Shire was in January, 1859. A considerable quantity of weed floated down the river for the first twenty-five miles, but not sufficient to interrupt navigation with canoes or with any other craft. Nearly the whole of this aquatic plant proceeds from a marsh on the west, and comes into the river a little beyond a lofty hill called Mount Morambala. Above that there is hardly any. As we approached the villages, the natives collected in large numbers, armed with bows and poisoned arrows; and some, dodging behind trees, were observed taking aim as if on the point of shooting. All the women had been sent out of the way, and the men were evidently prepared to resist aggression. At the village of a chief named Tingane, at least five hundred natives collected and ordered us to stop. Dr. Livingstone went ashore; and on his explaining that we were English and had come neither to take slaves nor to fight, but only to open a path by which our countrymen might follow to purchase cotton, or whatever else they might have to sell, except slaves, Tingane became at once quite friendly. The presence of the steamer, which showed that they had an entirely new people to deal with, probably contributed to this result; for Tingane was notorious for being the barrier to all intercourse between the Portuguese black traders and the natives further inland; none were allowed to pass him either way. He was an elderly, well-made man, grey-headed, and over six feet high. Though somewhat excited by our presence, he readily complied with the request to call his people together, in order that all might know what our objects were.

In commencing intercourse with any people we almost always referred to the English detestation of slavery. Most of them already possess some information respecting the efforts made by the English at sea to suppress the slave-trade; and our work being to induce them to raise and sell cotton, instead of capturing and selling their fellow-men, our errand appears quite natural; and as they all have clear ideas of their own self- interest, and are keen traders, the reasonableness of the proposal is at once admitted; and as a belief in a Supreme Being, the Maker and Ruler of all things, and in the continued existence of departed spirits, is universal, it becomes quite appropriate to explain that we possess a Book containing a Revelation of the will of Him to whom in their natural state they recognise no relationship. The fact that His Son appeared among men, and left His words in His Book, always awakens attention; but the great difficulty is to make them feel that they have any relationship to Him, and that He feels any interest in them. The numbness of moral perception exhibited, is often discouraging; but the mode of communication, either by interpreters, or by the imperfect knowledge of the language, which not even missionaries of talent can overcome save by the labour of many years, may, in part, account for the phenomenon. However, the idea of the Father of all being displeased with His children, for selling or killing each other, at once gains their ready assent: it harmonizes so exactly with their own ideas of right and wrong. But, as in our own case at home, nothing less than the instruction and example of many years will secure their moral elevation.

The dialect spoken here closely resembles that used at Senna and Tette. We understood it at first only enough to know whether our interpreter was saying what we bade him, or was indulging in his own version. After stating pretty nearly what he was told, he had an inveterate tendency to wind up with "The Book says you are to grow cotton, and the English are to come and buy it," or with some joke of his own, which might have been ludicrous, had it not been seriously distressing.

In the first ascent of the Shire our attention was chiefly directed to the river itself. The delight of threading out the meanderings of upwards of 200 miles of a hitherto unexplored river must be felt to be appreciated. All the lower part of the river was found to be at least two fathoms in depth. It became shallower higher up, where many departing and re-entering branches diminished the volume of water, but the absence of sandbanks made it easy of navigation. We had to exercise the greatest care lest anything we did should be misconstrued by the crowds who watched us. After having made, in a straight line, one hundred miles, although the windings of the river had fully doubled the distance, we found further progress with the steamer arrested, in 15 degrees 55 minutes south, by magnificent cataracts, which we called, "The Murchison," after one whose name has already a world-wide fame, and whose generous kindness we can never repay. The native name of that figured in the woodcut is Mamvira. It is that at which the progress of the steamer was first stopped. The angle of descent is much smaller than that of the five cataracts above it; indeed, so small as compared with them, that after they were discovered this was not included in the number.

A few days were spent here in the hope that there might be an opportunity of taking observations for longitude, but it rained most of the time, or the sky was overcast. It was deemed imprudent to risk a land journey whilst the natives were so very suspicious as to have a strong guard on the banks of the river night and day; the weather also was unfavourable. After sending presents and messages to two of the chiefs, we returned to Tette. In going down stream our progress was rapid, as we were aided by the current. The hippopotami never made a mistake, but got out of our way. The crocodiles, not so wise, sometimes rushed with great velocity at us, thinking that we were some huge animal swimming. They kept about a foot from the surface, but made three well-defined ripples from the feet and body, which marked their rapid progress; raising the head out of the water when only a few yards from the expected feast, down they went to the bottom like a stone, without touching the boat.

In the middle of March of the same year (1859), we started again for a second trip on the Shire. The natives were now friendly, and readily sold us rice, fowls, and corn. We entered into amicable relations with the chief, Chibisa, whose village was about ten miles below the cataract. He had sent two men on our first visit to invite us to drink beer; but the steamer was such a terrible apparition to them, that, after shouting the invitation, they jumped ashore, and left their canoe to drift down the stream. Chibisa was a remarkably shrewd man, the very image, save his dark hue, of one of our most celebrated London actors, {2} and the most intelligent chief, by far, in this quarter. A great deal of fighting had fallen to his lot, he said; but it was always others who began; he was invariably in the right, and they alone were to blame. He was moreover a firm believer in the divine right of kings. He was an ordinary man, he said, when his father died, and left him the chieftainship; but directly he succeeded to the high office, he was conscious of power passing into his head, and down his back; he felt it enter, and knew that he was a chief, clothed with authority, and possessed of wisdom; and people then began to fear and reverence him. He mentioned this, as one would a fact of natural history, any doubt being quite out of the question. His people, too, believed in him, for they bathed in the river without the slightest fear of crocodiles, the chief having placed a powerful medicine there, which protected them from the bite of these terrible reptiles.

A Popular Account of Dr. Livingstone's Expedition to the Zambesi 49

Leaving the vessel opposite Chibisa's village, Drs. Livingstone and Kirk and a number of the Makololo started on foot for Lake Shirwa. They travelled in a northerly direction over a mountainous country. The people were far from being well-disposed to them, and some of their guides tried to mislead them, and could not be trusted. Masakasa, a Makololo headman, overheard some remarks which satisfied him that the guide was leading them into trouble. He was quiet till they reached a lonely spot, when he came up to Dr. Livingstone, and said, "That fellow is bad, he is taking us into mischief; my spear is sharp, and there is no one here; shall I cast him into the long grass?" Had the Doctor given the slightest token of assent, or even kept silence, never more would any one have been led by that guide, for in a twinkling he would have been where "the wicked cease from troubling." It was afterwards found that in this case there was no treachery at all, but a want of knowledge on their part of the language and of the country. They asked to be led to "Nyanja Mukulu," or Great Lake, meaning, by this, Lake Shirwa; and the guide took them round a terribly rough piece of mountainous country, gradually edging away towards a long marsh, which from the numbers of those animals we had seen there we had called the Elephant Marsh, but which was really the place known to him by the name "Nyanja Mukulu," or Great Lake. Nyanja or Nyanza means, generally, a marsh, lake, river, or even a mere rivulet.

The party pushed on at last without guides, or only with crazy ones; for, oddly enough, they were often under great obligations to the madmen of the different villages: one of these honoured them, as they slept in the open air, by dancing and singing at their feet the whole night. These poor fellows sympathized with the explorers, probably in the belief that they belonged to their own class; and, uninfluenced by the general opinion of their countrymen, they really pitied, and took kindly to the strangers, and often guided them faithfully from place to place, when no sane man could be hired for love or money.

The bearing of the Manganja at this time was very independent; a striking contrast to the cringing attitude they afterwards assumed, when the cruel scourge of slave-hunting passed over their country. Signals were given from the different villages by means of drums, and notes of defiance and intimidation were sounded in the travellers' ears by day; and occasionally they were kept awake the whole night, in expectation of an instant attack. Drs. Livingstone and Kirk were desirous that nothing should occur to make the natives regard them as enemies; Masakasa, on the other hand, was anxious to show what he could do in the way of fighting them.

The perseverance of the party was finally crowned with success; for on the 18th of April they discovered Lake Shirwa, a considerable body of bitter water, containing leeches, fish, crocodiles, and hippopotami. From having probably no outlet, the water is slightly brackish, and it appears to be deep, with islands like hills rising out of it. Their point of view was at the base of Mount Pirimiti or Mopeu-peu, on its S.S.W. side. Thence the prospect northwards ended in a sea horizon with two small islands in the distance--a larger one, resembling a hill-top and covered with trees, rose more in the foreground. Ranges of hills appeared on the east; and on the west stood Mount Chikala, which seems to be connected with the great mountain-mass called Zomba.

The shore, near which they spent two nights, was covered with reeds and papyrus. Wishing to obtain the latitude by the natural horizon, they waded into the water some distance towards what was reported to be a sandbank, but were so assaulted by leeches, they were fain to retreat; and a woman told them that in enticing them into the water the men only wanted to kill them. The information gathered was that this lake was nothing in size compared to another in the north, from which it is separated by only a tongue of land. The northern end of Shirwa has not been seen, though it has been passed; the length of the lake may probably be 60 or 80 miles, and about 20 broad. The height above the sea is 1800 feet, and the taste of the water is like a weak solution of Epsom salts. The country around is very beautiful, and clothed with rich vegetation; and the waves, at the time they were there breaking and foaming over a rock on the south-eastern side, added to the beauty of the picture. Exceedingly lofty mountains, perhaps 8000 feet above the sea-level, stand near the eastern shore. When their lofty steep-sided summits appear, some above, some below the clouds, the scene is grand. This range is called Milanje; on the west stands Mount Zomba, 7000 feet in height, and some twenty miles long.

Their object being rather to gain the confidence of the people by degrees than to explore, they considered that they had advanced far enough into the country for one trip; and believing that they could secure their end by a repetition of their visit, as they had done on the Shire, they decided to return to the vessel at Dakanamoio island; but, instead of returning by the way they came, they passed down southwards close by Mount Chiradzuru, among the relatives of Chibisa, and thence by the pass Zedi, down to the Shire. The Kroomen had, while we were away, cut a good supply of wood for steaming, and we soon proceeded down the river.

The steamer reached Tette on the 23rd of June, and, after undergoing repairs, proceeded to the Kongone to receive provisions from one of H.M. cruisers. We had been very abundantly supplied with first-rate stores, but were unfortunate enough to lose a considerable portion of them, and had now to bear the privation as best we could. On the way down, we purchased a few gigantic cabbages and pumpkins at a native village below Mazaro. Our dinners had usually consisted of but a single course; but we were surprised the next day by our black cook from Sierra Leone bearing in a second course. "What have you got there?" was asked in wonder. "A tart, sir." "A tart! of what is it made?" "Of cabbage, sir." As we had no sugar, and could not "make believe," as in the days of boyhood, we did not enjoy the feast that Tom's genius had prepared. Her Majesty's brig "Persian," Lieutenant Saumarez commanding, called on her way to the Cape; and, though somewhat short of provisions herself, generously gave us all she could spare. We now parted with our Kroomen, as, from their inability to march, we could not use them in our land journeys. A crew was picked out from the Makololo, who, besides being good travellers, could cut wood, work the ship, and required only native food.

While at the Kongone it was found necessary to beach the steamer for repairs. She was built of a newly invented sort of steel plates, only a sixteenth of an inch in thickness, patented, but unfortunately never tried before. To build an exploring ship of untried material was a mistake. Some chemical action on this preparation of steel caused a minute hole; from this point, branches like lichens, or the little ragged stars we sometimes see in thawing ice, radiated in all directions. Small holes went through wherever a bend occurred in these branches. The bottom very soon became like a sieve, completely full of minute holes, which leaked perpetually. The engineer stopped the larger ones, but the vessel was no sooner afloat, than new ones broke out. The first news of a morning was commonly the unpleasant announcement of another leak in the forward compartment, or in the middle, which was worse still.

Frequent showers fell on our way up the Zambesi, in the beginning of August. On the 8th we had upwards of three inches of rain, which large quantity, more than falls in any single rainy day during the season at Tette, we owed to being near the sea. Sometimes the cabin was nearly flooded; for, in addition to the leakage from below, rain poured through the roof, and an umbrella had to be used whenever we wished to write: the mode of coupling the compartments, too, was a new one, and the action of the hinder compartment on the middle one pumped up the water of the river, and sent it in streams over the floor and lockers, where lay the cushions which did double duty as chairs and beds. In trying to form an opinion of the climate, it must be recollected that much of the fever, from which we suffered, was caused by sleeping on these wet cushions. Many of the botanical specimens, laboriously collected and carefully prepared by Dr. Kirk, were destroyed, or double work imposed, by their accidentally falling into wet places in the cabin.

About the middle of August, after cutting wood at Shamoara, we again steamed up the Shire, with the intention of becoming better acquainted with the people, and making another and longer journey on foot to the north of Lake Shirwa, in search of Lake Nyassa, of which we had already received some information, under the name Nyinyesi (the stars). The Shire is much narrower than the Zambesi, but deeper, and more easily navigated. It drains a low and exceedingly fertile valley of from fifteen to twenty miles in breadth. Ranges of wooded hills bound this valley on both sides. For the first twenty miles the hills on the left bank are close to the river; then comes Morambala, a detached mountain 500 yards from the river's brink, which rises, with steep sides on the west, to 4000 feet in height, and is about seven miles in length. It is wooded up to the very top, and very beautiful. The southern end, seen from a distance, has a fine gradual slope, and looks as if it might be of easy ascent; but the side which faces the Shire is steep and rocky, especially in the upper half. A small village peeps out about halfway up the mountain; it has a pure and bracing atmosphere; and is perched above mosquito range. The people on the summit have a very different climate and vegetation from those of the plains; but they have to spend a great portion of their existence amidst white fleecy clouds, which, in the rainy season, rest daily on the top of their favourite mountain. We were kindly treated by these mountaineers on our first ascent; before our second they were nearly all swept away by Mariano. Dr. Kirk found upwards of thirty species of ferns on this and other mountains, and even good-sized tree-ferns; though scarcely a single kind is to be met with on the plains. Lemon and orange trees grew wild, and pineapples had been planted by the people. Many large hornbills, hawks, monkeys, antelopes, and rhinoceroses found a home and food among the great trees round its base. A hot fountain boils up on the plain near the north end. It bubbles out of the earth, clear as crystal, at two points, or eyes, a few yards apart from each other, and sends off a fine flowing stream of hot water. The temperature was found to be 174 degrees Fahr., and it boiled an egg in about the usual time. Our guide threw in a small branch to show us how speedily the Madse-awira (boiling water) could kill the leaves. Unlucky lizards and insects did not seem to understand the nature of a hot-spring, as many of their remains were lying at the bottom. A large beetle had alighted on the water, and been killed before it had time to fold its wings. An incrustation, smelling of sulphur, has been deposited by the water on the stones. About a hundred feet from the eye of the fountain the mud is as hot as can be borne by the body. In taking a bath there, it makes the skin perfectly clean, and none of the mud adheres: it is strange that the Portuguese do not resort to it for the numerous cutaneous diseases with which they are so often afflicted.

A few clumps of the palm and acacia trees appear west of Morambala, on the rich plain forming the tongue of land between the rivers Shire and Zambesi. This is a good place for all sorts of game. The Zambesi canoe- men were afraid to sleep on it from the idea of lions being there; they preferred to pass the night on an island. Some black men, who accompanied us as volunteer workmen from Shupanga, called out one evening that a lion stood on the bank. It was very dark, and we could only see two sparkling lights, said to be the lion's eyes looking at us; for here, as elsewhere, they have a theory that the lion's eyes always flash fire at night. Not being fireflies--as they did not move when a shot was fired in their direction--they were probably glowworms.

Beyond Morambala the Shire comes winding through an extensive marsh. For many miles to the north a broad sea of fresh green grass extends, and is so level, that it might be used for taking the meridian altitude of the sun. Ten or fifteen miles north of Morambala, stands the dome-shaped mountain Makanga, or Chi-kanda; several others with granitic-looking peaks stretch away to the north, and form the eastern boundary of the valley; another range, but of metamorphic rocks, commencing opposite Senna, bounds the valley on the west. After streaming through a portion of this marsh, we came to a broad belt of palm and other trees, crossing the fine plain on the right bank. Marks of large game were abundant. Elephants had been feeding on the palm nuts, which have a pleasant fruity taste, and are used as food by man. Two pythons were observed coiled together among the branches of a large tree, and were both shot. The larger of the two, a female, was ten feet long. They are harmless, and said to be good eating. The Makololo having set fire to the grass where they were cutting wood, a solitary buffalo rushed out of the conflagration, and made a furious charge at an active young fellow named Mantlanyane. Never did his fleet limbs serve him better than during the few seconds of his fearful flight before the maddened animal. When he reached the bank, and sprang into the river, the infuriated beast was scarcely six feet behind him. Towards evening, after the day's labour in wood-cutting was over, some of the men went fishing. They followed the common African custom of agitating the water, by giving it a few sharp strokes with the top of the fishing-rod, immediately after throwing in the line, to attract the attention of the fish to the bait. Having caught nothing, the reason assigned was the same as would have been given in England under like circumstances, namely, that "the wind made the fish cold, and they would not bite." Many gardens of maize, pumpkins, and tobacco, fringed the marshy banks as we went on. They belong to natives of the hills, who come down in the dry season, and raise a crop on parts at other times flooded. While the crops are growing, large quantities of fish are caught, chiefly **Clarias capensis**, and **Mugil Africanus**; they are dried for sale or future consumption.

As we ascended, we passed a deep stream about thirty yards wide, flowing in from a body of open water several miles broad. Numbers of men were busy at different parts of it, filling their canoes with the lotus root, called **Nyika**, which, when boiled or roasted, resembles our chestnuts, and is extensively used in Africa as food. Out of this lagoon, and by this stream, the chief part of the duckweed of the Shire flows. The lagoon itself is called Nyanja ea Motope (Lake of Mud). It is also named Nyanja Pangono (Little Lake), while the elephant marsh goes by the name of Nyanja Mukulu (Great Lake). It is evident from the shore line still to be observed on the adjacent hills, that in ancient times these were really lakes, and the traditional names thus preserved are only another evidence of the general desiccation which Africa has undergone.

CHAPTER III.

The Steamer in difficulties--Elephant hunting--Arrival at Chibisa's--Search for Lake Nyassa--The Manganja country--Weavers and smelters--Lake Pamalombe.

Late in the afternoon of the first day's steaming, after we left the wooding-place, we called at the village of Chikanda-Kadze, a female chief, to purchase rice for our men; but we were now in the blissful region where time is absolutely of no account, and where men may sit down and rest themselves when tired; so they requested us to wait till next day, and they would then sell us some food. As our forty black men, however, had nothing to cook for supper, we were obliged to steam on to reach a village a few miles above. When we meet those who care not whether we purchase or let it alone, or who think men ought only to be in a hurry when fleeing from an enemy, our ideas about time being money, and the power of the purse, receives a shock. The state of eager competition, which in England wears out both mind and body, and makes life bitter, is here happily unknown. The cultivated spots are mere dots compared to the broad fields of rich soil which is never either grazed or tilled. Pity that the plenty in store for all, from our Father's bountiful hands, is not enjoyed by more.

The wretched little steamer could not carry all the hands we needed; so, to lighten her, we put some into the boats and towed them astern. In the dark, one of the boats was capsized; but all in it, except one poor fellow who could not swim, were picked up. His loss threw a gloom over us all, and added to the chagrin we often felt at having been so ill-served in our sorry craft.

Next day we arrived at the village of Mboma (16 degrees 56 minutes 30 seconds S.), where the people raised large quantities of rice, and were eager traders; the rice was sold at wonderfully low rates, and we could not purchase a tithe of the food brought for sale.

A native minstrel serenaded us in the evening, playing several quaint tunes on a species of one stringed fiddle, accompanied by wild, but not unmusical songs. He told the Makololo that he intended to play all night to induce us to give him a present. The nights being cold, the thermometer falling to 47 degrees, with occasional fogs, he was asked if he was not afraid of perishing from cold; but, with the genuine spirit of an Italian organ-grinder, he replied, "Oh, no; I shall spend the night with my white comrades in the big canoe; I have often heard of the white men, but have never seen them till now, and I must sing and play well to them." A small piece of cloth, however, bought him off, and he moved away in good humour. The water of the river was 70 degrees at sunrise, which was 23 degrees warmer than the air at the same time, and this caused fogs, which rose like steam off the river. When this is the case cold bathing in the mornings at this time of the year is improper, for, instead of a glow on coming out, one is apt to get a chill; the air being so much colder than the water.

A range of hills, commencing opposite Senna, comes to within two or three miles of Mboma village, and then runs in a north-westerly direction; the principal hill is named Malawe; a number of villages stand on its tree-covered sides, and coal is found cropping out in the rocks. The country improves as we ascend, the rich valley becoming less swampy, and adorned with a number of trees.

Both banks are dotted with hippopotamus traps, over every track which these animals have made in going up out of the water to graze. The hippopotamus feeds on grass alone, and, where there is any danger, only at night. Its enormous lips act like a mowing-machine, and form a path of short-cropped grass as it feeds. We never saw it eat aquatic plants or reeds. The tusks seem weapons of both offence and defence. The hippopotamus trap consists of a beam five or six feet long, armed with a spear-head or hard-wood spike, covered with poison, and suspended to a forked pole by a cord, which, coming down to the path, is held by a catch, to be set free when the beast treads on it. Being wary brutes, they are still very numerous. One got frightened by the ship, as she was steaming close to the bank. In its eager hurry to escape it rushed on shore, and ran directly under a trap, when down came the heavy beam on its back, driving the poisoned spear-head a foot deep into its flesh. In its agony it plunged back into the river, to die in a few hours, and afterwards furnished a feast for the natives. The poison on the spear-head does not affect the meat, except the part around the wound, and that is thrown away. In some places the descending beam is weighted with heavy stones, but here the hard heavy wood is sufficient.

"She is leaking worse than ever forward, sir, and there is a foot of water in the hold," was our first salutation on the morning of the 20th. But we have become accustomed to these things now; the cabin-floor is always wet, and one is obliged to mop up the water many times a day, giving some countenance to the native idea that Englishmen live in or on the water, and have no houses but ships. The cabin is now a favourite breeding-place for mosquitoes, and we have to support both the ship-bred and shore-bred bloodsuckers, of which several species show us their irritating attentions. A large brown sort, called by the Portuguese **mansos** (tame), flies straight to its victim, and goes to work at once, as though it were an invited guest. Some of the small kinds carry uncommonly sharp lancets, and very potent poison. "What would these insects eat, if we did not pass this way?" becomes a natural question.

The juices of plants, and decaying vegetable matter in the mud, probably form the natural food of mosquitoes, and blood is not necessary for their existence. They appear so commonly at malarious spots, that their presence may be taken as a hint to man to be off to more healthy localities. None appear on the high lands. On the low lands they swarm in myriads. The females alone are furnished with the biting apparatus, and their number appears to be out of all proportion in excess of the males. At anchor, on a still evening, they were excessively annoying; and the sooner we took refuge under our mosquito curtains, the better. The miserable and sleepless night that only one mosquito inside the curtain can cause, is so well known, and has been so often described, that it is needless to describe it here. One soon learns, from experience, that to beat out the curtains thoroughly before entering them, so that not one of these pests can possibly be harboured within, is the only safeguard against such severe trials to one's tranquillity and temper.

A few miles above Mboma we came again to the village (16 degrees 44 minutes 30 seconds S.) of the chief Tingane, the beat of whose war-drums can speedily muster some hundreds of armed men. The bows and poisoned arrows here are of superior workmanship to those below. Mariano's slave-hunting parties stood in great awe of these barbed arrows, and long kept aloof from Tingane's villages. His people were friendly enough with us now, and covered the banks with a variety of articles for sale. The majestic mountain, Chipirone, to which we have given the name of Mount Clarendon, now looms in sight, and further to the N.W. the southern end of the grand Milanje range rises in the form of an unfinished sphinx looking down on Lake Shirwa. The Ruo (16 degrees 31 minutes 0 seconds S.) is said to have its source in the Milanje mountains, and flows to the S.W., to join the Shire some distance above Tingane's. A short way beyond the Ruo lies the Elephant marsh, or Nyanja Mukulu, which is frequented by vast herds of these animals. We believe that we counted eight hundred elephants in sight at once. In the choice of such a strong hold, they have shown their usual sagacity, for no hunter can get near them through the swamps. They now keep far from the steamer; but, when she first came up, we steamed into the midst of a herd, and some were shot from the ship's deck. A single lesson was sufficient to teach them that the steamer was a thing to be avoided; and at the first glimpse they are now off two or three miles to the midst of the marsh, which is furrowed in every direction by wandering branches of the Shire. A fine young elephant was here caught alive, as he was climbing up the bank to follow his retreating dam. When laid hold of, he screamed with so much energy that, to escape a visit from the enraged mother, we steamed off, and dragged him through the water by the proboscis. As the men were holding his trunk over the gunwale, Monga, a brave Makololo elephant-hunter, rushed aft, and drew his knife across it in a sort of frenzy peculiar to the chase. The wound was skilfully sewn up, and the young animal soon became quite tame, but, unfortunately the breathing prevented the cut from healing, and he died in a few days from loss of blood. Had he lived, and had we been able to bring him home, he would have been the first *African* elephant ever seen in England. The African male elephant is from ten to a little over eleven feet in height, and differs from the Asiatic species more particularly in the convex shape of his forehead, and the enormous size of his ears. In Asia many of the males, and all the females, are without tusks, but in Africa both sexes are provided with these weapons. The enamel in the molar teeth is arranged differently in the two species. By an admirable provision, new teeth constantly come up at the part where in man the wisdom teeth appear, and these push the others along, and out at the front end of the jaws, thus keeping the molars sound by renewal, till the animal attains a very great age. The tusks of animals from dry rocky countries are very munch more dense and heavier than those from wet and marshy districts, but the latter attain much the larger size.

The Shire marshes support prodigious numbers of many kinds of water-fowl. An hour at the mast-head unfolds novel views of life in an African marsh. Near the edge, and on the branches of some favourite tree, rest scores of plotuses and cormorants, which stretch their snake-like necks, and in mute amazement turn one eye and then another towards the approaching monster. By-and-by the timid ones begin to fly off, or take "headers" into the stream; but a few of the bolder, or more composed, remain, only taking the precaution to spread their wings ready for instant flight. The pretty ardetta (**Herodias bubulcus**), of a light yellow colour when at rest, but seemingly of a pure white when flying, takes wing, and sweeps across the green grass in large numbers, often showing us where buffaloes and elephants are, by perching on their backs. Flocks of ducks, of which the kind called "Soriri" (**Dendrocygna personata**) is most abundant, being night feeders, meditate quietly by the small lagoons, until startled by the noise of the steam machinery. Pelicans glide over the water, catching fish, while the Scopus (**Scopus umbretta**) and large herons peer intently into pools. The large black and white spur-winged goose (a constant marauder of native gardens) springs up, and circles round to find out what the disturbance can be, and then settles down again with a splash. Hundreds of Linongolos (**Anastomus lamelligerus**) rise on the wing from the clumps of reeds, or low trees (the **Eschinomena**, from which pith hats are made), on which they build in colonies, and are speedily high in mid-air. Charming little red and yellow weavers (**Ploceidae**) remind one of butterflies, as they fly in and out of the tall grass, or hang to the mouths of their pendent nests, chattering briskly to their mates within. These weavers seem to have "cock nests," built with only a roof, and a perch beneath, with a doorway on each side. The natives say they are made to protect the bird from the rain. Though her husband is very attentive, we have seen the hen bird tearing her mate's nest to pieces, but why we cannot tell. Kites and vultures are busy overhead, beating the ground for their repast of carrion; and the solemn-looking, stately-stepping Marabout, with a taste for dead fish, or men, stalks slowly along the almost stagnant channels. Groups of men and boys are searching diligently in various places for lotus and other roots. Some are standing in canoes, on the weed-covered ponds, spearing fish, while others are punting over the small intersecting streams, to examine their sunken fish-baskets.

Towards evening, hundreds of pretty little hawks (***Erythropus vespertinus***) are seen flying in a southerly direction, and feeding on dragon-flies and locusts. They come, apparently, from resting on the palm-trees during the heat of the day. Flocks of scissor-bills (***Rhyncops***) are then also on the wing, and in search of food, ploughing the water with their lower mandibles, which are nearly half an inch longer than the upper ones.

At the north-eastern end of the marsh, and about three miles from the river, commences a great forest of palm-trees (***Borassus AEthiopium***). It extends many miles, and at one point comes close to the river. The grey trunks and green tops of this immense mass of trees give a pleasing tone of colour to the view. The mountain-range, which rises close behind the palms, is generally of a cheerful green, and has many trees, with patches of a lighter tint among them, as if spots of land had once been cultivated. The sharp angular rocks and dells on its sides have the appearance of a huge crystal broken; and this is so often the case in Africa, that one can guess pretty nearly at sight whether a range is of the old crystalline rocks or not. The Borassus, though not an oil-bearing palm, is a useful tree. The fibrous pulp round the large nuts is of a sweet fruity taste, and is eaten by men and elephants. The natives bury the nuts until the kernels begin to sprout; when dug up and broken, the inside resembles coarse potatoes, and is prized in times of scarcity as nutritious food. During several months of the year, palm- wine, or sura, is obtained in large quantities; when fresh, it is a pleasant drink, somewhat like champagne, and not at all intoxicating; though, after standing a few hours, it becomes highly so. Sticks, a foot long, are driven into notches in the hard outside of the tree--the inside being soft or hollow--to serve as a ladder; the top of the fruit-shoot is cut off, and the sap, pouring out at the fresh wound, is caught in an earthen pot, which is hung at the point. A thin slice is taken off the end, to open the pores, and make the juice flow every time the owner ascends to empty the pot. Temporary huts are erected in the forest, and men and boys remain by their respective trees day and night; the nuts, fish, and wine, being their sole food. The Portuguese use the palm-wine as yeast, and it makes bread so light, that it melts in the mouth like froth.

Beyond the marsh the country is higher, and has a much larger population.

We passed a long line of temporary huts, on a plain on the right bank, with crowds of men and women hard at work making salt. They obtain it by mixing the earth, which is here highly saline, with water, in a pot with a small hole in it, and then evaporating the liquid, which runs through, in the sun. From the number of women we saw carrying it off in bags, we concluded that vast quantities must be made at these works. It is worth observing that on soils like this, containing salt, the cotton is of larger and finer staple than elsewhere. We saw large tracts of this rich brackish soil both in the Shire and Zambesi valleys, and hence, probably, sea-island cotton would do well; a single plant of it, reared by Major Sicard, flourished and produced the long staple and peculiar tinge of this celebrated variety, though planted only in the street at Tette; and there also a salt efflorescence appears, probably from decomposition of the rock, off which the people scrape it for use.

The large village of the chief, Mankokwe, occupies a site on the right bank; he owns a number of fertile islands, and is said to be the Rundo, or paramount chief, of a large district. Being of an unhappy suspicious disposition, he would not see us; so we thought it best to move on, rather than spend time in seeking his favour.

On the 25th August we reached Dakanamoio island, opposite the perpendicular bluff on which Chibisa's village stands; he had gone, with most of his people, to live near the Zambesi, but his headman was civil, and promised us guides and whatever else we needed. A few of the men were busy cleaning, sorting, spinning, and weaving cotton. This is a common sight in nearly every village, and each family appears to have its patch of cotton, as our own ancestors in Scotland had each his patch of flax. Near sunset an immense flock of the large species of horn-bill (**Buceros cristatus**) came here to roost on the great trees which skirt the edge of the cliff. They leave early in the morning, often before sunrise, for their feeding-places, coming and going in pairs. They are evidently of a loving disposition, and strongly attached to each other, the male always nestling close beside his mate. A fine male fell to the ground, from fear, at the report of Dr. Kirk's gun; it was caught and kept on board; the female did not go off in the mornings to feed with the others, but flew round the ship, anxiously trying, by her plaintive calls, to induce her beloved one to follow her: she came again in the evenings to repeat the invitations. The poor disconsolate captive soon refused to eat, and in five days died of grief, because he could not have her company. No internal injury could be detected after death.

Chibisa and his wife, with a natural show of parental feeling, had told the Doctor, on his previous visit, that a few years before some of Chisaka's men had kidnapped and sold their little daughter, and that she was now a slave to the padre at Tette. On his return to Tette, the Doctor tried hard to ransom and restore the girl to her parents, and offered twice the value of a slave; the padre seemed willing, but she could not be found. This padre was better than the average men of the country; and, being always civil and obliging, would probably have restored her gratuitously, but she had been sold, it might be to the distant tribe Bazizulu, or he could not tell where. Custom had rendered his feelings callous, and Chibisa had to be told that his child would never return. It is this callous state of mind which leads some of our own blood to quote Scripture in support of slavery. If we could afford to take a backward step in civilization, we might find men among ourselves who would in like manner prove Mormonism or any other enormity to be divine.

We left the ship on the 28th of August, 1859, for the discovery of Lake Nyassa. Our party numbered forty-two in all--four whites, thirty-six Makololo, and two guides. We did not actually need so many, either for carriage or defence; but took them because we believed that, human nature being everywhere the same, blacks are as ready as whites to take advantage of the weak, and are as civil and respectful to the powerful. We armed our men with muskets, which gave us influence, although it did not add much to our strength, as most of the men had never drawn a trigger, and in any conflict would in all probability have been more dangerous to us than the enemy.

Our path crossed the valley, in a north-easterly direction, up the course of a beautiful flowing stream. Many of the gardens had excellent cotton growing in them. An hour's march brought us to the foot of the Manganja hills, up which lay the toilsome road. The vegetation soon changed; as we rose bamboos appeared, and new trees and plants were met with, which gave such incessant employment to Dr. Kirk, that he travelled the distance three times over. Remarkably fine trees, one of which has oil- yielding seeds, and belongs to the mahogany family, grow well in the hollows along the rivulet courses. The ascent became very fatiguing, and we were glad of a rest. Looking back from an elevation of a thousand feet, we beheld a lovely prospect. The eye takes in at a glance the valley beneath, and the many windings of its silver stream Makubula, or Kubvula, from the shady hill-side, where it emerges in foaming haste, to where it slowly glides into the tranquil Shire; then the Shire itself is seen for many a mile above and below Chibisa's, and the great level country beyond, with its numerous green woods; until the prospect, west and north-west, is bounded far away by masses of peaked and dome-shaped blue mountains, that fringe the highlands of the Maravi country.

After a weary march we halted at Makolongwi, the village of Chitimba. It stands in a woody hollow on the first of the three terraces of the Manganja hills, and, like all other Manganja villages, is surrounded by an impenetrable hedge of poisonous euphorbia. This tree casts a deep shade, which would render it difficult for bowmen to take aim at the villagers inside. The grass does not grow beneath it, and this may be the reason why it is so universally used, for when dry the grass would readily convey fire to the huts inside; moreover, the hedge acts as a fender to all flying sparks. As strangers are wont to do, we sat down under some fine trees near the entrance of the village. A couple of mats, made of split reeds, were spread for the white men to sit on; and the headman brought a seguati, or present, of a small goat and a basket of meal. The full value in beads and cotton cloth was handed to him in return. He measured the cloth, doubled it, and then measured that again. The beads were scrutinized; he had never seen beads of that colour before, and should like to consult with his comrades before accepting them, and this, after repeated examinations and much anxious talk, he concluded to do. Meal and peas were then brought for sale. A fathom of blue cotton cloth, a full dress for man or woman, was produced. Our Makololo headman, Sininyane, thinking a part of it was enough for the meal, was proceeding to tear it, when Chitimba remarked that it was a pity to cut such a nice dress for his wife, he would rather bring more meal. "All right," said Sininyane; "but look, the cloth is very wide, so see that the basket which carries the meal be wide too, and add a cock to make the meal taste nicely." A brisk trade sprang up at once, each being eager to obtain as fine things as his neighbour,--and all were in good humour. Women and girls began to pound and grind meal, and men and boys chased the screaming fowls over the village, until they ran them down. In a few hours the market was completely glutted with every sort of native food; the prices, however, rarely fell, as they could easily eat what was not sold.

We slept under the trees, the air being pheasant, and no mosquitoes on the hills. According to our usual plan of marching, by early dawn our camp was in motion. After a cup of coffee and a bit of biscuit we were on the way. The air was deliciously cool, and the path a little easier than that of yesterday. We passed a number of villages, occupying very picturesque spots among the hills, and in a few hours gained the upper terrace, 3000 feet above the level of the sea. The plateau lies west of the Milanje mountains, and its north-eastern border slopes down to Lake Shirwa. We were all charmed with the splendid country, and looked with never-failing delight on its fertile plains, its numerous hills, and majestic mountains. In some of the passes we saw bramble-berries growing; and the many other flowers, though of great beauty, did not remind us of youth and of home like the ungainly thorny bramble-bushes. We were a week in crossing the highlands in a northerly direction; then we descended into the Upper Shire Valley, which is nearly 1200 feet above the level of the sea. This valley is wonderfully fertile, and supports a large population. After leaving the somewhat flat-topped southern portion, the most prominent mountain of the Zomba range is Njongone, which has a fine stream running past its northern base. We were detained at the end of the chain some days by one of our companions being laid up with fever. One night we were suddenly aroused by buffaloes rushing close by the sick-bed. We were encamped by a wood on the border of a marsh, but our patient soon recovered, notwithstanding the unfavourable situation, and the poor accommodation.

The Manganja country is delightfully well watered. The clear, cool, gushing streams are very numerous. Once we passed seven fine brooks and a spring in a single hour, and this, too, near the close of the dry season. Mount Zomba, which is twenty miles long, and from 7000 to 8000 feet high, has a beautiful stream flowing through a verdant valley on its summit, and running away down into Lake Shirwa. The highlands are well wooded, and many trees, admirable for their height and timber, grow on the various watercourses. "Is this country good for cattle?" we inquired of a Makololo herdsman, whose occupation had given him skill in pasturage. "Truly," he replied, "do you not see abundance of those grasses which the cattle love, and get fat upon?" Yet the people have but few goats, and fewer sheep. With the exception of an occasional leopard, there are no beasts of prey to disturb domestic animals. Wool- sheep would, without doubt, thrive on these highlands. Part of the Upper Shire valley has a lady paramount, named Nyango; and in her dominions women rank higher and receive more respectful treatment than their sisters on the hills.

The hill chief, Mongazi, called his wife to take charge of a present we had given him. She dropped down on her knees, clapping her hands in reverence, before and after receiving our presents from his lordly hands. It was painful to see the abject manner in which the women of the hill tribes knelt beside the path as we passed; but a great difference took place when we got into Nyango's country.

On entering a village, we proceeded, as all strangers do, at once to the Boalo: mats of split reeds or bamboo were usually spread for us to sit on. Our guides then told the men who might be there, who we were, whence we had come, whither we wanted to go, and what were our objects. This information was duly carried to the chief, who, if a sensible man, came at once; but, if he happened to be timid and suspicious, waited until he had used divination, and his warriors had time to come in from outlying hamlets. When he makes his appearance, all the people begin to clap their hands in unison, and continue doing so till he sits down opposite to us. His counsellors take their places beside him. He makes a remark or two, and is then silent for a few seconds. Our guides then sit down in front of the chief and his counsellors, and both parties lean forward, looking earnestly at each other; the chief repeats a word, such as "Ambuiatu" (our Father, or master)--or "moio" (life), and all clap their hands. Another word is followed by two claps, a third by still more clapping, when each touches the ground with both hands placed together. Then all rise and lean forward with measured clap, and sit down again with clap, clap, clap, fainter, and still fainter, till the last dies away, or is brought to an end by a smart loud clap from the chief. They keep perfect time in this species of court etiquette. Our guides now tell the chief, often in blank verse, all they have already told his people, with the addition perhaps of their own suspicions of the visitors. He asks some questions, and then converses with us through the guides. Direct communication between the chief and the head of the stranger party is not customary. In approaching they often ask who is the spokesman, and the spokesman of the chief addresses the person indicated exclusively. There is no lack of punctilious good manners. The accustomed presents are exchanged with civil ceremoniousness; until our men, wearied and hungry, call out, "English do not buy slaves, they buy food," and then the people bring meal, maize, fowls, batatas, yams, beans, beer, for sale.

The Manganja are an industrious race; and in addition to working in iron, cotton, and basket-making, they cultivate the soil extensively. All the people of a village turn out to labour in the fields. It is no uncommon thing to see men, women, and children hard at work, with the baby lying close by beneath a shady bush. When a new piece of woodland is to be cleared, they proceed exactly as farmers do in America. The trees are cut down with their little axes of soft native iron; trunks and branches are piled up and burnt, and the ashes spread on the soil. The corn is planted among the standing stumps which are left to rot. If grass land is to be brought under cultivation, as much tall grass as the labourer can conveniently lay hold of is collected together and tied into a knot. He then strikes his hoe round the tufts to sever the roots, and leaving all standing, proceeds until the whole ground assumes the appearance of a field covered with little shocks of corn in harvest. A short time before the rains begin, these grass shocks are collected in small heaps, covered with earth, and burnt, the ashes and burnt soil being used to fertilize the ground. Large crops of the mapira, or Egyptian dura (**Holcus sorghum**), are raised, with millet, beans, and ground-nuts; also patches of yams, rice, pumpkins, cucumbers, cassava, sweet potatoes, tobacco, and hemp, or bang (**Cannabis setiva**). Maize is grown all the year round. Cotton is cultivated at almost every village. Three varieties of cotton have been found in the country, namely, two foreign and one native. The "tonje manga," or foreign cotton, the name showing that it has been introduced, is of excellent quality, and considered at Manchester to be nearly equal to the best New Orleans. It is perennial, but requires replanting once in three years. A considerable amount of this variety is grown in the Upper and Lower Shire valleys. Every family of any importance owns a cotton patch which, from the entire absence of weeds, seemed to be carefully cultivated. Most were small, none seen on this journey exceeding half an acre; but on the former trip some were observed of more than twice that size.

The "tonje cadja," or indigenous cotton, is of shorter staple, and feels in the hand like wool. This kind has to be planted every season in the highlands; yet, because it makes stronger cloth, many of the people prefer it to the foreign cotton; the third variety is not found here. It was remarked to a number of men near the Shire Lakelet, a little further on towards Nyassa, "You should plant plenty of cotton, and probably the English will come and buy it." "Truly," replied a far-travelled Babisa trader to his fellows, "the country is full of cotton, and if these people come to buy they will enrich us." Our own observation on the cotton cultivated convinced us that this was no empty flourish, but a fact. Everywhere we met with it, and scarcely ever entered a village without finding a number of men cleaning, spinning, and weaving. It is first carefully separated from the seed by the fingers, or by an iron roller, on a little block of wood, and rove out into long soft bands without twist. Then it receives its first twist on the spindle, and becomes about the thickness of coarse candlewick; after being taken off and wound into a large ball, it is given the final hard twist, and spun into a firm cop on the spindle again: all the processes being painfully slow.

Iron ore is dug out of the hills, and its manufacture is the staple trade of the southern highlands. Each village has its smelting-house, its charcoal-burners, and blacksmiths. They make good axes, spears, needles, arrowheads, bracelets and anklets, which, considering the entire absence of machinery, are sold at surprisingly low rates; a hoe over two pounds in weight is exchanged for calico of about the value of fourpence. In villages near Lake Shirwa and elsewhere, the inhabitants enter pretty largely into the manufacture of crockery, or pottery, making by hand all sorts of cooking, water, and grain pots, which they ornament with plumbago found in the hills. Some find employment in weaving neat baskets from split bamboos, and others collect the fibre of the buaze, which grows abundantly on the hills, and make it into fish-nets. These they either use themselves, or exchange with the fishermen on the river or lakes for dried fish and salt. A great deal of native trade is carried on between the villages, by means of barter in tobacco, salt, dried fish, skins, and iron. Many of the men are intelligent-looking, with well-shaped heads, agreeable faces, and high foreheads. We soon learned to forget colour, and we frequently saw countenances resembling those of white people we had known in England, which brought back the looks of forgotten ones vividly before the mind. The men take a good deal of pride in the arrangement of their hair; the varieties of style are endless. One trains his long locks till they take the admired form of the buffalo's horns; others prefer to let their hair hang in a thick coil down their backs, like that animal's tail; while another wears it in twisted cords, which, stiffened by fillets of the inner bark of a tree wound spirally round each curl, radiate from the head in all directions. Some have it hanging all round the shoulders in large masses; others shave it off altogether. Many shave part of it into ornamental figures, in which the fancy of the barber crops out conspicuously. About as many dandies run to seed among the blacks as among the whites. The Man ganja adorn their bodies extravagantly, wearing rings on their fingers and thumbs, besides throatlets, bracelets, and anklets of brass, copper, or iron. But the most wonderful of ornaments, if such it may be called, is the pelele, or upper-lip ring of the women. The middle of the upper lip of the girls is pierced close to the septum of the nose, and a small pin inserted to prevent the puncture closing up. After it has healed, the pin is taken out and a larger one is pressed into its place, and so on successively for weeks, and months, and years. The process of increasing the size of the lip goes on till its capacity becomes so great that a ring of two inches diameter can be introduced with ease. All the highland women wear the pelele, and it is common on the Upper and Lower Shire. The poorer classes make them of hollow or of solid bamboo, but the wealthier of ivory or tin. The tin pelele is often made in the form of a small dish. The ivory one is not unlike a napkin-ring. No woman ever appears in public without the pelele, except in times of mourning for the dead. It is frightfully ugly to see the upper lip projecting two inches beyond the tip of the nose. When an old wearer of a hollow bamboo ring smiles, by the action of the muscles of the cheeks, the ring and lip outside it are dragged back and thrown above the eyebrows. The nose is seen through the middle of the ring, amid the exposed teeth show how carefully they have been chipped to look like those of a cat or crocodile. The pelele of an old lady, Chikanda Kadze, a chieftainess, about twenty miles north of Morambala, hung down below her chin, with, of course, a piece of the upper lip around its border. The labial letters cannot be properly pronounced, but the under lip has to do its best for them, against the upper teeth and gum. Tell them it makes them ugly; they had better throw it away; they reply, "Kodi! Really! it is the fashion." How this hideous fashion originated is an enigma. Can thick lips ever have been thought beautiful, and this mode of artificial enlargement resorted to in consequence? The constant twiddling of the pelele with the tongue by the younger women suggested the irreverent idea that it might have been invented to give safe employment to that little member. "Why do the women wear these things?" we inquired of the old chief, Chinsunse. Evidently surprised at such a stupid question, he replied, "For beauty, to be sure! Men have beards and whiskers; women have none; and what kind of creature would a woman be without whiskers, and without the pelele? She would have a mouth like a man, and no beard; ha! ha! ha!" Afterwards on the Rovuma, we found men wearing the pelele, as well as women. An idea suggested itself on seeing the effects of the slight but constant pressure exerted on the upper gum and front teeth, of which our medical brethren will judge the value. In many cases the upper front teeth, instead of the natural curve outwards, which the row presents, had been pressed so as to appear as if the line of alveoli in which they were planted had an inward curve. As this was produced by the slight pressure of the pelele backwards, persons with too prominent teeth might by slight, but long-continued pressure, by some appliance only as elastic as the lip, have the upper gum and teeth depressed, especially in youth, more easily than is usually imagined. The pressure should be applied to the upper gum more than to the teeth.

The Manganja are not a sober people: they brew large quantities of beer, and like it well. Having no hops, or other means of checking fermentation, they are obliged to drink the whole brew in a few days, or it becomes unfit for use. Great merry-makings take place on these occasions, and drinking, drumming, and dancing continue day and night, till the beer is gone. In crossing the hills we sometimes found whole villages enjoying this kind of mirth. The veteran traveller of the party remarked, that he had not seen so much drunkenness during all the sixteen years he had spent in Africa. As we entered a village one afternoon, not a man was to be seen; but some women were drinking beer under a tree. In a few moments the native doctor, one of the innocents, "nobody's enemy but his own," staggered out of a hut, with his cupping-horn dangling from his neck, and began to scold us for a breach of etiquette. "Is this the way to come into a man's village, without sending him word that you are coming?" Our men soon pacified the fuddled but good-humoured medico, who, entering his beer-cellar, called on two of them to help him to carry out a huge pot of beer, which he generously presented to us. While the "medical practitioner" was thus hospitably employed, the chief awoke in a fright, and shouted to the women to run away, or they would all be killed. The ladies laughed at the idea of their being able to run away, and remained beside the beer-pots. We selected a spot for our camp, our men cooked the dinner as usual, and we were quietly eating it, when scores of armed men, streaming with perspiration, came pouring into the village. They looked at us, then at each other, and turning to the chief upbraided him for so needlessly sending for them. "These people are peaceable; they do not hurt you; you are killed with beer:" so saying, they returned to their homes.

Native beer has a pinkish colour, and the consistency of gruel. The grain is made to vegetate, dried in the sun, pounded into meal, and gently boiled. When only a day or two old, the beer is sweet, with a slight degree of acidity, which renders it a most grateful beverage in a hot climate, or when fever begets a sore craving for acid drinks. A single draught of it satisfies this craving at once. Only by deep and long-continued potations can intoxication be produced: the grain being in a minutely divided state, it is a good way of consuming it, and the decoction is very nutritious. At Tette a measure of beer is exchanged for an equal-sized pot full of grain. A present of this beer, so refreshing to our dark comrades, was brought to us in nearly every village. Beer-drinking does not appear to produce any disease, or to shorten life on the hills. Never before did we see so many old, grey-headed men and women; leaning on their staves they came with the others to see the white men. The aged chief, Muata Manga, could hardly have been less than ninety years of age; his venerable appearance struck the Makololo. "He is an old man," said they, "a very old man; his skin hangs in wrinkles, just like that on elephants' hips." "Did you never," he was asked, "have a fit of travelling come over you; a desire to see other lands and people?" No, he had never felt that, and had never been far from home in his life. For long life they are not indebted to frequent ablutions. An old man told us that he remembered to have washed once in his life, but it was so long since that he had forgotten how it felt. "Why do you wash?" asked Chinsunse's women of the Makololo; "our men never do."

The superstitious ordeal, by drinking the poisonous muave, obtains credit here; and when a person is suspected of crime, this ordeal is resorted to. If the stomach rejects the poison, the accused is pronounced innocent; but if it is retained, guilt is believed to be demonstrated. Their faith is so firm in its discriminating power, that the supposed criminal offers of his own accord to drink it, and even chiefs are not exempted. Chibisa, relying on its efficacy, drank it several times, in order to vindicate his character. When asserting that all his wars had been just, it was hinted that, as every chief had the same tale of innocence to tell, we ought to suspend our judgment. "If you doubt my word," said he, "give me the muave to drink." A chief at the foot of Mount Zomba successfully went through the ordeal the day we reached his village; and his people manifested their joy at his deliverance by drinking beer, dancing, and drumming for two days and nights. It is possible that the native doctor, who mixes the ingredients of the poisoned bowl, may be able to save those whom he considers innocent; but it is difficult to get the natives to speak about the matter, and no one is willing to tell what the muave poison consists of. We have been shown trees said to be used, but had always reason to doubt the accuracy of our informants. We once found a tree in a village, with many pieces of the bark chipped off, closely allied to the Tangena or Tanghina, the ordeal poison tree of Madagascar; but we could not ascertain any particulars about it. Death is inflicted on those found guilty of witchcraft, by the muave.

The women wail for the dead two days. Seated on the ground they chant a few plaintive words, and end each verse with the prolonged sound of a--a, or o--o, or ea-ea-ea--a. Whatever beer is in the house of the deceased, is poured out on the ground with the meal, and all cooking and water pots are broken, as being of no further use. Both men and women wear signs of mourning for their dead relatives. These consist of narrow strips of the palm-leaf wound round the head, the arms, legs, neck, and breasts, and worn till they drop off from decay. They believe in the existence of a supreme being, called Mpambe, and also Morungo, and in a future state. "We live only a few days here," said old Chinsunse, "but we live again after death: we do not know where, or in what condition, or with what companions, for the dead never return to tell us. Sometimes the dead do come back, and appear to us in dreams; but they never speak nor tell us where they have gone, nor how they fare."

CHAPTER IV.

The Upper Shire--Discovery of Lake Nyassa--Distressing exploration--Return to Zambesi--Unpleasant visitors--Start for Sekeletu's Country in the interior.

Our path followed the Shire above the cataracts, which is now a broad deep river, with but little current. It expands in one place into a lakelet, called Pamalombe, full of fine fish, and ten or twelve miles long by five or six in breadth. Its banks are low, and a dense wall of papyrus encircles it. On its western shore rises a range of hills running north. On reaching the village of the chief Muana-Moesi, and about a day's march distant from Nyassa, we were told that no lake had ever been heard of there; that the River Shire stretched on as we saw it now to a distance of "two months," and then came out from between perpendicular rocks, which towered almost to the skies. Our men looked blank at this piece of news, and said, "Let us go back to the ship, it is of no use trying to find the lake." "We shall go and see those wonderful rocks at any rate," said the Doctor. "And when you see them," replied Masakasa, "you will just want to see something else. But there *is* a lake," rejoined Masakasa, "for all their denying it, for it is down in a book." Masakasa, having unbounded faith in whatever was in a book, went and scolded the natives for telling him an untruth. "There is a lake," said he, "for how could the white men know about it in a book if it did not exist?" They then admitted that there was a lake a few miles off. Subsequent inquiries make it probable that the story of the "perpendicular rocks" may have had reference to a fissure, known to both natives and Arabs, in the north-eastern portion of the lake. The walls rise so high that the path along the bottom is said to be underground. It is probably a crack similar to that which made the Victoria Falls, and formed the Shire Valley.

The chief brought a small present of meal in the evening, and sat with us for a few minutes. On leaving us he said that he wished we might sleep well. Scarce had he gone, when a wild sad cry arose from the river, followed by the shrieking of women. A crocodile had carried off his principal wife, as she was bathing. The Makololo snatched up their arms, and rushed to the bank, but it was too late, she was gone. The wailing of the women continued all night, and next morning we met others coming to the village to join in the general mourning. Their grief was evidently heartfelt, as we saw the tears coursing down their cheeks. In reporting this misfortune to his neighbours, Muana-Moesi said, "that white men came to his village; washed themselves at the place where his wife drew water and bathed; rubbed themselves with a white medicine (soap); and his wife, having gone to bathe afterwards, was taken by a crocodile; he did not know whether in consequence of the medicine used or not." This we could not find fault with. On our return we were viewed with awe, and all the men fled at our approach; the women remained; and this elicited the remark from our men, "The women have the advantage of men, in not needing to dread the spear." The practice of bathing, which our first contact with Chinsunse's people led us to believe was unknown to the natives, we afterwards found to be common in other parts of the Manganja country.

We discovered Lake Nyassa a little before noon of the 16th September, 1859. Its southern end is in 14 degrees 25 minutes S. Lat., and 35 degrees 30 minutes E. Long. At this point the valley is about twelve miles wide. There are hills on both sides of the lake, but the haze from burning grass prevented us at the time from seeing far. A long time after our return from Nyassa, we received a letter from Captain R. B. Oldfield, R.N., then commanding H.M.S. "Lyra," with the information that Dr. Roscher, an enterprising German who unfortunately lost his life in his zeal for exploration, had also reached the Lake, but on the 19th November following our discovery; and on his arrival had been informed by the natives that a party of white men were at the southern extremity. On comparing dates (16th September and 19th November) we were about two months before Dr. Roscher.

It is not known where Dr. Roscher first saw its waters; as the exact position of Nusseewa on the borders of the Lake, where he lived some time, is unknown. He was three days north-east of Nusseewa, and on the Arab road back to the usual crossing-place of the Rovuma, when he was murdered. The murderers were seized by one of the chiefs, sent to Zanzibar, and executed. He is said to have kept his discoveries to himself, with the intention of publishing in Europe the whole at once, in a splendid book of travels.

The chief of the village near the confluence of the Lake and River Shire, an old man, called Mosauka, hearing that we were sitting under a tree, came and kindly invited us to his village. He took us to a magnificent banyan-tree, of which he seemed proud. The roots had been trained down to the ground into the form of a gigantic arm-chair, without the seat. Four of us slept in the space betwixt its arms. Mosauka brought us a present of a goat and basket of meal "to comfort our hearts." He told us that a large slave party, led by Arabs, were encamped close by. They had been up to Cazembe's country the past year, and were on their way back, with plenty of slaves, ivory, and malachite. In a few minutes half a dozen of the leaders came over to see us. They were armed with long muskets, and, to our mind, were a villanous-looking lot. They evidently thought the same of us, for they offered several young children for sale, but, when told that we were English, showed signs of fear, and decamped during the night. On our return to the Kongone, we found that H.M.S. "Lynx" had caught some of these very slaves in a dhow; for a woman told us she first saw us at Mosauka's, and that the Arabs had fled for fear of an **uncanny** sort of Basungu.

This is one of the great slave-paths from the interior, others cross the Shire a little below, and some on the lake itself. We might have released these slaves but did not know what to do with them afterwards. On meeting men, led in slave-sticks, the Doctor had to bear the reproaches of the Makololo, who never slave, "Ay, you call us bad, but are we yellow-hearted, like these fellows--why won't you let us choke them?" To liberate and leave them, would have done but little good, as the people of the surrounding villages would soon have seized them, and have sold them again into slavery. The Manganja chiefs sell their own people, for we met Ajawa and slave-dealers in several highland villages, who had certainly been encouraged to come among them for slaves. The chiefs always seemed ashamed of the traffic, and tried to excuse themselves. "We do not sell many, and only those who have committed crimes." As a rule the regular trade is supplied by the low and criminal classes, and hence the ugliness of slaves. Others are probably sold besides criminals, as on the accusation of witchcraft. Friendless orphans also sometimes disappear suddenly, and no one inquires what has become of them. The temptation to sell their people is peculiarly great, as there is but little ivory on the hills, and often the chief has nothing but human flesh with which to buy foreign goods. The Ajawa offer cloth, brass rings, pottery, and sometimes handsome young women, and agree to take the trouble of carrying off by night all those whom the chief may point out to them. They give four yards of cotton cloth for a man, three for a woman, and two for a boy or girl, to be taken to the Portuguese at Mozambique, Iboe, and Quillimane.

The Manganja were more suspicious and less hospitable than the tribes on the Zambesi. They were slow to believe that our object in coming into their country was really what we professed it to be. They naturally judge us by the motives which govern themselves. A chief in the Upper Shire Valley, whose scared looks led our men to christen him Kitlabolawa (I shall be killed), remarked that parties had come before, with as plausible a story as ours, and, after a few days, had jumped up and carried off a number of his people as slaves. We were not allowed to enter some of the villages in the valley, nor would the inhabitants even sell us food; Zimika's men, for instance, stood at the entrance of the euphorbia hedge, and declared we should not pass in. We sat down under a tree close by. A young fellow made an angry oration, dancing from side to side with his bow and poisoned arrows, and gesticulating fiercely in our faces. He was stopped in the middle of his harangue by an old man, who ordered him to sit down, and not talk to strangers in that way; he obeyed reluctantly, scowling defiance, and thrusting out his large lips very significantly. The women were observed leaving the village; and, suspecting that mischief might ensue, we proceeded on our journey, to the great disgust of our men. They were very angry with the natives for their want of hospitality to strangers, and with us, because we would not allow them to give "the things a thrashing." "This is what comes of going with white men," they growled out; "had we been with our own chief, we should have eaten their goats to-night, and had some of themselves to carry the bundles for us to-morrow." On our return by a path which left his village on our right, Zimika sent to apologize, saying that "he was ill, and in another village at the time; it was not by his orders we were sent away; his men did not know that we were a party wishing the land to dwell in peace."

We were not able, when hastening back to the men left in the ship, to remain in the villages belonging to this chief; but the people came after us with things for sale, and invited us to stop, and spend the night with them, urging, "Are we to have it said that white people passed through our country and we did not see them?" We rested by a rivulet to gratify these sight-seers. We appear to them to be red rather than white; and, though light colour is admired among themselves, our clothing renders us uncouth in aspect. Blue eyes appear savage, and a red beard hideous. From the numbers of aged persons we saw on the highlands, and the increase of mental and physical vigour we experienced on our ascent from the lowlands, we inferred that the climate was salubrious, and that our countrymen might there enjoy good health, and also be of signal benefit, by leading the multitude of industrious inhabitants to cultivate cotton, buaze, sugar, and other valuable produce, to exchange for goods of European manufacture; at the same time teaching them, by precept and example, the great truths of our Holy Religion.

Our stay at the Lake was necessarily short. We had found that the best plan for allaying any suspicions, that might arise in the minds of a people accustomed only to slave-traders, was to pay a hasty visit, and then leave for a while, and allow the conviction to form among the people that, though our course of action was so different from that of others, we were not dangerous, but rather disposed to be friendly. We had also a party at the vessel, and any indiscretion on their part might have proved fatal to the character of the Expedition.

The trade of Cazembe and Katanga's country, and of other parts of the interior, crosses Nyassa and the Shire, on its way to the Arab port, Kilwa, and the Portuguese ports of Iboe and Mozambique. At present, slaves, ivory, malachite, and copper ornaments, are the only articles of commerce. According to information collected by Colonel Rigby at Zanzibar, and from other sources, nearly all the slaves shipped from the above-mentioned ports come from the Nyassa district. By means of a small steamer, purchasing the ivory of the Lake and River above the cataracts, which together have a shore-line of at least 600 miles, the slave-trade in this quarter would be rendered unprofitable,--for it is only by the ivory being carried by the slaves, that the latter do not eat up all the profits of a trip. An influence would be exerted over an enormous area of country, for the Mazitu about the north end of the Lake will not allow slave-traders to pass round that way through their country. They would be most efficient allies to the English, and might themselves be benefited by more intercourse. As things are now, the native traders in ivory and malachite have to submit to heavy exactions; and if we could give them the same prices which they at present get after carrying their merchandise 300 miles beyond this to the Coast, it might induce them to return without going further. It is only by cutting off the supplies in the interior, that we can crush the slave-trade on the Coast. The plan proposed would stop the slave-trade from the Zambesi on one side and Kilwa on the other; and would leave, beyond this tract, only the Portuguese port of Inhambane on the south, and a portion of the Sultan of Zanzibar's dominion on the north, for our cruisers to look after. The Lake people grow abundance of cotton for their own consumption, and can sell it for a penny a pound or even less. Water-carriage exists by the Shire and Zambesi all the way to England, with the single exception of a portage of about thirty-five miles past the Murchison Cataracts, along which a road of less than forty miles could be made at a trifling expense; and it seems feasible that a legitimate and thriving trade might, in a short time, take the place of the present unlawful traffic.

Colonel Rigby, Captains Wilson, Oldfield, and Chapman, and all the most intelligent officers on the Coast, were unanimous in the belief, that one small vessel on the Lake would have decidedly more influence, and do more good in suppressing the slave-trade, than half a dozen men-of-war on the ocean. By judicious operations, therefore, on a small scale inland, little expense would be incurred, and the English slave-trade policy on the East would have the same fair chance of success, as on the West Coast.

After a land-journey of forty days, we returned to the ship on the 6th of October, 1859, in a somewhat exhausted condition, arising more from a sort of poisoning, than from the usual fatigue of travel. We had taken a little mulligatawney paste, for making soup, in case of want of time to cook other food. Late one afternoon, at the end of an unusually long march, we reached Mikena, near the base of Mount Njongone to the north of Zomba, and the cook was directed to use a couple of spoonfuls of the paste; but, instead of doing so, he put in the whole potful. The soup tasted rather hot, but we added boiled rice to it, and, being very hungry, partook freely of it; and, in consequence of the overdose, we were delayed several days in severe suffering, and some of the party did not recover till after our return to the ship. Our illness may partly have arisen from another cause. One kind of cassava (*Jatropha maligna*) is known to be, in its raw state, poisonous, but by boiling it carefully in two waters, which must be thrown off, the poison is extracted and the cassava rendered fit for food. The poisonous sort is easily known by raising a bit of the bark of the root, and putting the tongue to it. A bitter taste shows poison, but it is probable that even the sweet kind contains an injurious principle. The sap, which, like that of our potatoes, is injurious as an article of food, is used in the "Pepper-pot" of the West Indies, under the name of "Cassereep," as a perfect preservative of meat. This juice put into an earthen vessel with a little water and Chili pepper is said to keep meat, that is immersed in it, good for a great length of time; even for years. No iron or steel must touch the mixture, or it will become sour. This "Pepper-pot," of which we first heard from the late Archbishop Whately, is a most economical meat-safe in a hot climate; any beef, mutton, pork, or fowl that may be left at dinner, if put into the mixture and a little fresh cassereep added, keeps perfectly, though otherwise the heat of the climate or flies would spoil it. Our cook, however, boiled the cassava root as he was in the habit of cooking meat, namely, by filling the pot with it, and then pouring in water, which he allowed to stand on the fire until it had become absorbed and boiled away. This method did not expel the poisonous properties of the root, or render it wholesome; for, notwithstanding our systematic caution in purchasing only the harmless sort, we suffered daily from its effects, and it was only just before the end of our trip that this pernicious mode of boiling it was discovered by us.

In ascending 3000 feet from the lowlands to the highlands, or on reaching the low valley of the Shire from the higher grounds, the change of climate was very marked. The heat was oppressive below, the thermometer standing at from 84 degrees to 103 degrees in the shade; and our spirits were as dull and languid as they had been exhilarated on the heights in a temperature cooler by some 20 degrees. The water of the river was sometimes 84 degrees or higher, whilst that we had been drinking in the hill streams was only 65 degrees.

It was found necessary to send two of our number across from the Shire to Tette; and Dr. Kirk, with guides from Chibisa, and accompanied by Mr. Rae, the engineer, accomplished the journey. We had found the country to the north and east so very well watered, that no difficulty was anticipated in this respect in a march of less than a hundred miles; but on this occasion our friends suffered severely. The little water to be had at this time of the year, by digging in the beds of dry watercourses, was so brackish as to increase thirst--some of the natives indeed were making salt from it; and when at long intervals a less brackish supply was found, it was nauseous and muddy from the frequent visits of large game. The tsetse abounded. The country was level, and large tracts of it covered with mopane forest, the leaves of which afford but scanty shade to the baked earth, so that scarcely any grass grows upon it. The sun was so hot, that the men frequently jumped from the path, in the vain hope of cooling, for a moment, their scorched feet under the almost shadeless bushes; and the native who carried the provision of salt pork got lost, and came into Tette two days after the rest of the party, with nothing but the fibre of the meat left, the fat, melted by the blazing sun, having all run down his back. This path was soon made a highway for slaving parties by Captain Raposo, the Commandant. The journey nearly killed our two active young friends; and what the slaves must have since suffered on it no one can conceive; but slaving probably can never be conducted without enormous suffering and loss of life.

Mankokwe now sent a message to say that he wished us to stop at his village on our way down. He came on board on our arrival there with a handsome present, and said that his young people had dissuaded him from visiting us before; but now he was determined to see what every one else was seeing. A bald square-headed man, who had been his Prime Minister when we came up, was now out of office, and another old man, who had taken his place accompanied the chief. In passing the Elephant Marsh, we saw nine large herds of elephants; they sometimes formed a line two miles long.

On the 2nd of November we anchored off Shamoara, and sent the boat to Senna for biscuit and other provisions. Senhor Ferrao, with his wonted generosity, gave us a present of a bullock, which he sent to us in a canoe. Wishing to know if a second bullock would be acceptable to us, he consulted his Portuguese and English dictionary, and asked the sailor in charge if he would take *another*; but Jack, mistaking the Portuguese pronunciation of the letter h, replied, "Oh no, sir, thank you, I don't want an *otter* in the boat, they are such terrible biters!"

We had to ground the vessel on a shallow sandbank every night; she leaked so fast, that in deep water she would have sunk, and the pump had to be worked all day to keep her afloat. Heavy rains fell daily, producing the usual injurious effects in the cabin; and, unable to wait any longer for our associates, who had gone overland from the Shire to Tette, we ran down the Kongone and beached her for repairs. Her Majesty's ship "Lynx," Lieut. Berkeley commanding, called shortly afterwards with supplies; the bar, which had been perfectly smooth for some time before, became rather rough just before her arrival, so that it was two or three days before she could communicate with us. Two of her boats tried to come in on the second day, and one of them, mistaking the passage, capsized in the heavy breakers abreast of the island. Mr. Hunt, gunner, the officer in charge of the second boat, behaved nobly, and by his skilful and gallant conduct succeeded in rescuing every one of the first boat's crew. Of course the things that they were bringing to us were lost, but we were thankful that all the men were saved. The loss of the mail-bags, containing Government despatches and our friends' letters for the past year, was felt severely, as we were on the point of starting on an expedition into the interior, which might require eight or nine months; and twenty months is a weary time to be without news of friends and family. In the repairing of our crazy craft, we received kind and efficient aid from Lieutenant Berkeley, and we were enabled to leave for Tette on December 16th.

We had now frequent rains, and the river rose considerably; our progress up the stream was distressingly slow, and it was not until the 2nd of February, 1860, that we reached Tette. Mr. Thornton returned on the same day from a geological tour, by which some Portuguese expected that a fabulous silver-mine would be rediscovered. The tradition in the country is, that the Jesuits formerly knew and worked a precious lode at Chicova. Mr. Thornton had gone beyond Zumbo, in company with a trader of colour; he soon after this left the Zambesi and, joining the expedition of the Baron van der Decken, explored the snow mountain Kilimanjaro, north-west of Zanzibar. Mr. Thornton's companion, the trader, brought back much ivory, having found it both abundant and cheap. He was obliged, however, to pay heavy fines to the Banyai and other tribes, in the country which is coolly claimed in Europe as Portuguese. During this trip of six mouths 200 pieces of cotton cloth of sixteen yards each, besides beads and brass wire, were paid to the different chiefs, for leave to pass through their country. In addition to these sufficiently weighty exactions, the natives of **this dominion** have got into the habit of imposing fines for alleged milandos, or crimes, which the traders' men may have unwittingly committed. The merchants, however, submit rather than run the risk of fighting.

The general monotony of existence at Tette is sometimes relieved by an occasional death or wedding. When the deceased is a person of consequence, the quantity of gunpowder his slaves are allowed to expend is enormous. The expense may, in proportion to their means, resemble that incurred by foolishly gaudy funerals in England. When at Tette, we always joined with sympathizing hearts in aiding, by our presence at the last rites, to soothe the sorrows of the surviving relatives. We are sure that they would have done the same to us had we been the mourners. We never had to complain of want of hospitality. Indeed, the great kindness shown by many of whom we have often spoken, will never be effaced from our memory till our dying day. When we speak of their failings it is in sorrow, not in anger. Their trading in slaves is an enormous mistake. Their Government places them in a false position by cutting them off from the rest of the world; and of this they always speak with a bitterness which, were it heard, might alter the tone of the statesmen of Lisbon. But here there is no press, no booksellers' shops, and scarcely a schoolmaster. Had we been born in similar untoward circumstances--we tremble to think of it!

The weddings are celebrated with as much jollity as weddings are anywhere. We witnessed one in the house of our friend the Padre. It being the marriage of his goddaughter, he kindly invited us to be partakers in his joy; and we there became acquainted with old Donna Engenia, who was a married wife and had children, when the slaves came from Cassange, before any of us were born. The whole merry-making was marked by good taste amid propriety.

About the only interesting object in the vicinity of Tette is the coal a few miles to the north. There, in the feeders of the stream Revubue, it crops out in cliff sections. The seams are from four to seven feet in thickness; one measured was found to be twenty-five feet thick.

Learning that it would be difficult for our party to obtain food beyond Kebrabasa before the new crop came in and knowing the difficulty of hunting for so many men in the wet season, we decided on deferring our departure for the interior until May, and in the mean time to run down once more to the Kongone, in the hopes of receiving letters and despatches from the man-of-war that was to call in March. We left Tette on the 10th, and at Senna heard that our lost mail had been picked up on the beach by natives, west of the Milambe; carried to Quillimane, sent thence to Senna, and, passing us somewhere on the river, on to Tette. At Shupanga the governor informed us that it was a very large mail; no great comfort, seeing it was away up the river.

Mosquitoes were excessively troublesome at the harbour, and especially when a light breeze blew from the north over the mangroves. We lived for several weeks in small huts, built by our men. Those who did the hunting for the party always got wet, and were attacked by fever, but generally recovered in time to be out again before the meat was all consumed. No ship appearing, we started off on the 15th of March, and stopped to wood on the Luabo, near an encampment of hippopotamus hunters; our men heard again, through them, of the canoe path from this place to Quillimane, but they declined to point it out.

We found our friend Major Sicard at Mazaro with picks, shovels, hurdles, and slaves, having come to build a fort and custom-house at the Kongone. As we had no good reason to hide the harbour, but many for its being made known, we supplied him with a chart of the tortuous branches, which, running among the mangroves, perplex the search; and with such directions as would enable him to find his way down to the river. He had brought the relics of our fugitive mail, and it was a disappointment to find that all had been lost, with the exception of a bundle of old newspapers, two photographs, and three letters, which had been written before we left England.

The distance from Mazaro, on the Zambesi side, to the Kwakwa at Nterra, is about six miles, over a surprisingly rich dark soil. We passed the night in the long shed, erected at Nterra, on the banks of this river, for the use of travellers, who have often to wait several days for canoes; we tried to sleep, but the mosquitoes and rats were so troublesome as to render sleep impossible. The rats, or rather large mice, closely resembling ***Mus pumilio*** (Smith), of this region, are quite facetious, and, having a great deal of fun in them, often laugh heartily. Again and again they woke us up by scampering over our faces, and then bursting into a loud laugh of He! he! he! at having performed the feat. Their sense of the ludicrous appears to be exquisite; they screamed with laughter at the attempts which disturbed and angry human nature made in the dark to bring their ill-timed merriment to a close. Unlike their prudent European cousins, which are said to leave a sinking ship, a party of these took up their quarters in our leaky and sinking vessel. Quiet and invisible by day, they emerged at night, and cut their funny pranks. No sooner were we all asleep, than they made a sudden dash over the lockers and across our faces for the cabin door, where all broke out into a loud He! he! he! he! he! he! showing how keenly they enjoyed the joke. They next went forward with as much delight, and scampered over the men. Every night they went fore and aft, rousing with impartial feet every sleeper, and laughing to scorn the aimless blows, growls, and deadly rushes of outraged humanity. We observed elsewhere a species of large mouse, nearly allied to ***Euryotis unisulcatus*** (F. Cuvier), escaping up a rough and not very upright wall, with six young ones firmly attached to the perineum. They were old enough to be well covered with hair, and some were not detached by a blow which disabled the dam. We could not decide whether any involuntary muscles were brought into play in helping the young to adhere. Their weight seemed to require a sort of cataleptic state of the muscles of the jaw, to enable them to hold on.

Scorpions, centipedes, and poisonous spiders also were not unfrequently brought into the ship with the wood, and occasionally found their way into our beds; but in every instance we were fortunate enough to discover and destroy them before they did any harm. Naval officers on this coast report that, when scorpions and centipedes remain a few weeks after being taken on board in a similar manner, their poison loses nearly all its virulence; but this we did not verify. Snakes sometimes came in with the wood, but oftener floated down the river to us, climbing on board with ease by the chain-cable, and some poisonous ones were caught in the cabin. A green snake lived with us several weeks, concealing himself behind the casing of the deckhouse in the daytime. To be aroused in the dark by five feet of cold green snake gliding over one's face is rather unpleasant, however rapid the movement may be. Myriads of two varieties of cockroaches infested the vessel; they not only ate round the roots of our nails, but even devoured and defiled our food, flannels, and boots. Vain were all our efforts to extirpate these destructive pests; if you kill one, say the sailors, a hundred come down to his funeral! In the work of Commodore Owen it is stated that cockroaches, pounded into a paste, form a powerful carminative; this has not been confirmed, but when monkeys are fed on them they are sure to become lean.

On coming to Senna, we found that the Zulus had arrived in force for their annual tribute. These men are under good discipline, and never steal from the people. The tax is claimed on the ground of conquest, the Zulus having formerly completely overcome the Senna people, and chased them on to the islands in the Zambesi. Fifty-four of the Portuguese were slain on the occasion, and, notwithstanding the mud fort, the village has never recovered its former power. Fever was now very prevalent, and most of the Portuguese were down with it.

For a good view of the adjacent scenery, the hill, Baramuana, behind the village, was ascended. A caution was given about the probability of an attack of fever from a plant that grows near the summit. Dr. Kirk discovered it to be the **Paedevia foetida**, which, when smelt, actually does give headache and fever. It has a nasty fetor, as its name indicates. This is one instance in which fever and a foul smell coincide. In a number of instances offensive effluvia and fever seems to have no connection. Owing to the abundant rains, the crops in the Senna district were plentiful; this was fortunate, after the partial failure of the past two years. It was the 25th of April, 1860, before we reached Tette; here also the crops were luxuriant, and the people said that they had not had such abundance since 1856, the year when Dr. Livingstone came down the river. It is astonishing to any one who has seen the works for irrigation in other countries, as at the Cape and in Egypt, that no attempt has ever been made to lead out the water either of the Zambesi or any of its tributaries; no machinery has ever been used to raise it even from the stream, but droughts and starvations are endured, as if they were inevitable dispensations of Providence, incapable of being mitigated.

Feeling in honour bound to return with those who had been the faithful companions of Dr. Livingstone, in 1856, and to whose guardianship and services was due the accomplishment of a journey which all the Portuguese at Tette had previously pronounced impossible, the requisite steps were taken to convey them to their homes.

We laid the ship alongside of the island Kanyimbe, opposite Tette; and, before starting for the country of the Makololo, obtained a small plot of land, to form a garden for the two English sailors who were to remain in charge during our absence. We furnished them with a supply of seeds, and they set to work with such zeal, that they certainly merited success. Their first attempt at African horticulture met with failure from a most unexpected source; every seed was dug up and the inside of it eaten by mice. "Yes," said an old native, next morning, on seeing the husks, "that is what happens this month; for it is the mouse month, and the seed should have been sown last mouth, when I sowed mine." The sailors, however, sowed more next day; and, being determined to outwit the mice, they this time covered the beds over with grass. The onions, with other seeds of plants cultivated by the Portuguese, are usually planted in the beginning of April, in order to have the advantage of the cold season; the wheat a little later, for the same reason. If sown at the beginning of the rainy season in November, it runs, as before remarked, entirely to straw; but as the rains are nearly over in May, advantage is taken of low- lying patches, which have been flooded by the river. A hole is made in the mud with a hoe, a few seeds dropped in, and the earth shoved back with the foot. If not favoured with certain misty showers, which, lower down the river, are simply fogs, water is borne from the river to the roots of the wheat in earthern pots; and in about four months the crop is ready for the sickle. The wheat of Tette is exported, as the best grown in the country; but a hollow spot at Maruru, close by Mazaro, yielded very good crops, though just at the level of the sea, as a few inches rise of tide shows.

A number of days were spent in busy preparation for our journey; the cloth, beads, and brass wire, for the trip were sewn up in old canvas, and each package had the bearer's name printed on it. The Makololo, who had worked for the Expedition, were paid for their services, and every one who had come down with the Doctor from the interior received a present of cloth and ornaments, in order to protect them from the greater cold of their own country, and to show that they had not come in vain. Though called Makololo by courtesy, as they were proud of the name, Kanyata, the principal headman, was the only real Makololo of the party; and he, in virtue of his birth, had succeeded to the chief place on the death of Sekwebu. The others belonged to the conquered tribes of the Batoka, Bashubia, Ba-Selea, and Barotse. Some of these men had only added to their own vices those of the Tette slaves; others, by toiling during the first two years in navigating canoes, and hunting elephants, had often managed to save a little, to take back to their own country, but had to part with it all for food to support the rest in times of hunger, and, latterly, had fallen into the improvident habits of slaves, and spent their surplus earnings in beer and agua ardiente.

Everything being ready on the 15th of May, we started at 2 p.m. from the village where the Makololo had dwelt. A number of the men did not leave with the goodwill which their talk for months before had led us to anticipate; but some proceeded upon being told that they were not compelled to go unless they liked, though others altogether declined moving. Many had taken up with slave-women, whom they assisted in hoeing, and in consuming the produce of their gardens. Some fourteen children had been born to them; and in consequence of now having no chief to order them, or to claim their services, they thought that they were about as well off as they had been in their own country. They knew and regretted that they could call neither wives nor children their own; the slave-owners claimed the whole; but their natural affections had been so enchained, that they clave to the domestic ties. By a law of Portugal the baptized children of slave women are all free; by the custom of the Zambesi that law is void. When it is referred to, the officers laugh and say, "These Lisbon-born laws are very stringent, but somehow, possibly from the heat of the climate, here they lose all their force." Only one woman joined our party--the wife of a Batoka man: she had been given to him, in consideration of his skilful dancing, by the chief, Chisaka. A merchant sent three of his men along with us, with a present for Sekeletu, and Major Sicard also lent us three more to assist us on our return, and two Portuguese gentleman kindly gave us the loan of a couple of donkeys. We slept four miles above Tette, and hearing that the Banyai, who levy heavy fines on the Portuguese traders, lived chiefly on the right bank, we crossed over to the left, as we could not fully trust our men. If the Banyai had come in a threatening manner, our followers might, perhaps, from having homes behind them, have even put down their bundles and run. Indeed, two of them at this point made up their minds to go no further, and turned back to Tette. Another, Monga, a Batoka, was much perplexed, and could not make out what course to pursue, as he had, three years previously, wounded Kanyata, the headman, with a spear. This is a capital offence among the Makololo, and he was afraid of being put to death for it on his return. He tried, in vain, to console himself with the facts that he had neither father, mother, sisters, nor brothers to mourn for him, and that he could die but once. He was good, and would go up to the stars to Yesu, and therefore did not care for death. In spite, however, of these reflections, he was much cast down, until Kanyata assured him that he would never mention his misdeed to the chief; indeed, he had never even mentioned it to the Doctor, which he would assuredly have done had it lain heavy on his heart. We were right glad of Monga's company, for he was a merry good-tempered fellow, and his lithe manly figure had always been in the front in danger; and, from being left-handed, had been easily recognized in the fight with elephants.

We commenced, for a certain number of days, with short marches, walking gently until broken in to travel. This is of so much importance, that it occurs to us that more might be made out of soldiers if the first few days' marches were easy, and gradually increased in length and quickness. The nights were cold, with heavy dews and occasional showers, and we had several cases of fever. Some of the men deserted every night, and we fully expected that all who had children would prefer to return to Tette, for little ones are well known to prove the strongest ties, even to slaves. It was useless informing them, that if they wanted to return they had only to come and tell us so; we should not be angry with them for preferring Tette to their own country. Contact with slaves had destroyed their sense of honour; they would not go in daylight, but decamped in the night, only in one instance, however, taking our goods, though, in two more, they carried off their comrades' property. By the time we had got well into the Kebrabasa hills thirty men, nearly a third of the party, had turned back, and it became evident that, if many more left us, Sekeletu's goods could not be carried up. At last, when the refuse had fallen away, no more desertions took place.

Stopping one afternoon at a Kebrabasa village, a man, who pretended to be able to change himself into a lion, came to salute us. Smelling the gunpowder from a gun which had been discharged, he went on one side to get out of the wind of the piece, trembling in a most artistic manner, but quite overacting his part. The Makololo explained to us that he was a Pondoro, or a man who can change his form at will, and added that he trembles when he smells gunpowder. "Do you not see how he is trembling now?" We told them to ask him to change himself at once into a lion, and we would give him a cloth for the performance. "Oh no," replied they; "if we tell him so, he may change himself and come when we are asleep and kill us." Having similar superstitions at home, they readily became as firm believers in the Pondoro as the natives of the village. We were told that he assumes the form of a lion and remains in the woods for days, and is sometimes absent for a whole month. His considerate wife had built him a hut or den, in which she places food and beer for her transformed lord, whose metamorphosis does not impair his human appetite. No one ever enters this hut except the Pondoro and his wife, and no stranger is allowed even to rest his gun against the baobab-tree beside it: the Mfumo, or petty chief, of another small village wished to fine our men for placing their muskets against an old tumble-down hut, it being that of the Pondoro. At times the Pondoro employs his acquired powers in hunting for the benefit of the village; and after an absence of a day or two, his wife smells the lion, takes a certain medicine, places it in the forest, and there quickly leaves it, lest the lion should kill even her. This medicine enables the Pondoro to change himself back into a man, return to the village, and say, "Go and get the game that I have killed for you." Advantage is of course taken of what a lion has done, and they go and bring home the buffalo or antelope killed when he was a lion, or rather found when he was patiently pursuing his course of deception in the forest. We saw the Pondoro of another village dressed in a fantastic style, with numerous charms hung round him, and followed by a troop of boys who were honouring him with rounds of shrill cheering.

It is believed also that the souls of departed chiefs enter into lions, and render them sacred. On one occasion, when we had shot a buffalo in the path beyond the Kafue, a hungry lion, attracted probably by the smell of the meat, came close to our camp, and roused up all hands by his roaring. Tuba Mokoro, imbued with the popular belief that the beast was a chief in disguise, scolded him roundly during his brief intervals of silence. "You a chief, eh? You call yourself a chief, do you? What kind of chief are you to come sneaking about in the dark, trying to steal our buffalo meat! Are you not ashamed of yourself? A pretty chief truly; you are like the scavenger beetle, and think of yourself only. You have not the heart of a chief; why don't you kill your own beef? You must have a stone in your chest, and no heart at all, indeed!" Tuba Mokoro producing no impression on the transformed chief, one of the men, the most sedate of the party, who seldom spoke, took up the matter, and tried the lion in another strain. In his slow quiet way he expostulated with him on the impropriety of such conduct to strangers, who had never injured him. "We were travelling peaceably through the country back to our own chief. We never killed people, nor stole anything. The buffalo meat was ours, not his, and it did not become a great chief like him to be prowling round in the dark, trying, like a hyena, to steal the meat of strangers. He might go and hunt for himself, as there was plenty of game in the forest." The Pondoro, being deaf to reason, and only roaring the louder, the men became angry, and threatened to send a ball through him if he did not go away. They snatched up their guns to shoot him, but he prudently kept in the dark, outside the luminous circle made by our camp fires, and there they did not like to venture. A little strychnine was put into a piece of meat, and thrown to him, when he soon departed, and we heard no more of the majestic sneaker.

The Kebrabasa people were now plumper and in better condition than on our former visits; the harvest had been abundant; they had plenty to eat and drink, and they were enjoying life as much as ever they could. At Defwe's village, near where the ship lay on her first ascent, we found two Mfumos or headmen, the son and son-in-law of the former chief. A sister's son has much more chance of succeeding to a chieftainship than the chief's own offspring, it being unquestionable that the sister's child has the family blood. The men are all marked across the nose and up the middle of the forehead with short horizontal bars or cicatrices; and a single brass earring of two or three inches diameter, like the ancient Egyptian, is worn by the men. Some wear the hair long like the ancient Assyrians and Egyptians, and a few have eyes with the downward and inward slant of the Chinese.

After fording the rapid Luia, we left our former path on the banks of the Zambesi, and struck off in a N.W. direction behind one of the hill ranges, the eastern end of which is called Mongwa, the name of an acacia, having a peculiarly strong fetor, found on it. Our route wound up a valley along a small mountain-stream which was nearly dry, and then crossed the rocky spurs of some of the lofty hills. The country was all very dry at the time, and no water was found except in an occasional spring and a few wells dug in the beds of watercourses. The people were poor, and always anxious to convince travellers of the fact. The men, unlike those on the plains, spend a good deal of their time in hunting; this may be because they have but little ground on the hill-sides suitable for gardens, and but little certainty of reaping what may be sown in the valleys. No women came forward in the hamlet, east of Chiperiziwa, where we halted for the night. Two shots had been fired at guinea-fowl a little way off in the valley; the women fled into the woods, and the men came to know if war was meant, and a few of the old folks only returned after hearing that we were for peace. The headman, Kambira, apologized for not having a present ready, and afterwards brought us some meal, a roasted coney (***Hyrax cap-***

ensis), and a pot of beer; he wished to be thought poor. The beer had come to him from a distance; he had none of his own. Like the Manganja, these people salute by clapping their hands. When a man comes to a place where others are seated, before sitting down he claps his hands to each in succession, and they do the same to him. If he has anything to tell, both speaker and hearer clap their hands at the close of every paragraph, and then again vigorously at the end of the speech. The guide, whom the headman gave us, thus saluted each of his comrades before he started off with us. There is so little difference in the language, that all the tribes of this region are virtually of one family.

We proceeded still in the same direction, and passed only two small hamlets during the day. Except the noise our men made on the march, everything was still around us: few birds were seen. The appearance of a whydahbird showed that he had not yet parted with his fine long plumes. We passed immense quantities of ebony and lignum-vitae, and the tree from whose smooth and bitter bark granaries are made for corn. The country generally is clothed with a forest of ordinary-sized trees. We slept in the little village near Sindabwe, where our men contrived to purchase plenty of beer, and were uncommonly boisterous all the evening. We breakfasted next morning under green wild date-palms, beside the fine flowery stream, which runs through the charming valley of Zibah. We now had Mount Chiperiziwa between us, and part of the river near Morumbwa, having in fact come north about in order to avoid the difficulties of our former path. The last of the deserters, a reputed thief, took French leave of us here. He left the bundle of cloth he was carrying in the path a hundred yards in front of where we halted, but made off with the musket and most of the brass rings and beads of his comrade Shirimba, who had unsuspectingly intrusted them to his care.

Proceeding S.W. up this lovely valley, in about an hour's time we reached Sandia's village. The chief was said to be absent hunting, and they did not know when he would return. This is such a common answer to the inquiry after a headman, that one is inclined to think that it only means that they wish to know the stranger's object before exposing their superior to danger. As some of our men were ill, a halt was made here.

As we were unable to march next morning, six of our young men, anxious to try their muskets, went off to hunt elephants. For several hours they saw nothing, and some of them, getting tired, proposed to go to a village and buy food. "No!" said Mantlanyane, "we came to hunt, so let us go on." In a short time they fell in with a herd of cow elephants and calves. As soon as the first cow caught sight of the hunters on the rocks above her, she, with true motherly instinct, placed her young one between her fore-legs for protection. The men were for scattering, and firing into the herd indiscriminately. "That won't do," cried Mantlanyane, "let us all fire at this one." The poor beast received a volley, and ran down into the plain, where another shot killed her; the young one escaped with the herd. The men were wild with excitement, and danced round the fallen queen of the forest, with loud shouts and exultant songs. They returned, bearing as trophies the tail and part of the trunk, and marched into camp as erect as soldiers, and evidently feeling that their stature had increased considerably since the morning.

Sandia's wife was duly informed of their success, as here a law decrees that half the elephant belongs to the chief on whose ground it has been killed. The Portuguese traders always submit to this tax, and, were it of native origin, it could hardly be considered unjust. A chief must have some source of revenue; and, as many chiefs can raise none except from ivory or slaves, this tax is more free from objections than any other that a black Chancellor of the Exchequer could devise. It seems, however, to have originated with the Portuguese themselves, and then to have spread among the adjacent tribes. The Governors look sharply after any elephant that may be slain on the Crown lands, and demand one of the tusks from their vassals. We did not find the law in operation in any tribe beyond the range of Portuguese traders, or further than the sphere of travel of those Arabs who imitated Portuguese customs in trade. At the Kafue in 1855 the chiefs bought the meat we killed, and demanded nothing as their due; and so it was up the Shire during our visits. The slaves of the Portuguese, who are sent by their masters to shoot elephants, probably connive at the extension of this law, for they strive to get the good will of the chiefs to whose country they come, by advising them to make a demand of half of each elephant killed, and for this advice they are well paid in beer. When we found that the Portuguese argued in favour of this law, we told the natives that they might exact tusks from *them*, but that the English, being different, preferred the pure native custom. It was this which made Sandia, as afterwards mentioned, hesitate; but we did not care to insist on exemption in our favour, where the prevalence of the custom might have been held to justify the exaction.

The cutting up of an elephant is quite a unique spectacle. The men stand remind the animal in dead silence, while the chief of the travelling party declares that, according to ancient law, the head and right hind- leg belong to him who killed the beast, that is, to him who inflicted the first wound; the left leg to bins who delivered the second, or first touched the animal after it fell. The meat around the eye to the English, or chief of the travellers, and different parts to the headmen of the different fires, or groups, of which the camp is composed; not forgetting to enjoin the preservation of the fat and bowels for a second distribution. This oration finished, the natives soon become excited, and scream wildly as they cut away at the carcass with a score of spears, whose long handles quiver in the air above their heads. Their excitement becomes momentarily more and more intense, and reaches the culminating point when, as denoted by a roar of gas, the huge mass is laid fairly open. Some jump inside, and roll about there in their eagerness to seize the precious fat, while others run off, screaming, with pieces of the bloody meat, throw it on the grass, and run back for more: all keep talking and shouting at the utmost pitch of their voices. Sometimes two or three, regardless of all laws, seize the same piece of meat, and have a brief fight of words over it. Occasionally an agonized yell bursts forth, and a native emerges out of the moving mass of dead elephant and wriggling humanity, with his hand badly cut by the spear of his excited friend and neighbour: this requires a rag and some soothing words to prevent bad blood. In an incredibly short time tons of meat are cut up, and placed in separate heaps around.

Sandia arrived soon after the beast was divided: he is an elderly man, and wears a wig made of "ife" fibre (***sanseviera***) dyed black, and of a fine glossy appearance. This plant is allied to the aloes, and its thick fleshy leaves, in shape somewhat like our sedges, when bruised yield much fine strong fibre, which is made into ropes, nets, and wigs. It takes dyes readily, and the fibre might form a good article of commerce. "Ife" wigs, as we afterwards saw, are not uncommon in this country, though perhaps not so common as hair wigs at home. Sandia's mosamela, or small carved wooden pillow, exactly resembling the ancient Egyptian one, was hung from the back of his neck; this pillow and a sleeping mat are usually carried by natives when on hunting excursions.

We had the elephant's fore-foot cooked for ourselves, in native fashion. A large hole was dug in the ground, in which a fire was made; and, when the inside was thoroughly heated, the entire foot was placed in it, and covered over with the hot ashes and soil; another fire was made above the whole, and kept burning all night. We had the foot thus cooked for breakfast next morning, and found it delicious. It is a whitish mass, slightly gelatinous, and sweet, like marrow. A long march, to prevent biliousness, is a wise precaution after a meal of elephant's foot. Elephant's trunk and tongue are also good, and, after long simmering, much resemble the hump of a buffalo and the tongue of an ox; but all the other meat is tough, and, from its peculiar flavour, only to be eaten by a hungry man. The quantities of meat our men devour is quite astounding. They boil as much as their pots will hold, and eat till it becomes physically impossible for them to stow away any more. An uproarious dance follows, accompanied with stentorian song; and as soon as they have shaken their first course down, and washed off the sweat and dust of the after performance, they go to work to roast more: a short snatch of sleep succeeds, and they are up and at it again; all night long it is boil and eat, roast and devour, with a few brief interludes of sleep. Like other carnivora, these men can endure hunger for a much longer period than the mere porridge-eating tribes. Our men can cook meat as well as any reasonable traveller could desire; and, boiled in earthen pots, like Indian chatties, it tastes much better than when cooked in iron ones.

CHAPTER V.

Magnificent scenery--Method of marching--Hippopotamus killed--Lions and buffalo--Sequasha the ivory-trader.

Sandia gave us two guides; and on the 4th of June we left the Elephant valley, taking a westerly course; and, after crossing a few ridges, entered the Chingerere or Paguruguru valley, through which, in the rainy season, runs the streamlet Pajodze. The mountains on our left, between us and the Zambesi, our guides told us have the same name as the valley, but that at the confluence of the Pajodze is called Morumbwa. We struck the river at less than half a mile to the north of the cataract Morumbwa. On climbing up the base of this mountain at Pajodze, we found that we were distant only the diameter of the mountain from the cataract. In measuring the cataract we formerly stood on its southern flank; now we were perched on its northern flank, and at once recognized the onion-shaped mountain, here called Zakavuma, whose smooth convex surface overlooks the broken water. Its bearing by compass was 180 degrees from the spot to which we had climbed, and 700 or 800 yards distant. We now, from this standing-point, therefore, completed our inspection of all Kebrabasa, and saw what, as a whole, was never before seen by Europeans so far as any records show.

The remainder of the Kebrabasa path, on to Chicova, was close to the compressed and rocky river. Ranges of lofty tree-covered mountains, with deep narrow valleys, in which are dry watercourses, or flowing rivulets, stretch from the northwest, and are prolonged on the opposite side of the river in a south-easterly direction. Looking back, the mountain scenery in Kebrabasa was magnificent; conspicuous from their form and steep sides, are the two gigantic portals of the cataract; the vast forests still wore their many brilliant autumnal-coloured tints of green, yellow, red, purple, and brown, thrown into relief by the grey bark of the trunks in the background. Among these variegated trees were some conspicuous for their new livery of fresh light-green leaves, as though the winter of others was their spring. The bright sunshine in these mountain forests, and the ever-changing forms of the cloud shadows, gliding over portions of the surface, added fresh charms to scenes already surpassingly beautiful.

From what we have seen of the Kebrabasa rocks and rapids, it appears too evident that they must always form a barrier to navigation at the ordinary low water of the river; but the rise of the water in this gorge being as much as eighty feet perpendicularly, it is probable that a steamer might be taken up at high flood, when all the rapids are smoothed over, to run on the Upper Zambesi. The most formidable cataract in it, Morumbwa, has only about twenty feet of fall, in a distance of thirty yards, and it must entirely disappear when the water stands eighty feet higher. Those of the Makololo who worked on board the ship were not sorry at the steamer being left below, as they had become heartily tired of cutting the wood that the insatiable furnace of the "Asthmatic" required. Mbia, who was a bit of a wag, laughingly exclaimed in broken English, "Oh, Kebrabasa good, very good; no let shippee up to Sekeletu, too muchee work, cuttee woodyee, cuttee woodyee: Kebrabasa good." It is currently reported, and commonly believed, that once upon a time a Portuguese named Jose Pedra,--by the natives called Nyamatimbira,--chief, or capitao mor, of Zumbo, a man of large enterprise and small humanity,--being anxious to ascertain if Kebrabasa could be navigated, made two slaves fast to a canoe, and launched it from Chicova into Kebrabasa, in order to see if it would come out at the other end. As neither slaves nor canoe ever appeared again, his Excellency concluded that Kebrabasa was unnavigable. A trader had a large canoe swept away by a sudden rise of the river, and it was found without damage below; but the most satisfactory information was that of old Sandia, who asserted that in flood all Kebrabasa became quite smooth, and he had often seen it so.

We emerged from the thirty-five or forty miles of Kebrabasa hills into the Chicova plains on the 7th of June, 1860, having made short marches all the way. The cold nights caused some of our men to cough badly, and colds in this country almost invariably become fever. The Zambesi suddenly expands at Chicova, and assumes the size and appearance it has at Tette. Near this point we found a large seam of coal exposed in the left bank.

We met with native travellers occasionally. Those on a long journey carry with them a sleeping-mat and wooden pillow, cooking-pot and bag of meal, pipe and tobacco-pouch, a knife, bow, and arrows, and two small sticks, of from two to three feet in length, for making fire, when obliged to sleep away from human habitations. Dry wood is always abundant, and they get fire by the following method. A notch is cut in one of the sticks, which, with a close-grained outside, has a small core of pith, and this notched stick is laid horizontally on a knife-blade on the ground; the operator squatting, places his great toes on each end to keep all steady, and taking the other wand which is of very hard wood cut to a blunt point, fits it into the notch at right angles; the upright wand is made to spin rapidly backwards and forwards between the palms of the hands, drill fashion, and at the same time is pressed downwards; the friction, in the course of a minute or so, ignites portions of the pith of the notched stick, which, rolling over like live charcoal on to the knife-blade, are lifted into a handful of fine dry grass, and carefully blown, by waving backwards and forwards in the air. It is hard work for the hands to procure fire by this process, as the vigorous drilling and downward pressure requisite soon blister soft palms.

Having now entered a country where lions were numerous, our men began to pay greater attention to the arrangements of the camp at night. As they are accustomed to do with their chiefs, they place the white men in the centre; Kanyata, his men, and the two donkeys, camp on our right; Tuba Mokoro's party of Bashubia are in front; Masakasa, and Sininyane's body of Batoka, on the left; and in the rear six Tette men have their fires. In placing their fires they are careful to put them where the smoke will not blow in our faces. Soon after we halt, the spot for the English is selected, and all regulate their places accordingly, and deposit their burdens. The men take it by turns to cut some of the tall dry grass, and spread it for our beds on a spot, either naturally level, or smoothed by the hoe; some, appointed to carry our bedding, then bring our rugs and karosses, and place the three rugs in a row on the grass; Dr. Livingstone's being in the middle, Dr. Kirk's on the right, and Charles Livingstone's on the left. Our bags, rifles, and revolvers are carefully placed at our heads, and a fire made near our feet. We have no tent nor covering of any kind except the branches of the tree under which we may happen to lie; and it is a pretty sight to look up and see every branch, leaf, and twig of the tree stand out, reflected against the clear star-spangled and moonlit sky. The stars of the first magnitude have names which convey the same meaning over very wide tracts of country. Here when Venus comes out in the evenings, she is called Ntanda, the eldest or first-born, and Manjika, the first-born of morning, at other times: she has so much radiance when shining alone, that she casts a shadow. Sirius is named Kuewa usiko, "drawer of night," because supposed to draw the whole night after it. The moon has no evil influence in this country, so far as we know. We have lain and looked up at her, till sweet sleep closed our eyes, unharmed. Four or five of our men were affected with moon-blindness at Tette; though they had not slept out of doors there, they became so blind that their comrades had to guide their hands to the general dish of food; the affection is unknown in their own country. When our posterity shall have discovered what it is which, distinct from foul smells, causes fever, and what, apart from the moon, causes men to be moon-struck, they will pity our dulness of perception.

The men cut a very small quantity of grass for themselves, and sleep in fumbas or sleeping-bags, which are double mats of palm-leaf, six feet long by four wide, and sewn together round three parts of the square, and left open only on one side. They are used as a protection from the cold, wet, and mosquitoes, and are entered as we should get into our beds, were the blankets nailed to the top, bottom, and one side of the bedstead.

A dozen fires are nightly kindled in the camp; and these, being replenished from time to time by the men who are awakened by the cold, are kept burning until daylight. Abundance of dry hard wood is obtained with little trouble; and burns beautifully. After the great business of cooking and eating is over, all sit round the camp-fires, and engage in talking or singing. Every evening one of the Batoka plays his "sansa," and continues at it until far into the night; he accompanies it with an extempore song, in which he rehearses their deeds ever since they left their own country. At times animated political discussions spring up, and the amount of eloquence expended on these occasions is amazing. The whole camp is aroused, and the men shout to one another from the different fires; whilst some, whose tongues are never heard on any other subject, burst forth into impassioned speech.

As a specimen of our mode of marching, we rise about five, or as soon as dawn appears, take a cup of tea and a bit of biscuit; the servants fold up the blankets and stow them away in the bags they carry; the others tie their fumbas and cooking-pots to each end of their carrying-sticks, which are borne on the shoulder; the cook secures the dishes, and all are on the path by sunrise. If a convenient spot can be found we halt for breakfast about nine a.m. To save time, this meal is generally cooked the night before, and has only to be warmed. We continue the march after breakfast, rest a little in the middle of the day, and break off early in the afternoon. We average from two to two-and-a-half miles an hour in a straight line, or as the crow flies, and seldom have more than five or six hours a day of actual travel. This in a hot climate is as much as a man can accomplish without being oppressed; and we always tried to make our progress more a pleasure than a toil. To hurry over the ground, abuse, and look ferocious at one's native companions, merely for the foolish vanity of boasting how quickly a distance was accomplished, is a combination of silliness with absurdity quite odious; while kindly consideration for the feelings of even blacks, the pleasure of observing scenery and everything new as one moves on at an ordinary pace, and the participation in the most delicious rest with our fellows, render travelling delightful. Though not given to over haste, we were a little surprised to find that we could tire our men out; and even the headman, who carried but little more than we did, and never, as we often had to do, hunted in the afternoon, was no better than his comrades. Our experience tends to prove that the European constitution has a power of endurance, even in the tropics, greater than that of the hardiest of the meat-eating Africans.

After pitching our camp, one or two of us usually go off to hunt, more as a matter of necessity than of pleasure, for the men, as well as ourselves, must have meat. We prefer to take a man with us to carry home the game, or lead the others to where it lies; but as they frequently grumble and complain of being tired, we do not particularly object to going alone, except that it involves the extra labour of our making a second trip to show the men where the animal that has been shot is to be found. When it is a couple of miles off it is rather fatiguing to have to go twice; more especially on the days when it is solely to supply their wants that, instead of resting ourselves, we go at all. Like those who perform benevolent deeds at home, the tired hunter, though trying hard to live in charity with all men, is strongly tempted to give it up by bringing only sufficient meat for the three whites and leaving the rest; thus sending the "idle ungrateful poor" supperless to bed. And yet it is only by continuance in well-doing, even to the length of what the worldly-wise call weakness, that the conviction is produced anywhere, that our motives are high enough to secure sincere respect.

A jungle of mimosa, ebony, and "wait-a-bit" thorn lies between the Chicova flats and the cultivated plain, on which stand the villages of the chief, Chitora. He brought us a present of food and drink, because, as he, with the innate politeness of an African, said, he "did not wish us to sleep hungry: he had heard of the Doctor when he passed down, and had a great desire to see and converse with him; but he was a child then, and could not speak in the presence of great men. He was glad that he had seen the English now, and was sorry that his people were away, or he should have made them cook for us." All his subsequent conduct showed him to be sincere.

Many of the African women are particular about the water they use for drinking and cooking, and prefer that which is filtered through sand. To secure this, they scrape holes in the sandbanks beside the stream, and scoop up the water, which slowly filters through, rather than take it from the equally clear and limpid river. This practice is common in the Zambesi, the Rovuma, and Lake Nyassa; and some of the Portuguese at Tette have adopted the native custom, and send canoes to a low island in the middle of the river for water. Chitora's people also obtained their supply from shallow wells in the sandy bed of a small rivulet close to the village. The habit may have arisen from observing the unhealthiness of the main stream at certain seasons. During nearly nine months in the year, ordure is deposited around countless villages along the thousands of miles drained by the Zambesi. When the heavy rains come down, and sweep the vast fetid accumulation into the torrents, the water is polluted with filth; and, but for the precaution mentioned, the natives would prove themselves as little fastidious as those in London who drink the abomination poured into the Thames by Reading and Oxford. It is no wonder that sailors suffered so much from fever after drinking African river water, before the present admirable system of condensing it was adopted in our navy.

The scent of man is excessively terrible to game of all kinds, much more so, probably, than the sight of him. A herd of antelopes, a hundred yards off, gazed at us as we moved along the winding path, and timidly stood their ground until half our line had passed, but darted off the instant they "got the wind," or caught the flavour of those who had gone by. The sport is all up with the hunter who gets to the windward of the African beast, as it cannot stand even the distant aroma of the human race, so much dreaded by all wild animals. Is this the fear and the dread of man, which the Almighty said to Noah was to be upon every beast of the field? A lion may, while lying in wait for his prey, leap on a human being as he would on any other animal, save a rhinoceros or an elephant, that happened to pass; or a lioness, when she has cubs, might attack a man, who, passing "up the wind of her," had unconsciously, by his scent, alarmed her for the safety of her whelps; or buffaloes, amid other animals, might rush at a line of travellers, in apprehension of being surrounded by them; but neither beast nor snake will, as a general rule, turn on man except when wounded, or by mistake. If gorillas, unwounded, advance to do battle with him, and beat their breasts in defiance, they are an exception to all wild beasts known to us. From the way an elephant runs at the first glance of man, it is inferred that this huge brute, though really king of beasts, would run even from a child.

Our two donkeys caused as much admiration as the three white men. Great was the astonishment when one of the donkeys began to bray. The timid jumped more than if a lion had roared beside them. All were startled, and stared in mute amazement at the harsh-voiced one, till the last broken note was uttered; then, on being assured that nothing in particular was meant, they looked at each other, and burst into a loud laugh at their common surprise. When one donkey stimulated the other to try his vocal powers, the interest felt by the startled visitors, must have equalled that of the Londoners, when they first crowded to see the famous hippopotamus.

We were now, when we crossed the boundary rivulet Nyamatarara, out of Chicova and amongst sandstone rocks, similar to those which prevail between Lupata and Kebrabasa. In the latter gorge, as already mentioned, igneous and syenitic masses have been acted on by some great fiery convulsion of nature; the strata are thrown into a huddled heap of confusion. The coal has of course disappeared in Kebrabasa, but is found again in Chicova. Tette grey sandstone is common about Sinjere, and wherever it is seen with fossil wood upon it, coal lies beneath; and here, as at Chicova, some seams crop out on the banks of the Zambesi. Looking southwards, the country is open plain and woodland, with detached hills and mountains in the distance; but the latter are too far off, the natives say, for them to know their names. The principal hills on our right, as we look up stream, are from six to twelve miles away, and occasionally they send down spurs to the river, with brooks flowing through their narrow valleys. The banks of the Zambesi show two well-defined terraces; the first, or lowest, being usually narrow, and of great fertility, while the upper one is a dry grassy plain, a thorny jungle, or a mopane (*Bauhinia*) forest. One of these plains, near the Kafue, is covered with the large stumps and trunks of a petrified forest. We halted a couple of days by the fine stream Sinjere, which comes from the Chiroby-roby hills, about eight miles to the north. Many lumps of coal, brought down by the rapid current, lie in its channel. The natives never seem to have discovered that coal would burn, and, when informed of the fact, shook their heads, smiled incredulously, and said "*Kodi*" (really), evidently regarding it as a mere traveller's tale. They were astounded to see it burning freely on our fire of wood. They told us that plenty of it was seen among the hills; but, being long ago aware that we were now in an immense coalfield, we did not care to examine it further.

A dyke of black basaltic rock, called Kakolole, crosses the river near the mouth of the Sinjere; but it has two open gateways in it of from sixty to eighty yards in breadth, and the channel is very deep.

On a shallow sandbank, under the dyke, lay a herd of hippopotami in fancied security. The young ones were playing with each other like young puppies, climbing on the backs of their dams, trying to take hold of one another by the jaws and tumbling over into the water. Mbia, one of the Makololo, waded across to within a dozen yards of the drowsy beasts, and shot the father of the herd; who, being very fat, soon floated, and was secured at the village below. The headman of the village visited us while we were at breakfast. He wore a black "ife" wig and a printed shirt. After a short silence he said to Masakasa, "You are with the white people, so why do you not tell them to give me a cloth?" "We are strangers," answered Masakasa, "why do you not bring us some food?" He took the plain hint, and brought us two fowls, in order that we should not report that in passing him we got nothing to eat; and, as usual, we gave a cloth in return. In reference to the hippopotamus he would make no demand, but said he would take what we chose to give him. The men gorged themselves with meat for two days, and cut large quantities into long narrow strips, which they half-dried and half-roasted on wooden frames over the fire. Much game is taken in this neighbourhood in pitfalls. Sharp-pointed stakes are set in the bottom, on which the game tumbles and gets impaled. The natives are careful to warn strangers of these traps, and also of the poisoned beams suspended on the tall trees for the purpose of killing elephants and hippopotami. It is not difficult to detect the pitfalls after one's attention has been called to them; but in places where they are careful to carry the earth off to a distance, and a person is not thinking of such things, a sudden descent of nine feet is an experience not easily forgotten by the traveller. The sensations of one thus instantaneously swallowed up by the earth are peculiar. A momentary suspension of consciousness is followed by the rustling sound of a shower of sand and dry grass, and the half-bewildered thought of where he is, and how he came into darkness. Reason awakes to assure him that he must have come down through that small opening of daylight overhead, and that he is now where a hippopotamus ought to have been. The descent of a hippopotamus pitfall is easy, but to get out again into the upper air is a work of labour. The sides are smooth and treacherous, and the cross reeds, which support the covering, break in the attempt to get out by clutching them. A cry from the depths is unheard by those around, and it is only by repeated and most desperate efforts that the buried alive can regain the upper world. At Tette we are told of a white hunter, of unusually small stature, who plumped into a pit while stalking a guinea-fowl on a tree. It was the labour of an entire forenoon to get out; and he was congratulating himself on his escape, and brushing off the clay from his clothes, when down he went into a second pit, which happened, as is often the case, to be close beside the first, and it was evening before he could work himself out of *that*.

Elephants and buffaloes seldom return to the river by the same path on two successive nights, they become so apprehensive of danger from this human art. An old elephant will walk in advance of the herd, and uncover the pits with his trunk, that the others may see the openings and tread on firm ground. Female elephants are generally the victims: more timid by nature than the males, and very motherly in their anxiety for their calves, they carry their trunks up, trying every breeze for fancied danger, which often in reality lies at their feet. The tusker, fearing less, keeps his trunk down, and, warned in time by that exquisitely sensitive organ, takes heed to his ways.

Our camp on the Sinjere stood under a wide-spreading wild fig-tree. From the numbers of this family, of large size, dotted over the country, the fig or banyan species would seem to have been held sacred in Africa from the remotest times. The soil teemed with white ants, whose clay tunnels, formed to screen them from the eyes of birds, thread over the ground, up the trunks of trees, and along the branches, from which the little architects clear away all rotten or dead wood. Very often the exact shape of branches is left in tunnels on the ground and not a bit of the wood inside. The first night we passed here these destructive insects ate through our grass-beds, and attacked our blankets, and certain large red-headed ones even bit our flesh.

On some days not a single white ant is to be seen abroad; and on others, and during certain hours, they appear out of doors in myriads, and work with extraordinary zeal and energy in carrying bits of dried grass down into their nests. During these busy reaping-fits the lizards and birds have a good time of it, and enjoy a rich feast at the expense of thousands of hapless workmen; and when they swarm they are caught in countless numbers by the natives, and their roasted bodies are spoken of in an unctuous manner as resembling grains of soft rice fried in delicious fresh oil.

A strong marauding party of large black ants attacked a nest of white ones near the camp: as the contest took place beneath the surface, we could not see the order of the battle; but it soon became apparent that the blacks had gained the day, and sacked the white town, for they returned in triumph, bearing off the eggs, and choice bits of the bodies of the vanquished. A gift, analogous to that of language, has not been withheld from ants: if part of their building is destroyed, an official is seen coming out to examine the damage; and, after a careful survey of the ruins, he chirrups a few clear and distinct notes, and a crowd of workers begin at once to repair the breach. When the work is completed, another order is given, and the workmen retire, as will appear on removing the soft freshly-built portion. We tried to sleep one rainy might in a native hut, but could not because of attacks by the fighting battalions of a very small species of formica, not more than one-sixteenth of an inch in length. It soon became obvious that they were under regular discipline, and even attempting to carry out the skilful plans and stratagems of some eminent leader. Our hands and necks were the first objects of attack. Large bodies of these little pests were massed in silence round the point to be assaulted. We could hear the sharp shrill word of command two or three times repeated, though until then we had not believed in the vocal power of an ant; the instant after we felt the storming hosts range over head and neck, biting the tender skin, clinging with a death-grip to the hair, and parting with their jaws rather than quit their hold. On our lying down again in the hope of their having been driven off, no sooner was the light out, and all still, than the manoeuvre was repeated. Clear and audible orders were issued, and the assault renewed. It was as hard to sleep in that hut as in the trenches before Sebastopol. The white ant, being a vegetable feeder, devours articles of vegetable origin only, and leather, which, by tanning, is imbued with a vegetable flavour. "A man may be rich to-day and poor to-morrow, from the ravages of white ants," said a Portuguese merchant. "If he gets sick, and unable to look after his goods, his slaves neglect them, and they are soon destroyed by these insects." The reddish ant, in the west called drivers, crossed our path daily, in solid columns an inch wide, and never did the pugnacity of either man or beast exceed theirs. It is a sufficient cause of war if you only approach them, even by accident. Some turn out of the ranks and stand with open mandibles, or, charging with extended jaws, bite with savage ferocity. When hunting, we lighted among them too often; while we were intent on the game, and without a thought of ants, they quietly covered us from head to foot, then all began to bite at the same instant; seizing a piece of the skin with their powerful pincers, they twisted themselves round with it, as if determined to tear it out. Their bites are so terribly sharp that the bravest must run, and then strip to pick off those that still cling with their hooked jaws, as with steel forceps. This kind abounds in damp places, and is usually met with on the banks of streams. We have not heard of their actually killing any animal except the Python, and that only when gorged and quite lethargic, but they soon clear away any dead animal matter; this appears to be their principal food, and their use in the economy of nature is clearly in the scavenger line.

We started from the Sinjere on the 12th of June, our men carrying with them bundles of hippopotamus meat for sale, and for future use. We rested for breakfast opposite the Kakolole dyke, which confines the channel, west of the Manyerere mountain. A rogue monkey, the largest by far that we ever saw, and very fat and tame, walked off leisurely from a garden as we approached. The monkey is a sacred animal in this region, and is never molested or killed, because the people believe devoutly that the souls of their ancestors now occupy these degraded forms, and anticipate that they themselves must, sooner or later, be transformed in like manner; a future as cheerless for the black as the spirit-rapper's heaven is for the whites. The gardens are separated from each other by a single row of small stones, a few handfuls of grass, or a slight furrow made by the hoe. Some are enclosed by a reed fence of the flimsiest construction, yet sufficient to keep out the ever wary hippopotamus, who dreads a trap. His extreme caution is taken advantage of by the women, who hang, as a miniature trap-beam, a kigelia fruit with a bit of stick in the end. This protects the maize, of which he is excessively fond.

The quantity of hippopotamus meat eaten by our men made some of them ill, and our marches were necessarily short. After three hours' travel on the 13th, we spent the remainder of the day at the village of Chasiribera, on a rivulet flowing through a beautiful valley to the north, which is bounded by magnificent mountain-ranges. Pinkwe, or Mbingwe, otherwise Moeu, forms the south-eastern angle of the range. On the 16th June we were at the flourishing village of Senga, under the headman Manyame, which lies at the foot of the mount Motemwa. Nearly all the mountains in this country are covered with open forest and grass, in colour, according to the season, green or yellow. Many are between 2000 and 3000 feet high, with the sky line fringed with trees; the rocks show just sufficiently for one to observe their stratification, or their granitic form, and though not covered with dense masses of climbing plants, like those in moister eastern climates, there is still the idea conveyed that most of the steep sides are fertile, and none give the impression of that barrenness which, in northern mountains, suggests the idea that the bones of the world are sticking through its skin.

The villagers reported that we were on the footsteps of a Portuguese half-caste, who, at Senga, lately tried to purchase ivory, but, in consequence of his having murdered a chief near Zumbo and twenty of his men, the people declined to trade with him. He threatened to take the ivory by force, if they would not sell it; but that same night the ivory and the women were spirited out of the village, and only a large body of armed men remained. The trader, fearing that he might come off second best if it came to blows, immediately departed. Chikwanitsela, or Sekuanangila, is the paramount chief of some fifty miles of the northern bank of the Zambesi in this locality. He lives on the opposite, or southern side, and there his territory is still more extensive. We sent him a present from Senga, and were informed by a messenger next morning that he had a cough and could not come over to see us. "And has his present a cough too," remarked one of our party, "that it does not come to us? Is this the way your chief treats strangers, receives their present, and sends them no food in return?" Our men thought Chikwanitsela an uncommonly stingy fellow; but, as it was possible that some of them might yet wish to return this way, they did not like to scold him more than this, which was sufficiently to the point.

Men and women were busily engaged in preparing the ground for the November planting. Large game was abundant; herds of elephants and buffaloes came down to the river in the night, but were a long way off by daylight. They soon adopt this habit in places where they are hunted.

The plains we travel over are constantly varying in breadth, according as the furrowed and wooded hills approach or recede from the river. On the southern side we see the hill Bungwe, and the long, level, wooded ridge Nyangombe, the first of a series bending from the S.E. to the N.W. past the Zambesi. We shot an old pallah on the 16th, and found that the poor animal had been visited with more than the usual share of animal afflictions. He was stone-blind in both eyes, had several tumours, and a broken leg, which showed no symptoms of ever having begun to heal. Wild animals sometimes suffer a great deal from disease, and wearily drag on a miserable existence before relieved of it by some ravenous beast. Once we drove off a maneless lion and lioness from a dead buffalo, which had been in the last stage of a decline. They had watched him staggering to the river to quench his thirst, and sprang on him as he was crawling up the bank. One had caught him by the throat, and the other by his high projecting backbone, which was broken by the lion's powerful fangs. The struggle, if any, must have been short. They had only eaten the intestines when we frightened them off. It is curious that this is the part that wild animals always begin with, and that it is also the first choice of our men. Were it not a wise arrangement that only the strongest males should continue the breed, one could hardly help pitying the solitary buffalo expelled from the herd for some physical blemish, or on account of the weakness of approaching old age. Banished from female society, he naturally becomes morose and savage; the necessary watchfulness against enemies is now never shared by others; disgusted, he passes into a state of chronic war with all who enjoy life, and the sooner after his expulsion that he fills the lion's or the wild-dog's maw, the better for himself and for the peace of the country.

We encamped on the 20th of June at a spot where Dr. Livingstone, on his journey from the West to the East Coast, was formerly menaced by a chief named Mpende. No offence had been committed against him, but he had firearms, and, with the express object of showing his power, he threatened to attack the strangers. Mpende's counsellors having, however, found out that Dr. Livingstone belonged to a tribe of whom they had heard that "they loved the black man and did not make slaves," his conduct at once changed from enmity to kindness, and, as the place was one well selected for defence, it was perhaps quite as well for Mpende that he decided as he did. Three of his counsellors now visited us, and we gave them a handsome present for their chief, who came himself next morning and made us a present of a goat, a basket of boiled maize, and another of vetches. A few miles above this the headman, Chilondo of Nyamasusa, apologized for not formerly lending us canoes. "He was absent, and his children were to blame for not telling him when the Doctor passed; he did not refuse the canoes." The sight of our men, now armed with muskets, had a great effect. Without any bullying, firearms command respect, and lead men to be reasonable who might otherwise feel disposed to be troublesome. Nothing, however, our fracas with Mpende excepted, could be more peaceful than our passage through this tract of country in 1856. We then had nothing to excite the cupidity of the people, and the men maintained themselves, either by selling elephant's meat, or by exhibiting feats of foreign dancing. Most of the people were very generous and friendly; but the Banyai, nearer to Tette than this, stopped our march with a threatening war-dance. One of our party, terrified at this, ran away, as we thought, insane, and could not, after a painful search of three days, be found. The Banyai, evidently touched by our distress, allowed us to proceed. Through a man we left on an island a little below Mpende's, we subsequently learned that poor Monaheng had fled thither, and had been murdered by the headman for no reason except that he was defenceless. This headman had since become odious to his countrymen, and had been put to death by them.

On the 23rd of June we entered Pangola's principal village, which is upwards of a mile from the river. The ruins of a mud wall showed that a rude attempt had been made to imitate the Portuguese style of building. We established ourselves under a stately wild fig-tree, round whose trunk witchcraft medicine had been tied, to protect from thieves the honey of the wild bees, which had their hive in one of the limbs. This is a common device. The charm, or the medicine, is purchased of the dice doctors, and consists of a strip of palm-leaf smeared with something, and adorned with a few bits of grass, wood, or roots. It is tied round the tree, and is believed to have the power of inflicting disease and death on the thief who climbs over it. Superstition is thus not without its uses in certain states of society; it prevents many crimes and misdemeanours, which would occur but for the salutary fear that it produces.

Pangola arrived, tipsy and talkative.--"We are friends, we are great friends; I have brought you a basket of green maize--here it is!" We thanked him, and handed him two fathoms of cotton cloth, four times the market-value of his present. No, he would not take so small a present; he wanted a double-barrelled rifle--one of Dixon's best. "We are friends, you know; we are all friends together." But although we were willing to admit that, we could not give him our best rifle, so he went off in high dudgeon. Early next morning, as we were commencing Divine service, Pangola returned, sober. We explained to him that we wished to worship God, and invited him to remain; he seemed frightened, and retired: but after service he again importuned us for the rifle. It was of no use telling him that we had a long journey before us, and needed it to kill game for ourselves.--"He too must obtain meat for himself and people, for they sometimes suffered from hunger." He then got sulky, and his people refused to sell food except at extravagant prices. Knowing that we had nothing to eat, they felt sure of starving us into compliance. But two of our young men, having gone off at sunrise, shot a fine waterbuck, and down came the provision market to the lower figure; they even became eager to sell, but our men were angry with them for trying compulsion, and would not buy. Black greed had outwitted itself, as happens often with white cupidity; and not only here did the traits of Africans remind us of Anglo-Saxons elsewhere: the notoriously ready world- wide disposition to take an unfair advantage of a man's necessities shows that the same mean motives are pretty widely diffused among all races. It may not be granted that the same blood flows in all veins, or that all have descended from the same stock; but the traveller has no doubt that, practically, the white rogue and black are men and brothers.

Pangola is the child or vassal of Mpende. Sandia and Mpende are the only independent chiefs from Kebrabasa to Zumbo, and belong to the tribe Manganja. The country north of the mountains here in sight from the Zambesi is called Senga, and its inhabitants Asenga, or Basenga, but all appear to be of the same family as the rest of the Manganja and Maravi. Formerly all the Manganja were united under the government of their great chief, Undi, whose empire extended from Lake Shirwa to the River Loangwa; but after Undi's death it fell to pieces, and a large portion of it on the Zambesi was absorbed by their powerful southern neighbours the Banyai. This has been the inevitable fate of every African empire from time immemorial. A chief of more than ordinary ability arises and, subduing all his less powerful neighbours, founds a kingdom, which he governs more or less wisely till he dies. His successor not having the talents of the conqueror cannot retain the dominion, and some of the abler under-chiefs set up for themselves, and, in a few years, the remembrance only of the empire remains. This, which may be considered as the normal state of African society, gives rise to frequent and desolating wars, and the people long in vain for a power able to make all dwell in peace. In this light, a European colony would be considered by the natives as an inestimable boon to intertropical Africa. Thousands of industrious natives would gladly settle round it, and engage in that peaceful pursuit of agriculture and trade of which they are so fond, and, undistracted by wars or rumours of wars, might listen to the purifying and ennobling truths of the gospel of Jesus Christ. The Manganja on the Zambesi, like their countrymen on the Shire, are fond of agriculture; and, in addition to the usual varieties of food, cultivate tobacco and cotton in quantities more than equal to their wants. To the question, "Would they work for Europeans?" an affirmative answer may be given, if the Europeans belong to the class which can pay a reasonable price for labour, and not to that of adventurers who want employment for themselves. All were particularly well clothed from Sandia's to Pangola's; and it was noticed that all the cloth was of native manufacture, the product of their own looms. In Senga a great deal of iron is obtained from the ore and manufactured very cleverly.

As is customary when a party of armed strangers visits the village, Pangola took the precaution of sleeping in one of the outlying hamlets. No one ever knows, or at any rate will tell, where the chief sleeps. He came not next morning, so we went our way; but in a few moments we saw the rifle-loving chief approaching with some armed men. Before meeting us, he left the path and drew up his "following" under a tree, expecting us to halt, and give him a chance of bothering us again; but, having already had enough of that, we held right on: he seemed dumbfounded, and could hardly believe his own eyes. For a few seconds he was speechless, but at last recovered so far as to be able to say, "You are passing Pangola. Do you not see Pangola?" Mbia was just going by at the time with the donkey, and, proud of every opportunity of airing his small stock of English, shouted in reply, "All right! then get on." "Click, click, click."

On the 26th June we breakfasted at Zumbo, on the left bank of the Loangwa, near the ruins of some ancient Portuguese houses. The Loangwa was too deep to be forded, and there were no canoes on our side. Seeing two small ones on the opposite shore, near a few recently erected huts of two half-castes from Tette, we halted for the ferry-men to come over. From their movements it was evident that they were in a state of rollicking drunkenness. Having a waterproof cloak, which could be inflated into a tiny boat, we sent Mantlanyane across in it. Three half- intoxicated slaves then brought us the shaky canoes, which we lashed together and manned with our own canoe-men. Five men were all that we could carry over at a time; and after four trips had been made the slaves began to clamour for drink; not receiving any, as we had none to give, they grew more insolent, and declared that not another man should cross that day. Sininyane was remonstrating with them, when a loaded musket was presented at him by one of the trio. In an instant the gun was out of the rascal's hands, a rattling shower of blows fell on his back, and he took an involuntary header into the river. He crawled up the bank a sad and sober man, and all three at once tumbled from the height of saucy swagger to a low depth of slavish abjectness. The musket was found to have an enormous charge, and might have blown our man to pieces, but for the promptitude with which his companions administered justice in a lawless land. We were all ferried safely across by 8 o'clock in the evening.

In illustration of what takes place where no government, or law exists, the two half-castes, to whom these men belonged, left Tette, with four hundred slaves, armed with the old Sepoy Brown Bess, to hunt elephants and trade in ivory. On our way up, we heard from natives of their lawless deeds, and again, on our way down, from several, who had been eyewitnesses of the principal crime, and all reports substantially agreed. The story is a sad one. After the traders reached Zumbo, one of them, called by the natives Sequasha, entered into a plot with the disaffected headman, Namakusuru, to kill his chief, Mpangwe, in order that Namakusuru might seize upon the chieftainship; and for the murder of Mpangwe the trader agreed to receive ten large tusks of ivory. Sequasha, with a picked party of armed slaves, went to visit Mpangwe who received him kindly, and treated him with all the honour and hospitality usually shown to distinguished strangers, and the women busied themselves in cooking the best of their provisions for the repast to be set before him. Of this, and also of the beer, the half-caste partook heartily. Mpangwe was then asked by Sequasha to allow his men to fire their guns in amusement. Innocent of any suspicion of treachery, and anxious to hear the report of firearms, Mpangwe at once gave his consent; and the slaves rose and poured a murderous volley into the merry group of unsuspecting spectators, instantly killing the chief and twenty of his people. The survivors fled in horror. The children and young women were seized as slaves, and the village sacked. Sequasha sent the message to Namakusuru: "I have killed the lion that troubled you; come and let us talk over the matter." He came and brought the ivory. "No," said the half-caste, "let us divide the land:" and he took the larger share for himself, and compelled the would-be usurper to deliver up his bracelets, in token of subjection on becoming the child or vassal of Sequasha. These were sent in triumph to the authorities at Tette. The governor of Quillimane had told us that he had received orders from Lisbon to take advantage of our passing to re-establish Zumbo; and accordingly these traders had built a small stockade on the rich plain of the right bank of Loangwa, a mile above the site of the ancient mission church of Zumbo, as part of the royal policy. The bloodshed was quite unnecessary, because, the land at Zumbo having of old been purchased, the natives would have always of their own accord acknowledged the right thus acquired; they pointed it out to Dr. Livingstone in 1856 that, though they were cultivating it, is was not theirs, but white man's land. Sequasha and his mate had left their ivory in charge of some of their slaves, who, in the absence of their masters, were now having a gay time of it, and getting drunk every day with the produce of the sacked villages. The head slave came and begged for the musket of the delinquent ferryman, which was returned. He thought his master did perfectly right to kill Mpangwe, when asked to do it for the fee of ten tusks, and he even justified it thus: "If a man invites you to eat, will you not partake?"

We continued our journey on the 28th of June. Game was extremely abundant, and there were many lions. Mbia drove one off from his feast on a wild pig, and appropriated what remained of the pork to his own use. Lions are particularly fond of the flesh of wild pigs and zebras, and contrive to kill a large number of these animals. In the afternoon we arrived at the village of the female chief, Mamburuma, but she herself was now living on the opposite side of the river. Some of her people called, and said she had been frightened by seeing her son and other children killed by Sequasha, and had fled to the other bank; but when her heart was healed, she would return and live in her own village, and among her own people. She constantly inquired of the black traders, who came up the river, if they had any news of the white man who passed with the oxen. "He has gone down into the sea," was their reply, "but we belong to the same people." "Oh no; you need not tell me that; he takes no slaves, but wishes peace: you are not of his tribe." This antislavery character excites such universal attention, that any missionary who winked at the gigantic evils involved in the slave-trade would certainly fail to produce any good impression on the native mind.

CHAPTER VI.

Illness--The Honey-guide--Abundance of game--The Baenda pezi--The Batoka.

We left the river here, and proceeded up the valley which leads to the Mburuma or Mohango pass. The nights were cold, and on the 30th of June the thermometer was as low as 39 degrees at sunrise. We passed through a village of twenty large huts, which Sequasha had attacked on his return from the murder of the chief, Mpangwe. He caught the women and children for slaves, and carried off all the food, except a huge basket of bran, which the natives are wont to save against a time of famine. His slaves had broken all the water-pots and the millstones for grinding meal.

The buaze-trees and bamboos are now seen on the hills; but the jujube or zisyphus, which has evidently been introduced from India, extends no further up the river. We had been eating this fruit, which, having somewhat the taste of apples, the Portuguese call Macaas, all the way from Tette; and here they were larger than usual, though immediately beyond they ceased to be found. No mango-tree either is to be met with beyond this point, because the Portuguese traders never established themselves anywhere beyond Zumbo. Tsetse flies are more numerous and troublesome than we have ever before found them. They accompany us on the march, often buzzing round our heads like a swarm of bees. They are very cunning, and when intending to bite, alight so gently that their presence is not perceived till they thrust in their lance-like proboscis. The bite is acute, but the pain is over in a moment; it is followed by a little of the disagreeable itching of the mosquito's bite. This fly invariably kills all domestic animals except goats and donkeys; man and the wild animals escape. We ourselves were severely bitten on this pass, and so were our donkeys, but neither suffered from any after effects.

Water is scarce in the Mburuma pass, except during the rainy season. We however halted beside some fine springs in the bed of the now dry rivulet, Podebode, which is continued down to the end of the pass, and yields water at intervals in pools. Here we remained a couple of days in consequence of the severe illness of Dr. Kirk. He had several times been attacked by fever; and observed that when we were on the cool heights he was comfortable, but when we happened to descend from a high to a lower altitude, he felt chilly, though the temperature in the latter case was 25 degrees higher than it was above; he had been trying different medicines of reputed efficacy with a view to ascertain whether other combinations might not be superior to the preparation we generally used; in halting by this water he suddenly became blind, and unable to stand from faintness. The men, with great alacrity, prepared a grassy bed, on which we laid our companion, with the sad forebodings which only those who have tended the sick in a wild country can realize. We feared that in experimenting he had over-drugged himself; but we gave him a dose of our fever pills; on the third day he rode the one of the two donkeys that would allow itself to be mounted, and on the sixth he marched as well as any of us. This case is mentioned in order to illustrate what we have often observed, that moving the patient from place to place is most conducive to the cure; and the more pluck a man has--the less he gives in to the disease--the less likely he is to die.

Supplied with water by the pools in the Podebode, we again joined the Zambesi at the confluence of the rivulet. When passing through a dry district the native hunter knows where to expect water by the animals he sees. The presence of the gemsbuck, duiker or diver, springbucks, or elephants, is no proof that water is near; for these animals roam over vast tracts of country, and may be met scores of miles from it. Not so, however, the zebra, pallah, buffalo, and rhinoceros; their spoor gives assurance that water is not far off, as they never stray any distance from its neighbourhood. But when amidst the solemn stillness of the woods, the singing of joyous birds falls upon the ear, it is certain that water is close at hand.

Our men in hunting came on an immense herd of buffaloes, quietly resting in the long dry grass, and began to blaze away furiously at the astonished animals. In the wild excitement of the hunt, which heretofore had been conducted with spears, some forgot to load with ball, and, firing away vigorously with powder only, wondered for the moment that the buffaloes did not fall. The slayer of the young elephant, having buried his four bullets in as many buffaloes, fired three charges of No. 1 shot he had for killing guinea-fowl. The quaint remarks and merriment after these little adventures seemed to the listener like the pleasant prattle of children. Mbia and Mantlanyane, however, killed one buffalo each; both the beasts were in prime condition; the meat was like really excellent beef, with a smack of venison. A troop of hungry, howling hyenas also thought the savour tempting, as they hung round the camp at night, anxious to partake of the feast. They are, fortunately, arrant cowards, and never attack either men or beasts except they can catch them asleep, sick, or at some other disadvantage. With a bright fire at our feet their presence excites no uneasiness. A piece of meat hung on a tree, high enough to make him jump to reach it, and a short spear, with its handle firmly planted in the ground beneath, are used as a device to induce the hyena to commit suicide by impalement.

The honey-guide is an extraordinary bird; how is it that every member of its family has learned that all men, white or black, are fond of honey? The instant the little fellow gets a glimpse of a man, he hastens to greet him with the hearty invitation to come, as Mbia translated it, to a bees' hive, and take some honey. He flies on in the proper direction, perches on a tree, and looks back to see if you are following; then on to another and another, until he guides you to the spot. If you do not accept his first invitation he follows you with pressing importunities, quite as anxious to lure the stranger to the bees' hive as other birds are to draw him away from their own nest. Except while on the march, our men were sure to accept the invitation, and manifested the same by a peculiar responsive whistle, meaning, as they said, "All right, go ahead; we are coming." The bird never deceived them, but always guided them to a hive of bees, though some had but little honey in store. Has this peculiar habit of the honey-guide its origin, as the attachment of dogs, in friendship for man, or in love for the sweet pickings of the plunder left on the ground? Self-interest aiding in preservation from danger seems to be the rule in most cases, as, for instance, in the bird that guards the buffalo and rhinoceros. The grass is often so tall and dense that one could go close up to these animals quite unperceived; but the guardian bird, sitting on the beast, sees the approach of danger, flaps its wings and screams, which causes its bulky charge to rush off from a foe he has neither seen nor heard; for his reward the vigilant little watcher has the pick of the parasites on his fat friend. In other cases a chance of escape must be given even by the animal itself to its prey; as in the rattle-snake, which, when excited to strike, cannot avoid using his rattle, any more than the cat can resist curling its tail when excited in the chase of a mouse, or the cobra can refrain from inflating the loose skin of the neck and extending it laterally, before striking its poison fangs into its victim. There are many snakes in parts of this pass; they basked in the warm sunshine, but rustled off through the leaves as we approached. We observed one morning a small one of a deadly poisonous species, named Kakone, on a bush by the wayside, quietly resting in a horizontal position, digesting a lizard for breakfast. Though openly in view, its colours and curves so closely resembled a small branch that some failed to see it, even after being asked if they perceived anything on the bush. Here also one of our number had a glance at another species, rarely seen, and whose swift lightning-like motion has given rise to the native proverb, that when a man sees this snake he will forthwith become a rich man.

We slept near the ruined village of the murdered chief, Mpangwe, a lovely spot, with the Zambesi in front, and extensive gardens behind, backed by a semicircle of hills receding up to lofty mountains. Our path kept these mountains on our right, and crossed several streamlets, which seemed to be perennial, and among others the Selole, which apparently flows past the prominent peak Chiarapela. These rivulets have often human dwellings on their banks; but the land can scarcely be said to be occupied. The number of all sorts of game increases wonderfully every day. As a specimen of what may be met with where there are no human habitations, and where no firearms have been introduced, we may mention what at times has actually been seen by us. On the morning of July 3rd a herd of elephants passed within fifty yards of our sleeping-place, going down to the river along the dry bed of a rivulet. Starting a few minutes before the main body, we come upon large flocks of guinea-fowl, shoot what may be wanted for dinner, or next morning's breakfast, and leave them in the path to be picked up by the cook and his mates behind. As we proceed, francolins of three varieties run across the path, and hundreds of turtle-doves rise, with great blatter of wing, and fly off to the trees. Guinea-fowls, francolins, turtle-doves, ducks, and geese are the game birds of this region. At sunrise a herd of pallahs, standing like a flock of sheep, allow the first man of our long

Indian file to approach within about fifty yards; but having meat, we let them trot off leisurely and unmolested. Soon afterwards we come upon a herd of waterbucks, which here are very much darker in colour, and drier in flesh, than the same species near the sea. They look at us and we at them; and we pass on to see a herd of doe koodoos, with a magnificently horned buck or two, hurrying off to the dry hillsides. We have ceased shooting antelopes, as our men have been so often gorged with meat that they have become fat and dainty. They say that they do not want more venison, it is so dry and tasteless, and ask why we do not give them shot to shoot the more savoury guinea-fowl.

About eight o'clock the tsetse commence to buzz about us, and bite our hands and necks sharply. Just as we are thinking of breakfast, we meet some buffaloes grazing by the path; but they make off in a heavy gallop at the sight of man. We fire, and the foremost, badly wounded, separates from the herd, and is seen to stop amongst the trees; but, as it is a matter of great danger to follow a wounded buffalo, we hold on our way. It is this losing of wounded animals which makes firearms so annihilating to these beasts of the field, and will in time sweep them all away. The small Enfield bullet is worse than the old round one for this. It often goes through an animal without killing him, and he afterwards perishes, when he is of no value to man. After breakfast we draw near a pond of water; a couple of elephants stand on its bank, and, at a respectful distance behind these monarchs of the wilderness, is seen a herd of zebras, and another of waterbucks. On getting our wind the royal beasts make off at once; but the zebras remain till the foremost man is within eighty yards of them, when old and young canter gracefully away. The zebra has a great deal of curiosity; and this is often fatal to him, for he has the habit of stopping to look at the hunter. In this particular he is the exact opposite of the diver antelope, which rushes off like the wind, and never for a moment stops to look behind, after having once seen or smelt danger. The finest zebra of the herd is sometimes shot, our men having taken a sudden fancy to the flesh, which all declare to be the "king of good meat." On the plains of short grass between us and the river many antelopes of different species are calmly grazing, or reposing. Wild pigs are common, and walk abroad during the day; but are so shy as seldom to allow a close approach. On taking alarm they erect their slender tails in the air, and trot off swiftly in a straight line, keeping their bodies as steady as a locomotive on a railroad. A mile beyond the pool three cow buffaloes with their calves come from the woods, and move out into the plain. A troop of monkeys, on the edge of the forest, scamper back to its depths on hearing the loud song of Singeleka, and old surly fellows, catching sight of the human party, insult it with a loud and angry bark. Early in the afternoon we may see buffaloes again, or other animals. We camp on the dry higher ground, after, as has happened, driving off a solitary elephant. The nights are warmer now, and possess nearly as much of interest and novelty as the days. A new world awakes and comes forth, more numerous, if we may judge by the noise it makes, than that which is abroad by sunlight. Lions and hyenas roar around us, and sometimes come disagreeably near, though they have never ventured into our midst. Strange birds sing their agreeable songs, while others scream and call harshly as if in fear or anger. Marvellous insect-sounds fall upon the ear; one, said by natives to proceed from a large beetle, resembles a succession of measured musical blows upon an anvil, while many others are perfectly indescribable. A little lemur was once seen to leap about from branch to branch with the agility of a frog; it chirruped like a bird, and is not larger than a robin red-breast. Reptiles, though numerous, seldom troubled us; only two men suffered from stings, and that very slightly, during the entire journey, the one supposed that he was bitten by a snake, and the other was stung by a scorpion.

Grass-burning has begun, and is producing the blue hazy atmosphere of the American Indian summer, which in Western Africa is called the "smokes." Miles of fire burn on the mountain-sides in the evenings, but go out during the night. From their height they resemble a broad zigzag line of fire in the heavens.

We slept on the night of the 6th of July on the left bank of the Chongwe, which comes through a gap in the hills on our right, and is twenty yards wide. A small tribe of the Bazizulu, from the south, under Dadanga, have recently settled here and built a village. Some of their houses are square, and they seem to be on friendly terms with the Bakoa, who own the country. They, like the other natives, cultivate cotton, but of a different species from any we have yet seen in Africa, the staple being very long, and the boll larger than what is usually met with; the seeds cohere as in the Pernambuco kind. They brought the seed with them from their own country, the distant mountains of which in the south, still inhabited by their fellow-countrymen, who possess much cattle and use shields, can be seen from this high ground. These people profess to be children of the great paramount chief, Kwanyakarombe, who is said to be lord of all the Bazizulu. The name of this tribe is known to geographers, who derive their information from the Portuguese, as the *Morusurus*, and the hills mentioned above are said to have been the country of Changamira, the warrior-chief of history, whom no Portuguese ever dared to approach. The Bazizulu seem, by report, to be brave mountaineers; nearer the river, the Sidima inhabit the plains; just as on the north side, the Babimpe live on the heights, about two days off, and the Makoa on or near the river. The chief of the Bazizulu we were now with was hospitable and friendly. A herd of buffaloes came trampling through the gardens and roused up our men; a feat that roaring lions seldom achieved.

Our course next day passed over the upper terrace and through a dense thorn jungle. Travelling is always difficult where there is no path, but it is even more perplexing where the forest is cut up by many game-tracks. Here we got separated from one another, and a rhinoceros with angry snort dashed at Dr. Livingstone as he stooped to pick up a specimen of the wild fruit morula; but she strangely stopped stock-still when less than her own length distant, and gave him time to escape; a branch pulled out his watch as he ran, and turning half round to grasp it, he got a distant glance of her and her calf still standing on the selfsame spot, as if arrested in the middle of her charge by an unseen hand. When about fifty yards off, thinking his companions close behind, he shouted "Look out there!" when off she rushed, snorting loudly, in another direction. The Doctor usually went unarmed before this, but never afterwards.

A fine eland was shot by Dr. Kirk this afternoon, the first we have killed. It was in first-rate condition, and remarkably fat; but the meat, though so tempting in appearance, severely deranged all who partook of it heartily, especially those who ate of the fat. Natives who live in game countries, and are acquainted with the different kinds of wild animals, have a prejudice against the fat of the eland, the pallah, the zebra, hippopotamus, and pig; they never reject it, however, the climate making the desire for all animal food very strong; but they consider that it causes ulcers and leprosy, while the fat of sheep and of oxen never produces any bad effects, unless the animal is diseased.

On the morning of the 9th, after passing four villages, we breakfasted at an old friend's, Tombanyama, who lives now on the mainland, having resigned the reedy island, where he was first seen, to the buffaloes, which used to take his crops and show fight to his men. He keeps a large flock of tame pigeons, and some fine fat capons, one of which he gave us, with a basket of meal. They have plenty of salt in this part of the country, obtaining it from the plains in the usual way.

The half-caste partner of Sequasha and a number of his men were staying near. The fellow was very munch frightened when he saw us, and trembled so much when he spoke, that the Makololo and other natives noticed and remarked on it. His fears arose from a sense of guilt, as we said nothing to frighten him, and did not allude to the murder till a few minutes before starting; when it was remarked that Dr. Livingstone having been accredited to the murdered chief, it would be his duty to report on it; and that not even the Portuguese Government would approve of the deed. He defended it by saying that they had put in the right man, the other was a usurper. He was evidently greatly relieved when we departed. In the afternoon we came to an outlying hamlet of Kambadzo, whose own village is on an island, Nyampungo, or Nyangalule, at the confluence of the Kafue. The chief was on a visit here, and they had been enjoying a regular jollification. There had been much mirth, music, drinking, and dancing. The men, and women too, had taken "a wee drap too much," but had not passed the complimentary stage. The wife of the headman, after looking at us a few moments, called out to the others, "Black traders have come before, calling themselves Bazungu, or white men, but now, for the first time, have we seen the real Bazungu." Kambadzo also soon appeared; he was sorry that we had not come before the beer was all done, but he was going back to see if it was all really and entirely finished, and not one little potful left somewhere.

This was, of course, mere characteristic politeness, as he was perfectly aware that every drop had been swallowed; so we proceeded on to the Kafue, or Kafuje, accompanied by the most intelligent of his headmen. A high ridge, just before we reached the confluence, commands a splendid view of the two great rivers, and the rich country beyond. Behind, on the north and east, is the high mountain-range, along whose base we have been travelling; the whole range is covered with trees, which appear even on the prominent peaks, Chiarapela, Morindi, and Chiava; at this last the chain bends away to the N.W., and we could see the distant mountains where the chief, Semalembue, gained all our hearts in 1856.

On the 9th of July we tried to send Semalembue a present, but the people here refused to incur the responsibility of carrying it. We, who have the art of writing, cannot realize the danger one incurs of being accused of purloining a portion of goods sent from one person to another, when the carrier cannot prove that he delivered all committed to his charge. Rumours of a foray having been made, either by Makololo or Batoka, as far as the fork of the Kafue, were received here by our men with great indignation, as it looked as if the marauders were shutting up the country, which they had been trying so much to open. Below the junction of the rivers, on a shallow sandbank, lay a large herd of hippopotami, their bodies out of the water, like masses of black rock. Kambadzo's island, called Nyangalule, a name which occurs again at the mouth of the Zambesi, has many choice Motsikiri (*Trachelia*) trees on it; and four very conspicuous stately palms growing out of a single stem. The Kafue reminds us a little of the Shire, flowing between steep banks, with fertile land on both sides. It is a smaller river, and has less current. Here it seems to come from the west. The headman of the village, near which we encamped, brought a present of meal, fowls, and sweet potatoes. They have both the red and white varieties of this potato. We have, on several occasions during this journey, felt the want of vegetables, in a disagreeable craving which our diet of meat and native meal could not satisfy. It became worse and worse till we got a meal of potatoes, which allayed it at once. A great scarcity of vegetables prevails in these parts of Africa. The natives collect several kinds of wild plants in the woods, which they use no doubt for the purpose of driving off cravings similar to those we experienced.

Owing to the strength of the wind, and the cranky state of the canoes, it was late in the afternoon of the 11th before our party was ferried over the Kafue. After crossing, we were in the Bawe country. Fishhooks here, of native workmanship, were observed to have barbs like the European hooks: elsewhere the point of the hook is merely bent in towards the shank, to have the same effect in keeping on the fish as the barb. We slept near a village a short distance above the ford. The people here are of Batoka origin, the same as many of our men, and call themselves Batonga (independents), or Balengi, and their language only differs slightly from that of the Bakoa, who live between the two rivers Kafue and Loangwa. The paramount chief of the district lives to the west of this place, and is called Nchomokela--an hereditary title: the family burying-place is on a small hill near this village. The women salute us by clapping their hands and lullilooing as we enter and leave a village, and the men, as they think, respectfully clap their hands on their hips. Immense crops of mapira (*holcus sorghum*) are raised; one species of it forms a natural bend on the seed-stalk, so that the massive ear hangs down. The grain was heaped up on wooden stages, and so was a variety of other products. The men are skilful hunters, and kill elephants and buffaloes with long heavy spears. We halted a few minutes on the morning of the 12th July, opposite the narrow island of Sikakoa, which has a village on its lower end. We were here told that Moselekatse's chief town is a month's distance from this place. They had heard, moreover, that the English had come to Moselekatse, and told him it was wrong to kill men; and he had replied that he was born to kill people, but would drop the habit; and, since the English came, he had sent out his men, not to kill as of yore, but to collect tribute of cloth and ivory. This report referred to the arrival of the Rev. R. Moffat, of Kuruman, who, we afterwards found, had established a mission. The statement is interesting as showing that, though imperfectly expressed, the purport of the missionaries' teaching had travelled, in a short time, over 300 miles, and we know not how far the knowledge of the English operations on the coast spread inland.

When abreast of the high wooded island Kalabi we came in contact with one of the game-laws of the country, which has come down from the most ancient times. An old buffalo crossed the path a few yards in front of us; our guide threw his small spear at its hip, and it was going off scarcely hurt, when three rifle balls knocked it over. "It is mine," said the guide. He had wounded it first, and the established native game- law is that the animal belongs to the man who first draws blood; the two legs on one side, by the same law, belonged to us for killing it. This beast was very old, blind of one eye, and scabby; the horns, mere stumps, not a foot long, must have atrophied, when by age he lost the strength distinctive of his sex; some eighteen or twenty inches of horn could not well be worn down by mere rubbing against the trees. We saw many buffaloes next day, standing quietly amidst a thick thorn-jungle, through which we were passing. They often stood until we were within fifty or a hundred yards of them.

On the 14th July we left the river at the mountain-range, which, lying northeast and south-west across the river, forms the Kariba gorge. Near the upper end of the Kariba rapids, the stream Sanyati enters from the south, and is reported to have

Moselekatse's principal cattle-posts at its sources; our route went round the end of the mountains, and we encamped beside the village of the generous chief Moloi, who brought us three immense baskets of fine mapira meal, ten fowls, and two pots of beer. On receiving a present in return, he rose, and, with a few dancing gestures, said or sang, "Motota, Motota, Motota," which our men translated into "thanks." He had visited Moselekatse a few months before our arrival, and saw the English missionaries, living in their wagons. "They told Moselekatse," said he, "they were of his family, or friends, and would plough the land and live at their own expense;" and he had replied, "The land is before you, and I shall come and see you plough." This again was substantially what took place, when Mr. Moffat introduced the missionaries to his old friend, and shows still further that the notion of losing their country by admitting foreigners does not come as the first idea to the native mind. One might imagine that, as mechanical powers are unknown to the heathen, the almost magic operations of machinery, the discoveries of modern science and art, or the presence of the prodigious force which, for instance, is associated with the sight of a man-of-war, would have the effect which miracles once had of arresting the attention and inspiring awe. But, though we have heard the natives exclaim in admiration at the sight of even small illustrations of what science enables us to do--"Ye are gods, and not men"--the heart is unaffected. In attempting their moral elevation, it is always more conducive to the end desired, that the teacher should come unaccompanied by any power to cause either jealousy or fear. The heathen, who have not become aware of the greed and hate which too often characterize the advancing tide of emigration, listen with most attention to the message of Divine love when delivered by men who evidently possess the same human sympathies with themselves. A chief is rather envied his good fortune in first securing foreigners in his town. Jealousy of strangers belongs more to the Arab than to the African character; and if the women are let alone by the traveller, no danger need be apprehended from any save the slave-trading tribes, and not often even from them.

We passed through a fertile country, covered with open forest, accompanied by the friendly Bawe. They are very hospitable; many of them were named, among themselves, "the Baenda pezi," or "Go-nakeds," their only clothing being a coat of red ochre. Occasionally stopping at their villages we were duly lullilooed, and regaled with sweet new-made beer, which, being yet unfermented, was not intoxicating. It is in this state called Liting or Makonde. Some of the men carry large shields of buffalo-hide, and all are well supplied with heavy spears. The vicinity of the villages is usually cleared and cultivated in large patches; but nowhere can the country be said to be stocked with people. At every village stands were erected, and piles of the native corn, still unthrashed, placed upon them; some had been beaten out, put into oblong parcels made of grass, and stacked in wooden frames.

We crossed several rivulets in our course, as the Mandora, the Lofia, the Manzaia (with brackish water), the Rimbe, the Chibue, the Chezia, the Chilola (containing fragments of coal), which did little more than mark our progress. The island and rapid of Nakansalo, of which we had formerly heard, were of no importance, the rapid being but half a mile long, and only on one side of the island. The island Kaluzi marks one of the numerous places where astronomical observations were made; Mozia, a station where a volunteer poet left us; the island Mochenya, and Mpande island, at the mouth of the Zungwe rivulet, where we left the Zambesi.

When favoured with the hospitality and company of the "Go-nakeds," we tried to discover if nudity were the badge of a particular order among the Bawe, but they could only refer to custom. Some among them had always liked it for no reason in particular: shame seemed to lie dormant, and the sense could not be aroused by our laughing and joking them on their appearance. They evidently felt no less decent than we did with our clothes on; but, whatever may be said in favour of nude statues, it struck us that man, in a state of nature, is a most ungainly animal. Could we see a number of the degraded of our own lower classes in like guise, it is probable that, without the black colour which acts somehow as a dress, they would look worse still.

In domestic contentions the Bawe are careful not to kill each other; but, when one village goes to war with another, they are not so particular. The victorious party are said to quarter one of the bodies of the enemies they may have killed, and to perform certain ceremonies over the fragments. The vanquished call upon their conquerors to give them a portion also; and, when this request is complied with, they too perform the same ceremonies, and lament over their dead comrade, after which the late combatants may visit each other in peace. Sometimes the head of the slain is taken and buried in an ant-hill, till all the flesh is gone; and the lower jaw is then worn as a trophy by the slayer; but this we never saw, and the foregoing information was obtained only through an interpreter.

We left the Zambesi at the mouth of the Zungwe or Mozama or Dela rivulet, up which we proceeded, first in a westerly and then in a north-westerly direction. The Zungwe at this time had no water in its sandy channel for the first eight or ten miles. Willows, however, grow on the banks, and water soon began to appear in the hollows; and a few miles further up it was a fine flowing stream deliciously cold. As in many other streams from Chicova to near Sinamane shale and coal crop out in the bank; and here the large roots of stigmaria or its allied plants were found. We followed the course of the Zungwe to the foot of the Batoka highlands, up whose steep and rugged sides of red and white quartz we climbed till we attained an altitude of upwards of 3000 feet. Here, on the cool and bracing heights, the exhilaration of mind and body was delightful, as we looked back at the hollow beneath covered with a hot sultry glare, not unpleasant now that we were in the mild radiance above. We had a noble view of the great valley in which the Zambesi flows. The cultivated portions are so small in comparison to the rest of the landscape that the valley appears nearly all forest, with a few grassy glades. We spent the night of the 28th July high above the level of the sea, by the rivulet Tyotyo, near Tabacheu or Chirebuechina, names both signifying white mountain; in the morning hoar frost covered the ground, and thin ice was on the pools. Skirting the southern flank of Tabacheu, we soon passed from the hills on to the portion of the vast table-land called Mataba, and looking back saw all the way across the Zambesi valley to the lofty ridge some thirty miles off, which, coming from the Mashona, a country in the S.E., runs to the N.W. to join the ridge at the angle of which are the Victoria Falls, and then bends far to the N.E. from the same point. Only a few years since these extensive highlands were peopled by the Batoka; numerous herds of cattle furnished abundance of milk, and the rich soil amply repaid the labour of the husbandman; now large herds of buffaloes, zebras, and antelopes fatten on the excellent pasture; and on that land, which formerly supported multitudes, not a man is to been seen. In travelling from Monday morning till late on Saturday afternoon, all the way from Tabacheu to Moachemba, which is only twenty-one miles of latitude from the Victoria Falls, and constantly passing the ruined sites of utterly deserted Botoka villages, we did not fall in with a single person. The Batoka were driven out of their noble country by the invasions of Moselekatse and Sebetuane. Several tribes of Bechuana and Basutu, fleeing from the Zulu or Matebele chief Moselekatse reached the Zambesi above the Falls. Coming from a land without rivers, none of them knew how to swim; and one tribe, called the Bamangwato, wishing to cross the Zambesi, was ferried over, men and women separately, to different islands, by one of the Batoka chiefs; the men were then left to starve and the women appropriated by the ferryman and his people. Sekomi, the present chief of the Bamangwato, then an infant in his mother's arms, was enabled, through the kindness of a private Batoka, to escape. This act seems to have made an indelible impression on Sekomi's heart, for though otherwise callous, he still never fails to inquire after the welfare of his benefactor.

Sebetuane, with his wonted ability, outwitted the treacherous Batoka, by insisting in the politest manner on their chief remaining at his own side until the people and cattle were all carried safe across; the chief was then handsomely rewarded, both with cattle and brass rings off Sebetuane's own wives. No sooner were the Makololo, then called Basuto, safely over, than they were confronted by the whole Batoka nation; and to this day the Makololo point with pride to the spot on the Lekone, near to which they were encamped, where Sebetuane, with a mere handful of warriors in comparison to the vast horde that surrounded him, stood waiting the onslaught, the warriors in one small body, the women and children guarding the cattle behind them. The Batoka, of course, melted away before those who had been made veterans by years of continual fighting, and Sebetuane always justified his subsequent conquests in that country by alleging that the Batoka had come out to fight with a man fleeing for his life, who had never done them any wrong. They seem never to have been a warlike race; passing through their country, we once observed a large stone cairn, and our guide favoured us with the following account of it:--"Once upon a time, our forefathers were going to fight another tribe, and here they halted and sat down. After a long consultation, they came to the unanimous conclusion that, instead of proceeding to fight and kill their neighbours, and perhaps be killed themselves, it would be more like men to raise this heap of stones, as their protest against the wrong the other tribe had done them, which, having accomplished, they returned quietly home." Such men of peace could not stand before the Makololo, nor, of course, the more warlike Matebele, who coming afterwards, drove even their conquerors, the Makololo, out of the country. Sebetuane, however, profiting by the tactics which he had learned of the Batoka, inveigled a large body of this new enemy on to another island, and after due starvation there overcame the whole. A much greater army of "Moselekatse's own" followed with canoes, but were now baffled by Sebetuane's placing all his people and cattle on an island and so guarding it that none could approach. Dispirited, famished, borne down by fever, they returned to the Falls, and all except five were cut off.

But though the Batoka appear never to have had much inclination to fight with men, they are decidedly brave hunters of buffaloes and elephants. They go fearlessly close up to these formidable animals, and kill them with large spears. The Banyai, who have long bullied all Portuguese traders, were amazed at the daring and bravery of the Batoka in coming at once to close quarters with the elephant; and Chisaka, a Portuguese rebel, having formerly induced a body of this tribe to settle with him, ravaged all the Portuguese villas around Tette. They bear the name of Basimilongwe, and some of our men found relations among them. Sininyane and Matenga also, two of our party, were once inveigled into a Portuguese expedition against Mariano, by the assertion that the Doctor had arrived and had sent for them to come down to Senna. On finding that they were entrapped to fight, they left, after seeing an officer with a large number of Tette slaves killed.

The Batoka had attained somewhat civilized ideas, in planting and protecting various fruit and oil-seed yielding trees of the country. No other tribe either plants or abstains from cutting down fruit trees, but here we saw some which had been planted in regular rows, and the trunks of which were quite two feet in diameter. The grand old Mosibe, a tree yielding a bean with a thin red pellicle, said to be very fattening, had probably seen two hundred summers. Dr. Kirk found that the Mosibe is peculiar, in being allied to a species met with only in the West Indies. The Motsikiri, sometimes called Mafuta, yields a hard fat, and an oil which is exported from Inhambane. It is said that two ancient Batoka travellers went down as far as the Loangwa, and finding the Macaa tree (*jujube* or *zisyphus*) in fruit, carried the seed all the way back to the great Falls, in order to plant them. Two of these trees are still to be seen there, the only specimens of the kind in that region.

The Batoka had made a near approach to the custom of more refined nations and had permanent graveyards, either on the sides of hills, thus rendered sacred, or under large old shady trees; they reverence the tombs of their ancestors, and plant the largest elephants' tusks, as monuments at the head of the grave, or entirely enclose it with the choicest ivory. Some of the other tribes throw the dead body into the river to be devoured by crocodiles, or, sewing it up in a mat, place it on the branch of a baobab, or cast it in some lonely gloomy spot, surrounded by dense tropical vegetation, where it affords a meal to the foul hyenas; but the Batoka reverently bury their dead, and regard the spot henceforth as sacred. The ordeal by the poison of the muave is resorted to by the Batoka, as well as by the other tribes; but a cock is often made to stand proxy for the supposed witch. Near the confluence of the Kafue the Mambo, or chief, with some of his headmen, came to our sleeping-place with a present; their foreheads were smeared with white flour, and an unusual seriousness marked their demeanour. Shortly before our arrival they had been accused of witchcraft; conscious of innocence, they accepted the ordeal, and undertook to drink the poisoned muave. For this purpose they made a journey to the sacred hill of Nchomokela, on which repose the bodies of their ancestors; and, after a solemn appeal to the unseen spirits to attest the innocence of their children, they swallowed the muave, vomited, and were therefore declared not guilty. It is evident that they believe that the soul has a continued existence; and that the spirits of the departed know what those they have left behind them are doing, and are pleased or not according as their deeds are good or evil; this belief is universal. The owner of a large canoe refused to sell it, because it belonged to the spirit of his father, who helped him when he killed the hippopotamus. Another, when the bargain for his canoe was nearly completed, seeing a large serpent on a branch of the tree overhead, refused to complete the sale, alleging that this was the spirit of his father come to protest against it.

Some of the Batoka chiefs must have been men of considerable enterprise; the land of one, in the western part of this country, was protected by the Zambesi on the S., and on the N. and E. lay an impassable reedy marsh, filled with water all the year round, leaving only his western border open to invasion: he conceived the idea of digging a broad and deep canal nearly a mile in length, from the reedy marsh to the Zambesi, and, having actually carried the scheme into execution, he formed a large island, on which his cattle grazed in safety, and his corn ripened from year to year secure from all marauders.

Another chief, who died a number of years ago, believed that he had discovered a remedy for tsetse-bitten cattle; his son Moyara showed us a plant, which was new to our botanist, and likewise told us how the medicine was prepared; the bark of the root, and, what might please our homoeopathic friends, a dozen of the tsetse are dried, and ground together into a fine powder. This mixture is administered internally; and the cattle are fumigated by burning under them the rest of the plant collected. The treatment must be continued for weeks, whenever the symptoms of poison appear. This medicine, he frankly admitted, would not cure all the bitten cattle. "For," said he, "cattle, and men too, die in spite of medicine; but should a herd by accident stray into a tsetse district and be bitten, by this medicine of my father, Kampa-kampa, some of them could be saved, while, without it, all would inevitably die." He stipulated that we were not to show the medicine to other people, and if ever we needed it in this region we must employ him; but if we were far off we might make it ourselves; and when we saw it cure the cattle think of him, and send him a present.

Our men made it known everywhere that we wished the tribes to live in peace, and would use our influence to induce Sekeletu to prevent the Batoka of Moshobotwane and the Makololo under-chiefs making forays into their country: they had already suffered severely, and their remonstrances with their countryman, Moshobotwane, evoked only the answer, "The Makololo have given me a spear; why should I not use it?" He, indeed, it was who, being remarkably swift of foot, first guided the Makololo in their conquest of the country. In the character of peace-makers, therefore, we experienced abundant hospitality; and, from the Kafue to the Falls, none of our party was allowed to suffer hunger. The natives sent to our sleeping-places generous presents of the finest white meal, and fat capons to give it a relish, great pots of beer to comfort our hearts, together with pumpkins, beans, and tobacco, so that we "should sleep neither hungry nor thirsty."

In travelling from the Kafue to the Zungwe we frequently passed several villages in the course of a day's march. In the evening came deputies from the villages, at which we could not stay to sleep, with liberal presents of food. It would have pained them to have allowed strangers to pass without partaking of their hospitality; repeatedly were we hailed from huts, and asked to wait a moment and drink a little of the beer, which was brought with alacrity. Our march resembled a triumphant procession. We entered and left every village amidst the cheers of its inhabitants; the men clapping their hands, and the women lullilooing, with the shrill call, "Let us sleep," or "Peace." Passing through a hamlet one day, our guide called to the people, "Why do you not clap your hands and salute when you see men who are wishing to bring peace to the land?" When we halted for the night it was no uncommon thing for the people to prepare our camp entirely of their own accord; some with hoes quickly smoothed the ground for our beds, others brought dried grass and spread it carefully over the spot; some with their small axes speedily made a bush fence to shield us from the wind; and if, as occasionally happened, the water was a little distance off, others hastened and brought it with firewood to cook our food with. They are an industrious people, and very fond of agriculture. For hours together we marched through unbroken fields of mapira, or native corn, of a great width; but one can give no idea of the extent of land under the hoe as compared with any European country. The extent of surface is so great that the largest fields under culture, when viewed on a wide landscape, dwindle to mere spots. When taken in connection with the wants of the people, the cultivation on the whole is most creditable to their industry. They erect numerous granaries which give their villages the appearance of being large; and, when the water of the Zambesi has subsided, they place large quantities of grain, tied up in bundles of grass, and well plastered over with clay, on low sand islands for protection from the attacks of marauding mice and men. Owing to the ravages of the weevil, the native corn can hardly be preserved until the following crop comes in. However largely they may cultivate, and however abundant the harvest, it must all be consumed in a year. This may account for their making so much of it into beer. The beer these Batoka or Bawe brew is not the sour and intoxicating boala or pombe found among some other tribes, but sweet, and highly nutritive, with only a slight degree of acidity, sufficient to render it a pleasant drink. The people were all plump, and in good condition; and we never saw a single case of intoxication among them, though all drank abundance of this liting, or sweet beer. Both men and boys were eager to work for very small pay. Our men could hire any number of them to carry their burdens for a few beads a day. Our miserly and dirty ex-cook had an old pair of trousers that some one had given to him; after he had long worn them himself, with one of the sorely decayed legs he hired a man to carry his heavy load a whole day; a second man carried it the next day for the other leg, and what remained of the old garment, without the buttons, procured the labour of another man for the third day.

Men of remarkable ability have risen up among the Africans from time to time, as amongst other portions of the human family. Some have attracted the attention, and excited the admiration of large districts by their wisdom. Others, apparently by the powers of ventriloquism, or by peculiar dexterity in throwing the spear, or shooting with the bow, have been the wonder of their generation; but the total absence of literature leads to the loss of all former experience, and the wisdom of the wise has not been handed down. They have had their minstrels too, but mere tradition preserves not their effusions. One of these, and apparently a genuine poet, attached himself to our party for several days, and whenever we halted, sang our praises to the villagers, in smooth and harmonious numbers. It was a sort of blank verse, and each line consisted of five syllables. The song was short when it first began, but each day he picked up more information about us, and added to the poem until our praises became an ode of respectable length. When distance from home compelled his return he expressed his regret at leaving us, and was, of course, paid for his useful and pleasant flatteries. Another, though a less gifted son of song, belonged to the Batoka of our own party. Every evening, while the others were cooking, talking, or sleeping, he rehearsed his songs, containing a history of everything he had seen in the land of the white men, and on the way back. In composing, extempore, any new piece, he was never at a loss; for if the right word did not come he halted not, but eked out the measure with a peculiar musical sound meaning nothing at all. He accompanied his recitations on the *sansa*, an instrument figured in the woodcut, the nine iron keys of which are played with the thumbs, while the fingers pass behind to hold it. The hollow end and ornaments face the breast of the player. Persons of a musical turn, if too poor to buy a sansa, may be seen playing vigorously on an instrument made with a number of thick corn-stalks sewn together, as a sansa frame, and keys of split bamboo, which, though making but little sound, seems to soothe the player himself. When the instrument is played with a calabash as a sounding board, it emits a greater volume of sound. Pieces of shells and tin are added to make a jingling accompaniment, and the calabash is also ornamented.

After we had passed up, a party of slaves, belonging to the two native Portuguese who assassinated the chief, Mpangwe, and took possession of his lands at

Zumbo, followed on our footsteps, and representing themselves to be our "children," bought great quantities of ivory from the Bawe, for a few coarse beads a tusk. They also purchased ten large new canoes to carry it, at the rate of six strings of red or white beads, or two fathoms of grey calico, for each canoe, and, at the same cheap rate, a number of good-looking girls.

CHAPTER VII.

The Victoria Falls of the Zambesi--Marvellous grandeur of the Cataracts--
The Makololo's town--The Chief Sekeletu.

During the time we remained at Motunta a splendid meteor was observed to lighten the whole heavens. The observer's back was turned to it, but on looking round the streak of light was seen to remain on its path some seconds. This streak is usually explained to be only the continuance of the impression made by the shining body on the retina. This cannot be, as in this case the meteor was not actually seen and yet the streak was clearly perceived. The rays of planets and stars also require another explanation than that usually given.

Fruit-trees and gigantic wild fig-trees, and circles of stones on which corn safes were placed, with worn grindstones, point out where the villages once stood. The only reason now assigned for this fine country remaining desolate is the fear of fresh visitations by the Matebele. The country now slopes gradually to the west into the Makololo Valley. Two days' march from the Batoka village nearest the highlands, we met with some hunters who were burning the dry grass, in order to attract the game by the fresh vegetation which speedily springs up afterwards. The grass, as already remarked, is excellent for cattle. One species, with leaves having finely serrated edges, and of a reddish-brown colour, we noticed our men eating: it tastes exactly like liquorice-root, and is named kezu-kezu. The tsetse, known to the Batoka by the name "ndoka," does not exist here, though buffaloes and elephants abound.

A small trap in the path, baited with a mouse, to catch spotted cats (**F. Genetta**), is usually the first indication that we are drawing near to a village; but when we get within the sounds of pounding corn, cockcrowing, or the merry shouts of children at play, we know that the huts are but a few yards off, though the trees conceal them from view. We reached, on the 4th of August, Moachemba, the first of the Batoka villages which now owe allegiance to Sekeletu, and could see distinctly with the naked eye, in the great valley spread out before us, the columns of vapour rising from the Victoria Falls, though upwards of 20 miles distant. We were informed that, the rains having failed this year, the corn crops had been lost, and great scarcity and much hunger prevailed from Sesheke to Linyanti. Some of the reports which the men had heard from the Batoka of the hills concerning their families, were here confirmed. Takelang's wife had been killed by Mashotlane, the headman at the Falls, on a charge, as usual, of witchcraft. Inchikola's two wives, believing him to be dead, had married again; and Masakasa was intensely disgusted to hear that two years ago his friends, upon a report of his death, threw his shield over the Falls, slaughtered all his oxen, and held a species of wild Irish wake, in honour of his memory: he said he meant to disown them, and to say, when they come to salute him, "I am dead. I am not here. I belong to another world, and should stink if I came among you."

All the sad news we had previously heard, of the disastrous results which followed the attempt of a party of missionaries, under the Rev. H. Helmore, to plant the gospel at Linyanti, were here fully confirmed. Several of the missionaries and their native attendants, from Kuruman, had succumbed to the fever, and the survivors had retired some weeks before our arrival. We remained the whole of the 7th beside the village of the old Batoka chief, Moshobotwane, the stoutest man we have seen in Africa. The cause of our delay here was a severe attack of fever in Charles Livingstone. He took a dose of our fever pills; was better on the 8th, and marched three hours; then on the 9th marched eight miles to the Great Falls, and spent the rest of the day in the fatiguing exercise of sight-seeing. We were in the very same valley as Linyanti, and this was the same fever which treated, or rather maltreated, with only a little Dover's powder, proved so fatal to poor Helmore; the symptoms, too, were identical with those afterwards described by non-medical persons as those of poison.

We gave Moshobotwane a present, and a pretty plain exposition of what we thought of his bloody forays among his Batoka brethren. A scolding does most good to the recipient, when put alongside some obliging act. He certainly did not take it ill, as was evident from what he gave us in return; which consisted of a liberal supply of meal, milk, and an ox. He has a large herd of cattle, and a tract of fine pasture-land on the beautiful stream Lekone. A home-feeling comes over one, even in the interior of Africa, at seeing once more cattle grazing peacefully in the meadows. The tsetse inhabits the trees which bound the pasture-land on the west; so, should the herdsman forget his duty, the cattle straying might be entirely lost. The women of this village were more numerous than the men, the result of the chief's marauding. The Batoko wife of Sima came up from the Falls, to welcome her husband back, bringing a present of the best fruits of the country. Her husband was the only one of the party who had brought a wife from Tette, namely, the girl whom he obtained from Chisaka for his feats of dancing. According to our ideas, his first wife could hardly have been pleased at seeing the second and younger one; but she took her away home with her, while the husband remained with us. In going down to the Fall village we met several of the real Makololo. They are lighter in colour than the other tribes, being of a rich warm brown; and they speak in a slow deliberate manner, distinctly pronouncing every word. On reaching the village opposite Kalai, we had an interview with the Makololo headman, Mashotlane: he came to the shed in which we were seated, a little boy carrying his low three- legged stool before him: on this he sat down with becoming dignity, looked round him for a few seconds, then at us, and, saluting us with "Rumela" (good morning, or hail), he gave us some boiled hippopotamus meat, took a piece himself, and then handed the rest to his attendants, who soon ate it up. He defended his forays on the ground that, when he went to collect tribute, the Batoka attacked him, and killed some of his attendants. The excuses made for their little wars are often the very same as those made by Caesar in his "Commentaries." Few admit, like old Moshobotwane, that they fought because they had the power, and a fair prospect of conquering. We found here Pitsane, who had accompanied the Doctor to St. Paul de Loanda. He had been sent by Sekeletu to purchase three horses from a trading party of Griquas from Kuruman, who charged nine large tusks apiece for very wretched animals.

In the evening, when all was still, one of our men, Takelang, fired his musket, and cried out, "I am weeping for my wife: my court is desolate: I have no home;" and then uttered a loud wail of anguish.

We proceeded next morning, 9th August, 1860, to see the Victoria Falls. Mosi-oa-tunya is the Makololo name and means smoke sounding; Seongo or Chongwe, meaning the Rainbow, or the place of the Rainbow, was the more ancient term they bore. We embarked in canoes, belonging to Tuba Mokoro, "smasher of canoes," an ominous name; but he alone, it seems, knew the medicine which insures one against shipwreck in the rapids above the Falls. For some miles the river was smooth and tranquil, and we glided pleasantly over water clear as crystal, and past lovely islands densely covered with a tropical vegetation. Noticeable among the many trees were the lofty Hyphaene and Borassus palms; the graceful wild date-palm, with its fruit in golden clusters, and the umbrageous mokononga, of cypress form, with its dark-green leaves and scarlet fruit. Many flowers peeped out near the water's edge, some entirely new to us, and others, as the convolvulus, old acquaintances.

But our attention was quickly called from the charming islands to the dangerous rapids, down which Tuba might unintentionally shoot us. To confess the truth, the very ugly aspect of these roaring rapids could scarcely fail to cause some uneasiness in the minds of new-comers. It is only when the river is very low, as it was now, that any one durst venture to the island to which we were bound. If one went during the period of flood, and fortunately hit the island, he would be obliged to remain there till the water subsided again, if he lived so long. Both hippopotami and elephants have been known to be swept over the Falls, and of course smashed to pulp.

Before entering the race of waters, we were requested not to speak, as our talking might diminish the virtue of the medicine; and no one with such boiling eddying rapids before his eyes, would think of disobeying the orders of a "canoe-smasher." It soon became evident that there was sound sense in this request of Tuba's, although the reason assigned was not unlike that of the canoe-man from Sesheke, who begged one of our party not to whistle, because whistling made the wind come. It was the duty of the man at the bow to look out ahead for the proper course, and when he saw a rock or snag, to call out to the steersman. Tuba doubtless thought that talking on board might divert the attention of his steersman, at a time when the neglect of an order, or a slight mistake, would be sure to spill us all into the chafing river. There were places where the utmost exertions of both men had to be put forth in order to force the canoe to the only safe part of the rapid, and to prevent it from sweeping down broadside on, where in a twinkling we should have found ourselves floundering among the plotuses and cormorants, which were engaged in diving for their breakfast of small fish. At times it seemed as if nothing could save us from dashing in our headlong race against the rocks which, now that the river was low, jutted out of the water; but just at the very nick of time, Tuba passed the word to the steersman, and then with ready pole turned the canoe a little aside, and we glided swiftly past the threatened danger. Never was canoe more admirably managed: once only did the medicine seem to have lost something of its efficacy. We were driving swiftly down, a black rock over which the white foam flew, lay directly in our path, the pole was planted against it as readily as ever, but it slipped, just as Tuba put forth his strength to turn the bow off. We struck hard, and were half-full of water in a moment; Tuba recovered himself as speedily, shoved off the bow, and shot the canoe into a still shallow place, to bale out the water. Here we were given to understand that it was not the medicine which was at fault; that had lost none of its virtue; the accident was owing entirely to Tuba having started without his breakfast. Need it be said we never let Tuba go without that meal again?

We landed at the head of Garden Island, which is situated near the middle of the river and on the lip of the Falls. On reaching that lip, and peering over the giddy height, the wondrous and unique character of the magnificent cascade at once burst upon us.

It is rather a hopeless task to endeavour to convey an idea of it in words, since, as was remarked on the spot, an accomplished painter, even by a number of views, could but impart a faint impression of the glorious scene. The probable mode of its formation may perhaps help to the conception of its peculiar shape. Niagara has been formed by a wearing back of the rock over which the river falls; and during a long course of ages, it has gradually receded, and left a broad, deep, and pretty straight trough in front. It goes on wearing back daily, and may yet discharge the lakes from which its river--the St. Lawrence--flows. But the Victoria Falls have been formed by a crack right across the river, in the hard, black, basaltic rock which there formed the bed of the Zambesi. The lips of the crack are still quite sharp, save about three feet of the edge over which the river rolls. The walls go sheer down from the lips without any projecting crag, or symptoms of stratification or dislocation. When the mighty rift occurred, no change of level took place in the two parts of the bed of the river thus rent asunder, consequently, in coming down the river to Garden Island, the water suddenly disappears, and we see the opposite side of the cleft, with grass and trees growing where once the river ran, on the same level as that part of its bed on which we sail. The first crack is, in length, a few yards more than the breadth of the Zambesi, which by measurement we found to be a little over 1860 yards, but this number we resolved to retain as indicating the year in which the Fall was for the first time carefully examined. The main stream here runs nearly north and south, and the cleft across it is nearly east and west. The depth of the rift was measured by lowering a line, to the end of which a few bullets and a foot of white cotton cloth were tied. One of us lay with his head over a projecting crag, and watched the descending calico, till, after his companions had paid out 310 feet, the weight rested on a sloping projection, probably 50 feet from the water below, the actual bottom being still further down. The white cloth now appeared the size of a crown-piece. On measuring the width of this deep cleft by sextant, it was found at Garden Island, its narrowest part, to be eighty yards, and at its broadest somewhat more. Into this chasm, of twice the depth of Niagara-fall, the river, a full mile wide, rolls with a deafening roar; and this is Mosi-oa-tunya, or the Victoria Falls.

Looking from Garden Island, down to the bottom of the abyss, nearly half a mile of water, which has fallen over that portion of the Falls to our right, or west of our point of view, is seen collected in a narrow channel twenty or thirty yards wide, and flowing at exactly right angles to its previous course, to our left; while the other half, or that which fell over the eastern portion of the Falls, is seen in the left of the narrow channel below, coming towards our right. Both waters unite midway, in a fearful boiling whirlpool, and find an outlet by a crack situated at right angles to the fissure of the Falls. This outlet is about 1170 yards from the western end of the chasm, and some 600 from its eastern end; the whirlpool is at its commencement. The Zambesi, now apparently not more than twenty or thirty yards wide, rushes and surges south, through the narrow escape-channel for 130 yards; then enters a second chasm somewhat deeper, and nearly parallel with the first. Abandoning the bottom of the eastern half of this second chasm to the growth of large trees, it turns sharply off to the west, and forms a promontory, with the escape-channel at its point, of 1170 yards long, and 416 yards broad at the base. After reaching this base, the river runs abruptly round the head of another promontory, and flows away to the east, in a third chasm; then glides round a third promontory, much narrower than the rest, and away back to the west, in a fourth chasm; and we could see in the distance that it appeared to round still another promontory, and bend once more in another chasm towards the east. In this gigantic, zigzag, yet narrow trough, the rocks are all so sharply cut and angular, that the idea at once arises that the hard basaltic trap must have been riven into its present shape by a force acting from beneath, and that this probably took place when the ancient inland seas were let off by similar fissures nearer the ocean.

The land beyond, or on the south of the Falls, retains, as already remarked, the same level as before the rent was made. It is as if the trough below Niagara were bent right and left, several times before it reached the railway bridge. The land in the supposed bends being of the same height as that above the Fall, would give standing-places, or points of view, of the same nature as that from the railway-bridge, but the nearest would be only eighty yards, instead of two miles (the distance to the bridge) from the face of the cascade. The tops of the promontories are in general flat, smooth, and studded with trees. The first, with its base on the east, is at one place so narrow, that it would be dangerous to walk to its extremity. On the second, however, we found a broad rhinoceros path and a hut; but, unless the builder were a hermit, with a pet rhinoceros, we cannot conceive what beast or man ever went there for. On reaching the apex of this second eastern promontory we saw the great river, of a deep sea-green colour, now sorely compressed, gliding away, at least 400 feet below us.

Garden Island, when the river is low, commands the best view of the Great Fall chasm, as also of the promontory opposite, with its grove of large evergreen trees, and brilliant rainbows of three-quarters of a circle, two, three, and sometimes even four in number, resting on the face of the vast perpendicular rock, down which tiny streams are always running to be swept again back by the upward rushing vapour. But as, at Niagara, one has to go over to the Canadian shore to see the chief wonder--the Great Horse-shoe Fall--so here we have to cross over to Moselekatse's side to the promontory of evergreens, for the best view of the principal Falls of Mosi-oa-tunya. Beginning, therefore, at the base of this promontory, and facing the Cataract, at the west end of the chasm, there is, first, a fall of thirty-six yards in breadth, and of course, as they all are, upwards of 310 feet in depth. Then Boaruka, a small island, intervenes, and next comes a great fall, with a breadth of 573 yards; a projecting rock separates this from a second grand fall of 325 yards broad; in all, upwards of 900 yards of perennial Falls. Further east stands Garden Island; then, as the river was at its lowest, came a good deal of the bare rock of its bed, with a score of narrow falls, which, at the time of flood, constitute one enormous cascade of nearly another half-mile. Near the east end of the chasm are two larger falls, but they are nothing at low water compared to those between the islands.

The whole body of water rolls clear over, quite unbroken; but, after a descent of ten or more feet, the entire mass suddenly becomes like a huge sheet of driven snow. Pieces of water leap off it in the form of comets with tails streaming behind, till the whole snowy sheet becomes myriads of rushing, leaping, aqueous comets. This peculiarity was not observed by Charles Livingstone at Niagara, and here it happens, possibly from the dryness of the atmosphere, or whatever the cause may be which makes every drop of Zambesi water appear to possess a sort of individuality. It runs off the ends of the paddles, and glides in beads along the smooth surface, like drops of quicksilver on a table. Here we see them in a conglomeration, each with a train of pure white vapour, racing down till lost in clouds of spray. A stone dropped in became less and less to the eye, and at last disappeared in the dense mist below.

Charles Livingstone had seen Niagara, and gave Mosi-oa-tunya the palm, though now at the end of a drought, and the river at its very lowest. Many feel a disappointment on first seeing the great American Falls, but Mosi-oa-tunya is so strange, it must ever cause wonder. In the amount of water, Niagara probably excels, though not during the months when the Zambesi is in flood. The vast body of water, separating in the comet- like forms described, necessarily encloses in its descent a large volume of air, which, forced into the cleft, to an unknown depth, rebounds, and rushes up loaded with vapour to form the three or even six columns, as if of steam, visible at the Batoka village Moachemba, twenty-one miles distant. On attaining a height of 200, or at most 300 feet from the level of the river above the cascade, this vapour becomes condensed into a perpetual shower of fine rain. Much of the spray, rising to the west of Garden Island, falls on the grove of evergreen trees opposite; and from their leaves, heavy drops are for ever falling, to form sundry little rills, which, in running down the steep face of rock, are blown off and turned back, or licked off their perpendicular bed, up into the column from which they have just descended.

The morning sun gilds these columns of watery smoke with all the glowing colours of double or treble rainbows. The evening sun, from a hot yellow sky, imparts a sulphureous hue, and gives one the impression that the yawning gulf might resemble the mouth of the bottomless pit. No bird sits and sings on the branches of the grove of perpetual showers, or ever builds its nest there. We saw hornbills and flocks of little black weavers flying across from the mainland to the islands, and from the islands to the points of the promontories and back again, but they uniformly shunned the region of perpetual rain, occupied by the evergreen grove. The sunshine, elsewhere in this land so overpowering, never penetrates the deep gloom of that shade. In the presence of the strange Mosi-oa-tunya, we can sympathize with those who, when the world was young, peopled earth, air, and river, with beings not of mortal form. Sacred to what deity would be this awful chasm and that dark grove, over which hovers an ever-abiding "pillar of cloud"?

The ancient Batoka chieftains used Kazeruka, now Garden Island, and Boaruka, the island further west, also on the lip of the Falls, as sacred spots for worshipping the Deity. It is no wonder that under the cloudy columns, and near the brilliant rainbows, with the ceaseless roar of the cataract, with the perpetual flow, as if pouring forth from the hand of the Almighty, their souls should be filled with reverential awe. It inspired wonder in the native mind throughout the interior. Among the first questions asked by Sebituane of Mr. Oswell and Dr. Livingstone, in 1851, was, "Have you any smoke soundings in your country," and "what causes the smoke to rise for ever so high out of water?" In that year its fame was heard 200 miles off, and it was approached within two days; but it was seen by no European till 1855, when Dr. Livingstone visited it on his way to the East Coast. Being then accompanied as far as this Fall by Sekeletu and 200 followers, his stay was necessarily short; and the two days there were employed in observations for fixing the geographical position of the place, and turning the showers, that at times sweep from the columns of vapour across the island, to account, in teaching the Makololo arboriculture, and making that garden from which the natives named the island; so that he did not visit the opposite sides of the cleft, nor see the wonderful course of the river beyond the Falls. The hippopotami had destroyed the trees which were then planted; and, though a strong stockaded hedge was made again, and living orange-trees, cashew- nuts, and coffee seeds put in afresh, we fear that the perseverance of the hippopotami will overcome the obstacle of the hedge. It would require a resident missionary to rear European fruit-trees. The period at which the peach and apricot come into blossom is about the end of the dry season, and artificial irrigation is necessary. The Batoka, the only arboriculturists in the country, rear native fruit-trees alone--the mosibe, the motsikiri, the boma, and others. When a tribe takes an interest in trees, it becomes more attached to the spot on which they are planted, and they prove one of the civilizing influences.

Where one Englishman goes, others are sure to follow. Mr. Baldwin, a gentleman from Natal, succeeded in reaching the Falls guided by his pocket-compass alone. On meeting the second subject of Her Majesty, who had ever beheld the greatest of African wonders, we found him a sort of prisoner at large. He had called on Mashotlane to ferry him over to the north side of the river, and, when nearly over, he took a bath, by jumping in and swimming ashore. "If," said Mashotlane, "he had been devoured by one of the crocodiles which abound there, the English would have blamed us for his death. He nearly inflicted a great injury upon us, therefore, we said, he must pay a fine." As Mr. Baldwin had nothing with him wherewith to pay, they were taking care of him till he should receive beads from his wagon, two days distant.

Mashotlane's education had been received in the camp of Sebituane, where but little regard was paid to human life. He was not yet in his prime, and his fine open countenance presented to us no indication of the evil influences which unhappily, from infancy, had been at work on his mind. The native eye was more penetrating than ours; for the expression of our men was, "He has drunk the blood of men-- you may see it in his eyes." He made no further difficulty about Mr. Baldwin; but the week after we left he inflicted a severe wound on the head of one of his wives with his rhinoceros-horn club. She, being of a good family, left him, and we subsequently met her and another of his wives proceeding up the country.

The ground is strewn with agates for a number of miles above the Falls; but the fires, which burn off the grass yearly, have injured most of those on the surface. Our men were delighted to hear that they do as well as flints for muskets; and this with the new ideas of the value of gold (*dalama*) and malachite, that they had acquired at Tette, made them conceive that we were not altogether silly in picking up and looking at stones.

Marching up the river, we crossed the Lekone at its confluence, about eight miles above the island Kalai, and went on to a village opposite the Island Chundu. Nambowe, the headman, is one of the Matebele or Zulus, who have had to flee from the anger of Moselekatse, to take refuge with the Makololo.

We spent Sunday, the 12th, at the village of Molele, a tall old Batoka, who was proud of having formerly been a great favourite with Sebituane. In coming hither we passed through patches of forest abounding in all sorts of game. The elephants' tusks, placed over graves, are now allowed to decay, and the skulls, which the former Batoka stuck on poles to ornament their villages, not being renewed, now crumble into dust. Here the famine, of which we had heard, became apparent, Molele's people being employed in digging up the *tsitla* root out of the marshes, and cutting out the soft core of the young palm-trees, for food.

The village, situated on the side of a wooded ridge, commands an extensive view of a great expanse of meadow and marsh lying along the bank of the river. On these holmes herds of buffaloes and waterbucks daily graze in security, as they have in the reedy marshes a refuge into which they can run on the approach of danger. The pretty little tianyane or ourebi is abundant further on, and herds of blue weldebeests or brindled gnus (**Katoblepas Gorgon**) amused us by their fantastic capers. They present a much more ferocious aspect than the lion himself, but are quite timid. We never could, by waving a red handkerchief, according to the prescription, induce them to venture near to us. It may therefore be that the red colour excites their fury only when wounded or hotly pursued. Herds of lechee or lechwe now enliven the meadows; and they and their younger brother, the graceful poku, smaller, and of a rounder contour, race together towards the grassy fens. We venture to call the poku after the late Major Vardon, a noble-hearted African traveller; but fully anticipate that some aspiring Nimrod will prefer that his own name should go down to posterity on the back of this buck.

Midway between Tabacheu and the Great Falls the streams begin to flow westward. On the other side they begin to flow east. Large round masses of granite, somewhat like old castles, tower aloft about the Kalomo. The country is an elevated plateau, and our men knew and named the different plains as we passed them by.

On the 13th we met a party from Sekeletu, who was now at Sesheke. Our approach had been reported, and they had been sent to ask the Doctor what the price of a horse ought to be; and what he said, that they were to give and no more. In reply they were told that by their having given nine large tusks for one horse before the Doctor came, the Griquas would naturally imagine that the price was already settled. It was exceedingly amusing to witness the exact imitation they gave of the swagger of a certain white with whom they had been dealing, and who had, as they had perceived, evidently wished to assume an air of indifference. Holding up the head and scratching the beard it was hinted might indicate not indifference, but vermin. It is well that we do not always know what they say about us. The remarks are often not quite complimentary, and resemble closely what certain white travellers say about the blacks.

We made our camp in the afternoon abreast of the large island called Mparira, opposite the mouth of the Chobe. Francolins, quails, and guinea-fowls, as well as larger game, were abundant. The Makololo headman, Mokompa, brought us a liberal present; and in the usual way, which is considered politeness, regretted he had no milk, as his cows were all dry. We got some honey here from the very small stingless bee, called, by the Batoka, moandi, and by others, the kokomatsane. This honey is slightly acid, and has an aromatic flavour. The bees are easily known from their habit of buzzing about the eyes, and tickling the skin by sucking it as common flies do. The hive has a tube of wax like a quill, for its entrance, and is usually in the hollows of trees.

Mokompa feared that the tribe was breaking up, and lamented the condition into which they had fallen in consequence of Sekeletu's leprosy; he did not know what was to become of them. He sent two canoes to take us up to Sesheke; his best canoe had taken ivory up to the chief, to purchase goods of some native traders from Benguela. Above the Falls the paddlers always stand in the canoes, using long paddles, ten feet in length, and changing from side to side without losing the stroke.

Mochokotsa, a messenger from Sekeletu, met us on the 17th, with another request for the Doctor to take ivory and purchase a horse. He again declined to interfere. None were to come up to Sekeletu but the Doctor; and all the men who had had smallpox at Tette, three years ago, were to go back to Moshobotwane, and he would sprinkle medicine over them, to drive away the infection, and prevent it spreading in the tribe. Mochokotsa was told to say to Sekeletu that the disease was known of old to white men, and we even knew the medicine to prevent it; and, were there any danger now, we should be the first to warn him of it. Why did not he go himself to have Moshobotwane sprinkle medicine to drive away his leprosy. We were not afraid of his disease, nor of the fever that had killed the teachers and many Makololo at Linyanti. As this attempt at quarantine was evidently the suggestion of native doctors to increase their own importance, we added that we had no food, and would hunt next day for game, and the day after; and, should we be still ordered purification by their medicine, we should then return to our own country.

The message was not all of our dictation, our companions interlarded it with their own indignant protests, and said some strong things in the Tette dialect about these "doctor things" keeping them back from seeing their father; when to their surprise Mochokotsa told them he knew every word they were saying, as he was of the tribe Bazizulu, and defied them to deceive him by any dialect, either of the Mashona on the east, or of the Mambari on the west. Mochokotsa then repeated our message twice, to be sure that he had it every word, and went back again. These chiefs' messengers have most retentive memories; they carry messages of considerable length great distances, and deliver them almost word for word. Two or three usually go together, and when on the way the message is rehearsed every night, in order that the exact words may be kept to. One of the native objections to learning to write is, that these men answer the purpose of transmitting intelligence to a distance as well as a letter would; and, if a person wishes to communicate with any one in the town, the best way to do so is either to go to or send for him. And as for corresponding with friends very far off, that is all very well for white people, but the blacks have no friends to whom to write. The only effective argument for the learning to read is, that it is their duty to know the revelation from their Father in Heaven, as it stands in the Book.

Our messenger returned on the evening of the following day with "You speak truly," says Sekeletu, "the disease is old, come on at once, do not sleep in the path; for I am greatly desirous (*tlologelecoe*) to see the Doctor."

After Mochokotsa left us, we met some of Mokompa's men bringing back the ivory, as horses were preferred to the West-Coast goods. They were the bearers of instructions to Mokompa, and as these instructions illustrate the government of people who have learned scarcely anything from Europeans, they are inserted, though otherwise of no importance. Mashotlane had not behaved so civilly to Mr. Baldwin as Sekeletu had ordered him to do to all Englishmen. He had been very uncivil to the messengers sent by Moselekatse with letters from Mr. Moffat, treated them as spies, and would not land to take the bag until they moved off. On our speaking to him about this, he justified his conduct on the plea that he was set at the Falls for the very purpose of watching these, their natural enemies; and how was he to know that they had been sent by Mr. Moffat? Our men thereupon reported at head-quarters that Mashotlane had cursed the Doctor. The instructions to Mokompa, from Sekeletu, were to "go and tell Mashotlane that he had offended greatly. He had not cursed Monare (Dr. Livingstone) but Sebituane, as Monare was now in the place of Sebituane, and he reverenced him as he had done his father. Any fine taken from Mr. Baldwin was to be returned at once, as he was not a Boer but an Englishman. Sekeletu was very angry, and Mokompa must not conceal the message."

On finding afterwards that Mashotlane's conduct had been most outrageous to the Batoka, Sekeletu sent for him to come to Sesheke, in order that he might have him more under his own eye; but Mashotlane, fearing that this meant the punishment of death, sent a polite answer, alleging that he was ill and unable to travel. Sekeletu tried again to remove Mashotlane from the Falls, but without success. In theory the chief is absolute and quite despotic; in practice his authority is limited, and he cannot, without occasionally putting refractory headmen to death, force his subordinates to do his will.

Except the small rapids by Mparira island, near the mouth of the Chobe, the rest of the way to Sesheke by water is smooth. Herds of cattle of two or three varieties graze on the islands in the river: the Batoka possessed a very small breed of beautiful shape, and remarkably tame, and many may still be seen; a larger kind, many of which have horns pendent, and loose at the roots; and a still larger sort, with horns of extraordinary dimensions,--apparently a burden for the beast to carry. This breed was found in abundance at Lake Ngami. We stopped at noon at one of the cattle-posts of Mokompa, and had a refreshing drink of milk. Men of his standing have usually several herds placed at different spots, and the owner visits each in turn, while his head-quarters are at his village. His son, a boy of ten, had charge of the establishment during his father's absence. According to Makololo ideas, the cattle-post is the proper school in which sons should be brought up. Here they receive the right sort of education--the knowledge of pasture and how to manage cattle.

Strong easterly winds blow daily from noon till midnight, and continue till the October or November rains set in. Whirlwinds, raising huge pillars of smoke from burning grass and weeds, are common in the forenoon. We were nearly caught in an immense one. It crossed about twenty yards in front of us, the wind apparently rushing into it from all points of the compass. Whirling round and round in great eddies, it swept up hundreds of feet into the air a continuous dense dark cloud of the black pulverized soil, mixed with dried grass, off the plain. Herds of the new antelopes, lechwe, and poku, with the kokong, or gnus, and zebras stood gazing at us as we passed. The mirage lifted them at times halfway to the clouds, and twisted them and the clumps of palms into strange unearthly forms. The extensive and rich level plains by the banks, along the sides of which we paddled, would support a vast population, and might be easily irrigated from the Zambesi. If watered, they would yield crops all the year round, and never suffer loss by drought. The hippopotamus is killed here with long lance-like spears. We saw two men, in a light canoe, stealing noiselessly down on one of these animals thought to be asleep; but it was on the alert, and they had quickly to retreat. Comparatively few of these animals now remain between Sesheke and the Falls, and they are uncommonly wary, as it is certain death for one to be caught napping in the daytime.

On the 18th we entered Sesheke. The old town, now in ruins, stands on the left bank of the river. The people have built another on the same side, a quarter of a mile higher up, since their headman Moriantsiane was put to death for bewitching the chief with leprosy. Sekeletu was on the right bank, near a number of temporary huts. A man hailed us from the chiefs quarters, and requested us to rest under the old Kotla, or public meeting-place tree. A young Makololo, with the large thighs which Zulus and most of this tribe have, crossed over to receive orders from the chief, who had not shown himself to the people since he was affected with leprosy. On returning he ran for Mokele, the headman of the new town, who, after going over to Sekeletu, came back and conducted us to a small but good hut, and afterwards brought us a fine fat ox, as a present from the chief. "This is a time of hunger," he said, "and we have no meat, but we expect some soon from the Barotse Valley." We were entirely out of food when we reached Sesheke. Never was better meat than that of the ox Sekeletu sent, and infinitely above the flesh of all kinds of game is beef!

A constant stream of visitors rolled in on us the day after our arrival. Several of them, who had suffered affliction during the Doctor's absence, seemed to be much affected on seeing him again. All were in low spirits. A severe drought had cut off the crops, and destroyed the pasture of Linyanti, and the people were scattered over the country in search of wild fruits, and the hospitality of those whose ground-nuts (**Arachis hypogoea**) had not failed. Sekeletu's leprosy brought troops of evils in its train. Believing himself bewitched, he had suspected a number of his chief men, and had put some, with their families, to death; others had fled to distant tribes, and were living in exile. The chief had shut himself up, and allowed no one to come into his presence but his uncle Mamire. Ponwane, who had been as "head and eyes" to him, had just died; evidence, he thought, of the potent spells of those who hated all who loved the chief. The country was suffering grievously, and Sebituane's grand empire was crumbling to pieces. A large body of young Barotse had revolted and fled to the north; killing a man by the way, in order to put a blood-feud between Masiko, the chief to whom they were going, and Sekeletu. The Batoka under Sinamane, and Muemba, were independent, and Mashotlane at the Falls was setting Sekeletu's authority virtually at defiance. Sebituane's wise policy in treating the conquered tribes on equal terms with his own Makololo, as all children of the chief, and equally eligible to the highest honours, had been abandoned by his son, who married none but Makololo women, and appointed to office none but Makololo men. He had become unpopular among the black tribes, conquered by the spear but more effectually won by the subsequent wise and just government of his father.

Strange rumours were afloat respecting the unseen Sekeletu; his fingers were said to have grown like eagle's claws, and his face so frightfully distorted that no one could recognize him. Some had begun to hint that he might not really be the son of the great Sebituane, the founder of the nation, strong in battle, and wise in the affairs of state. "In the days of the Great Lion" (Sebituane), said his only sister, Moriantsiane's widow, whose husband Sekeletu had killed, "we had chiefs and little chiefs and elders to carry on the government, and the great chief, Sebituane, knew them all, and everything they did, and the whole country was wisely ruled; but now Sekeletu knows nothing of what his underlings do, and they care not for him, and the Makololo power is fast passing away." {3}

The native doctors had given the case of Sekeletu up. They could not cure him, and pronounced the disease incurable. An old doctress from the Manyeti tribe had come to see what she could do for him, and on her skill he now hung his last hopes. She allowed no one to see him, except his mother and uncle, making entire seclusion from society an essential condition of the much longed-for cure. He sent, notwithstanding, for the Doctor; and on the following day we all three were permitted to see him. He was sitting in a covered wagon, which was enclosed by a high wall of close-set reeds; his face was only slightly disfigured by the thickening of the skin in parts, where the leprosy had passed over it; and the only peculiarity about his hands was the extreme length of his finger-nails, which, however, was nothing very much out of the way, as all the Makololo gentlemen wear them uncommonly long. He has the quiet, unassuming manners of his father, Sebituane, speaks distinctly, in a low pleasant voice, and appears to be a sensible man, except perhaps on the subject of his having been bewitched; and in this, when alluded to, he exhibits as firm a belief as if it were his monomania. "Moriantsiane, my aunt's husband, tried the bewitching medicine first on his wife, and she is leprous, and so is her head-servant; then, seeing that it succeeded, he gave me a stronger dose in the cooked flesh of a goat, and I have had the disease ever since. They have lately killed Ponwane, and, as you see, are now killing me." Ponwane had died of fever a short time previously. Sekeletu asked us for medicine and medical attendance, but we did not like to take the case out of the hands of the female physician already employed, it being bad policy to appear to undervalue any of the profession; and she, being anxious to go on with her remedies, said "she had not given him up yet, but would try for another month; if he was not cured by that time, then she would hand him over to the white doctors." But we intended to leave the country before a month was up; so Mamire, with others, induced the old lady to suspend her treatment for a little. She remained, as the doctors stipulated, in the chief's establishment, and on full pay.

Sekeletu was told plainly that the disease was unknown in our country, and was thought exceedingly obstinate of cure; that we did not believe in his being bewitched, and we were willing to do all we could to help him. This was a case for disinterested benevolence; no pay was expected, but considerable risk incurred; yet we could not decline it, as we had the trading in horses. Having, however, none of the medicines usually employed in skin diseases with us, we tried the local application of lunar caustic, and hydriodate of potash internally; and with such gratifying results, that Mamire wished the patient to be smeared all over with a solution of lunar caustic, which he believed to be of the same nature as the blistering fluid formerly applied to his own knee by Mr. Oswell. *Its* power he considered irresistible, and he would fain have had anything like it tried on Sekeletu.

It was a time of great scarcity and hunger, but Sekeletu treated us hospitably, preparing tea for us at every visit we paid him. With the tea we had excellent American biscuit and preserved fruits, which had been brought to him all the way from Benguela. The fruits he most relished were those preserved in their own juices; plums, apples, pears, strawberries, and peaches, which we have seen only among Portuguese and Spaniards. It made us anxious to plant the fruit-tree seeds we had brought, and all were pleased with the idea of having these same fruits in their own country. Mokele, the headman of Sesheke, and Sebituane's sister, Manchunyane, were ordered to provide us with food, as Sekeletu's wives, to whom this duty properly belonged, were at Linyanti. We found a black trader from the West Coast, and some Griqua traders from the South, both in search of ivory. Ivory is dear at Sesheke; but cheaper in the Batoka country, from Sinamane's to the Kafue, than anywhere else. The trader from Benguela took orders for goods for his next year's trip, and offered to bring tea, coffee, and sugar at cent. per cent. prices. As, in consequence of a hint formerly given, the Makololo had secured all the ivory in the Batoga country to the east, by purchasing it with hoes, the Benguela traders found it unprofitable to go thither for slaves. They assured us that without ivory the trade in slaves did not pay. In this way, and by the orders of Sekeletu, an extensive slave-mart was closed. These orders were never infringed except secretly. We discovered only two or three cases of their infraction.

Sekeletu was well pleased with the various articles we brought for him, and inquired if a ship could not bring his sugar-mill and the other goods we had been obliged to leave behind at Tette. On hearing that there was a possibility of a powerful steamer ascending as far as Sinamane's, but never above the Grand Victoria Falls, he asked, with charming simplicity, if a cannon could not blow away the Falls, so as to allow the vessel to come up to Sesheke.

To save the tribe from breaking up, by the continual loss of real Makololo, it ought at once to remove to the healthy Batoka highlands, near the Kafue. Fully aware of this, Sekeletu remarked that all his people, save two, were convinced that, if they remained in the lowlands, a few years would suffice to cut off all the real Makololo; they came originally from the healthy South, near the confluence of the Likwa and Namagari, where fever is almost unknown, and its ravages had been as frightful among them here, as amongst Europeans on the Coast. Sebituane's sister described its first appearance among the tribe, after their settling in the Barotse Valley on the Zambesi. Many of them were seized with a shivering sickness, as if from excessive cold; they had never seen the like before. They made great fires, and laid the shivering wretches down before them; but, pile on wood as they might, they could not raise heat enough to drive the cold out of the bodies of the sufferers, and they shivered on till they died. But, though all preferred the highlands, they were afraid to go there, lest the Matebele should come and rob them of their much-loved cattle. Sebituane, with all his veterans, could not withstand that enemy; and how could they be resisted, now that most of the brave warriors were dead? The young men would break, and run away the moment they saw the terrible Matebele, being as much afraid of them as the black conquered tribes are of the Makololo. "But if the Doctor and his wife," said the chiefs and counsellors, "would come and live with us, we would remove to the highlands at once, as Moselekatse would not attack a place where the daughter of his friend, Moffat, was living."

The Makololo are by far the most intelligent and enterprising of the tribes we have met. None but brave and daring men remained long with Sebituane, his stern discipline soon eradicated cowardice from his army. Death was the inevitable doom of the coward. If the chief saw a man running away from the fight, he rushed after him with amazing speed, and cut him down; or waited till he returned to the town, and then summoned the deserter into his presence. "You did not wish to die on the field, you wished to die at home, did you? you shall have your wish!" and he was instantly led off and executed. The present race of young men are inferior in most respects to their fathers. The old Makololo had many manly virtues; they were truthful, and never stole, excepting in what they considered the honourable way of lifting cattle in fair fight. But this can hardly be said of their sons; who, having been brought up among the subjected tribes, have acquired some of the vices peculiar to a menial and degraded race. A few of the old Makololo cautioned us not to leave any of our property exposed, as the blacks were great thieves; and some of our own men advised us to be on our guard, as the Makololo also would steal. A very few trifling articles were stolen by a young Makololo; and he, on being spoken to on the subject, showed great ingenuity in excusing himself, by a plausible and untruthful story. The Makololo of old were hard workers, and did not consider labour as beneath them; but their sons never work, regarding it as fit only for the Mashona and Makalaka servants. Sebituane, seeing that the rival tribes had the advantage over his, in knowing how to manage canoes, had his warriors taught to navigate; and his own son, with his companions, paddled the chief's canoe. All the dishes, baskets, stools, and canoes are made by the black tribes called Manyeti and Matlotlora. The houses are built by the women and servants. The Makololo women are vastly superior to any we have yet seen. They are of a light warm brown complexion, have pleasant countenances, and are remarkably quick of apprehension. They dress neatly, wearing a kilt and mantle, and have many ornaments. Sebituane's sister, the head lady of Sesheke, wore eighteen solid brass rings, as thick as one's finger, on each leg, and three of copper under each knee; nineteen brass rings on her left arm, and eight of brass and copper on her right, also a large ivory ring above each elbow. She had a pretty bead necklace, and a bead sash encircled her waist. The weight of the bright brass rings round her legs impeded her walking, and chafed her ankles; but, as it was the fashion, she did not mind the inconvenience, and guarded against the pain by putting soft rag round the lower rings.

Justice appears upon the whole to be pretty fairly administered among the Makololo. A headman took some beads and a blanket from one of his men who had been with us; the matter was brought before the chief, and he immediately ordered the goods to be restored, and decreed, moreover, that no headman should take the property of the men who had returned. In theory, all the goods brought back belonged to the chief; the men laid them at his feet, and made a formal offer of them all; he looked at the articles, and told the men to keep them. This is almost invariably the case. Tuba Mokoro, however, fearing lest Sekeletu might take a fancy to some of his best goods, exhibited only a few of his old and least valuable acquisitions. Masakasa had little to show; he had committed some breach of native law in one of the villages on the way, and paid a heavy fine rather than have the matter brought to the Doctor's ears. Each carrier is entitled to a portion of the goods in his bundle, though purchased by the chief's ivory, and they never hesitate to claim their rights; but no wages can be demanded from the chief, if he fails to respond to the first application. Our men, accustomed to our ways, thought that the English system of paying a man for his labour was the only correct one, and some even said it would be better to live under a government where life and labour were more secure and valuable than here. While with us, they always conducted themselves with propriety during Divine service, and not only maintained decorum themselves, but insisted on other natives who might be present doing the same. When Moshobotwane, the Batoka chief, came on one occasion with a number of his men, they listened in silence to the reading of the Bible in the Makololo tongue; but, as soon as we all knelt down to pray, they commenced a vigorous clapping of hands, their mode of asking a favour. Our indignant Makololo soon silenced their noisy accompaniment, and looked with great contempt on this display of ignorance. Nearly all our men had learned to repeat the Lord's Prayer and the Apostles' Creed in their own language, and felt rather proud of being able to do so; and when they reached home, they liked to recite them to groups of admiring friends. Their ideas of right and wrong differ in no respect from our own, except in their professed inability to see how it can be improper for a man to have more than one wife. A year or two ago several of the wives of those who had been absent with us petitioned the chief for leave to marry again. They thought that it was of no use waiting any longer, their husbands must be dead; but Sekeletu refused permission; he himself had bet a number of oxen that the Doctor would return with their husbands, and he had promised the absent men that their wives should be kept for them. The impatient spouses had therefore to wait a little longer. Some of them, however, eloped with other men; the wife of Mantlanyane, for instance, ran off and left his little boy among strangers. Mantlanyane was very angry when he heard of it, not that he cared much about her deserting him, for he had two other wives at Tette, but he was indignant at her abandoning his boy.

CHAPTER VIII.

Life amongst the Makololo--Return journey--Native hospitality--A canoe voyage on the Zambesi.

While we were at Sesheke, an ox was killed by a crocodile; a man found the carcass floating in the river, and appropriated the meat. When the owner heard of this, he requested him to come before the chief, as he meant to complain of him; rather than go, the delinquent settled the matter by giving one of his own oxen in lieu of the lost one. A headman from near Linyanti came with a complaint that all his people had run off, owing to the "hunger." Sekeletu said, "You must not be left to grow lean alone, some of them must come back to you." He had thus an order to compel their return, if he chose to put it in force. Families frequently leave their own headman and flee to another village, and sometimes a whole village decamps by night, leaving the headman by himself. Sekeletu rarely interfered with the liberty of the subject to choose his own headman, and, as it is often the fault of the latter which causes the people to depart, it is punishment enough for him to be left alone. Flagrant disobedience to the chief's orders is punished with death. A Moshubia man was ordered to cut some reeds for Sekeletu: he went off, and hid himself for two days instead. For this he was doomed to die, and was carried in a canoe to the middle of the river, choked, and tossed into the stream. The spectators hooted the executioners, calling out to them that they too would soon be carried out and strangled. Occasionally when a man is sent to beat an offender, he tells him his object, returns, and assures the chief he has nearly killed him. The transgressor then keeps for a while out of sight, and the matter is forgotten. The river here teems with monstrous crocodiles, and women are frequently, while drawing water, carried off by these reptiles.

We met a venerable warrior, sole survivor, probably, of the Mantatee host which threatened to invade the colony in 1824. He retained a vivid recollection of their encounter with the Griquas: "As we looked at the men and horses, puffs of smoke arose, and some of us dropped down dead!" "Never saw anything like it in my life, a man's brains lying in one place and his body in another!" They could not understand what was killing them; a ball struck a man's shield at an angle; knocked his arm out of joint at the shoulder; and leaving a mark, or burn, as he said, on the shield, killed another man close by. We saw the man with his shoulder still dislocated. Sebetuane was present at the fight, and had an exalted opinion of the power of white people ever afterwards.

The ancient costume of the Makololo consisted of the skin of a lamb, kid, jackal, ocelot, or other small animal, worn round and below the loins: and in cold weather a kaross, or skin mantle, was thrown over the shoulders. The kaross is now laid aside, and the young men of fashion wear a monkey-jacket and a skin round the hips; but no trousers, waistcoat, or shirt. The river and lake tribes are in general very cleanly, bathing several times a day. The Makololo women use water rather sparingly, rubbing themselves with melted butter instead: this keeps off parasites, but gives their clothes a rancid odour. One stage of civilization often leads of necessity to another--the possession of clothes creates a demand for soap; give a man a needle, and he is soon back to you for thread.

This being a time of mourning, on account of the illness of the chief, the men were negligent of their persons, they did not cut their hair, or have merry dances, or carry spear and shield when they walked abroad. The wife of Pitsane was busy making a large hut, while we were in the town: she informed us that the men left house-building entirely to the women and servants. A round tower of stakes and reeds, nine or ten feet high, is raised and plastered; a floor is next made of soft tufa, or ant-hill material and cowdung. This plaster prevents the poisonous insects, called tumpans, whose bite causes fever in some, and painful sores in all, from harbouring in the cracks or soil. The roof, which is much larger in diameter than the tower, is made on the ground, and then, many persons assisting, lifted up and placed on the tower, and thatched. A plastered reed fence is next built up to meet the outer part of the roof, which still projects a little over this fence, and a space of three feet remains between it and the tower. We slept in this space, instead of in the tower, as the inner door of the hut we occupied was uncomfortably small, being only nineteen inches high, and twenty-two inches wide at the floor. A foot from the bottom it measured seventeen inches in breadth, and close to the top only twelve inches, so it was a difficult matter to get through it. The tower has no light or ventilation, except through this small door. The reason a lady assigned for having the doors so very small was to keep out the mice!

The children have merry times, especially in the cool of the evening. One of their games consists of a little girl being carried on the shoulders of two others. She sits with outstretched arms, as they walk about with her, and all the rest clap their hands, and stopping before each hut sing pretty airs, some beating time on their little kilts of cowskin, others making a curious humming sound between the songs. Excepting this and the skipping-rope, the play of the girls consists in imitation of the serious work of their mothers, building little huts, making small pots, and cooking, pounding corn in miniature mortars, or hoeing tiny gardens. The boys play with spears of reeds pointed with wood, and small shields, or bows and arrows; or amuse themselves in making little cattle-pens, or in moulding cattle in clay; they show great ingenuity in the imitation of various-shaped horns. Some too are said to use slings, but as soon as they can watch the goats, or calves, they are sent to the field. We saw many boys riding on the calves they had in charge, but this is an innovation since the arrival of the English with their horses. Tselane, one of the ladies, on observing Dr. Livingstone noting observations on the wet and dry bulb thermometers, thought that he too was engaged in play; for on receiving no reply to her question, which was rather difficult to answer, as the native tongue has no scientific terms, she said with roguish glee, "Poor thing, playing like a little child!"

Like other Africans, the Makololo have great faith in the power of medicine; they believe that there is an especial medicine for every ill that flesh is heir to. Mamire is anxious to have children; he has six wives, and only one boy, and he begs earnestly for "child medicine." The mother of Sekeletu came from the Barotse Valley to see her son. Thinks she has lost flesh since Dr. Livingstone was here before, and asks for "the medicine of fatness." The Makololo consider plumpness an essential part of beauty in women, but the extreme stoutness, mentioned by Captain Speke, in the north, would be considered hideous here, for the men have been overheard speaking of a lady whom we call "inclined to **embonpoint**," as "fat unto ugliness."

Two packages from the Kuruman, containing letters and newspapers, reached Linyanti previous to our arrival, and Sekeletu, not knowing when we were coming, left them there; but now at once sent a messenger for them. This man returned on the seventh day, having travelled 240 geographical miles. One of the packages was too heavy for him, and he left it behind. As the Doctor wished to get some more medicine and papers out of the wagon left at Linyanti in 1853, he decided upon going thither himself. The chief gave him his own horse, now about twelve years old, and some men. He found everything in his wagon as safe as when he left it seven years before. The headmen, Mosale and Pekonyane, received him cordially, and lamented that they had so little to offer him. Oh! had he only arrived the year previous, when there was abundance of milk and corn and beer.

Very early the next morning the old town-crier, Ma-Pulenyane, of his own accord made a public proclamation, which, in the perfect stillness of the town long before dawn, was striking: "I have dreamed! I have dreamed! I have dreamed! Thou Mosale and thou Pekonyane, my lords, be not faint-hearted, nor let your hearts be sore, but believe all the words of Monare (the Doctor) for his heart is white as milk towards the Makololo. I dreamed that he was coming, and that the tribe would live, if you prayed to God and give heed to the word of Monare." Ma-Pulenyane showed Dr. Livingstone the burying-place where poor Helmore and seven others were laid, distinguishing those whom he had put to rest, and those for whom Mafale had performed that last office. Nothing whatever marked the spot, and with the native idea of ***hiding*** the dead, it was said, "it will soon be all overgrown with bushes, for no one will cultivate there." None but Ma-Pulenyane approached the place, the others stood at a respectful distance; they invariably avoid everything connected with the dead, and no such thing as taking portions of human bodies to make charms of, as is the custom further north, has ever been known among the Makololo.

Sekeletu's health improved greatly during our visit, the melancholy foreboding left his spirits, and he became cheerful, but resolutely refused to leave his den, and appear in public till he was perfectly cured, and had regained what he considered his good looks. He also feared lest some of those who had bewitched him originally might still be among the people, and neutralize our remedies. {4}

As we expected another steamer to be at Kongone in November, it was impossible for us to remain in Sesheke more than one month. Before our departure, the chief and his principal men expressed in a formal manner their great desire to have English people settled on the Batoka highlands. At one time he proposed to go as far as Phori, in order to select a place of residence; but as he afterwards saw reasons for remaining where he was, till his cure was completed, he gave orders to those sent with us, in the event of our getting, on our return, past the rapids near Tette, not to bring us to Sesheke, but to send forward a messenger, and he with the whole tribe would come to us. Dr. Kirk being of the same age, Sekeletu was particularly anxious that he should come and live with him. He said that he would cut off a section of the country for the special use of the English; and on being told that in all probability their descendants would cause disturbance in his country, he replied, "These would be only domestic feuds, and of no importance." The great extent of uncultivated land on the cool and now unpeopled highlands has but to be seen to convince the spectator how much room there is, and to spare, for a vastly greater population than ever, in our day, can be congregated there.

On the last occasion of our holding Divine service at Sesheke, the men were invited to converse on the subject on which they had been addressed. So many of them had died since we were here before, that not much probability existed of our all meeting again, and this had naturally led to the subject of a future state. They replied that they did not wish to offend the speaker, but they could not believe that all the dead would rise again: "Can those who have been killed in the field and devoured by the vultures; or those who have been eaten by the hyenas or lions; or those who have been tossed into the river, and eaten by more than one crocodile,--can they all be raised again to life?" They were told that men could take a leaden bullet, change it into a salt (acetate of lead), which could be dissolved as completely in water as our bodies in the stomachs of animals, and then reconvert it into lead; or that the bullet could be transformed into the red and white paint of our wagons, and again be reconverted into the original lead; and that if men exactly like themselves could do so much, how much more could He do who has made the eye to see, and the ear to hear! We added, however, that we believed in a resurrection, not because we understood how it would be brought about, but because our Heavenly Father assured us of it in His Book. The reference to the truth of the Book and its Author seems always to have more influence on the native mind than the cleverness of the illustration. The knowledge of the people is scanty, but their reasoning is generally clear as far as their information goes.

We left Sesheke on the 17th September, 1860, convoyed by Pitsane and Leshore with their men. Pitsane was ordered by Sekeletu to make a hedge round the garden at the Falls, to protect the seeds we had brought; and also to collect some of the tobacco tribute below the Falls. Leshore, besides acting as a sort of guard of honour to us, was sent on a diplomatic mission to Sinamane. No tribute was exacted by Sekeletu from Sinamane; but, as he had sent in his adhesion, he was expected to act as a guard in case of the Matebele wishing to cross and attack the Makololo. As we intended to purchase canoes of Sinamane in which to descend the river, Leshore was to commend us to whatever help this Batoka chief could render. It must be confessed that Leshore's men, who were all of the black subject tribes, really needed to be viewed by us in the most charitable light; for Leshore, on entering any village, called out to the inhabitants, "Look out for your property, and see that my thieves don't steal it."

Two young Makololo with their Batoka servants accompanied us to see if Kebrabasa could be surmounted, and to bring a supply of medicine for Sekeletu's leprosy; and half a dozen able canoe-men, under Mobito, who had previously gone with Dr. Livingstone to Loanda, were sent to help us in our river navigation. Some men on foot drove six oxen which Sekeletu had given us as provisions for the journey. It was, as before remarked, a time of scarcity; and, considering the dearth of food, our treatment had been liberal.

By day the canoe-men are accustomed to keep close under the river's bank from fear of the hippopotami; by night, however, they keep in the middle of the stream, as then those animals are usually close to the bank on their way to their grazing grounds. Our progress was considerably impeded by the high winds, which at this season of the year begin about eight in the morning, and blow strongly up the river all day. The canoes were poor leaky affairs, and so low in parts of the gunwale, that the paddlers were afraid to follow the channel when it crossed the river, lest the waves might swamp us. A rough sea is dreaded by all these inland canoe-men; but though timid, they are by no means unskilful at their work. The ocean rather astonished them afterwards; and also the admirable way that the Nyassa men managed their canoes on a rough lake, and even amongst the breakers, where no small boat could possibly live.

On the night of the 17th we slept on the left bank of the Majeele, after having had all the men ferried across. An ox was slaughtered, and not an ounce of it was left next morning. Our two young Makololo companions, Maloka and Ramakukane, having never travelled before, naturally clung to some of the luxuries they had been accustomed to at home. When they lay down to sleep, their servants were called to spread their blankets over their august persons, not forgetting their feet. This seems to be the duty of the Makololo wife to her husband, and strangers sometimes receive the honour. One of our party, having wandered, slept at the village of Nambowe. When he laid down, to his surprise two of Nambowe's wives came at once, and carefully and kindly spread his kaross over him.

A beautiful silvery fish with reddish fins, called Ngwesi, is very abundant in the river; large ones weigh fifteen or twenty pounds each. Its teeth are exposed, and so arranged that, when they meet, the edges cut a hook like nippers. The Ngwesi seems to be a very ravenous fish. It often gulps down the Konokono, a fish armed with serrated bones more than an inch in length in the pectoral and dorsal fins, which, fitting into a notch at the roots, can be put by the fish on full cock or straight out,--they cannot be folded down, without its will, and even break in resisting. The name "Konokono," elbow-elbow, is given it from a resemblance its extended fins are supposed to bear to a man's elbows stuck out from his body. It often performs the little trick of cocking its fins in the stomach of the Ngwesi, and, the elbows piercing its enemy's sides, he is frequently found floating dead. The fin bones seem to have an acrid secretion on them, for the wound they make is excessively painful. The Konokono barks distinctly when landed with the hook. Our canoe-men invariably picked up every dead fish they saw on the surface of the water, however far gone. An unfragrant odour was no objection; the fish was boiled and eaten, and the water drunk as soup. It is a curious fact that many of the Africans keep fish as we do woodcocks, until they are extremely offensive, before they consider them fit to eat. Our paddlers informed us on our way down that iguanas lay their eggs in July and August, and crocodiles in September. The eggs remain a month or two under the sand where they are laid, and the young come out when the rains have fairly commenced. The canoe-men were quite positive that crocodiles frequently stun men by striking them with their tails, and then squat on them till they are drowned. We once caught a young crocodile, which certainly did use its tail to inflict sharp blows, and led us to conclude that the native opinion is correct. They believed also that, if a person shuts the beast's eyes, it lets go its hold. Crocodiles have been known to unite and kill a large one of their own species and eat it. Some fishermen throw the bones of the fish into the river but in most of the fishing villages there are heaps of them in various places. The villagers can walk over them without getting them into their feet; but the Makololo, from having softer soles, are unable to do so. The explanation offered was, that the fishermen have a medicine against fish-bones, but that they will not reveal it to the Makololo.

We spent a night on Mparira island, which is four miles long and about one mile broad. Mokompa, the headman, was away hunting elephants. His wife sent for him on our arrival, and he returned next morning before we left. Taking advantage of the long-continued drought, he had set fire to the reeds between the Chobe and Zambesi, in such a manner as to drive the game out at one corner, where his men laid in wait with their spears. He had killed five elephants and three buffaloes, wounding several others which escaped.

On our land party coming up, we were told that the oxen were bitten by the tsetse: they could see a great difference in their looks. One was already eaten, and they now wished to slaughter another. A third fell into a buffalo-pit next day, so our stock was soon reduced.

The Batoka chief, Moshobotwane, again treated us with his usual hospitality, giving us an ox, some meal, and milk. We took another view of the grand Mosi-oa-tunya, and planted a quantity of seeds in the garden on the island; but, as no one will renew the hedge, the hippopotami will, doubtless, soon destroy what we planted. Mashotlane assisted us. So much power was allowed to this under-chief, that he appeared as if he had cast off the authority of Sekeletu altogether. He did not show much courtesy to his messengers; instead of giving them food, as is customary, he took the meat out of a pot in their presence, and handed it to his own followers. This may have been because Sekeletu's men bore an order to him to remove to Linyanti. He had not only insulted Baldwin, but had also driven away the Griqua traders; but this may all end in nothing. Some of the natives here, and at Sesheke, know a few of the low tricks of more civilized traders. A pot of milk was brought to us one evening, which was more indebted to the Zambesi than to any cow. Baskets of fine- looking white meal, elsewhere, had occasionally the lower half filled with bran. Eggs are always a perilous investment. The native idea of a good egg differs as widely from our own as is possible on such a trifling subject. An egg is eaten here with apparent relish, though an embryo chick be inside.

We left Mosi-oa-tunya on the 27th, and slept close to the village of Bakwini. It is built on a ridge of loose red soil, which produces great crops of mapira and ground-nuts; many magnificent mosibe-trees stand near the village. Machimisi, the headman of the village, possesses a herd of cattle and a large heart; he kept us company for a couple of days to guide us on our way.

We had heard a good deal of a stronghold some miles below the Falls, called Kalunda. Our return path was much nearer the Zambesi than that of our ascent,--in fact, as near as the rough country would allow,--but we left it twice before we reached Sinamane's, in order to see Kalunda and a Fall called Moomba, or Moamba. The Makololo had once dispossessed the Batoka of Kalunda, but we could not see the fissure, or whatever it is, that rendered it a place of security, as it was on the southern bank. The crack of the Great Falls was here continued: the rocks are the same as further up, but perhaps less weather-worn--and now partially stratified in great thick masses. The country through which we were travelling was covered with a cindery-looking volcanic tufa, and might be called "Katakaumena."

The description we received of the Moamba Falls seemed to promise something grand. They were said to send up "smoke" in the wet season, like Mosi-oa-tunya; but when we looked down into the cleft, in which the dark-green narrow river still rolls, we saw, about 800 or 1000 feet below us, what, after Mosi-oa-tunya, seemed two insignificant cataracts. It was evident that Pitsane, observing our delight at the Victoria Falls, wished to increase our pleasure by a second wonder. One Mosi-oa-tunya, however, is quite enough for a continent.

We had now an opportunity of seeing more of the Batoka, than we had on the highland route to our north. They did not wait till the evening before offering food to the strangers. The aged wife of the headman of a hamlet, where we rested at midday, at once kindled a fire, and put on the cooking-pot to make porridge. Both men and women are to be distinguished by greater roundness of feature than the other natives, and the custom of knocking out the upper front teeth gives at once a distinctive character to the face. Their colour attests the greater altitude of the country in which many of them formerly lived. Some, however, are as dark as the Bashubia and Barotse of the great valley to their west, in which stands Sesheke, formerly the capital of the Balui, or Bashubia.

The assertion may seem strange, yet it is none the less true, that in all the tribes we have visited we never saw a really black person. Different shades of brown prevail, and often with a bright bronze tint, which no painter, except Mr. Angus, seems able to catch. Those who inhabit elevated, dry situations, and who are not obliged to work much in the sun, are frequently of a light warm brown, "dark but comely." Darkness of colour is probably partly caused by the sun, and partly by something in the climate or soil which we do not yet know. We see something of the same sort in trout and other fish which take their colour from the ponds or streams in which they live. The members of our party were much less embrowned by free exposure to the sun for years than Dr. Livingstone and his family were by passing once from Kuruman to Cape Town, a journey which occupied only a couple of months.

We encamped on the Kalomo, on the 1st of October, and found the weather very much warmer than when we crossed this stream in August. At 3 p.m. the thermometer, four feet from the ground, was 101 degrees in the shade; the wet bulb only 61 degrees: a difference of 40 degrees. Yet, notwithstanding this extreme dryness of the atmosphere, without a drop of rain having fallen for months, and scarcely any dew, many of the shrubs and trees were putting forth fresh leaves of various hues, while others made a profuse display of lovely blossoms.

Two old and very savage buffaloes were shot for our companions on the 3rd October. Our Volunteers may feel an interest in knowing that balls sometimes have but little effect: one buffalo fell, on receiving a Jacob's shell; it was hit again twice, and lost a large amount of blood; and yet it sprang up, and charged a native, who, by great agility, had just time to climb a tree, before the maddened beast struck it, battering- ram fashion, hard enough almost to have split both head and tree. It paused a few seconds--drew back several paces--glared up at the man--and then dashed at the tree again and again, as if determined to shake him out of it. It took two more Jacob's shells, and five other large solid rifle-balls to finish the beast at last. These old surly buffaloes had been wandering about in a sort of miserable fellowship; their skins were diseased and scabby, as if leprous, and their horns atrophied or worn down to stumps--the first was killed outright, by one Jacob's shell, the second died hard. There is so much difference in the tenacity of life in wounded animals of the same species, that the inquiry is suggested where the seat of life can be?--We have seen a buffalo live long enough, after a large bullet had passed right through the heart, to allow firm adherent clots to be formed in the two holes.

One day's journey above Sinamane's, a mass of mountain called Gorongue, or Golongwe, is said to cross the river, and the rent through which the river passes is, by native report, quite fearful to behold. The country round it is so rocky, that our companions dreaded the fatigue, and were not much to blame, if, as is probably the case, the way be worse than that over which we travelled. As we trudged along over the black slag- like rocks, the almost leafless trees affording no shade, the heat was quite as great as Europeans could bear. It was 102 degrees in the shade, and a thermometer placed under the tongue or armpit showed that our blood was 99.5 degrees, or 1.5 degrees hotter than that of the natives, which stood at 98 degrees. Our shoes, however, enable us to pass over the hot burning soil better than they can. Many of those who wear sandals have corns on the sides of the feet, and on the heels, where the straps pass. We have seen instances, too, where neither sandals nor shoes were worn, of corns on the soles of the feet. It is, moreover, not at all uncommon to see toes cocked up, as if pressed out of their proper places; at home, we should have unhesitatingly ascribed this to the vicious fashions perversely followed by our shoemakers.

On the 5th, after crossing some hills, we rested at the village of Simariango. The bellows of the blacksmith here were somewhat different from the common goat-skin bags, and more like those seen in Madagascar. They consisted of two wooden vessels, like a lady's bandbox of small dimensions, the upper ends of which were covered with leather, and looked something like the heads of drums, except that the leather bagged in the centre. They were fitted with long nozzles, through which the air was driven by working the loose covering of the tops up and down by means of a small piece of wood attached to their centres. The blacksmith said that tin was obtained from a people in the north, called Marendi, and that he had made it into bracelets; we had never heard before of tin being found in the country.

Our course then lay down the bed of a rivulet, called Mapatizia, in which there was much calc spar, with calcareous schist, and then the Tette grey sandstone, which usually overlies coal. On the 6th we arrived at the islet Chilombe, belonging to Sinamane, where the Zambesi runs broad and smooth again, and were well received by Sinamane himself. Never was Sunday more welcome to the weary than this, the last we were to spend with our convoy.

We now saw many good-looking young men and women. The dresses of the ladies are identical with those of Nubian women in Upper Egypt. To a belt on the waist a great number of strings are attached to hang all round the person. These fringes are about six or eight inches long. The matrons wear in addition a skin cut like the tails of the coatee formerly worn by our dragoons. The younger girls wear the waist-belt exhibited in the woodcut, ornamented with shells, and have the fringes only in front. Marauding parties of Batoka, calling themselves Makololo, have for some time had a wholesome dread of Sinamane's "long spears." Before going to Tette our Batoka friend, Masakasa, was one of a party that came to steal some of the young women; but Sinamane, to their utter astonishment, attacked them so furiously that the survivors barely escaped with their lives. Masakasa had to flee so fast that he threw away his shield, his spear, and his clothes, and returned home a wiser and a sadder man.

Sinamane's people cultivate large quantities of tobacco, which they manufacture into balls for the Makololo market. Twenty balls, weighing about three-quarters of a pound each, are sold for a hoe. The tobacco is planted on low moist spots on the banks of the Zambesi; and was in flower at the time we were there, in October. Sinamane's people appear to have abundance of food, and are all in good condition. He could sell us only two of his canoes; but lent us three more to carry us as far as Moemba's, where he thought others might be purchased. They were manned by his own canoe-men, who were to bring them back. The river is about 250 yards wide, and flows serenely between high banks towards the North-east. Below Sinamane's the banks are often worn down fifty feet, and composed of shingle and gravel of igneous rocks, sometimes set in a ferruginous matrix. The bottom is all gravel and shingle, how formed we cannot imagine, unless in pot-holes in the deep fissure above. The bottom above the Falls, save a few rocks close by them, is generally sandy or of soft tufa. Every damp spot is covered with maize, pumpkins, water-melons, tobacco, and hemp. There is a pretty numerous Batoka population on both sides of the river. As we sailed slowly down, the people saluted us from the banks, by clapping their hands. A headman even hailed us, and brought a generous present of corn and pumpkins.

Moemba owns a rich island, called Mosanga, a mile in length, on which his village stands. He has the reputation of being a brave warrior, and is certainly a great talker; but he gave us strangers something better than a stream of words. We received a handsome present of corn, and the fattest goat we had ever seen; it resembled mutton. His people were as liberal as their chief. They brought two large baskets of corn, and a lot of tobacco, as a sort of general contribution to the travellers. One of Sinamane's canoe-men, after trying to get his pay, deserted here, and went back before the stipulated time, with the story, that the Englishman had stolen the canoes. Shortly after sunrise next morning, Sinamane came into the village with fifty of his "long spears," evidently determined to retake his property by force; he saw at a glance that his man had deceived him. Moemba rallied him for coming on a wildgoose chase. "Here are your canoes left with me, your men have all been paid, and the Englishmen are now asking me to sell my canoes." Sinamane said little to us; only observing that he had been deceived by his follower. A single remark of his chief's caused the foolish fellow to leave suddenly, evidently much frightened and crestfallen. Sinamane had been very kind to us, and, as he was looking on when we gave our present to Moemba, we made him also an additional offering of some beads, and parted good friends. Moemba, having heard that we had called the people of Sinamane together to tell them about our Saviour's mission to man, and to pray with them, associated the idea of Sunday with the meeting, and, before anything of the sort was proposed, came and asked that he and his people might be "sundayed" as well as his neighbours; and be given a little seed wheat, and fruit-tree seeds; with which request of course we very willingly complied. The idea of praying direct to the Supreme Being, though not quite new to all, seems to strike their minds so forcibly that it will not be forgotten. Sinamane said that he prayed to God, Morungo, and made drink-offerings to him. Though he had heard of us, he had never seen white men before.

Beautiful crowned cranes, named from their note "ma-wang," were seen daily, and were beginning to pair. Large flocks of spur-winged geese, or machikwe, were common. This goose is said to lay her eggs in March. We saw also pairs of Egyptian geese, as well as a few of the knob-nosed, or, as they are called in India, combed geese. When the Egyptian geese, as at the present time, have young, the goslings keep so steadily in the wake of their mother, that they look as if they were a part of her tail; and both parents, when on land, simulate lameness quite as well as our plovers, to draw off pursuers. The ostrich also adopts the lapwing fashion, but no quadrupeds do: they show fight to defend their young instead. In some places the steep banks were dotted with the holes which lead into the nests of bee-eaters. These birds came out in hundreds as we passed. When the red-breasted species settle on the trees, they give them the appearance of being covered with red foliage.

On the morning of the 12th October we passed through a wild, hilly country, with fine wooded scenery on both sides, but thinly inhabited. The largest trees were usually thorny acacias, of great size and beautiful forms. As we sailed by several villages without touching, the people became alarmed, and ran along the banks, spears in hand. We employed one to go forward and tell Mpande of our coming. This allayed their fears, and we went ashore, and took breakfast near the large island with two villages on it, opposite the mouth of the Zungwe, where we had left the Zambesi on our way up. Mpande was sorry that he had no canoes of his own to sell, but he would lend us two. He gave us cooked pumpkins and a water-melon. His servant had lateral curvature of the spine. We have often seen cases of humpback, but this was the only case of this kind of curvature we had met with. Mpande accompanied us himself in his own vessel, till we had an opportunity of purchasing a fine large canoe elsewhere. We paid what was considered a large price for it: twelve strings of blue cut glass neck beads, an equal number of large blue ones of the size of marbles, and two yards of grey calico. Had the beads been coarser, they would have been more valued, because such were in fashion. Before concluding the bargain the owner said "his bowels yearned for his canoe, and we must give a little more to stop their yearning." This was irresistible. The trading party of Sequasha, which we now met, had purchased ten large new canoes for six strings of cheap coarse white beads each, or their equivalent, four yards of calico, and had bought for the merest trifle ivory enough to load them all. They were driving a trade in slaves also, which was something new in this part of Africa, and likely soon to change the character of the inhabitants. These men had been living in clover, and were uncommonly fat and plump. When sent to trade, slaves wisely never stint themselves of beer or anything else, which their master's goods can buy.

The temperature of the Zambesi had increased 10 degrees since August, being now 80 degrees. The air was as high as 96 degrees after sunset; and, the vicinity of the water being the coolest part, we usually made our beds close by the river's brink, though there in danger of crocodiles. Africa differs from India in the air always becoming cool and refreshing long before the sun returns, and there can be no doubt that we can in this country bear exposure to the sun, which would be fatal in India. It is probably owing to the greater dryness of the African atmosphere that sunstroke is so rarely met with. In twenty-two years Dr. Livingstone never met or heard of a single case, though the protective head-dresses of India are rarely seen.

When the water is nearly at its lowest, we occasionally meet with small rapids which are probably not in existence during the rest of the year. Having slept opposite the rivulet Bume, which comes from the south, we passed the island of Nakansalo, and went down the rapids of the same name on the 17th, and came on the morning of the 19th to the more serious ones of Nakabele, at the entrance to Kariba. The Makololo guided the canoes admirably through the opening in the dyke. When we entered the gorge we came on upwards of thirty hippopotami: a bank near the entrance stretches two-thirds across the narrowed river, and in the still place behind it they were swimming about. Several were in the channel, and our canoe-men were afraid to venture down among them, because, as they affirm, there is commonly an ill-natured one in a herd, which takes a malignant pleasure in upsetting canoes. Two or three boys on the rocks opposite amused themselves by throwing stones at the frightened animals, and hit several on the head. It would have been no difficult matter to have shot the whole herd. We fired a few shots to drive them off; the balls often glance off the skull, and no more harm is done than when a schoolboy gets a bloody nose; we killed one, which floated away down the rapid current, followed by a number of men on the bank. A native called to us from the left bank, and said that a man on his side knew how to pray to the Kariba gods, and advised us to hire him to pray for our safety, while we were going down the rapids, or we should certainly all be drowned. No one ever risked his life in Kariba without first paying the river-doctor, or priest, for his prayers. Our men asked if there was a cataract in front, but he declined giving any information; they were not on his side of the river; if they would come over, then he might be able to tell them. We crossed, but he went off to the village. We then landed and walked over the hills to have a look at Karaba before trusting our canoes in it. The current was strong, and there was broken water in some places, but the channel was nearly straight, and had no cataract, so we determined to risk it. Our men visited the village while we were gone, and were treated to beer and tobacco. The priest who knows how to pray to the god that rules the rapids followed us with several of his friends, and they were rather surprised to see us pass down in safety, without the aid of his intercession. The natives who followed the dead hippopotamus caught it a couple of miles below, and, having made it fast to a rock, were sitting waiting for us on the bank beside the dead animal. As there was a considerable current there, and the rocky banks were unfit for our beds, we took the hippopotamus in tow, telling the villagers to follow, and we would give them most of the meat. The crocodiles tugged so hard at the carcass, that we were soon obliged to cast it adrift, to float down in the current, to avoid upsetting the canoe. We had to go on so far before finding a suitable spot to spend the night in, that the natives concluded we did not intend to share the meat with them, and returned to the village. We slept two nights at the place where the hippopotamus was cut up. The crocodiles had a busy time of it in the dark, tearing away at what was left in the river, and thrashing the water furiously with their powerful tails. The hills on both sides of Kariba are much like those of Kebrabasa, the strata tilted and twisted in every direction, with no level ground.

Although the hills confine the Zambesi within a narrow channel for a number of miles, there are no rapids beyond those near the entrance. The river is smooth and apparently very deep. Only one single human being was seen in the gorge, the country being too rough for culture. Some rocks in the water, near the outlet of Kariba, at a distance look like a fort; and such large masses dislocated, bent, and even twisted to a remarkable degree, at once attest some tremendous upheaving and convulsive action of nature, which probably caused Kebrabasa, Kariba, and the Victoria Falls to assume their present forms; it took place after the formation of the coal, that mineral having then been tilted up. We have probably nothing equal to it in the present quiet operations of nature.

On emerging we pitched our camp by a small stream, the Pendele, a few miles below the gorge. The Palabi mountain stands on the western side of the lower end of the Kariba strait; the range to which it belongs crosses the river, and runs to the south-east. Chikumbula, a hospitable old headman, under Nchomokela, the paramount chief of a large district, whom we did not see, brought us next morning a great basket of meal, and four fowls, with some beer, and a cake of salt, "to make it taste good." Chikumbula said that the elephants plagued them, by eating up the cotton-plants; but his people seem to be well off.

A few days before we came, they caught three buffaloes in pitfalls in one night, and, unable to eat them all, left one to rot. During the night the wind changed and blew from the dead buffalo to our sleeping-place; and a hungry lion, not at all dainty in his food, stirred up the putrid mass, and growled and gloated over his feast, to the disturbance of our slumbers. Game of all kinds is in most extraordinary abundance, especially from this point to below the Kafue, and so it is on Moselekatso's side, where there are no inhabitants. The drought drives all the game to the river to drink. An hour's walk on the right bank, morning or evening, reveals a country swarming with wild animals: vast herds of pallahs, many waterbucks, koodoos, buffaloes, wild pigs, elands, zebras, and monkeys appear; francolins, guinea-fowls, and myriads of turtledoves attract the eye in the covers, with the fresh spoor of elephants and rhinoceroses, which had been at the river during the night. Every few miles we came upon a school of hippopotami, asleep on some shallow sandbank; their bodies, nearly all out of the water, appeared like masses of black rock in the river. When these animals are hunted much, they become proportionably wary, but here no hunter ever troubles them, and they repose in security, always however taking the precaution of sleeping just above the deep channel, into which they can plunge when alarmed. When a shot is fired into a sleeping herd, all start up on their feet, and stare with peculiar stolid looks of hippopotamic surprise, and wait for another shot before dashing into deep water. A few miles below Chikumbula's we saw a white hippopotamus in a herd. Our men had never seen one like it before. It was of a pinkish white, exactly like the colour of the Albino. It seemed to be the father of a number of others, for there were many marked with large light patches. The so-called ***white*** elephant is just such a pinkish Albino as this hippopotamus. A few miles above Kariba we observed that, in two small hamlets, many of the inhabitants had a similar affection of the skin. The same influence appeared to have affected man and beast. A dark coloured hippopotamus stood alone, as if expelled from the herd, and bit the water, shaking his head from side to side in a most frantic manner. When the female has twins, she is said to kill one of them.

We touched at the beautiful tree-covered island of Kalabi, opposite where Tuba-mokoro lectured the lion in our way up. The ancestors of the people who now inhabit this island possessed cattle. The tsetse has taken possession of the country since "the beeves were lifted." No one knows where these insects breed; at a certain season all disappear, and as suddenly come back, no one knows whence. The natives are such close observers of nature, that their ignorance in this case surprised us. A solitary hippopotamus had selected the little bay in which we landed, and where the women drew water, for his dwelling-place. Pretty little lizards, with light blue and red tails, run among the rocks, catching flies and other insects. These harmless--though to new-comers repulsive--creatures sometimes perform good service to man, by eating great numbers of the destructive white ants.

At noon on the 24th October, we found Sequasha in a village below the Kafue, with the main body of his people. He said that 210 elephants had been killed during his trip; many of his men being excellent hunters. The numbers of animals we saw renders this possible. He reported that, after reaching the Kafue, he went northwards into the country of the Zulus, whose ancestors formerly migrated from the south and set up a sort of Republican form of government. Sequasha is the greatest Portuguese traveller we ever became acquainted with, and he boasts that he is able to speak a dozen different dialects; yet, unfortunately, he can give but a very meagre account of the countries and people he has seen, and his statements are not very much to be relied on. But considering the influence among which he has been reared, and the want of the means of education at Tette, it is a wonder that he possesses the good traits that he sometimes exhibits. Among his wares were several cheap American clocks; a useless investment rather, for a part of Africa where no one cares for the artificial measurement of time. These clocks got him into trouble among the Banyai: he set them all agoing in the presence of a chief, who became frightened at the strange sounds they made, and looked upon them as so many witchcraft agencies at work to bring all manner of evils upon himself and his people. Sequasha, it was decided, had been guilty of a milando, or crime, and he had to pay a heavy fine of cloth and beads for his exhibition. He alluded to our having heard that he had killed Mpangwe, and he denied having actually done so; but in his absence his name had got mixed up in the affair, in consequence of his slaves, while drinking beer one night with Namakusuru, the man who succeeded Mpangwe, saying that they would kill the chief for him. His partner had not thought of this when we saw him on the way up, for he tried to excuse the murder, by saying that now they had put the right man into the chieftainship.

After three hours' sail, on the morning of the 29th, the river was narrowed again by the mountains of Mburuma, called Karivua, into one channel, and another rapid dimly appeared. It was formed by two currents guided by rocks to the centre. In going down it, the men sent by Sekeletu behaved very nobly. The canoes entered without previous survey, and the huge jobbling waves of mid-current began at once to fill them. With great presence of mind, and without a moment's hesitation, two men lightened each by jumping overboard; they then ordered a Botoka man to do the same, as "the white men must be saved." "I cannot swim," said the Batoka. "Jump out, then, and hold on to the canoe;" which he instantly did. Swimming alongside, they guided the swamping canoes down the swift current to the foot of the rapid, and then ran them ashore to bale them out. A boat could have passed down safely, but our canoes were not a foot above the water at the gunwales.

Thanks to the bravery of these poor fellows, nothing was lost, although everything was well soaked. This rapid is nearly opposite the west end of the Mburuma mountains or Karivua. Another soon begins below it. They are said to be all smoothed over when the river rises. The canoes had to be unloaded at this the worst rapid, and the goods carried about a hundred yards. By taking the time in which a piece of stick floated past 100 feet, we found the current to be running six knots, by far the greatest velocity noted in the river. As the men were bringing the last canoe down close to the shore, the stern swung round into the current, and all except one man let go, rather than be dragged off. He clung to the bow, and was swept out into the middle of the stream. Having held on when he ought to have let go, he next put his life in jeopardy by letting go when he ought to have held on; and was in a few seconds swallowed up by a fearful whirlpool. His comrades launched out a canoe below, and caught him as he rose the third time to the surface, and saved him, though much exhausted and very cold.

The scenery of this pass reminded us of Kebrabasa, although it is much inferior. A band of the same black shining glaze runs along the rocks about two feet from the water's edge. There was not a blade of grass on some of the hills, it being the end of the usual dry season succeeding a previous severe drought; yet the hill-sides were dotted over with beautiful green trees. A few antelopes were seen on the rugged slopes, where some people too appeared lying down, taking a cup of beer. The Karivua narrows are about thirty miles in length. They end at the mountain Roganora. Two rocks, twelve or fifteen feet above the water at the time we were there, may in flood be covered and dangerous. Our chief danger was the wind, a very slight ripple being sufficient to swamp canoes.

CHAPTER IX.

The waterbuck--Disaster in Kebrabasa rapids--The "Ma Robert" founders--Arrival of the "Pioneer" and Bishop Mackenzie's party--Portuguese slave-trade--Interference and liberation.

We arrived at Zumbo, at the mouth of the Loangwa, on the 1st of November. The water being scarcely up to the knee, our land party waded this river with ease. A buffalo was shot on an island opposite Pangola's, the ball lodging in the spleen. It was found to have been wounded in the same organ previously, for an iron bullet was imbedded in it, and the wound entirely healed. A great deal of the plant **Pistia stratiotes** was seen floating in the river. Many people inhabit the right bank about this part, yet the game is very abundant.

As we were taking our breakfast on the morning of the 2nd, the Mambo Kazai, of whom we knew nothing, and his men came with their muskets and large powder-horns to levy a fine, and obtain payment for the wood we used in cooking. But on our replying to his demand that we were English, "Oh! are you?" he said; "I thought you were Bazungu (Portuguese). They are the people I take payments from:" and he apologized for his mistake. Bazungu, or Azungu, is a term applied to all foreigners of a light colour, and to Arabs; even to trading slaves if clothed; it probably means foreigners, or visitors,--from **zunga**, to visit or wander,--and the Portuguese were the only foreigners these men had ever seen. As we had no desire to pass for people of that nation--quite the contrary--we usually made a broad line of demarcation by saying that we were English, and the English neither bought, sold, nor held black people as slaves, but wished to put a stop to the slave-trade altogether.

We called upon our friend, Mpende, in passing. He provided a hut for us, with new mats spread on the floor. Having told him that we were hurrying on because the rains were near, "Are they near?" eagerly inquired an old counsellor, "and are we to have plenty of rain this year?" We could only say that it was about the usual time for the rains to commence; and that there were the usual indications in great abundance of clouds floating westwards, but that we knew nothing more than they did themselves.

The hippopotami are more wary here than higher up, as the natives hunt them with guns. Having shot one on a shallow sandbank, our men undertook to bring it over to the left bank, in order to cut it up with greater ease. It was a fine fat one, and all rejoiced in the hope of eating the fat for butter, with our hard dry cakes of native meal. Our cook was sent over to cut a choice piece for dinner, but returned with the astonishing intelligence that the carcass was gone. They had been hoodwinked, and were very much ashamed of themselves. A number of Banyai came to assist in rolling it ashore, and asserted that it was all shallow water. They rolled it over and over towards the land, and, finding the rope we had made fast to it, as they said, an encumbrance, it was unloosed. All were shouting and talking as loud as they could bawl, when suddenly our expected feast plumped into a deep hole, as the Banyai intended it should do. When sinking, all the Makololo jumped in after it. One caught frantically at the tail; another grasped a foot; a third seized the hip; "but, by Sebituane, it would go down in spite of all that we could do." Instead of a fat hippopotamus we had only a lean fowl for dinner, and were glad enough to get even that. The hippopotamus, however, floated during the night, and was found about a mile below. The Banyai then assembled on the bank, and disputed our right to the beast: "It might have been shot by somebody else." Our men took a little of it and then left it, rather than come into collision with them.

A fine waterbuck was shot in the Kakolole narrows, at Mount Manyerere; it dropped beside the creek where it was feeding; an enormous crocodile, that had been watching it at the moment, seized and dragged it into the water, which was not very deep. The mortally wounded animal made a desperate plunge, and hauling the crocodile several yards tore itself out of the hideous jaws. To escape the hunter, the waterbuck jumped into the river, and was swimming across, when another crocodile gave chase, but a ball soon sent it to the bottom. The waterbuck swam a little longer, the fine head dropped, the body turned over, and one of the canoes dragged it ashore. Below Kakolole, and still at the base of Manyerere mountain, several coal-seams, not noticed on our ascent, were now seen to crop out on the right bank of the Zambesi.

Chitora, of Chicova, treated us with his former hospitality. Our men were all much pleased with his kindness, and certainly did not look upon it as a proof of weakness. They meant to return his friendliness when they came this way on a marauding expedition to eat the sheep of the Banyai, for insulting them in the affair of the hippopotamus; they would then send word to Chitora not to run away, for they, being his friends, would do such a good-hearted man no harm.

We entered Kebrabasa rapids, at the east end of Chicova, in the canoes, and went down a number of miles, until the river narrowed into a groove of fifty or sixty yards wide, of which we have already spoken in describing the flood-bed and channel of low water. The navigation then became difficult and dangerous. A fifteen feet fall of the water in our absence had developed many cataracts. Two of our canoes passed safely down a narrow channel, which, bifurcating, had an ugly whirlpool at the rocky partition between the two branches, the deep hole in the whirls at times opening and then shutting. The Doctor's canoe came next, and seemed to be drifting broadside into the open vortex, in spite of the utmost exertions of the paddlers. The rest were expecting to have to pull to the rescue; the men saying, "Look where these people are going!--look, look!"--when a loud crash burst on our ears. Dr. Kirk's canoe was dashed on a projection of the perpendicular rocks, by a sudden and mysterious boiling up of the river, which occurs at irregular intervals. Dr. Kirk was seen resisting the sucking-down action of the water, which must have been fifteen fathoms deep, and raising himself by his arms on to the ledge, while his steersman, holding on to the same rocks, saved the canoe; but nearly all its contents were swept away down the stream. Dr. Livingstone's canoe, meanwhile, which had distracted the men's attention, was saved by the cavity in the whirlpool filling up as the frightful eddy was reached. A few of the things in Dr. Kirk's canoe were left; but all that was valuable, including a chronometer, a barometer, and, to our great sorrow, his notes of the journey and botanical drawings of the fruit-trees of the interior, perished.

We now left the river, and proceeded on foot, sorry that we had not done so the day before. The men were thoroughly frightened, they had never seen such perilous navigation. They would carry all the loads, rather than risk Kebrabasa any longer; but the fatigue of a day's march over the hot rocks and burning sand changed their tune before night; and then they regretted having left the canoes; they thought they should have dragged them past the dangerous places, and then launched them again. One of the two donkeys died from exhaustion near the Luia. Though the men eat zebras and quaggas, blood relations of the donkey, they were shocked at the idea of eating the ass; "it would be like eating man himself, because the donkey lives with man, and is his bosom companion." We met two large trading parties of Tette slaves on their way to Zumbo, leading, to be sold for ivory, a number of Manganja women, with ropes round their necks, and all made fast to one long rope.

Panzo, the headman of the village east of Kebrabasa, received us with great kindness. After the usual salutation he went up the hill, and, in a loud voice, called across the valley to the women of several hamlets to cook supper for us. About eight in the evening he returned, followed by a procession of women, bringing the food. There were eight dishes of nsima, or porridge, six of different sorts of very good wild vegetables, with dishes of beans and fowls; all deliciously well cooked, and scrupulously clean. The wooden dishes were nearly as white as the meal itself: food also was brought for our men. Ripe mangoes, which usually indicate the vicinity of the Portuguese, were found on the 21st November; and we reached Tette early on the 23rd, having been absent a little over six months.

The two English sailors, left in charge of the steamer, were well, had behaved well, and had enjoyed excellent health all the time we were away. Their farm had been a failure. We left a few sheep, to be slaughtered when they wished for fresh meat, and two dozen fowls. Purchasing more, they soon had double the number of the latter, and anticipated a good supply of eggs; but they also bought two monkeys, and *they* ate all the eggs. A hippopotamus came up one night, and laid waste their vegetable garden; the sheep broke into their cotton patch, when it was in flower, and ate it all, except the stems; then the crocodiles carried off the sheep, and the natives stole the fowls. Nor were they more successful as gun-smiths: a Portuguese trader, having an exalted opinion of the ingenuity of English sailors, showed them a double-barrelled rifle, and inquired if they could put on the ***browning***, which had rusted off. "I think I knows how," said one, whose father was a blacksmith, "it's very easy; you have only to put the barrels in the fire." A great fire of wood was made on shore, and the unlucky barrels put over it, to secure the handsome rifle colour. To Jack's utter amazement the barrels came asunder. To get out of the scrape, his companion and he stuck the pieces together with resin, and sent it to the owner, with the message, "It was all they could do for it, and they would not charge him anything for the job!" They had also invented an original mode of settling a bargain; having ascertained the market price of provisions, they paid that, but no more. If the traders refused to leave the ship till the price was increased, a chameleon, of which the natives have a mortal dread, was brought out of the cabin; and the moment the natives saw the creature, they at once sprang overboard. The chameleon settled every dispute in a twinkling.

But besides their good-humoured intercourse, they showed humanity worthy of English sailors. A terrible scream roused them up one night, and they pushed off in a boat to the rescue. A crocodile had caught a woman, and was dragging her across a shallow sandbank. Just as they came up to her, she gave a fearful shriek: the horrid reptile had snapped off her leg at the knee. They took her on board, bandaged the limb as well as they could, and, not thinking of any better way of showing their sympathy, gave her a glass of rum, and carried her to a hut in the village. Next morning they found the bandages torn off, and the unfortunate creature left to die. "I believe," remarked Rowe, one of the sailors, "her master was angry with us for saving her life, seeing as how she had lost her leg."

The Zambesi being unusually low, we remained at Tette till it rose a little, and then left on the 3rd of December for the Kongone. It was hard work to keep the vessel afloat; indeed, we never expected her to remain above water. New leaks broke out every day; the engine pump gave way; the bridge broke down; three compartments filled at night; except the cabin and front compartment all was flooded; and in a few days we were assured by Rowe that "she can't be worse than she is, sir." He and Hutchins had spent much of their time, while we were away, in patching her bottom, puddling it with clay, and shoring it, and it was chiefly to please them that we again attempted to make use of her. We had long been fully convinced that the steel plates were thoroughly unsuitable. On the morning of the 21st the uncomfortable "Asthmatic" grounded on a sandbank and filled. She could neither be emptied nor got off. The river rose during the night, and all that was visible of the worn-out craft next day was about six feet of her two masts. Most of the property we had on board was saved; and we spent the Christmas of 1860 encamped on the island of Chimba. Canoes were sent for from Senna; and we reached it on the 27th, to be again hospitably entertained by our friend, Senhor Ferrao.

We reached the Kongone on the 4th of January, 1861. A flagstaff and a Custom-house had been erected during our absence; a hut, also, for a black lance-corporal and three privates. By the kind permission of the lance-corporal, who came to see us as soon as he had got into his trousers and shirt, we took up our quarters in the Custom-house, which, like the other buildings, is a small square floorless hut of mangrove stakes overlaid with reeds. The soldiers complained of hunger, they had nothing to eat but a little mapira, and were making palm wine to deaden their cravings. While waiting for a ship, we had leisure to read the newspapers and periodicals we found in the mail which was waiting our arrival at Tette. Several were a year and a half old.

Our provisions began to run short; and towards the end of the month there was nothing left but a little bad biscuit and a few ounces of sugar. Coffee and tea were expended, but scarcely missed, as our sailors discovered a pretty good substitute in roasted mapira. Fresh meat was obtained in abundance from our antelope preserves on the large island made by a creek between the Kongone and East Luabo.

In this focus of decaying vegetation, nothing is so much to be dreaded as inactivity. We had, therefore, to find what exercise and amusement we could, when hunting was not required, in peering about in the fetid swamps; to have gone mooning about, in listless idleness, would have ensured fever in its worst form, and probably with fatal results.

A curious little blenny-fish swarms in the numerous creeks which intersect the mangrove topes. When alarmed, it hurries across the surface of the water in a series of leaps. It may be considered amphibious, as it lives as much out of the water as in it, and its most busy time is during low water. Then it appears on the sand or mud, near the little pools left by the retiring tide; it raises itself on its pectoral fins into something of a standing attitude, and with its large projecting eyes keeps a sharp look-out for the light-coloured fly, on which it feeds. Should the fly alight at too great a distance for even a second leap, the blenny moves slowly towards it like a cat to its prey, or like a jumping spider; and, as soon as it gets within two or three inches of the insect, by a sudden spring contrives to pop its underset mouth directly over the unlucky victim. He is, moreover, a pugnacious little fellow; and rather prolonged fights may be observed between him and his brethren. One, in fleeing from an apparent danger, jumped into a pool a foot square, which the other evidently regarded as his by right of prior discovery; in a twinkling the owner, with eyes flashing fury, and with dorsal fin bristling up in rage, dashed at the intruding foe. The fight waxed furious, no tempest in a teapot ever equalled the storm of that miniature sea. The warriors were now in the water, and anon out of it, for the battle raged on sea and shore. They struck hard, they bit each other; until, becoming exhausted, they seized each other by the jaws like two bull-dogs, then paused for breath, and at it again as fiercely as before, until the combat ended by the precipitate retreat of the invader.

The muddy ground under the mangrove-trees is covered with soldier-crabs, which quickly slink into their holes on any symptom of danger. When the ebbing tide retires, myriads of minute crabs emerge from their underground quarters, and begin to work like so many busy bees. Soon many miles of the smooth sand become rough with the results of their labour. They are toiling for their daily bread: a round bit of moist sand appears at the little labourer's mouth, and is quickly brushed off by one of the claws; a second bit follows the first; and another, and still another come as fast as they can be laid aside. As these pellets accumulate, the crab moves sideways, and the work continues. The first impression one receives is, that the little creature has swallowed a great deal of sand, and is getting rid of it as speedily as possible: a habit he indulges in of darting into his hole at intervals, as if for fresh supplies, tends to strengthen this idea; but the size of the heaps formed in a few seconds shows that this cannot be the case, and leads to the impression that, although not readily seen, at the distance at which he chooses to keep the observer, yet that possibly he raises the sand to his mouth, where whatever animalcule it may contain is sifted out of it, and the remainder rejected in the manner described. At times the larger species of crabs perform a sort of concert; and from each subterranean abode strange sounds arise, as if, in imitation of the songsters of the groves, for very joy they sang!

We found some natives pounding the woody stems of a poisonous climbing-plant (***Dirca palustris***) called Busungu, or poison, which grows abundantly in the swamps. When a good quantity was bruised, it was tied up in bundles. The stream above and below was obstructed with bushes, and with a sort of rinsing motion the poison was diffused through the water. Many fish were soon affected, swain in shore, and died, others were only stupefied. The plant has pink, pea-shaped blossoms, and smooth, pointed, glossy leaves, and the brown bark is covered with minute white points. The knowledge of it might prove of use to a shipwrecked party by enabling them to catch the fish.

The poison is said to be deleterious to man if the water is drunk; but not when the fish is cooked. The Busungu is repulsive to some insects, and is smeared round the shoots of the palm-trees to prevent the ants from getting into the palm wine while it is dropping from the tops of the palm-trees into the little pots suspended to collect it.

We were in the habit of walking from our beds into the salt water at sunrise, for a bath, till a large crocodile appeared at the bathing-place, and from that time forth we took our dip in the sea, away from the harbour, about midday. This is said to be unwholesome, but we did not find it so. It is certainly better not to bathe in the mornings, when the air is colder than the water--for then, on returning to the cooler air, one is apt to get a chill and fever. In the mouth of the river, many sawfish are found. Rowe saw one while bathing--caught it by the tail, and shoved it, "snout on," ashore. The saw is from a foot to eighteen inches long. We never heard of any one being wounded by this fish; nor, though it goes hundreds of miles up the river in fresh water, could we learn that it was eaten by the people. The hippopotami delighted to spend the day among the breakers, and seemed to enjoy the fun as much as we did.

Severe gales occurred during our stay on the Coast, and many small sea-birds (***Prion Banksii***, Smith) perished: the beach was strewn with their dead bodies, and some were found hundreds of yards inland; many were so emaciated as to dry up without putrefying. We were plagued with myriads of mosquitoes, and had some touches of fever; the men we brought from malarious regions of the interior suffered almost as much from it here as we did ourselves. This gives strength to the idea that the civilized withstand the evil influences of strange climates better than the uncivilized. When negroes return to their own country from healthy lands, they suffer as severely as foreigners ever do.

On the 31st of January, 1861, our new ship, the "Pioneer," arrived from England, and anchored outside the bar; but the weather was stormy, and she did not venture in till the 4th of February.

Two of H.M. cruisers came at the same time, bringing Bishop Mackenzie, and the Oxford and Cambridge Mission to the tribes of the Shire and Lake Nyassa. The Mission consisted of six Englishmen, and five coloured men from the Cape. It was a puzzle to know what to do with so many men. The estimable Bishop, anxious to commence his work without delay, wished the "Pioneer" to carry the Mission up the Shire, as far as Chibisa's, and there leave them. But there were grave objections to this. The "Pioneer" was under orders to explore the Rovuma, as the Portuguese Government had refused to open the Zambesi to the ships of other nations, and their officials were very effectually pursuing a system, which, by abstracting the labour, was rendering the country of no value either to foreigners or to themselves. She was already two months behind her time, and the rainy season was half over. Then, if the party were taken to Chibisa's, the Mission would he left without a medical attendant, in an unhealthy region, at the beginning of the most sickly season of the year, and without means of reaching the healthy highlands, or of returning to the sea. We dreaded that, in the absence of medical aid and all knowledge of the treatment of fever, there might be a repetition of the sorrowful fate which befell the similar non-medical Mission at Linyanti.

On the 25th of February the "Pioneer" anchored in the mouth of the Rovuma, which, unlike most African rivers, has a magnificent bay and no bar. We wooded, and then waited for the Bishop till the 9th of March, when he came in the "Lyra." On the 11th we proceeded up the river, and saw that it had fallen four or five feet during our detention. The scenery on the lower part of the Rovuma is superior to that on the Zambesi, for we can see the highlands from the sea. Eight miles from the mouth the mangroves are left behind, and a beautiful range of well-wooded hills on each bank begins. On these ridges the tree resembling African blackwood, of finer grain than ebony, grows abundantly, and attains a large size. Few people were seen, and those were of Arab breed, and did not appear to be very well off. The current of the Rovuma was now as strong as that of the Zambesi, but the volume of water is very much less. Several of the crossings had barely water enough for our ship, drawing five feet, to pass. When we were thirty miles up the river, the water fell suddenly seven inches in twenty-four hours. As the March flood is the last of the season, and it appeared to be expended, it was thought prudent to avoid the chance of a year's detention, by getting the ship back to the sea without delay. Had the Expedition been alone, we would have pushed up in boats, or afoot, and done what we could towards the exploration of the river and upper end of the lake; but, though the Mission was a private one, and entirely distinct from our own, a public one, the objects of both being similar, we felt anxious to aid our countrymen in their noble enterprise; and, rather than follow our own inclination, decided to return to the Shire, see the Mission party settled safely, and afterwards explore Lake Nyassa and the Rovuma, from the Lake downwards. Fever broke out on board the "Pioneer," at the mouth of the Rovuma, as we thought from our having anchored close to a creek coming out of the mangroves; and it remained in her until we completely isolated the engine-room from the rest of the ship. The coal-dust rotting sent out strong effluvia, and kept up the disease for more than a twelvemonth.

Soon after we started the fever put the "Pioneer" almost entirely into the hands of the original Zambesi Expedition, and not long afterwards the leader had to navigate the ocean as well as the river. The habit of finding the geographical positions on land renders it an easy task to steer a steamer with only three or four sails at sea; where, if one does not run ashore, no one follows to find out an error, and where a current affords a ready excuse for every blunder.

Touching at Mohilla, one of the Comoro Islands, on our return, we found a mixed race of Arabs, Africans, and their conquerors, the natives of Madagascar. Being Mahometans, they have mosques and schools, in which we were pleased to see girls as well as boys taught to read the Koran. The teacher said he was paid by the job, and received ten dollars for teaching each child to read. The clever ones learn in six months; but the dull ones take a couple of years. We next went over to Johanna for our friends; and, after a sojourn of a few days at the beautiful Comoro Islands, we sailed for the Kongone mouth of the Zambesi with Bishop Mackenzie and his party. We reached the coast in seven days, and passed up the Zambesi to the Shire.

The "Pioneer," constructed under the skilful supervision of Admiral Sir Baldwin Walker and the late Admiral Washington, warm-hearted and highly esteemed friends of the Expedition, was a very superior vessel, and well suited for our work in every respect, except in her draught of water. Five feet were found to be too much for the navigation of the upper part of the Shire. Designed to draw three feet only, the weight necessary to impart extra strength, and fit her for the ocean, brought her down two feet more, and caused us a great deal of hard and vexatious work, in laying out anchors, and toiling at the capstan to get her off sandbanks. We should not have minded this much, but for the heavy loss of time which might have been more profitably, and infinitely more pleasantly, spent in intercourse with the people, exploring new regions, and otherwise carrying out the objects of the Expedition. Once we were a fortnight on a bank of soft yielding sand, having only two or three inches less water than the ship drew; this delay was occasioned by the anchors coming home, and the current swinging the ship broadside on the bank, which, immediately on our touching, always formed behind us. We did not like to leave the ship short of Chibisa's, lest the crew should suffer from the malaria of the lowland around; and it would have been difficult to have got the Mission goods carried up. We were daily visited by crowds of natives, who brought us abundance of provisions far beyond our ability to consume. In hauling the "Pioneer" over the shallow places, the Bishop, with Horace Waller and Mr. Scudamore, were ever ready and anxious to lend a hand, and worked as hard as any on board. Had our fine little ship drawn but three feet, she could have run up and down the river at any time of the year with the greatest ease, but as it was, having once passed up over a few shallow banks, it was impossible to take her down again until the river rose in December. She could go up over a bank, but not come down over it, as a heap of sand always formed instantly astern, while the current washed it away from under her bows.

On at last reaching Chibisa's, we heard that there was war in the Manganja country, and the slave-trade was going on briskly. A deputation from a chief near Mount Zomba had just passed on its way to Chibisa, who was in a distant village, to implore him to come himself, or send medicine, to drive off the Waiao, Waiau, or Ajawa, whose marauding parties were desolating the land. A large gang of recently enslaved Manganja crossed the river, on their way to Tette, a few days before we got the ship up. Chibisa's deputy was civil, and readily gave us permission to hire as many men to carry the Bishop's goods up to the hills as were willing to go. With a sufficient number, therefore, we started for the highlands on the 15th of July, to show the Bishop the country, which, from its altitude and coolness, was most suitable for a station. Our first day's march was a long and fatiguing one. The few hamlets we passed were poor, and had no food for our men, and we were obliged to go on till 4 p.m., when we entered the small village of Chipindu. The inhabitants complained of hunger, and said they had no food to sell, and no hut for us to sleep in; but, if we would only go on a little further, we should come to a village where they had plenty to eat; but we had travelled far enough, and determined to remain where we were. Before sunset as much food was brought as we cared to purchase, and, as it threatened to rain, huts were provided for the whole party.

Next forenoon we halted at the village of our old friend Mbame, to obtain new carriers, because Chibisa's men, never before having been hired, and not having yet learned to trust us, did not choose to go further. After resting a little, Mbame told us that a slave party on its way to Tette would presently pass through his village. "Shall we interfere?" we inquired of each other. We remembered that all our valuable private baggage was in Tette, which, if we freed the slaves, might, together with some Government property, be destroyed in retaliation; but this system of slave-hunters dogging us where previously they durst not venture, and, on pretence of being "our children," setting one tribe against another, to furnish themselves with slaves, would so inevitably thwart all the efforts, for which we had the sanction of the Portuguese Government, that we resolved to run all risks, and put a stop, if possible, to the slave-trade, which had now followed on the footsteps of our discoveries. A few minutes after Mbame had spoken to us, the slave party, a long line of manacled men, women, and children, came wending their way round the hill and into the valley, on the side of which the village stood. The black drivers, armed with muskets, and bedecked with various articles of finery, marched jauntily in the front, middle, and rear of the line; some of them blowing exultant notes out of long tin horns. They seemed to feel that they were doing a very noble thing, and might proudly march with an air of triumph. But the instant the fellows caught a glimpse of the English, they darted off like mad into the forest; so fast, indeed, that we caught but a glimpse of their red caps and the soles of their feet. The chief of the party alone remained; and he, from being in front, had his hand tightly grasped by a Makololo! He proved to be a well-known slave of the late Commandant at

Tette, and for some time our own attendant while there. On asking him how he obtained these captives, he replied he had bought them; but on our inquiring of the people themselves, all, save four, said they had been captured in war. While this inquiry was going on, he bolted too. The captives knelt down, and, in their way of expressing thanks, clapped their hands with great energy. They were thus left entirely on our hands, and knives were soon busy at work cutting the women and children loose. It was more difficult to cut the men adrift, as each had his neck in the fork of a stout stick, six or seven feet long, and was kept in by an iron rod which was riveted at both ends across the throat. With a saw, luckily in the Bishop's baggage, one by one the men were sawn out into freedom. The women, on being told to take the meal they were carrying and cook breakfast for themselves and the children, seemed to consider the news too good to be true; but after a little coaxing went at it with alacrity, and made a capital fire by which to boil their pots with the slave sticks and bonds, their old acquaintances through many a sad night and weary day. Many were mere children about five years of age and under. One little boy, with the simplicity of childhood, said to our men, "The others tied and starved us, you cut the ropes and tell us to eat; what sort of people are you?--Where did you come from?" Two of the women had been shot the day before for attempting to untie the thongs. This, the rest were told, was to prevent them from attempting to escape. One woman had her infant's brains knocked out, because she could not carry her load and it. And a man was dispatched with an axe, because he had broken down with fatigue. Self-interest would have set a watch over the whole rather than commit murder; but in this traffic we invariably find self-interest overcome by contempt of human life and by bloodthirstiness.

    The Bishop was not present at this scene, having gone to bathe in a little stream below the village; but on his return he warmly approved of what had been done; he at first had doubts, but now felt that, had he been present, he would have joined us in the good work. Logic is out of place when the question with a true-hearted man is, whether his brother man is to be saved or not. Eighty-four, chiefly women and children, were liberated; and on being told that they were now free, and might go where they pleased, or remain with us, they all chose to stay; and the Bishop wisely attached them to his Mission, to be educated as members of a Christian family. In this way a great difficulty in the commencement of a Mission was overcome. Years are usually required before confidence is so far instilled into the natives' mind as to induce them, young or old, to submit to the guidance of strangers professing to be actuated by motives the reverse of worldly wisdom, and inculcating customs strange and unknown to them and their fathers.

We proceeded next morning to Soche's with our liberated party, the men cheerfully carrying the Bishop's goods. As we had begun, it was of no use to do things by halves, so eight others were freed in a hamlet on our path; but a party of traders, with nearly a hundred slaves, fled from Soche's on hearing of our proceedings. Dr. Kirk and four Makololo followed them with great energy, but they made clear off to Tette. Six more captives were liberated at Mongazi's, and two slave-traders detained for the night, to prevent them from carrying information to a large party still in front. Of their own accord they volunteered the information that the Governor's servants had charge of the next party; but we did not choose to be led by them, though they offered to guide us to his Excellency's own agents. Two of the Bishop's black men from the Cape, having once been slaves, were now zealous emancipators, and volunteered to guard the prisoners during the night. So anxious were our heroes to keep them safe, that instead of relieving each other, by keeping watch and watch, both kept watch together, till towards four o'clock in the morning, when sleep stole gently over them both; and the wakeful prisoners, seizing the opportunity, escaped: one of the guards, perceiving the loss, rushed out of the hut, shouting, "They are gone, the prisoners are off, and they have taken my rifle with them, and the women too! Fire! everybody fire!" The rifle and the women, however, were all safe enough, the slave-traders being only too glad to escape alone. Fifty more slaves were freed next day in another village; and, the whole party being stark-naked, cloth enough was left to clothe them, better probably than they had ever been clothed before. The head of this gang, whom we knew as the agent of one of the principal merchants of Tette, said that they had the license of the Governor for all they did. This we were fully aware of without his stating it. It is quite impossible for any enterprise to be undertaken there without the Governor's knowledge and connivance.

The portion of the highlands which the Bishop wished to look at before deciding on a settlement belonged to Chiwawa, or Chibaba, the most manly and generous Manganja chief we had met with on our previous journey. On reaching Nsambo's, near Mount Chiradzuru, we heard that Chibaba was dead, and that Chigunda was chief instead. Chigunda, apparently of his own accord, though possibly he may have learnt that the Bishop intended to settle somewhere in the country, asked him to come and live with him at Magomero, adding that there was room enough for both. This hearty and spontaneous invitation had considerable influence on the Bishop's mind, and seemed to decide the question. A place nearer the Shire would have been chosen had he expected his supplies to come up that river; but the Portuguese, claiming the river Shire, though never occupying even its mouth, had closed it, as well as the Zambesi.

Our hopes were turned to the Rovuma, as a free highway into Lake Nyassa and the vast interior. A steamer was already ordered for the Lake, and the Bishop, seeing the advantageous nature of the highlands which stretch an immense way to the north, was more anxious to be near the Lake and the Rovuma, than the Shire. When he decided to settle at Magomero, it was thought desirable, to prevent the country from being depopulated, to visit the Ajawa chief, and to try and persuade him to give up his slaving and kidnapping courses, and turn the energies of his people to peaceful pursuits.

On the morning of the 22nd we were informed that the Ajawa were near, and were burning a village a few miles off. Leaving the rescued slaves, we moved off to seek an interview with these scourges of the country. On our way we met crowds of Manganja fleeing from the war in front. These poor fugitives from the slave hunt had, as usual, to leave all the food they possessed, except the little they could carry on their heads. We passed field after field of Indian corn or beans, standing ripe for harvesting, but the owners were away. The villages were all deserted: one where we breakfasted two years before, and saw a number of men peacefully weaving cloth, and, among ourselves, called it the "Paisley of the hills," was burnt; the stores of corn were poured out in cartloads, and scattered all over the plain, and all along the paths, neither conquerors nor conquered having been able to convey it away. About two o'clock we saw the smoke of burning villages, and heard triumphant shouts, mingled with the wail of the Manganja women, lamenting over their slain. The Bishop then engaged us in fervent prayer; and, on rising from our knees, we saw a long line of Ajawa warriors, with their captives, coming round the hill-side. The first of the returning conquerors were entering their own village below, and we heard women welcoming them back with "lillilooings." The Ajawa headman left the path on seeing us, and stood on an anthill to obtain a complete view of our party. We called out that we had come to have an interview with them, but some of the Manganja who followed us shouted "Our Chibisa is come:" Chibisa being well known as a great conjurer and general. The Ajawa ran off yelling and screaming, "Nkondo! Nkondo!" (War! War!) We heard the words of the Manganja, but they did not strike us at the moment as neutralizing all our assertions of peace. The captives threw down their loads on the path, and fled to the hills: and a large body of armed men came running up from the village, and in a few seconds they were all around us, though mostly concealed by the projecting rocks and long grass. In vain we protested that we had not come to fight, but to talk with them. They would not listen, having, as we remembered afterwards, good reason, in the cry of "Our Chibisa." Flushed with recent victory over three villages, and confident of an easy triumph over a mere handful of men, they began to shoot their poisoned arrows, sending them with great force upwards of a hundred yards, and wounding one of our followers through the arm. Our retiring slowly up the ascent from the village only made them more eager to prevent our escape; and, in the belief that this retreat was evidence of fear, they closed upon us in bloodthirsty fury. Some came within fifty yards, dancing hideously; others having quite surrounded us, and availing themselves of the rocks and long grass hard by, were intent on cutting us off, while others made off with their women and a large body of slaves. Four were armed with muskets, and we were obliged in self-defence to return their fire and drive them off. When they saw the range of rifles, they very soon desisted, and ran away; but some shouted to us from the hills the consoling intimation, that they would follow, and kill us where we slept. Only two of the captives escaped to us, but probably most of those made prisoners that day fled elsewhere in the confusion. We returned to the village which we had left in the morning, after a hungry, fatiguing, and most unpleasant day.

Though we could not blame ourselves for the course we had followed, we felt sorry for what had happened. It was the first time we had ever been attacked by the natives or come into collision with them; though we had always taken it for granted that we might be called upon to act in self- defence, we were on this occasion less prepared than usual, no game having been expected here. The men had only a single round of cartridge each; their leader had no revolver, and the rifle he usually fired with was left at the ship to save it from the damp of the season. Had we known better the effect of slavery and murder on the temper of these bloodthirsty marauders, we should have tried messages and presents before going near them.

The old chief, Chinsunse, came on a visit to us next day, and pressed the Bishop to come and live with him. "Chigunda," he said, "is but a child, and the Bishop ought to live with the father rather than with the child." But the old man's object was so evidently to have the Mission as a shield against the Ajawa, that his invitation was declined. While begging us to drive away the marauders, that he might live in peace, he adopted the stratagem of causing a number of his men to rush into the village, in breathless haste, with the news that the Ajawa were close upon us. And having been reminded that we never fought, unless attacked, as we were the day before, and that we had come among them for the purpose of promoting peace, and of teaching them to worship the Supreme, to give up selling His children, and to cultivate other objects for barter than each other, he replied, in a huff, "Then I am dead already."

The Bishop, feeling, as most Englishmen would, at the prospect of the people now in his charge being swept off into slavery by hordes of men-stealers, proposed to go at once to the rescue of the captive Manganja, and drive the marauding Ajawa out of the country. All were warmly in favour of this, save Dr. Livingstone, who opposed it on the ground that it would be better for the Bishop to wait, and see the effect of the check the slave-hunters had just experienced. The Ajawa were evidently goaded on by Portuguese agents from Tette, and there was no bond of union among the Manganja on which to work. It was possible that the Ajawa might be persuaded to something better, though, from having long been in the habit of slaving for the Quillimane market, it was not very probable. But the Manganja could easily be overcome piecemeal by any enemy; old feuds made them glad to see calamities befall their next neighbours. We counselled them to unite against the common enemies of their country, and added distinctly that we English would on no account enter into their quarrels. On the Bishop inquiring whether, in the event of the Manganja again asking aid against the Ajawa, it would be his duty to accede to their request,--"No," replied Dr. Livingstone, "you will be oppressed by their importunities, but do not interfere in native quarrels." This advice the good man honourably mentions in his journal. We have been rather minute in relating what occurred during the few days of our connection with the Mission of the English Universities, on the hills, because, the recorded advice having been discarded, blame was thrown on Dr. Livingstone's shoulders, as if the missionaries had no individual responsibility for their subsequent conduct. This, unquestionably, good Bishop Mackenzie had too much manliness to have allowed. The connection of the members of the Zambesi Expedition, with the acts of the Bishop's Mission, now ceased, for we returned to the ship and prepared for our journey to Lake Nyassa. We cheerfully, if necessary, will bear all responsibility up to this point; and if the Bishop afterwards made mistakes in certain collisions with the slavers, he had the votes of all his party with him, and those who best knew the peculiar circumstances, and the loving disposition of this good-hearted man, will blame him least. In this position, and in these circumstances, we left our friends at the Mission Station.

As a temporary measure the Bishop decided to place his Mission Station on a small promontory formed by the windings of the little, clear stream of Magomero, which was so cold that the limbs were quite benumbed by washing in it in the July mornings. The site chosen was a pleasant spot to the eye, and completely surrounded by stately, shady trees. It was expected to serve for a residence, till the Bishop had acquired an accurate knowledge of the adjacent country, and of the political relations of the people, and could select a healthy and commanding situation, as a permanent centre of Christian civilization. Everything promised fairly. The weather was delightful, resembling the pleasantest part of an English summer; provisions poured in very cheap and in great abundance. The Bishop, with characteristic ardour, commenced learning the language, Mr. Waller began building, and Mr. Scudamore improvised a sort of infant school for the children, than which there is no better means for acquiring an unwritten tongue.

On the 6th of August, 1861, a few days after returning from Magomero, Drs. Livingstone and Kirk, and Charles Livingstone started for Nyassa with a light four-oared gig, a white sailor, and a score of attendants. We hired people along the path to carry the boat past the forty miles of the Murchison Cataracts for a cubit of cotton cloth a day. This being deemed great wages, more than twice the men required eagerly offered their services. The chief difficulty was in limiting their numbers. Crowds followed us; and, had we not taken down in the morning the names of the porters engaged, in the evening claims would have been made by those who only helped during the last ten minutes of the journey. The men of one village carried the boat to the next, and all we had to do was to tell the headman that we wanted fresh men in the morning. He saw us pay the first party, and had his men ready at the time appointed, so there was no delay in waiting for carriers. They often make a loud noise when carrying heavy loads, but talking and bawling does not put them out of breath. The country was rough and with little soil on it, but covered with grass and open forest. A few small trees were cut down to clear a path for our shouting assistants, who were good enough to consider the boat as a certificate of peaceful intentions at least to them. Several small streams were passed, the largest of which were the Mukuru-Madse and Lesungwe. The inhabitants on both banks were now civil and obliging. Our possession of a boat, and consequent power of crossing independently of the canoes, helped to develop their good manners, which were not apparent on our previous visit.

There is often a surprising contrast between neighbouring villages. One is well off and thriving, having good huts, plenty of food, and native cloth; and its people are frank, trusty, generous, and eager to sell provisions; while in the next the inhabitants may be ill-housed, disobliging, suspicious, ill-fed, and scantily clad, and with nothing for sale, though the land around is as fertile as that of their wealthier neighbours. We followed the river for the most part to avail ourselves of the still reaches for sailing; but a comparatively smooth country lies further inland, over which a good road could be made. Some of the five main cataracts are very grand, the river falling 1200 feet in the 40 miles. After passing the last of the cataracts, we launched our boat for good on the broad and deep waters of the Upper Shire, and were virtually on the lake, for the gentle current shows but little difference of level. The bed is broad and deep, but the course is rather tortuous at first, and makes a long bend to the east till it comes within five or six miles of the base of Mount Zomba. The natives regarded the Upper Shire as a prolongation of Lake Nyassa; for where what we called the river approaches Lake Shirwa, a little north of the mountains, they said that the hippopotami, "which are great night travellers," pass from **one lake into the other**. There the land is flat, and only a short land journey would be necessary. Seldom does the current here exceed a knot an hour, while that of the Lower Shire is from two to two-and-a-half knots. Our land party of

Makololo accompanied us along the right bank, and passed thousands of Manganja fugitives living in temporary huts on that side, who had recently been driven from their villages on the opposite hills by the Ajawa.

The soil was dry and hard, and covered with mopane-trees; but some of the Manganja were busy hoeing the ground and planting the little corn they had brought with them. The effects of hunger were already visible on those whose food had been seized or burned by the Ajawa and Portuguese slave-traders. The spokesman or prime minister of one of the chiefs, named Kalonjere, was a humpbacked dwarf, a fluent speaker, who tried hard to make us go over and drive off the Ajawa; but he could not deny that by selling people Kalonjere had invited these slave-hunters to the country. This is the second humpbacked dwarf we have found occupying the like important post, the other was the prime minister of a Batonga chief on the Zambesi.

As we sailed along, we disturbed many white-breasted cormorants; we had seen the same species fishing between the cataracts. Here, with many other wildfowls, they find subsistence on the smooth water by night, and sit sleepily on trees and in the reeds by day. Many hippopotami were seen in the river, and one of them stretched its wide jaws, as if to swallow the whole stern of the boat, close to Dr. Kirk's back; the animal was so near that, in opening its mouth, it lashed a quantity of water on to the stern-sheets, but did no damage. To avoid large marauding parties of Ajawa, on the left bank of the Shire, we continued on the right, or western side, with our land party, along the shore of the small lake Pamalombe. This lakelet is ten or twelve miles in length, and five or six broad. It is nearly surrounded by a broad belt of papyrus, so dense that we could scarcely find an opening to the shore. The plants, ten or twelve feet high, grew so closely together that air was excluded, and so much sulphuretted hydrogen gas evolved that by one night's exposure the bottom of the boat was blackened. Myriads of mosquitoes showed, as probably they always do, the presence of malaria.

We hastened from this sickly spot, trying to take the attentions of the mosquitoes as hints to seek more pleasant quarters on the healthy shores of Lake Nyassa; and when we sailed into it, on the 2nd September, we felt refreshed by the greater coolness of the air off this large body of water. The depth was the first point of interest. This is indicated by the colour of the water, which, on a belt along the shore, varying from a quarter to half a mile in breadth, is light green, and this is met by the deep blue or indigo tint of the Indian Ocean, which is the colour of the great body of Nyassa. We found the Upper Shire from nine to fifteen feet in depth; but skirting the western side of the lake about a mile from the shore the water deepened from nine to fifteen fathoms; then, as we rounded the grand mountainous promontory, which we named Cape Maclear, after our excellent friend the Astronomer Royal at the Cape of Good Hope, we could get no bottom with our lead-line of thirty-five fathoms. We pulled along the western shore, which was a succession of bays, and found that where the bottom was sandy near the beach, and to a mile out, the depth varied from six to fourteen fathoms. In a rocky bay about latitude 11 degrees 40 minutes we had soundings at 100 fathoms, though outside the same bay we found none with a fishing-line of 116 fathoms; but this cast was unsatisfactory, as the line broke in coming up. According to our present knowledge, a ship could anchor only near the shore.

Looking back to the southern end of Lake Nyassa, the arm from which the Shire flows was found to be about thirty miles long and from ten to twelve broad. Rounding Cape Maclear, and looking to the south-west, we have another arm, which stretches some eighteen miles southward, and is from six to twelve miles in breadth. These arms give the southern end a forked appearance, and with the help of a little imagination it may be likened to the "boot-shape" of Italy. The narrowest part is about the ankle, eighteen or twenty miles. From this it widens to the north, and in the upper third or fourth it is fifty or sixty miles broad. The length is over 200 miles. The direction in which it lies is as near as possible due north and south. Nothing of the great bend to the west, shown in all the previous maps, could be detected by either compass or chronometer, and the watch we used was an excellent one. The season of the year was very unfavourable. The "smokes" filled the air with an impenetrable haze, and the equinoctial gales made it impossible for us to cross to the eastern side. When we caught a glimpse of the sun rising from behind the mountains to the east, we made sketches and bearings of them at different latitudes, which enabled us to secure approximate measurements of the width. These agreed with the times taken by the natives at the different crossing-places--as Tsenga and Molamba. About the beginning of the upper third the lake is crossed by taking advantage of the island Chizumara, which name in the native tongue means the "ending;" further north they go round the end instead, though that takes several days.

The lake appeared to be surrounded by mountains, but it was afterwards found that these beautiful tree-covered heights were, on the west, only the edges of high table-lands. Like all narrow seas encircled by highlands, it is visited by sudden and tremendous storms. We were on it in September and October, perhaps the stormiest season of the year, and were repeatedly detained by gales. At times, while sailing pleasantly over the blue water with a gentle breeze, suddenly and without any warning was heard the sound of a coming storm, roaring on with crowds of angry waves in its wake. We were caught one morning with the sea breaking all around us, and, unable either to advance or recede, anchored a mile from shore, in seven fathoms. The furious surf on the beach would have shivered our boat to atoms, had we tried to land. The waves most dreaded came rolling on in threes, with their crests, driven into spray, streaming behind them. A short lull followed each triple charge. Had one of these seas struck our boat, nothing could have saved us; for they came on with resistless force; seaward, in shore, and on either side of us, they broke in foam, but we escaped. For six weary hours we faced those terrible trios. A low, dark, detached, oddly shaped cloud came slowly from the mountains, and hung for hours directly over our heads. A flock of night-jars (***Cometornis vexillarius***), which on no other occasion come out by day, soared above us in the gale, like birds of evil omen. Our black crew became sea-sick and unable to sit up or keep the boat's head to the sea. The natives and our land party stood on the high cliffs looking at us and exclaiming, as the waves seemed to swallow up the boat, "They are lost! they are all dead!" When at last the gale moderated and we got safely ashore, they saluted us warmly, as after a long absence. From this time we trusted implicitly to the opinions of our seaman, John Neil, who, having been a fisherman on the coast of Ireland, understood boating on a stormy coast, and by his advice we often sat cowering on the land for days together waiting for the surf to go down. He had never seen such waves before. We had to beach the boat every night to save her from being swamped at anchor; and, did we not believe the gales to be peculiar to one season of the year, would call Nyassa the "Lake of Storms."

Distinct white marks on the rocks showed that, for some time during the rainy season, the water of the lake is three feet above the point to which it falls towards the close of the dry period of the year. The rains begin here in November, and the permanent rise of the Shire does not take place till January. The western side of Lake Nyassa, with the exception of the great harbour to the west of Cape Maclear, is, as has been said before, a succession of small bays of nearly similar form, each having an open sandy beach and pebbly shore, and being separated from its neighbour by a rocky headland, with detached rocks extending some distance out to sea. The great south-western bay referred to would form a magnificent harbour, the only really good one we saw to the west.

The land immediately adjacent to the lake is low and fertile, though in some places marshy and tenanted by large flocks of ducks, geese, herons, crowned cranes, and other birds. In the southern parts we have sometimes ten or a dozen miles of rich plains, bordered by what seem high ranges of well-wooded hills, running nearly parallel with the lake. Northwards the mountains become loftier and present some magnificent views, range towering beyond range, until the dim, lofty outlines projected against the sky bound the prospect. Still further north the plain becomes more narrow, until, near where we turned, it disappears altogether, and the mountains rise abruptly out of the lake, forming the north-east boundary of what was described to us as an extensive table-land; well suited for pasturage and agriculture, and now only partially occupied by a tribe of Zulus, who came from the south some years ago. These people own large herds of cattle, and are constantly increasing in numbers by annexing other tribes.

CHAPTER X.

The Lake tribes--The Mazitu--Quantities of elephants--Distressing journey--Detention on the Shire.

Never before in Africa have we seen anything like the dense population on the shores of Lake Nyassa. In the southern part there was an almost unbroken chain of villages. On the beach of wellnigh of every little sandy bay, dark crowds were standing, gazing at the novel sight of a boat under sail; and wherever we landed we were surrounded in a few seconds by hundreds of men, women, and children, who hastened to have a stare at the "chirombo" (wild animals).

During a portion of the year, the northern dwellers on the lake have a harvest which furnishes a singular sort of food. As we approached our limit in that direction, clouds, as of smoke rising from miles of burning grass, were observed bending in a south-easterly direction, and we thought that the unseen land on the opposite side was closing in, and that we were near the end of the lake. But next morning we sailed through one of the clouds on our own side, and discovered that it was neither smoke nor haze, but countless millions of minute midges called "kungo" (a cloud or fog). They filled the air to an immense height, and swarmed upon the water, too light to sink in it. Eyes and mouth had to be kept closed while passing through this living cloud: they struck upon the face like fine drifting snow. Thousands lay in the boat when she emerged from the cloud of midges. The people gather these minute insects by night, and boil them into thick cakes, to be used as a relish--millions of midges in a cake. A kungo cake, an inch thick, and as large as the blue bonnet of a Scotch ploughman, was offered to us; it was very dark in colour, and tasted not unlike caviare, or salted locusts.

Abundance of excellent fish is found in the lake, and nearly all were new to us. The mpasa, or sanjika, found by Dr. Kirk to be a kind of carp, was running up the rivers to spawn, like our salmon at home: the largest we saw was over two feet in length; it is a splendid fish, and the best we have ever eaten in Africa. They were ascending the rivers in August and September, and furnished active and profitable employment to many fishermen, who did not mind their being out of season. Weirs were constructed full of sluices, in each of which was set a large basket-trap, through whose single tortuous opening the fish once in has but small chance of escape. A short distance below the weir, nets are stretched across from bank to bank, so that it seemed a marvel how the most sagacious sanjika could get up at all without being taken. Possibly a passage up the river is found at night; but this is not the country of Sundays or "close times" for either men or fish. The lake fish are caught chiefly in nets, although men, and even women with babies on their backs, are occasionally seen fishing from the rocks with hooks.

A net with small meshes is used for catching the young fry of a silvery kind like pickerel, when they are about two inches long; thousands are often taken in a single haul. We had a present of a large bucketful one day for dinner: they tasted as if they had been cooked with a little quinine, probably from their gall-bladders being left in. In deep water, some sorts are taken by lowering fish-baskets attached by a long cord to a float, around which is often tied a mass of grass or weeds, as an alluring shade for the deep-sea fish. Fleets of fine canoes are engaged in the fisheries. The men have long paddles, and stand erect while using them. They sometimes venture out when a considerable sea is running. Our Makololo acknowledge that, in handling canoes, the Lake men beat them; they were unwilling to cross the Zambesi even, when the wind blew fresh.

Though there are many crocodiles in the lake, and some of an extraordinary size, the fishermen say that it is a rare thing for any one to be carried off by these reptiles. When crocodiles can easily obtain abundance of fish--their natural food--they seldom attack men; but when unable to see to catch their prey, from the muddiness of the water in floods, they are very dangerous.

Many men and boys are employed in gathering the buaze, in preparing the fibre, and in making it into long nets. The knot of the net is different from ours, for they invariably use what sailors call the reef knot, but they net with a needle like that we use. From the amount of native cotton cloth worn in many of the southern villages, it is evident that a great number of hands and heads must be employed in the cultivation of cotton, and in the various slow processes through which it has to pass, before the web is finished in the native loom. In addition to this branch of industry, an extensive manufacture of cloth, from the inner bark of an undescribed tree, of the botanical group, **Caesalpineae**, is ever going on, from one end of the lake to the other; and both toil and time are required to procure the bark, and to prepare it by pounding and steeping it to render it soft and pliable. The prodigious amount of the bark clothing worn indicates the destruction of an immense number of trees every year; yet the adjacent heights seem still well covered with timber.

The Lake people are by no means handsome: the women are **very** plain; and really make themselves hideous by the means they adopt to render themselves attractive. The **pelele**, or ornament for the upper lip, is universally worn by the ladies; the most valuable is of pure tin, hammered into the shape of a small dish; some are made of white quartz, and give the wearer the appearance of having an inch or more of one of Price's patent candles thrust through the lip, and projecting beyond the tip of the nose.

In character, the Lake tribes are very much like other people; there are decent men among them, while a good many are no better than they should be. They are open-handed enough: if one of us, as was often the case, went to see a net drawn, a fish was always offered. Sailing one day past a number of men, who had just dragged their nets ashore, at one of the fine fisheries at Pamalombe, we were hailed and asked to stop, and received a liberal donation of beautiful fish. Arriving late one afternoon at a small village on the lake, a number of the inhabitants manned two canoes, took out their seine, dragged it, and made us a present of the entire haul. The northern chief, Marenga, a tall handsome man, with a fine aquiline nose, whom we found living in his stockade in a forest about twenty miles north of the mountain Kowirwe, behaved like a gentleman to us. His land extended from Dambo to the north of Makuza hill. He was specially generous, and gave us bountiful presents of food and beer. "Do they wear such things in your country?" he asked, pointing to his iron bracelet, which was studded with copper, and highly prized. The Doctor said he had never seen such in his country, whereupon Marenga instantly took it off, and presented it to him, and his wife also did the same with hers. On our return south from the mountains near the north end of the lake, we reached Marenga's on the 7th October. When he could not prevail upon us to forego the advantage of a fair wind for his invitation to "spend the whole day drinking his beer, which was," he said, "quite ready," he loaded us with provisions, all of which he sent for before we gave him any present. In allusion to the boat's sail, his people said that they had no Bazimo, or none worth having, seeing they had never invented the like for them. The chief, Mankambira, likewise treated us with kindness; but wherever the slave-trade is carried on, the people are dishonest and uncivil; that invariably leaves a blight and a curse in its path. The first question put to us at the lake crossing-places, was, "Have you come to buy slaves?" On hearing that we were English, and never purchased slaves, the questioners put on a supercilious air, and sometimes refused to sell us food. This want of respect to us may have been owing to the impressions conveyed to them by the Arabs, whose dhows have sometimes been taken by English cruisers when engaged in lawful trade. Much foreign cloth, beads, and brass-wire were worn by these ferrymen--and some had muskets.

By Chitanda, near one of the slave crossing-places, we were robbed for the first time in Africa, and learned by experience that these people, like more civilized nations, have expert thieves among them. It might be only a coincidence; but we never suffered from impudence, loss of property, or were endangered, unless among people familiar with slaving. We had such a general sense of security, that never, save when we suspected treachery, did we set a watch at night. Our native companions had, on this occasion, been carousing on beer, and had removed to a distance of some thirty yards, that we might not overhear their free and easy after-dinner remarks, and two of us had a slight touch of fever; between three and four o'clock in the morning some thieves came, while we slept ingloriously--rifles and revolvers all ready,--and relieved us of most of our goods. The boat's sail, under which we slept, was open all around, so the feat was easy.

Awaking as honest men do, at the usual hour, the loss of one was announced by "My bag is gone--with all my clothes; and my boots too!" "And mine!" responded a second. "And mine also!" chimed in the third, "with the bag of beads, and the rice!" "Is the cloth taken?" was the eager inquiry, as that would have been equivalent to all our money. It had been used for a pillow that night, and thus saved. The rogues left on the beach, close to our beds, the Aneroid Barometer and a pair of boots, thinking possibly that they might be of use to us, or, at least, that they could be of none to them. They shoved back some dried plants and fishes into one bag, but carried off many other specimens we had collected; some of our notes also, and nearly all our clothing.

We could not suspect the people of the village near which we lay. We had probably been followed for days by the thieves watching for an opportunity. And our suspicions fell on some persons who had come from the East Coast; but having no evidence, and expecting to hear if our goods were exposed for sale in the vicinity, we made no fuss about it, and began to make new clothing. That our rifles and revolvers were left untouched was greatly to our advantage: yet we felt it was most humiliating for armed men to have been so thoroughly fleeced by a few black rascals.

Some of the best fisheries appear to be private property. We found shelter from a storm one morning in a spacious lagoon, which communicated with the lake by a narrow passage. Across this strait stakes were driven in, leaving only spaces for the basket fish-traps. A score of men were busily engaged in taking out the fish. We tried to purchase some, but they refused to sell. The fish did not belong to them, they would send for the proprietor of the place. The proprietor arrived in a short time, and readily sold what we wanted.

Some of the burying-grounds are very well arranged, and well cared for; this was noticed at Chitanda, and more particularly at a village on the southern shore of the fine harbour at Cape Maclear. Wide and neat paths were made in the burying-ground on its eastern and southern sides. A grand old fig-tree stood at the northeast corner, and its wide-spreading branches threw their kindly shade over the last resting-place of the dead. Several other magnificent trees grew around the hallowed spot. Mounds were raised as they are at home, but all lay north and south, the heads apparently north. The graves of the sexes were distinguished by the various implements which the buried dead had used in their different employments during life; but they were all broken, as if to be employed no more. A piece of fishing-net and a broken paddle told where a fisherman lay. The graves of the women had the wooden mortar, and the heavy pestle used in pounding the corn, and the basket in which the meal is sifted, while all had numerous broken calabashes and pots arranged around them. The idea that the future life is like the present does not appear to prevail; yet a banana-tree had been carefully planted at the head of several of the graves; the fruit might be considered an offering to those who still possess human tastes. The people of the neighbouring villages were friendly and obliging, and willingly brought us food for sale.

Pursuing our exploration, we found that the northern part of the lake was the abode of lawlessness and bloodshed. The Mazite, or Mazitu, live on the highlands, and make sudden swoops on the villages of the plains. They are Zulus who came originally from the south, inland of Sofalla and Inhambane; and are of the same family as those who levy annual tribute from the Portuguese on the Zambesi. All the villages north of Mankambira's (lat. 11 degrees 44 minutes south) had been recently destroyed by these terrible marauders, but they were foiled in their attacks upon that chief and Marenga. The thickets and stockades round their villages enabled the bowmen to pick off the Mazitu in security, while they were afraid to venture near any place where they could not use their shields. Beyond Mankambira's we saw burned villages, and the putrid bodies of many who had fallen by Mazitu spears only a few days before. Our land party were afraid to go further. This reluctance to proceed without the presence of a white man was very natural, because bands of the enemy who had ravaged the country were supposed to be still roaming about; and if these marauders saw none but men of their own colour, our party might forthwith be attacked. Compliance with their request led to an event which might have been attended by very serious consequences. Dr. Livingstone got separated from the party in the boat for four days. Having taken the first morning's journey along with them, and directing the boat to call for him in a bay in sight, both parties proceeded north. In an hour Dr. Livingstone and his party struck inland, on approaching the foot of the mountains which rise abruptly from the lake. Supposing that they had heard of a path behind the high range which there forms the shore, those in the boat held on their course; but it soon began to blow so fresh that they had to run ashore for safety. While delayed a couple of hours, two men were sent up the hills to look for the land party, but they could see nothing of them, and the boat party sailed as soon as it was safe to put to sea, with the conviction that the missing ones would regain the lake in front.

In a short time a small island or mass of rocks was passed, on which were a number of armed Mazitu with some young women, apparently their wives. The headman said that he had been wounded in the foot by Mankambira, and that they were staying there till he could walk to his chief, who lived over the hills. They had several large canoes, and it was evident that this was a nest of lake pirates, who sallied out by night to kill and plunder. They reported a path behind the hills, and, the crew being reassured, the boat sailed on. A few miles further, another and still larger band of pirates were fallen in with, and hundreds of crows and kites hovered over and round the rocks on which they lived. Dr. Kirk and Charles Livingstone, though ordered in a voice of authority to come ashore, kept on their course. A number of canoes then shot out from the rocks and chased them. One with nine strong paddlers persevered for some time after all the others gave up the chase. A good breeze, however, enabled the gig to get away from them with ease. After sailing twelve or fifteen miles, north of the point where Dr. Livingstone had left them, it was decided that he must be behind; but no sooner had the boat's head been turned south, than another gale compelled her to seek shelter in a bay. Here a number of wretched fugitives from the slave-trade on the opposite shore of the lake were found; the original inhabitants of the place had all been swept off the year before by the Mazitu. In the deserted gardens beautiful cotton was seen growing, much of it had the staple an inch and a half long, and of very fine quality. Some of the plants were uncommonly large, deserving to be ranked with trees.

On their trying to purchase food, the natives had nothing to sell except a little dried cassava-root, and a few fish: and they demanded two yards of calico for the head only of a large fish. When the gale admitted of their return, their former pursuers tried to draw them ashore by asserting that they had quantities of ivory for sale. Owing to a succession of gales, it was the fourth day from parting that the boat was found by Dr. Livingstone, who was coming on in search of it with only two of his companions.

After proceeding a short distance up the path in which they had been lost sight of, they learned that it would take several days to go round the mountains, and rejoin the lake; and they therefore turned down to the bay, expecting to find the boat, but only saw it disappearing away to the north. They pushed on as briskly as possible after it, but the mountain flank which forms the coast proved excessively tedious and fatiguing; travelling all day, the distance made, in a straight line, was under five miles. As soon as day dawned, the march was resumed; and, after hearing at the first inhabited rock that their companions had passed it the day before, a goat was slaughtered out of the four which they had with them, when suddenly, to the evident consternation of the men, seven Mazitu appeared armed with spears and shields, with their heads dressed fantastically with feathers. To hold a parley, Dr. Livingstone and Moloka, a Makololo man who spoke Zulu, went unarmed to meet them. On Dr. Livingstone approaching them, they ordered him to stop, and sit down in the sun, while they sat in the shade. "No, no!" was the reply, "if you sit in the shade, so will we." They then rattled their shields with their clubs, a proceeding which usually inspires terror; but Moloka remarked, "It is not the first time we have heard shields rattled." And all sat down together. They asked for a present, to show their chief that they had actually met strangers--something as evidence of having seen men who were not Arabs. And they were requested in turn to take these strangers to the boat, or to their chief. All the goods were in the boat, and to show that no present such as they wanted was in his pockets, Dr. Livingstone emptied them, turning out, among other things, a note-book: thinking it was a pistol they started up, and said, "Put that in again." The younger men then became boisterous, and demanded a goat. That could not be spared, as they were the sole provisions. When they insisted, they were asked how many of the party they had killed, that they thus began to divide the spoil; this evidently made them ashamed. The elders were more reasonable; they dreaded treachery, and were as much afraid of Dr. Livingstone and his party as his men were of them; for on leaving they sped away up the hills like frightened deer. One of them, and probably the leader, was married, as seen by portions of his hair sewn into a ring; all were observed by their teeth to be people of the country, who had been incorporated into the Zulu tribe.

The way still led over a succession of steep ridges with ravines of from 500 to 1000 feet in depth; some of the sides had to be scaled on hands and knees, and no sooner was the top reached than the descent began again. Each ravine had a running stream; and the whole country, though so very rugged, had all been cultivated, and densely peopled. Many banana-trees, uncared for patches of corn, and Congo-bean bushes attested former cultivation. The population had all been swept away; ruined villages, broken utensils, and human skeletons, met with at every turn, told a sad tale. So numerous were the slain, that it was thought the inhabitants had been slaughtered in consequence of having made raids on the Zulus for cattle.

Continuing the journey that night as long as light served, they slept unconsciously on the edge of a deep precipice, without fire, lest the Mazitu should see it. Next morning most of the men were tired out, the dread of the apparition of the day before tending probably to increase the lameness of which they complained. When told, however, that all might return to Mankambira's save two, Moloka and Charlie, they would not, till assured that the act would not be considered one of cowardice. Giving them one of the goats as provision, another was slaughtered for the remainder of the party who, having found on the rocks a canoe which had belonged to one of the deserted villages, determined to put to sea again; but the craft was very small, and the remaining goat, spite of many a threat of having its throat cut, jumped and rolled about so, as nearly to capsize it; so Dr. Livingstone took to the shore again, and after another night spent without fire, except just for cooking, was delighted to see the boat coming back.

We pulled that day to Mankambira's, a distance that on shore, with the most heartbreaking toil, had taken three days to travel. This was the last latitude taken, 11 degrees 44 minutes S. The boat had gone about 24 minutes further to the north, the land party probably half that distance, but fever prevented the instruments being used. Dr. Kirk and Charles Livingstone were therefore furthest up the lake, and they saw about 20 minutes beyond their turning-point, say into the tenth degree of south latitude. From the heights of at least a thousand feet, over which the land party toiled, the dark mountain masses on both sides of the lake were seen closing in. At this elevation the view extended at least as far as that from the boats, and it is believed the end of the lake lies on the southern borders of 10 degrees, or the northern limits of 11 degrees south latitude.

Elephants are numerous on the borders of the lake, and surprisingly tame, being often found close to the villages. Hippopotami swarm very much at their ease in the creeks and lagoons, and herds are sometimes seen in the lake itself. Their tameness arises from the fact that poisoned arrows have no effect on either elephant or hippopotamus. Five of each were shot for food during our journey. Two of the elephants were females, and had only a single tusk apiece, and were each killed by the first shot. It is always a case of famine or satiety when depending on the rifle for food--a glut of meat or none at all. Most frequently it is scanty fare, except when game is abundant, as it is far up the Zambesi. We had one morning two hippopotami and an elephant, perhaps in all some eight tons of meat, and two days after the last of a few sardines only for dinner.

One morning when sailing past a pretty thickly-inhabited part, we were surprised at seeing nine large bull-elephants standing near the beach quietly flapping their gigantic ears. Glad of an opportunity of getting some fresh meat, we landed and fired into one. They all retreated into a marshy piece of ground between two villages. Our men gave chase, and fired into the herd. Standing on a sand hummock, we could see the bleeding animals throwing showers of water with their trunks over their backs. The herd was soon driven back upon us, and a wounded one turned to bay. Yet neither this one, nor any of the others, ever attempted to charge. Having broken his legs with a rifle-ball, we fired into him at forty yards as rapidly as we could load and discharge the rifles. He simply shook his head at each shot, and received at least sixty Enfield balls before he fell. Our excellent sailor from the north of Ireland happened to fire the last, and, as soon as he saw the animal fall, he turned with an air of triumph to the Doctor and exclaimed, "It was *my* shot that done it, sir!"

In a few minutes upwards of a thousand natives were round the prostrate king of beasts; and, after our men had taken all they wanted, an invitation was given to the villagers to take the remainder. They rushed at it like hungry hyenas, and in an incredibly short time every inch of it was carried off. It was only by knowing that the meat would all be used that we felt justified in the slaughter of this noble creature. The tusks weighed 62 lbs. each. A large amount of ivory might be obtained from the people of Nyassa, and we were frequently told of their having it in their huts.

While detained by a storm on the 17th October at the mouth of the Kaombe, we were visited by several men belonging to an Arab who had been for fourteen years in the interior at Katanga's, south of Cazembe's. They had just brought down ivory, malachite, copper rings, and slaves to exchange for cloth at the lake. The malachite was said to be dug out of a large vein on the side of a hill near Katanga's. They knew Lake Tanganyika well, but had not heard of the Zambesi. They spoke quite positively, saying that the water of Lake Tanganyika flowed out by the opposite end to that of Nyassa. As they had seen neither of the overflows, we took it simply as a piece of Arab geography. We passed their establishment of long sheds next day, and were satisfied that the Arabs must be driving a good trade.

The Lake slave-trade was going on at a terrible rate. Two enterprising Arabs had built a dhow, and were running her, crowded with slaves, regularly across the Lake. We were told she sailed the day before we reached their head-quarters. This establishment is in the latitude of the Portuguese slave-exporting town of Iboe, and partly supplies that vile market; but the greater number of the slaves go to Kilwa. We did not see much evidence of a wish to barter. Some ivory was offered for sale; but the chief traffic was in human chattels. Would that we could give a comprehensive account of the horrors of the slave-trade, with an approximation to the number of lives it yearly destroys! for we feel sure that were even half the truth told and recognized, the feelings of men would be so thoroughly roused, that this devilish traffic in human flesh would be put down at all risks; but neither we, nor any one else, have the statistics necessary for a work of this kind. Let us state what we do know of one portion of Africa, and then every reader who believes our tale can apply the ratio of the known misery to find out the unknown. We were informed by Colonel Rigby, late H.M. Political Agent, and Consul at Zanzibar, that 19,000 slaves from this Nyassa country alone pass annually through the Custom-house of that island. This is exclusive of course of those sent to Portuguese slave-ports. Let it not be supposed for an instant that this number, 19,000, represents all the victims. Those taken out of the country are but a very small section of the sufferers. We never realized the atrocious nature of the traffic, until we saw it at the fountain-head. There truly "Satan has his seat." Besides those actually captured, thousands are killed and die of their wounds and famine, driven from their villages by the slave raid proper. Thousands perish in internecine war waged for slaves with their own clansmen and neighbours, slain by the lust of gain, which is stimulated, be it remembered always, by the slave purchasers of Cuba and elsewhere. The many skeletons we have seen, amongst rocks and woods, by the little pools, and along the paths of the wilderness, attest the awful sacrifice of human life, which must be attributed, directly or indirectly, to this trade of hell. We would ask our countrymen to believe us when we say, as we conscientiously can, that it is our deliberate opinion, from what we know and have seen, that not one-fifth of the victims of the slave-trade ever become slaves. Taking the Shire Valley as an average, we should say not even one-tenth arrive at their destination. As the system, therefore, involves such an awful waste of human life,--or shall we say of human labour?--and moreover tends directly to perpetuate the barbarism of those who remain in the country, the argument for the continuance of this wasteful course because, forsooth, a fraction of the enslaved may find good masters, seems of no great value. This reasoning, if not the result of ignorance, may be of maudlin philanthropy. A small armed steamer on Lake Nyassa could easily, by exercising a control, and furnishing goods in exchange for ivory and other products, break the neck of this infamous traffic in that quarter; for nearly all must cross the Lake or the Upper Shire.

Our exploration of the Lake extended from the 2nd September to the 27th October, 1861; and, having expended or lost most of the goods we had brought, it was necessary to go back to the ship. When near the southern end, on our return, we were told that a very large slave-party had just crossed to the eastern side. We heard the fire of three guns in the evening, and judged by the report that they must be at least six-pounders. They were said to belong to an Ajawa chief named Mukata.

In descending the Shire, we found concealed in the broad belt of papyrus round the lakelet Pamalombe, into which the river expands, a number of Manganja families who had been driven from their homes by the Ajawa raids. So thickly did the papyrus grow, that when beat down it supported their small temporary huts, though when they walked from one hut to another, it heaved and bent beneath their feet as thin ice does at home.

A dense and impenetrable forest of the papyrus was left standing between them and the land, and no one passing by on the same side would ever have suspected that human beings lived there. They came to this spot from the south by means of their canoes, which enabled them to obtain a living from the fine fish which abound in the lakelet. They had a large quantity of excellent salt sewed up in bark, some of which we bought, our own having run out. We anchored for the night off their floating camp, and were visited by myriads of mosquitoes. Some of the natives show a love of country quite surprising. We saw fugitives on the mountains, in the north of the lake, who were persisting in clinging to the haunts of their boyhood and youth, in spite of starvation and the continual danger of being put to death by the Mazitu.

A few miles below the lakelet is the last of the great slave-crossings. Since the

Ajawa invasion the villages on the left bank had been abandoned, and the people, as we saw in our ascent, were living on the right or western bank.

As we were resting for a few minutes opposite the valuable fishery at Movunguti, a young effeminate-looking man from some sea-coast tribe came in great state to have a look at us. He walked under a large umbrella, and was followed by five handsome damsels gaily dressed and adorned with a view to attract purchasers. One was carrying his pipe for smoking bang, here called "chamba;" another his bow and arrows; a third his battle-axe; a fourth one of his robes; while the last was ready to take his umbrella when he felt tired. This show of his merchandise was to excite the cupidity of any chief who had ivory, and may be called the lawful way of carrying on the slave-trade. What proportion it bears to the other ways in which we have seen this traffic pursued, we never found means of forming a judgment. He sat and looked at us for a few minutes, the young ladies kneeling behind him; and having satisfied himself that we were not likely to be customers, he departed.

On our first trip we met, at the landing opposite this place, a middle- aged woman of considerable intelligence, and possessing more knowledge of the country than any of the men. Our first definite information about Lake Nyassa was obtained from her. Seeing us taking notes, she remarked that she had been to the sea, and had there seen white men writing. She had seen camels also, probably among the Arabs. She was the only Manganja woman we ever met who was ashamed of wearing the "pelele," or lip-ring. She retired to her hut, took it out, and kept her hand before her mouth to hide the hideous hole in the lip while conversing with us. All the villagers respected her, and even the headmen took a secondary place in her presence. On inquiring for her now, we found that she was dead. We never obtained sufficient materials to estimate the relative mortality of the highlands and lowlands; but, from many very old white- headed blacks having been seen on the highlands, we think it probable that even native races are longer lived the higher their dwelling-places are.

We landed below at Mikena's and took observations for longitude, to verify those taken two years before. The village was deserted, Mikena and his people having fled to the other side of the river. A few had come across this morning to work in their old gardens. After completing the observations we had breakfast; and, as the last of the things were being carried into the boat, a Manganja man came running down to his canoe, crying out, "The Ajawa have just killed my comrade!" We shoved off, and in two minutes the advanced guard of a large marauding party were standing with their muskets on the spot where we had taken breakfast. They were evidently surprised at seeing us there, and halted; as did also the main body of perhaps a thousand men. "Kill them," cried the Manganja; "they are going up to the hills to kill the English," meaning the missionaries we had left at Magomero. But having no prospect of friendly communication with them, nor confidence in Manganja's testimony, we proceeded down the river; leaving the Ajawa sitting under a large baobab, and the Manganja cursing them most energetically across the river.

On our way up, we had seen that the people of Zimika had taken refuge on a long island in the Shire, where they had placed stores of grain to prevent it falling into the hands of the Ajawa; supposing afterwards that the invasion and war were past, they had removed back again to the mainland on the east, and were living in fancied security. On approaching the chief's village, which was built in the midst of a beautiful grove of lofty wild-fig and palm trees, sounds of revelry fell upon our ears. The people were having a merry time--drumming, dancing, and drinking beer--while a powerful enemy was close at hand, bringing death or slavery to every one in the village. One of our men called out to several who came to the bank to look at us, that the Ajawa were coming and were even now at Mikena's village; but they were dazed with drinking, and took no notice of the warning.

Crowds of carriers offered their services after we left the river. Several sets of them placed so much confidence in us, as to decline receiving payment at the end of the first day; they wished to work another day, and so receive both days' wages in one piece. The young headman of a new village himself came on with his men. The march was a pretty long one, and one of the men proposed to lay the burdens down beside a hut a mile or more from the next village. The headman scolded the fellow for his meanness in wishing to get rid of our goods where we could not procure carriers, and made him carry them on. The village, at the foot of the cataracts, had increased very much in size and wealth since we passed it on our way up. A number of large new huts had been built; and the people had a good stock of cloth and beads. We could not account for this sudden prosperity, until we saw some fine large canoes, instead of the two old, leaky things which lay there before. This had become a crossing-place for the slaves that the Portuguese agents were carrying to

Tette, because they were afraid to take them across nearer to where the ship lay, about seven miles off. Nothing was more disheartening than this conduct of the Manganja, in profiting by the entire breaking up of their nation.

We reached the ship on the 8th of November, 1861, in a very weak condition, having suffered more from hunger than on any previous trip. Heavy rains commenced on the 9th, and continued several days; the river rose rapidly, and became highly discoloured. Bishop Mackenzie came down to the ship on the 14th, with some of the "Pioneer's" men, who had been at Magomero for the benefit of their health, and also for the purpose of assisting the Mission. The Bishop appeared to be in excellent spirits, and thought that the future promised fair for peace and usefulness. The Ajawa having been defeated and driven off while we were on the Lake, had sent word that they desired to live at peace with the English. Many of the Manganja had settled round Magomero, in order to be under the protection of the Bishop; and it was hoped that the slave-trade would soon cease in the highlands, and the people be left in the secure enjoyment of their industry. The Mission, it was also anticipated, might soon become, to a considerable degree, self-supporting, and raise certain kinds of food, like the Portuguese of Senna and Quillimane. Mr. Burrup, an energetic young man, had arrived at Chibisa's the day before the Bishop, having come up the Shire in a canoe. A surgeon and a lay brother followed behind in another canoe. The "Pioneer's" draught being too much for the upper part of the Shire, it was not deemed advisable to bring her up, on the next trip, further than the Ruo; the Bishop, therefore, resolved to explore the country from Magomero to the mouth of that river, and to meet the ship with his sisters and Mrs. Burrup, in January. This was arranged before parting, and then the good Bishop and Burrup, whom we were never to meet again, left us; they gave and received three hearty English cheers as they went to the shore, and we steamed off.

The rains ceased on the 14th, and the waters of the Shire fell, even more rapidly than they had risen. A shoal, twenty miles below Chibisa's, checked our further progress, and we lay there five weary weeks, till the permanent rise of the river took place. During this detention, with a large marsh on each side, the first death occurred in the Expedition which had now been three-and-a-half years in the country. The carpenter's mate, a fine healthy young man, was seized with fever. The usual remedies had no effect; he died suddenly while we were at evening prayers, and was buried on shore. He came out in the "Pioneer," and, with the exception of a slight touch of fever at the mouth of the Rovuma, had enjoyed perfect health all the time he had been with us. The Portuguese are of opinion that the European who has immunity from this disease for any length of time after he enters the country is more likely to be cut off by it when it does come, than the man who has it frequently at first.

The rains became pretty general towards the close of December, and the Shire was in flood in the beginning of January, 1862. At our wooding- place, a mile above the Ruo, the water was three feet higher than it was when we were here in June; and on the night of the 6th it rose eighteen inches more, and swept down an immense amount of brushwood and logs which swarmed with beetles and the two kinds of shells which are common all over the African continent. Natives in canoes were busy spearing fish in the meadows and creeks, and appeared to be taking them in great numbers. Spur-winged geese, and others of the knob-nosed species, took advantage of the low gardens being flooded, and came to pilfer the beans. As we passed the Ruo, on the 7th, and saw nothing of the Bishop, we concluded that he had heard from his surgeon of our detention, and had deferred his journey. He arrived there five days after, on the 12th.

After paying our Senna men, as they wished to go home, we landed them here. All were keen traders, and had invested largely in native iron- hoes, axes, and ornaments. Many of the hoes and spears had been taken from the slaving parties whose captives we liberated; for on these occasions our Senna friends were always uncommonly zealous and active. The remainder had been purchased with the old clothes we had given them and their store of hippopotamus meat: they had no fear of losing them, or of being punished for aiding us. The system, in which they had been trained, had eradicated the idea of personal responsibility from their minds. The Portuguese slaveholders would blame the English alone, they said; they were our servants at the time. No white man on board could purchase so cheaply as these men could. Many a time had their eloquence persuaded a native trader to sell for a bit of dirty worn cloth things for which he had, but a little before, refused twice the amount of clean new calico. "Scissors" being troubled with a cough at night, received a present of a quilted coverlet, which had seen a good deal of service. A few days afterwards, a good chance of investing in hoes offering itself, he ripped off both sides, tore them into a dozen pieces, and purchased about a dozen hoes with them.

We entered the Zambesi on the 11th of January, and steamed down towards the coast, taking the side on which we had come up; but the channel had changed to the other side during the summer, as it sometimes does, and we soon grounded. A Portuguese gentleman, formerly a lieutenant in the army, and now living on Sangwisa, one of the islands of the Zambesi, came over with his slaves, to aid us in getting the ship off. He said frankly, that his people were all great thieves, and we must be on our guard not to leave anything about. He next made a short speech to his men, told them he knew what thieves they were, but implored them not to steal from us, as we would give them a present of cloth when the work was done. "The natives of this country," he remarked to us, "think only of three things, what they shall eat and drink, how many wives they can have, and what they may steal from their master, if not how they may murder him." He always slept with a loaded musket by his side. This opinion may apply to slaves, but decidedly does not in our experience apply to freemen. We paid his men for helping us, and believe that even they, being paid, stole nothing from us. Our friend farms pretty extensively the large island called Sangwisa,--lent him for nothing by Senhor Ferrao,--and raises large quantities of mapira and beans, and also beautiful white rice, grown from seed brought a few years ago from South Carolina. He furnished us with some, which was very acceptable; for though not in absolute want, we were living on beans, salt pork, and fowls, all the biscuit and flour on board having been expended.

We fully expected that the owners of the captives we had liberated would show their displeasure, at least by their tongues; but they seemed ashamed; only one ventured a remark, and he, in the course of common conversation, said, with a smile, "You took the Governor's slaves, didn't you?" "Yes, we did free several gangs that we met in the Manganja country." The Portuguese of Tette, from the Governor downwards, were extensively engaged in slaving. The trade is partly internal and partly external: they send some of the captives, and those bought, into the interior, up the Zambesi: some of these we actually met on their way up the river. The young women were sold there for ivory: an ordinary-looking one brought two arrobas, sixty-four pounds weight, and an extra beauty brought twice that amount. The men and boys were kept as carriers, to take the ivory down from the interior to

Tette, or were retained on farms on the Zambesi, ready for export if a slaver should call: of this last mode of slaving we were witnesses also. The slaves were sent down the river chained, and in large canoes. This went on openly at Tette, and more especially so while the French "Free Emigration" system was in full operation. This double mode of disposing of the captives pays better than the single system of sending them down to the coast for exportation. One merchant at Tette, with whom we were well acquainted, sent into the interior three hundred Manganja women to be sold for ivory, and another sent a hundred and fifty.

CHAPTER XI.

Arrival of H.M.S. "Gorgon"--Dr. Livingstone's new steamer and Mrs. Livingstone--Death of Mrs. Livingstone--Voyage to Johanna and the Rovuma--An attack upon the "Pioneer's" boats.

We anchored on the Great Luabo mouth of the Zambesi, because wood was much more easily obtained there than at the Kongone.

On the 30th, H.M.S. "Gorgon" arrived, towing the brig which brought Mrs. Livingstone, some ladies about to join their relatives in the Universities' Mission, and the twenty-four sections of a new iron steamer intended for the navigation of Lake Nyassa. The "Pioneer" steamed out, and towed the brig into the Kongone harbour. The new steamer was called the "Lady of the Lake," or the "Lady Nyassa," and as much as could be carried of her in one trip was placed, by the help of the officers and men of the "Gorgon," on board the "Pioneer," and the two large paddle-box boats of H.M.'s ship. We steamed off for Ruo on the 10th of February, having on board Captain Wilson, with a number of his officers and men to help us to discharge the cargo. Our progress up was distressingly slow. The river was in flood, and we had a three-knot current against us in many places. These delays kept us six months in the delta, instead of, as we anticipated, only six days; for, finding it impossible to carry the sections up to the Ruo without great loss of time, it was thought best to land them at Shupanga, and, putting the hull of the "Lady Nyassa" together there, to tow her up to the foot of the Murchison Cataracts.

A few days before the "Pioneer" reached Shupanga, Captain Wilson, seeing the hopeless state of affairs, generously resolved to hasten with the Mission ladies up to those who, we thought, were anxiously awaiting their arrival, and therefore started in his gig for the Ruo, taking Miss Mackenzie, Mrs. Burrup, and his surgeon,

Dr. Ramsay. They were accompanied by Dr. Kirk and Mr. Sewell, paymaster of the "Gorgon," in the whale-boat of the "Lady Nyassa." As our slow-paced-launch, "Ma Robert," had formerly gone up to the foot of the cataracts in nine days' steaming, it was supposed that the boats might easily reach the expected meeting- place at the Ruo in a week; but the Shire was now in flood, and in its most rapid state; and they were longer in getting up about half the distance, than it was hoped they would be in the whole navigable part of the river. They could hear nothing of the Bishop from the chief of the island, Malo, at the mouth of the Ruo. "No white man had ever come to his village," he said. They proceeded on to Chibisa's, suffering terribly from mosquitoes at night. Their toil in stemming the rapid current made them estimate the distance, by the windings, as nearer 300 than 200 miles. The Makololo who had remained at Chibisa's told them the sad news of the death of the good Bishop and of Mr. Burrup. Other information received there awakened fresh anxiety on behalf of the survivors; so, leaving the ladies with Dr. Ramsay and the Makololo, Captain Wilson and Dr. Kirk went up the hills, in hopes of being able to render assistance, and on the way they met some of the Mission party at Soche's. The excessive fatigue that our friends had undergone in the voyage up to Chibisa's in no wise deterred them from this further attempt for the benefit of their countrymen, but the fresh labour, with diminished rations, was too much for their strength. They were reduced to a diet of native beans and an occasional fowl. Both became very ill of fever, Captain Wilson so dangerously that his fellow-sufferer lost all hopes of his recovery. His strong able-bodied cockswain did good service in cheerfully carrying his much-loved Commander, and they managed to return to the boat, and brought the two bereaved and sorrow-stricken ladies back to the "Pioneer."

We learnt that the Bishop, wishing to find a shorter route down to the Shire, had sent two men to explore the country between Magomero and the junction of the Ruo; and in December Messrs. Proctor and Scudamore, with a number of Manganja carriers, left Magomero for the same purpose. They were to go close to Mount Choro, and then skirt the Elephant Marsh, with Mount Clarendon on their left. Their guides seem to have led them away to the east, instead of south; to the upper waters of the Ruo in the Shirwa valley, instead of to its mouth. Entering an Anguru slave-trading village, they soon began to suspect that the people meant mischief, and just before sunset a woman told some of their men that if they slept there they would all be killed. On their preparing to leave, the Anguru followed them and shot their arrows at the retreating party. Two of the carriers were captured, and all the goods were taken by these robbers. An arrow-head struck deep into the stock of Proctor's gun; and the two missionaries, barely escaping with their lives, swam a deep river at night, and returned to Magomero famished and exhausted.

The wives of the captive carriers came to the Bishop day after day weeping and imploring him to rescue their husbands from slavery. The men had been caught while in his service, no one else could be entreated; there was no public law nor any power superior to his own, to which an appeal could be made; for in him Church and State were, in the disorganized state of the country, virtually united. It seemed to him to be clearly his duty to try and rescue these kidnapped members of the Mission family. He accordingly invited the veteran Makololo to go with him on this somewhat hazardous errand. Nothing could have been proposed to them which they would have liked better, and they went with alacrity to eat the sheep of the Anguru, only regretting that the enemy did not keep cattle as well. Had the matter been left entirely in their hands, they would have made a clean sweep of that part of the country; but the Bishop restrained them, and went in an open manner, thus commending the measure to all the natives, as one of justice. This deliberation, however, gave the delinquents a chance of escape.

The missionaries were successful; the offending village was burned, and a few sheep and goats were secured which could not be considered other than a very mild punishment for the offence committed; the headman, Muana-somba, afraid to retain the prisoners any longer, forthwith liberated them, and they returned to their homes. This incident took place at the time we were at the Ruo and during the rains, and proved very trying to the health of the missionaries; they were frequently wetted, and had hardly any food but roasted maize. Mr. Scudamore was never well afterwards. Directly on their return to Magomero, the Bishop and Mr. Burrup, both suffering from diarrhoea in consequence of wet, hunger, and exposure, started for Chibisa's to go down to the Ruo by the Shire. So fully did the Bishop expect a renewal of the soaking wet from which he had just returned, that on leaving Magomero he walked through the stream. The rivulets were so swollen that it took five days to do a journey that would otherwise have occupied only two days and a half.

None of the Manganja being willing to take them down the river during the flood, three Makololo canoe-men agreed to go with them. After paddling till near sunset, they decided to stop and sleep on shore; but the mosquitoes were so numerous that they insisted on going on again; the Bishop, being a week behind the time he had engaged to be at the Ruo, reluctantly consented, and in the darkness the canoe was upset in one of the strong eddies or whirlpools, which suddenly boil up in flood time near the outgoing branches of the river; clothing, medicines, tea, coffee, and sugar were all lost. Wet and weary, and tormented by mosquitoes, they lay in the canoe till morning dawned, and then proceeded to Malo, an island at the mouth of the Ruo, where the Bishop was at once seized with fever.

Had they been in their usual health, they would doubtless have pushed on to Shupanga, or to the ship; but fever rapidly prostrates the energies, and induces a drowsy stupor, from which, if not roused by medicine, the patient gradually sinks into the sleep of death. Still mindful, however, of his office, the Bishop consoled himself by thinking that he might gain the friendship of the chief, which would be of essential service to him in his future labours. That heartless man, however, probably suspicious of all foreigners from the knowledge he had acquired of white slave-traders, wanted to turn the dying Bishop out of the hut, as he required it for his corn, but yielded to the expostulations of the Makololo. Day after day for three weeks did these faithful fellows remain beside his mat on the floor; till, without medicine or even proper food, he died. They dug his grave on the edge of the deep dark forest where the natives buried their dead. Mr. Burrup, himself far gone with dysentery, staggered from the hut, and, as in the dusk of evening they committed the Bishop's body to the grave, repeated from memory portions of our beautiful service for the Burial of the Dead--"earth to earth, ashes to ashes, dust to dust; in sure and certain hope of the resurrection of the dead through our Lord Jesus Christ." And in this sad way ended the earthly career of one, of whom it can safely be said that for unselfish goodness of heart, and earnest devotion to the noble work he had undertaken, none of the commendations of his friends can exceed the reality. The grave in which his body rests is about a hundred yards from the confluence of the Ruo, on the left bank of the Shire, and opposite the island of Malo. The Makololo then took Mr. Burrup up in the canoe as far as they could, and, making a litter of branches, carried him themselves, or got others to carry him, all the way back to his countrymen at Magomero. They hurried him on lest he should die in their hands, and blame be attached to them. Soon after his return he expired, from the disease which was on him when he started to meet his wife.

Captain Wilson arrived at Shupanga on the 11th of March, having been three weeks on the Shire. On the 15th the "Pioneer" steamed down to the Kongone. The "Gorgon" had been driven out to sea in a gale, and had gone to Johanna for provisions, and it was the 2nd of April before she returned. It was fortunate for us that she had obtained a supply, as our provisions were exhausted, and we had to buy some from the master of the brig. The "Gorgon" left for the Cape on the 4th, taking all, except one, of the Mission party who had come in January. We take this opportunity of expressing our heartfelt gratitude to the gallant Captain I. C. Wilson and his officers for innumerable acts of kindness and hearty co-operation. Our warmest thanks are also due to Captain R. B. Oldfield and the other officers from the Admiral downwards, and we beg to assure them that nothing could be more encouraging to us in our difficulties and trials, than the knowledge that we possessed their friendship and sympathy in our labours.

The Rev. James Stewart, of the Free Church of Scotland, arrived in the "Gorgon." He had wisely come out to inspect the country, before deciding on the formation of a Mission in the interior. To this object he devoted many months of earnest labour. This Mission was intended to embrace both the industrial and the religious element; and as the route by the Zambesi and Shire forms the only one at present known, with but a couple of days' land journey to the highlands, which stretch to an unknown distance into the continent, and as no jealousy was likely to be excited in the mind of a man of Bishop Mackenzie's enlarged views--there being moreover room for hundreds of Missions--we gladly extended the little aid in our power to an envoy from the energetic body above mentioned, but recommended him to examine the field with his own eyes.

During our subsequent detention at Shupanga, he proceeded as far up the Shire as the Upper Cataracts, and saw the mere remnants of that dense population, which we at first had found living in peace and plenty, but which was now scattered and destroyed by famine and slave-hunting. The land, which both before and after we found so fair and fruitful, was burned up by a severe drought; in fact, it was at its very worst. With most praiseworthy energy, and in spite of occasional attacks of fever, he then ascended the Zambesi as far as Kebrabasa; and, what may be of interest to some, compared it, in parts, to the Danube. His estimate of the highlands would naturally be lower than ours. The main drawbacks in his opinion, however, were the slave-trade, and the power allowed the effete Portuguese of shutting up the country from all except a few convicts of their own nation. The time of his coming was inopportune; the disasters which, from inexperience, had befallen the Mission of the Universities, had a depressing effect on the minds of many at home, and rendered a new attempt unadvisable; though, had the Scotch perseverance and energy been introduced, it is highly probable that they would have reacted, most beneficially, on the zeal of our English brethren, and desertion would never have been heard of. After examining the country, Mr. Stewart descended the Zambesi in the beginning of the following year, and proceeded homewards with his report, by Mosambique and the Cape.

On the 7th of April we had only one man fit for duty; all the rest were down with fever, or with the vile spirit secretly sold to them by the Portuguese officer of customs, in spite of our earnest request to him to refrain from the pernicious traffic.

We started on the 11th for Shupanga with another load of the "Lady Nyassa." As we steamed up the delta, we observed many of the natives wearing strips of palm-leaf, the signs of sickness and mourning; for they too suffer from fever. This is the unhealthy season; the rains are over, and the hot sun draws up malaria from the decayed vegetation; disease seemed peculiarly severe this year. On our way up we met Mr. Waller, who had come from Magomero for provisions; the missionaries were suffering severely from want of food; the liberated people were starving, and dying of diarrhoea, and loathsome sores. The Ajawa, stimulated in their slave raids by supplies of ammunition and cloth from the Portuguese, had destroyed the large crops of the past year; a drought had followed, and little or no food could be bought. With his usual energy, Mr. Waller hired canoes, loaded them with stores, and took them up the long weary way to Chibisa's. Before he arrived he was informed that the Mission of the Universities, now deprived of its brave leader, had retired from the highlands down to the Low Shire Valley. This appeared to us, who knew the danger of leading a sedentary life, the greatest mistake they could have made, and was the result of no other counsel or responsibility than their own. Waller would have reascended at once to the higher altitude, but various objections stood in the way. The loss of poor Scudamore and Dickinson, in this low-lying situation, but added to the regret that the highlands had not received a fair trial.

When the news of the Bishop's unfortunate collisions with the natives, and of his untimely end, reached England, much blame was imputed to him. The policy, which with the formal sanction of all his companions he had adopted, being directly contrary to the advice which Dr. Livingstone tendered, and to the assurances of the peaceable nature of the Mission which the Doctor had given to the natives, a friendly disapproval of a bishop's engaging in war was ventured on, when we met him at Chibisa's in November. But when we found his conduct regarded with so much bitterness in England, whether from a disposition to "stand by the down man," or from having an intimate knowledge of the peculiar circumstances of the country in which he was placed, or from the thorough confidence which intimacy caused us to repose in his genuine piety, and devout service of God, we came to think much more leniently of his proceedings, than his assailants did. He never seemed to doubt but that he had done his duty; and throughout he had always been supported by his associates.

The question whether a Bishop, in the event of his flock being torn from his bosom, may make war to rescue them, requires serious consideration. It seems to narrow itself into whether a Christian man may lawfully use the civil power or the sword at all in defensive war, as police or otherwise. We would do almost anything to avoid a collision with degraded natives; but in case of an invasion--our blood boils at the very thought of our wives, daughters, or sisters being touched--we, as men with human feelings, would unhesitatingly fight to the death, with all the fury in our power.

The good Bishop was as intensely averse to using arms, before he met the slave-hunters, as any man in England. In the course he pursued he may have made a mistake, but it is a mistake which very few Englishmen on meeting bands of helpless captives, or members of his family in bonds, would have failed to commit likewise.

During unhealthy April, the fever was more severe in Shupanga and Mazaro than usual. We had several cases on board--they were quickly cured, but, from our being in the delta, as quickly returned. About the middle of the month Mrs.

Livingstone was prostrated by this disease; and it was accompanied by obstinate vomiting. Nothing is yet known that can allay this distressing symptom, which of course renders medicine of no avail, as it is instantly rejected. She received whatever medical aid could be rendered from Dr. Kirk, but became unconscious, and her eyes were closed in the sleep of death as the sunset on the evening of the Christian Sabbath, the 27th April, 1862. A coffin was made during the night, a grave was dug next day under the branches of the great baobab-tree, and with sympathizing hearts the little band of his countrymen assisted the bereaved husband in burying his dead. At his request, the Rev. James Stewart read the burial-service; and the seamen kindly volunteered to mount guard for some nights at the spot where her body rests in hope. Those who are not aware how this brave, good, English wife made a delightful home at Kolobeng, a thousand miles inland from the Cape, and as the daughter of Moffat and a Christian lady exercised most beneficial influence over the rude tribes of the interior, may wonder that she should have braved the dangers and toils of this down-trodden land. She knew them all, and, in the disinterested and dutiful attempt to renew her labours, was called to her rest instead. "***Fiat, Domine, voluntas tua***!"

On the 5th of May Dr. Kirk and Charles Livingstone started in the boat for Tette, in order to see the property of the Expedition brought down in canoes. They took four Mazaro canoe-men to manage the boat, and a white sailor to cook for them; but, unfortunately, he caught fever the very day after leaving the ship, and was ill most of the trip; so they had to cook for themselves, and to take care of him besides.

We now proceeded with preparations for the launch of the "Lady Nyassa." Ground was levelled on the bank at Shupanga, for the purpose of arranging the compartments in order: she was placed on palm-trees which were brought from a place lower down the river for ways, and the engineer and his assistants were soon busily engaged; about a fortnight after they were all brought from Kongone, the sections were screwed together. The blacks are more addicted to stealing where slavery exists than elsewhere. We were annoyed by thieves who carried off the iron screw-bolts, but were gratified to find that strychnine saved us from the man-thief as well as the hyena-thief. A hyena was killed by it, and after the natives saw the dead animal and knew how we had destroyed it, they concluded that it was not safe to steal from men who possessed a medicine so powerful. The half-caste, who kept Shupanga-house, said he wished to have some to give to the Zulus, of whom he was mortally afraid, and to whom he had to pay an unwilling tribute.

The "Pioneer" made several trips to the Kongone, and returned with the last load on the 12th of June. On the 23rd the "Lady Nyassa" was safely launched, the work of putting her together having been interrupted by fever and dysentery, and many other causes which it would only weary the reader to narrate in detail. Natives from all parts of the country came to see the launch, most of them quite certain that, being made of iron, she must go to the bottom as soon as she entered the water. Earnest discussions had taken place among them with regard to the propriety of using iron for ship-building. The majority affirmed that it would never answer. They said, "If we put a hoe into the water, or the smallest bit of iron, it sinks immediately. How then can such a mass of iron float? it must go to the bottom." The minority answered that this might be true with them, but white men had medicine for everything. "They could even make a woman, all except the speaking; look at that one on the figure- head of the vessel." The unbelievers were astonished, and could hardly believe their eyes, when they saw the ship float lightly and gracefully on the river, instead of going to the bottom, as they so confidently predicted. "Truly," they said, "these men have powerful medicine."

Birds are numerous on the Shupanga estate. Some kinds remain all the year round, while many others are there only for a few months. Flocks of green pigeons come in April to feed on the young fruit of the wild fig- trees, which is also eaten by a large species of bat in the evenings. The pretty little black weaver, with yellow shoulders, appears to enjoy life intensely after assuming his wooing dress. A hearty breakfast is eaten in the mornings and then come the hours for making merry. A select party of three or four perch on the bushes which skirt a small grassy plain, and cheer themselves with the music of their own quiet and self-complacent song. A playful performance on the wind succeeds. Expanding his soft velvet-like plumage, one glides with quivering pinions to the centre of the open space, singing as he flies, then turns with a rapid whirring sound from his wings--somewhat like a child's rattle--and returns to his place again. One by one the others perform the same feat, and continue the sport for hours, striving which can produce the loudest brattle while turning. These games are only played during the season of courting and of the gay feathers; the merriment seems never to be thought of while the bird wears his winter suit of sober brown.

We received two mules from the Cape to aid us in transporting the pieces of the "Lady Nyassa" past the cataracts and landed them at Shupanga, but they soon perished. A Portuguese gentleman kindly informed us, **after** both the mules were dead, that he knew they would die; for the land there had been often tried, and nothing would live on it--not even a pig. He said he had not told us so before, because he did not like to appear officious!

By the time everything had been placed on board the "Lady Nyassa," the waters of the Zambesi and the Shire had fallen so low that it was useless to attempt taking her up to the cataracts before the rains in December. Draught oxen and provisions also were required, and could not be obtained nearer than the Island of Johanna. The Portuguese, without refusing positively to let trade enter the Zambesi, threw impediments in the way; they only wanted a small duty! They were about to establish a river police, and rearrange the Crown lands, which have long since become Zulu lands; meanwhile they were making the Zambesi, by slaving, of no value to any one.

The Rovuma, which was reported to come from Lake Nyassa, being out of their claims and a free river, we determined to explore it in our boats immediately on our return from Johanna, for which place, after some delay at the Kongone, in repairing engines, paddle-wheel, and rudder, we sailed on the 6th of August. A store of naval provisions had been formed on a hulk in Pomone Bay of that island for the supply of the cruisers, and was in charge of Mr. Sunley, the Consul, from whom we always received the kindest attentions and assistance. He now obliged us by parting with six oxen, trained for his own use in sugar-making. Though sadly hampered in his undertaking by being obliged to employ slave labour, he has by indomitable energy overcome obstacles under which most persons would have sunk. He has done all that under the circumstances could be done to infuse a desire for freedom, by paying regular wages; and has established a large factory, and brought 300 acres of rich soil under cultivation with sugar-cane. We trust he will realize the fortune which he so well deserves to earn. Had Mr. Sunley performed the same experiment on the mainland, where people would have flocked to him for the wages he now gives, he would certainly have inaugurated a new era on the East Coast of Africa.

On a small island where the slaveholders have complete power over the slaves, and where there is no free soil such as is everywhere met with in Africa, the experiment ought not to be repeated. Were Mr. Sunley commencing again, it should neither be in Zanzibar nor Johanna, but on African soil, where, if even a slave is ill-treated, he can easily by flight become free. On an island under native rule a joint manufacture by Arabs and Englishmen might only mean that the latter were to escape the odium of flogging the slaves.

On leaving Johanna and our oxen for a time, H.M.S. "Orestes" towed us thence to the mouth of the Rovuma at the beginning of September. Captain Gardner, her commander, and several of his officers, accompanied us up the river for two days in the gig and cutter. The water was unusually low, and it was rather dull work for a few hours in the morning; but the scene became livelier and more animated when the breeze began to blow. Our four boats they swept on under full sail, the men on the look out in the gig and cutter calling, "Port, sir!" "Starboard, sir!" "As you go, sir!" while the black men in the bows of the others shouted the practical equivalents, "Pagombe! Pagombe!" "Enda quete!" "Berane! Berane!" Presently the leading-boat touches on a sandbank; down comes the fluttering sail; the men jump out to shove her off, and the other boats, shunning the obstruction, shoot on ahead to be brought up each in its turn by mistaking a sandbank for the channel, which had often but a very little depth of water.

A drowsy herd of hippopotami were suddenly startled by a score of rifle-shots, and stared in amazement at the strange objects which had invaded their peaceful domains, until a few more bullets compelled them to seek refuge at the bottom of the deep pool, near which they had been quietly reposing. On our return, one of the herd retaliated. He followed the boat, came up under it, and twice tried to tear the bottom out of it; but fortunately it was too flat for his jaws to get a good grip, so he merely damaged one of the planks with his tusks, though he lifted the boat right up, with ten men and a ton of ebony in it.

We slept, one of the two nights Captain Gardner was with us, opposite the lakelet Chidia, which is connected with the river in flood time, and is nearly surrounded by hills some 500 or 600 feet high, dotted over with trees. A few small groups of huts stood on the hill-sides, with gardens off which the usual native produce had been reaped. The people did not seem much alarmed by the presence of the large party which had drawn up on the sandbanks below their dwellings. There is abundance of large ebony in the neighbourhood. The pretty little antelope (***Cephalophus caeruleus***), about the size of a hare, seemed to abound, as many of their skins were offered for sale. Neat figured date-leaf mats of various colours are woven here, the different dyes being obtained from the barks of trees. Cattle could not live on the banks of the Rovuma on account of the tsetse, which are found from near the mouth, up as far as we could take the boats. The navigation did not improve as we ascended; snags, brought down by the floods, were common, and left in the channel on the sudden subsidence of the water. In many places, where the river divided into two or three channels, there was not water enough in any of them for a boat drawing three feet, so we had to drag ours over the shoals; but we saw the river at its very lowest, and it may be years before it is so dried up again.

The valley of the Rovuma, bounded on each side by a range of highlands, is from two to four miles in width, and comes in a pretty straight course from the W.S.W.; but the channel of the river is winding, and now at its lowest zigzagged so perversely, that frequently the boats had to pass over three miles to make one in a straight line. With a full stream it must of course be much easier work. Few natives were seen during the first week. Their villages are concealed in the thick jungle on the hill- sides, for protection from marauding slave-parties. Not much of interest was observed on this part of the silent and shallow river. Though feeling convinced that it was unfit for navigation, except for eight months of the year, we pushed on, resolved to see if, further inland, the accounts we had received from different naval officers of its great capabilities would prove correct; or if, by communication with Lake Nyassa, even the upper part could be turned to account. Our exploration showed us that the greatest precaution is required in those who visit new countries.

The reports we received from gentlemen, who had entered the river and were well qualified to judge, were that the Rovuma was infinitely superior to the Zambesi, in the absence of any bar at its mouth, in its greater volume of water, and in the beauty of the adjacent lands. We probably came at a different season from that in which they visited it, and our account ought to be taken with theirs to arrive at the truth. It might be available as a highway for commerce during three quarters of each year; but casual visitors, like ourselves and others, are all ill able to decide.

The absence of animal life was remarkable. Occasionally we saw pairs of the stately jabirus, or adjutant-looking marabouts, wading among the shoals, and spur-winged geese, and other water-fowl, but there was scarcely a crocodile or a hippopotamus to be seen.

At the end of the first week, an old man called at our camp, and said he would send a present from his village, which was up among the hills. He appeared next morning with a number of his people, bringing meal, cassava- root, and yams. The language differs considerably from that on the Zambesi, but it is of the same family. The people are Makonde, and are on friendly terms with the Mabiha, and the Makoa, who live south of the Rovuma. When taking a walk up the slopes of the north bank, we found a great variety of trees we had seen nowhere else. Those usually met with far inland seem here to approach the coast. African ebony, generally named ***mpingu***, is abundant within eight miles of the sea; it attains a larger size, and has more of the interior black wood than usual. A good timber tree called ***mosoko*** is also found; and we saw half-caste Arabs near the coast cutting up a large log of it into planks. Before reaching the top of the rise we were in a forest of bamboos. On the plateau above, large patches were cleared and cultivated. A man invited us to take a cup of beer; on our complying with his request, the fear previously shown by the bystanders vanished. Our Mazaro men could hardly understand what they said. Some of them waded in the river and caught a curious fish in holes in the claybank. Its ventral fin is peculiar, being unusually large, and of a circular shape, like boys' playthings called "suckers." We were told that this fish is found also in the Zambesi, and is called Chirire. Though all its fins are large, it is asserted that it rarely ventures out into the stream, but remains near its hole, where it is readily caught by the hand.

The Zambesi men thoroughly understood the characteristic marks of deep or shallow water, and showed great skill in finding out the proper channel. The Molimo is the steersman at the helm, the Mokadamo is the head canoe- man, and he stands erect on the bows with a long pole in his hands, and directs the steersman where to go, aiding the rudder, if necessary, with his pole. The others preferred to stand and punt our boat, rather than row with our long oars, being able to shove her ahead faster than they could pull her. They are accustomed to short paddles. Our Mokadamo was affected with moon-blindness, and could not see at all at night.

His comrades then led him about, and handed him his food. They thought that it was only because his eyes rested all night, that he could see the channel so well by day. At difficult places the Mokadamo sometimes, however, made mistakes, and ran us aground; and the others, evidently imbued with the spirit of resistance to constituted authority, and led by Joao an aspirant for the office, jeered him for his stupidity. "Was he asleep? Why did he allow the boat to come there? Could he not see the channel was somewhere else?" At last the Mokadamo threw down the pole in disgust, and told Joao he might be a Mokadamo himself. The office was accepted with alacrity; but in a few minutes he too ran us into a worse difficulty than his predecessor ever did, and was at once disrated amidst the derision of his comrades.

On the 16th September, we arrived at the inhabited island of Kichokomane. The usual way of approaching an unknown people is to call out in a cheerful tone "Malonda!" Things for sale, or do you want to sell anything? If we can obtain a man from the last village, he is employed, though only useful in explaining to the next that we come in a friendly way. The people here were shy of us at first, and could not be induced to sell any food; until a woman, more adventurous than the rest, sold us a fowl. This opened the market, and crowds came with fowls and meal, far beyond our wants. The women are as ugly as those on Lake Nyassa, for who can be handsome wearing the pelele, or upper-lip ring, of large dimensions? We were once surprised to see young men wearing the pelele, and were told that in the tribe of the Mabiha, on the south bank, men as well as women wore them.

Along the left bank, above Kichokomane, is an exceedingly fertile plain, nearly two miles broad, and studded with a number of deserted villages. The inhabitants were living in temporary huts on low naked sandbanks; and we found this to be the case as far as we went. They leave most of their property and food behind, because they are not afraid of these being stolen, but only fear being stolen themselves. The great slave-route from Nyassa to Kilwa passes to N.E. from S.W., just beyond them; and it is dangerous to remain in their villages at this time of year, when the kidnappers are abroad. In one of the temporary villages, we saw, in passing, two human heads lying on the ground. We slept a couple of miles above this village.

Before sunrise next morning, a large party armed with bows and arrows and muskets came to the camp, two or three of them having a fowl each, which we refused to purchase, having bought enough the day before. They followed us all the morning, and after breakfast those on the left bank swam across and joined the main party on the other side. It was evidently their intention to attack us at a chosen spot, where we had to pass close to a high bank, but their plan was frustrated by a stiff breeze sweeping the boat past, before the majority could get to the place. They disappeared then, but came out again ahead of us, on a high wooded bank, walking rapidly to the bend, near which we were obliged to sail. An arrow was shot at the foremost boat; and seeing the force at the bend, we pushed out from the side, as far as the shoal water would permit, and tried to bring them to a parley, by declaring that we had not come to fight, but to see the river. "Why did you fire a gun, a little while ago?" they asked. "We shot a large puff-adder, to prevent it from killing men; you may see it lying dead on the beach." With great courage, our Mokadamo waded to within thirty yards of the bank, and spoke with much earnestness, assuring them that we were a peaceable party, and had not come for war, but to see the river. We were friends, and our countrymen bought cotton and ivory, and wished to come and trade with them. All we wanted was to go up quietly to look at the river, and then return to the sea. While he was talking with those on the shore, the old rogue, who appeared to be the ringleader, stole up the bank, and with a dozen others, waded across to the island, near which the boats lay, and came down behind us. Wild with excitement, they rushed into the water, and danced in our rear, with drawn bows, taking aim, and making various savage gesticulations. Their leader urged them to get behind some snags, and then shoot at us. The party on the bank in front had many muskets--and those of them, who had bows, held them with arrows ready set in the bowstrings. They had a mass of thick bush and trees behind them, into which they could in a moment dart, after discharging their muskets and arrows, and be completely hidden from our sight; a circumstance that always gives people who use bows and arrows the greatest confidence. Notwithstanding these demonstrations, we were exceedingly loath to come to blows. We spent a full half-hour exposed at any moment to be struck by a bullet or poisoned arrow. We explained that we were better armed than they were, and had plenty of ammunition, the suspected want of which often inspires them with courage, but that we did not wish to shed the blood of the children of the same Great Father with ourselves; that if we must fight, the guilt would be all theirs.

This being a common mode of expostulation among themselves, we so far succeeded, that with great persuasion the leader and others laid down their arms, and waded over from the bank to the boats to talk the matter over. "This was their river; they did not allow white men to use it. We must pay toll for leave to pass." It was somewhat humiliating to do so, but it was pay or fight; and, rather than fight, we submitted to the humiliation of paying for their friendship, and gave them thirty yards of cloth. They pledged themselves to be our friends ever afterwards, and said they would have food cooked for us on our return. We then hoisted sail, and proceeded, glad that the affair had been amicably settled. Those on shore walked up to the bend above to look at the boat, as we supposed; but the moment she was abreast of them, they gave us a volley of musket-balls and poisoned arrows, without a word of warning. Fortunately we were so near, that all the arrows passed clear over us, but four musket-balls went through the sail just above our heads. All our assailants bolted into the bushes and long grass the instant after firing, save two, one of whom was about to discharge a musket and the other an arrow, when arrested by the fire of the second boat. Not one of them showed their faces again, till we were a thousand yards away. A few shots were then fired over their heads, to give them an idea of the range of our rifles, and they all fled into the woods. Those on the sand-bank rushed off too, with the utmost speed; but as they had not shot at us, we did not molest them, and they went off safely with their cloth. They probably expected to kill one of our number, and in the confusion rob the boats. It is only where the people are slavers that the natives of this part of Africa are bloodthirsty.

These people have a bad name in the country in front, even among their own tribe. A slave-trading Arab we met above, thinking we were then on our way down the river, advised us not to land at the villages, but to stay in the boats, as the inhabitants were treacherous, and attacked at once, without any warning or provocation. Our experience of their conduct fully confirmed the truth of what he said. There was no trade on the river where they lived, but beyond that part there was a brisk canoe- trade in rice and salt; those further in the interior cultivating rice, and sending it down the river to be exchanged for salt, which is extracted from the earth in certain places on the banks. Our assailants hardly anticipated resistance, and told a neighbouring chief that, if they had known who we were, they would not have attacked English, who can "bite hard." They offered no molestations on our way down, though we were an hour in passing their village. Our canoe-men plucked up courage on finding that we had come off unhurt. One of them, named Chiku, acknowledging that he had been terribly frightened, said. "His fear was not the kind which makes a man jump overboard and run away; but that which brings the heart up to the mouth, and renders the man powerless, and no more able to fight than a woman."

In the country of Chonga Michi, about 80 or 90 miles up the river, we found decent people, though of the same tribe, who treated strangers with civility. A body of Makoa had come from their own country in the south, and settled here. The Makoa are known by a cicatrice in the forehead shaped like the new moon with the horns turned downwards. The tribe possesses all the country west of Mosambique; and they will not allow any of the Portuguese to pass into their country more than two hours' distance from the fort. A hill some ten or twelve miles distant, called Pau, has been visited during the present generation only by one Portuguese and one English officer, and this visit was accomplished only by the influence of the private friendship of a chief for this Portuguese gentleman. Our allies have occupied the Fort of Mosambique for three hundred years, but in this, as in all other cases, have no power further than they can see from a gun-carriage.

The Makoa chief, Matingula, was hospitable and communicative, telling us all he knew of the river and country beyond. He had been once to Iboe and once at Mosambique with slaves. Our men understood his language easily. A useless musket he had bought at one of the above places was offered us for a little cloth. Having received a present of food from him, a railway rug was handed to him: he looked at it--had never seen cloth like that before--did not approve of it, and would rather have cotton cloth. "But this will keep you warm at night."--"Oh, I do not wish to be kept warm at night."--We gave him a bit of cotton cloth, not one-third the value of the rug, but it was more highly prized. His people refused to sell their fowls for our splendid prints and drab cloths. They had probably been taken in with gaudy-patterned sham prints before. They preferred a very cheap, plain, blue stuff of which they had experience. A great quantity of excellent honey is collected all along the river, by bark hives being placed for the bees on the high trees on both banks. Large pots of it, very good and clear, were offered in exchange for a very little cloth. No wax was brought for sale; there being no market for this commodity, it is probably thrown away as useless.

At Michi we lose the tableland which, up to this point, bounds the view on both sides of the river, as it were, with ranges of flat-topped hills, 600 or 800 feet high; and to this plateau a level fertile plain succeeds, on which stand detached granite hills. That portion of the tableland on the right bank seems to bend away to the south, still preserving the appearance of a hill range. The height opposite extends a few miles further west, and then branches off in a northerly direction. A few small pieces of coal were picked up on the sandbanks, showing that this useful mineral exists on the Rovuma, or on some of its tributaries: the natives know that it will burn. At the lakelet Chidia, we noticed the same sandstone rock, with fossil wood on it, which we have on the Zambesi, and knew to be a sure evidence of coal beneath. We mentioned this at the time to Captain Gardner, and our finding coal now seemed a verification of what we then said; the coal-field probably extends from the Zambesi to the Rovuma, if not beyond it. Some of the rocks lower down have the permanent water-line three feet above the present height of the water.

A few miles west of the Makoa of Matingula, we came again among the Makonde, but now of good repute. War and slavery have driven them to seek refuge on the sand-banks. A venerable-looking old man hailed us as we passed, and asked us if we were going by without speaking. We landed, and he laid down his gun and came to us; he was accompanied by his brother, who shook hands with every one in the boat, as he had seen people do at Kilwa. "Then you have seen white men before?" we said. "Yes," replied the polite African, "but never people of your quality." These men were very black, and wore but little clothing. A young woman, dressed in the highest style of Makonde fashion, punting as dexterously as a man could, brought a canoe full of girls to see us. She wore an ornamental head-dress of red beads tied to her hair on one side of her head, a necklace of fine beads of various colours, two bright figured brass bracelets on her left arm, and scarcely a farthing's worth of cloth, though it was at its cheapest.

As we pushed on westwards, we found that the river makes a little southing, and some reaches were deeper than any near the sea; but when we had ascended about 140 miles by the river's course from the sea, soft tufa rocks began to appear; ten miles beyond, the river became more narrow and rocky, and when, according to our measurement, we had ascended 156 miles, our further progress was arrested. We were rather less than two degrees in a straight line from the Coast. The incidents worth noticing were but few: seven canoes with loads of salt and rice kept company with us for some days, and the further we went inland, the more civil the people became.

When we came to a stand, just below the island of Nyamatolo, Long. 38 degrees 36 minutes E., and Lat. 11 degrees 53 minutes, the river was narrow, and full of rocks. Near the island there is a rocky rapid with narrow passages fit only for native canoes; the fall is small, and the banks quite low; but these rocks were an effectual barrier to all further progress in boats. Previous reports represented the navigable part of this river as extending to the distance of a month's sail from its mouth; we found that, at the ordinary heights of the water, a boat might reach the obstructions which seem peculiar to all African rivers in six or eight days. The Rovuma is remarkable for the high lands that flank it for some eighty miles from the ocean. The cataracts of other rivers occur in mountains, those of the Rovuma are found in a level part, with hills only in the distance. Far away in the west and north we could see high blue heights, probably of igneous origin from their forms, rising out of a plain.

The distance from Ngomano, a spot thirty miles further up, to the Arab crossing-places of Lake Nyassa Tsenga or Kotakota was said to be twelve days. The way we had discovered to Lake Nyassa by Murchison's Cataracts had so much less land carriage, that we considered it best to take our steamer thither, by the route in which we were well known, instead of working where we were strangers; and accordingly we made up our minds to return.

The natives reported a worse place above our turning-point--the passage being still narrower than this. An Arab, they said, once built a boat above the rapids, and sent it down full of slaves; but it was broken to pieces in these upper narrows. Many still maintained that the Rovuma came from Nyassa, and that it is very narrow as it issues out of the lake. One man declared that he had seen it with his own eyes as it left the lake, and seemed displeased at being cross-questioned, as if we doubted his veracity.

More satisfactory information, as it appeared to us, was obtained from others. Two days, or thirty miles, beyond where we turned back, the Rovuma is joined by the Liende, which, coming from the south-west, rises in the mountains on the east side of Nyassa. The great slave route to Kilwa runs up the banks of this river, which is only ankle-deep at the dry season of the year. The Rovuma itself comes from the W.N.W., and after the traveller passes the confluence of the Liende at Ngomano or "meeting-place," the chief of which part is named Ndonde, he finds the river narrow, and the people Ajawa.

Crocodiles in the Rovuma have a sorry time of it. Never before were reptiles so persecuted and snubbed. They are hunted with spears, and spring traps are set for them. If one of them enters an inviting pool after fish, he soon finds a fence thrown round it, and a spring trap set in the only path out of the enclosure. Their flesh is eaten, and relished. The banks, on which the female lays her eggs by night, are carefully searched by day, and all the eggs dug out and devoured. The fish-hawk makes havoc among the few young ones that escape their other enemies. Our men were constantly on the look-out for crocodiles' nests. One was found containing thirty-five newly-laid eggs, and they declared that the crocodile would lay as many more the second night in another place. The eggs were a foot deep in the sand on the top of a bank ten feet high. The animal digs a hole with its foot, covers the eggs, and leaves them till the river rises over the nest in about three months afterwards, when she comes back, and assists the young ones out. We once saw opposite Tette young crocodiles in December, swimming beside an island in company with an old one. The yolk of the egg is nearly as white as the real white. In taste they resemble hen's eggs with perhaps a smack of custard, and would be as highly relished by whites as by blacks, were it not for their unsavoury origin in men-eaters.

Hunting the Senze (***Aulacodus Swindernianus***), an animal the size of a large cat, but in shape more like a pig, was the chief business of men and boys as we passed the reedy banks and low islands. They set fire to a mass of reeds, and, armed with sticks, spears, bows and arrows, stand in groups guarding the outlets through which the seared Senze may run from the approaching flames. Dark dense volumes of impenetrable smoke now roll over on the lee side of the islet, and shroud the hunters. At times vast sheets of lurid flames bursting forth, roaring, crackling and exploding, leap wildly far above the tall reeds. Out rush the terrified animals, and amid the smoke are seen the excited hunters dancing about with frantic gesticulations, and hurling stick, spear, and arrow at their burned out victims. Kites hover over the smoke, ready to pounce on the mantis and locusts as they spring from the fire. Small crows and hundreds of swallows are on eager wing, darting into the smoke and out again, seizing fugitive flies. Scores of insects, in their haste to escape from the fire, jump into the river, and the active fish enjoy a rare feast.

We returned to the "Pioneer" on the 9th of October, having been away one month. The ship's company had used distilled water, a condenser having been sent out from England; and there had not been a single case of sickness on board since we left, though there were so many cases of fever the few days she lay in the same spot last year. Our boat party drank the water of the river, and the three white sailors, who had never been in an African river before, had some slight attacks of fever.

CHAPTER XII.

Return to the Zambesi--Bishop Mackenzie's grave--Frightful scenes with crocodiles--Death of Mr. Thornton--African poisons--Recall of the Expedition.

We put to sea on the 18th of October, and, again touching at Johanna, obtained a crew of Johanna men and some oxen, and sailed for the Zambesi; but our fuel failing before we reached it, and the wind being contrary, we ran into Quillimane for wood.

Quillimane must have been built solely for the sake of carrying on the slave-trade, for no man in his senses would ever have dreamed of placing a village on such a low, muddy, fever-haunted, and mosquito-swarming site, had it not been for the facilities it afforded for slaving. The bar may at springs and floods be easily crossed by sailing-vessels, but, being far from the land, it is always dangerous for boats. Slaves, under the name of "free emigrants," have gone by thousands from Quillimane, during the last six years, to the ports a little to the south, particularly to Massangano. Some excellent brick-houses still stand in the place, and the owners are generous and hospitable: among them our good friend, Colonel Nunez. His disinterested kindness to us and to all our countrymen can never be forgotten. He is a noble example of what energy and uprightness may accomplish even here. He came out as a cabin- boy, and, without a single friend to help him, he has persevered in an honourable course until he is the richest man on the East Coast. When Dr. Livingstone came down the Zambesi in 1856, Colonel Nunez was the chief of the only four honourable, trustworthy men in the country. But while he has risen a whole herd has sunk, making loud lamentations, through puffs of cigar-smoke, over negro laziness; they might add, their own.

All agricultural enterprise is virtually discouraged by Quillimane Government.

A man must purchase a permit from the Governor, when he wishes to visit his country farm; and this tax, in a country where labour is unpopular, causes the farms to be almost entirely left in the hands of a head slave, who makes returns to his master as interest or honesty prompts him. A passport must also be bought whenever a man wishes to go up the river to Mazaro, Senna, or Tette, or even to reside for a month at Quillimane. With a soil and a climate well suited for the growth of the cane, abundance of slave labour, and water communication to any market in the world, they have never made their own sugar. All they use is imported from Bombay. "The people of Quillimane have no enterprise," said a young European Portuguese, "they do nothing, and are always wasting their time in suffering, or in recovering from fever."

We entered the Zambesi about the end of November and found it unusually low, so we did not get up to Shupanga till the 19th of December. The friends of our Mazaro men, who had now become good sailors and very attentive servants, turned out and gave them a hearty welcome back from the perils of the sea: they had begun to fear that they would never return. We hired them at a sixteen-yard piece of cloth a month--about ten shillings' worth, the Portuguese market-price of the cloth being then sevenpence halfpenny a yard,--and paid them five pieces each, for four- and-a-half months' work. A merchant at the same time paid other Mazaro men three pieces for seven months, and they were with him in the interior. If the merchants do not prosper, it is not because labour is dear, but because it is scarce, and because they are so eager on every occasion to sell the workmen out of the country. Our men had also received quantities of good clothes from the sailors of the "Pioneer" and of the "Orestes," and were now regarded by their neighbours and by themselves as men of importance. Never before had they possessed so much wealth: they believed that they might settle in life, being now of sufficient standing to warrant their entering the married state; and a wife and a hut were among their first investments. Sixteen yards were paid to the wife's parents, and a hut cost four yards. We should have liked to have kept them in the ship, for they were well-behaved and had learned a great deal of the work required. Though they would not themselves go again, they engaged others for us; and brought twice as many as we could take, of their brothers and cousins, who were eager to join the ship and go with us up the Shire, or anywhere else. They all agreed to take half-pay until they too had learned to work; and we found no scarcity of labour, though all that could be exported is now out of the country.

There had been a drought of unusual severity during the past season in the country between Lupata and Kebrabasa, and it had extended north-east to the Manganja highlands. All the Tette slaves, except a very few household ones, had been driven away by hunger, and were now far off in the woods, and wherever wild fruit, or the prospect of obtaining anything whatever to keep the breath of life in them, was to be found. Their masters were said never to expect to see them again. There have been two years of great hunger at Tette since we have been in the country, and a famine like the present prevailed in 1854, when thousands died of starvation. If men like the Cape farmers owned this country, their energy and enterprise would soon render the crops independent of rain. There being plenty of slope or fall, the land could be easily irrigated from the Zambesi and its tributary streams. A Portuguese colony can never prosper: it is used as a penal settlement, and everything must be done military fashion. "What do I care for this country?" said the most enterprising of the Tette merchants, "all I want is to make money as soon possible, and then go to Bombay and enjoy it." All business at Tette was now suspended. Carriers could not be found to take the goods into the interior, and the merchants could barely obtain food for their own families. At Mazaro more rain had fallen, and a tolerable crop followed. The people of Shupanga were collecting and drying different wild fruits, nearly all of which are far from palatable to a European taste. The root of a small creeper called "bise" is dug up and eaten. In appearance it is not unlike the small white sweet potato, and has a little of the flavour of our potato. It would be very good, if it were only a little larger. From another tuber, called "ulanga," very good starch can be made. A few miles from Shupanga there is an abundance of large game, but the people here, though fond enough of meat, are not a hunting race, and seldom kill any.

The Shire having risen, we steamed off on the 10th of January, 1863, with the "Lady Nyassa" in tow. It was not long before we came upon the ravages of the notorious Mariano. The survivors of a small hamlet, at the foot of Morambala, were in a state of starvation, having lost their food by one of his marauding parties. The women were in the fields collecting insects, roots, wild fruits, and whatever could be eaten, in order to drag on their lives, if possible, till the next crop should be ripe.

Two canoes passed us, that had been robbed by Mariano's band of everything they had in them; the owners were gathering palm-nuts for their subsistence. They wore palm-leaf aprons, as the robbers had stripped them of their clothing and ornaments. Dead bodies floated past us daily, and in the mornings the paddles had to be cleared of corpses, caught by the floats during the night. For scores of miles the entire population of the valley was swept away by this scourge Mariano, who is again, as he was before, the great Portuguese slave-agent. It made the heart ache to see the widespread desolation; the river-banks, once so populous, all silent; the villages burned down, and an oppressive stillness reigning where formerly crowds of eager sellers appeared with the various products of their industry. Here and there might be seen on the bank a small dreary deserted shed, where had sat, day after day, a starving fisherman, until the rising waters drove the fish from their wonted haunts, and left him to die. Tingane had been defeated; his people had been killed, kidnapped, and forced to flee from their villages. There were a few wretched survivors in a village above the Ruo; but the majority of the population was dead. The sight and smell of dead bodies was everywhere. Many skeletons lay beside the path, where in their weakness they had fallen and expired. Ghastly living forms of boys and girls, with dull dead eyes, were crouching beside some of the huts. A few more miserable days of their terrible hunger, and they would be with the dead.

Oppressed with the shocking scenes around, we visited the Bishop's grave; and though it matters little where a good Christian's ashes rest, yet it was with sadness that we thought over the hopes which had clustered around him, as he left the classic grounds of Cambridge, all now buried in this wild place. How it would have torn his kindly heart to witness the sights we now were forced to see!

In giving vent to the natural feelings of regret, that a man so eminently endowed and learned, as was Bishop Mackenzie, should have been so soon cut off, some have expressed an opinion that it was wrong to use an instrument so valuable *merely* to convert the heathen. If the attempt is to be made at all, it is "penny wise and pound foolish" to employ any but the very best men, and those who are specially educated for the work. An ordinary clergyman, however well suited for a parish, will not, without special training, make a Missionary; and as to their comparative usefulness, it is like that of the man who builds an hospital, as compared with that of the surgeon who in after years only administers for a time the remedies which the founder had provided in perpetuity. Had the Bishop succeeded in introducing Christianity, his converts might have been few, but they would have formed a continuous roll for all time to come.

The Shire fell two feet, before we reached the shallow crossing where we had formerly such difficulty, and we had now two ships to take up. A hippopotamus was shot two miles above a bank on which the ship lay a fortnight: it floated in three hours. As the boat was towing it down, the crocodiles were attracted by the dead beast, and several shots had to be fired to keep them off. The bullet had not entered the brain of the animal, but driven a splinter of bone into it. A little moisture with some gas issued from the wound, and this was all that could tell the crocodiles down the stream of a dead hippopotamus; and yet they came up from miles below. Their sense of smell must be as acute as their hearing; both are quite extraordinary. Dozens fed on the meat we left. Our Krooman, Jumbo, used to assert that the crocodile never eats fresh meat, but always keeps it till it is high and tender--and the stronger it smells the better he likes it. There seems to be some truth in this. They can swallow but small pieces at a time, and find it difficult to tear fresh meat. In the act of swallowing, which is like that of a dog, the head is raised out of the water. We tried to catch some, and one was soon hooked; it required half-a-dozen hands to haul him up the river, and the shark-hook straightened, and he got away. A large iron hook was next made, but, as the creatures could not swallow it, their jaws soon pressed it straight--and our crocodile-fishing was a failure. As one might expect,-- from the power even of a salmon--the tug of a crocodile was terribly strong.

The corpse of a boy floated past the ship; a monstrous crocodile rushed at it with the speed of a greyhound, caught it and shook it, as a terrier dog does a rat. Others dashed at the prey, each with his powerful tail causing the water to churn and froth, as he furiously tore off a piece. In a few seconds it was all gone. The sight was frightful to behold. The Shire swarmed with crocodiles; we counted sixty-seven of these repulsive reptiles on a single bank, but they are not as fierce as they are in some rivers. "Crocodiles," says Captain Tuckey, "are so plentiful in the Congo, near the rapids, and so frequently carry off the women, who at daylight go down to the river for water, that, while they are filling their calabashes, one of the party is usually employed in throwing large stones into the water outside." Here, either a calabash on a long pole is used in drawing water, or a fence is planted. The natives eat the crocodile, but to us the idea of tasting the musky-scented, fishy-looking flesh carried the idea of cannibalism. Humboldt remarks, that in South America the alligators of some rivers are more dangerous than in others. Alligators differ from crocodiles in the fourth or canine tooth going into a hole or socket in the upper jaw, while in the crocodile it fits into a notch. The forefoot of the crocodile has five toes not webbed, the hindfoot has four toes which are webbed; in the alligator the web is altogether wanting. They are so much alike that they would no doubt breed together.

One of the crocodiles which was shot had a piece snapped off the end of his tail, another had lost a forefoot in fighting; we saw actual leeches between the teeth, such as are mentioned by Herodotus, but we never witnessed the plover picking them out. Their greater fierceness in one part of the country than another is doubtless owing to a scarcity of fish; in fact, Captain Tuckey says, of that part of the Congo, mentioned above, "There are no fish here but catfish," and we found that the lake crocodiles, living in clear water, and with plenty of fish, scarcely ever attacked man. The Shire teems with fish of many different kinds. The only time, as already remarked, when its crocodiles are particularly to be dreaded, is when the river is in flood. Then the fish are driven from their usual haunts, and no game comes down to the river to drink, water being abundant in pools inland. Hunger now impels the crocodile to lie in wait for the women who come to draw water, and on the Zambesi numbers are carried off every year. The danger is not so great at other seasons; though it is never safe to bathe, or to stoop to drink, where one cannot see the bottom, especially in the evening. One of the Makololo ran down in the dusk of the river; and, as he was busy tossing the water to his mouth with his hand, in the manner peculiar to the natives, a crocodile rose suddenly from the bottom, and caught him by the hand. The limb of a tree was fortunately within reach, and he had presence of mind to lay hold of it. Both tugged and pulled; the crocodile for his dinner, and the man for dear life. For a time it appeared doubtful whether a dinner or a life was to be sacrificed; but the man held on, and the monster let the hand go, leaving the deep marks of his ugly teeth in it.

During our detention, in expectation of the permanent rise of the river in March, Dr. Kirk and Mr. C. Livingstone collected numbers of the wading- birds of the marshes--and made pleasant additions to our salted provisions, in geese, ducks, and hippopotamus flesh. One of the comb or knob-nosed geese, on being strangled in order to have its skin preserved without injury, continued to breathe audibly by the broken humerus, or wing-bone, and other means had to be adopted to put it out of pain. This was as if a man on the gallows were to continue to breathe by a broken armbone, and afforded us an illustration of the fact, that in birds, the vital air penetrates every part of the interior of their bodies. The breath passes through and round about the lungs--bathes the surfaces of the viscera, and enters the cavities of the bones; it even penetrates into some spaces between the muscles of the neck--and thus not only is the most perfect oxygenation of the blood secured, but, the temperature of the blood being very high, the air in every part is rarefied, and the great lightness and vigour provided for, that the habits of birds require. Several birds were found by Dr. Kirk to have marrow in the tibiae, though these bones are generally described as hollow.

During the period of our detention on the shallow part of the river in March, Mr. Thornton came up to us from Shupanga: he had, as before narrated, left the Expedition in 1859, and joined Baron van der Decken, in the journey to Kilimanjaro, when, by an ascent of the mountain to the height of 8000 feet, it was first proved to be covered with perpetual snow, and the previous information respecting it, given by the Church of England Missionaries, Krapf and Rebman, confirmed. It is now well known that the Baron subsequently ascended the Kilimanjaro to 14,000 feet, and ascertained its highest peak to be at least 20,000 feet above the sea. Mr. Thornton made the map of the first journey, at Shupanga, from materials collected when with the Baron; and when that work was accomplished, followed us. He was then directed to examine geologically the Cataract district, but not to expose himself to contact with the Ajawa until the feelings of that tribe should be ascertained.

The members of Bishop Mackenzie's party, on the loss of their head, fell back from Magomero on the highlands, to Chibisa's, in the low-lying Shire Valley; and Thornton, finding them suffering from want of animal food, kindly volunteered to go across thence to Tette, and bring a supply of goats and sheep. We were not aware of this step, to which the generosity of his nature prompted him, till two days after he had started. In addition to securing supplies for the Universities' Mission, he brought some for the Expedition, and took bearings, by which he hoped to connect his former work at Tette with the mountains in the Shire district. The toil of this journey was too much for his strength, as with the addition of great scarcity of water, it had been for that of Dr. Kirk and Rae, and he returned in a sadly haggard and exhausted condition; diarrhoea supervened, and that ended in dysentery and fever, which terminated fatally on the 21st of April, 1863. He received the unremitting attentions of Dr. Kirk, and Dr. Meller, surgeon of the "Pioneer," during the fortnight of his illness; and as he had suffered very little from fever, or any other disease, in Africa, we had entertained strong hopes that his youth and unimpaired constitution would have carried him through. During the night of the 20th his mind wandered so much, that we could not ascertain his last wishes; and on the morning of the 21st, to our great sorrow, he died. He was buried on the 22nd, near a large tree on the right bank of the Shire, about five hundred yards from the lowest of the Murchison Cataracts--and close to a rivulet, at which the "Lady Nyassa" and "Pioneer" lay.

No words can convey an adequate idea of the scene of widespread desolation which the once pleasant Shire Valley now presented. Instead of smiling villages and crowds of people coming with things for sale, scarcely a soul was to be seen; and, when by chance one lighted on a native, his frame bore the impress of hunger, and his countenance the look of a cringing broken-spiritedness. A drought had visited the land after the slave-hunting panic swept over it. Had it been possible to conceive the thorough depopulation which had ensued, we should have avoided coming up the river. Large masses of the people had fled down to the Shire, only anxious to get the river between them and their enemies. Most of the food had been left behind; and famine and starvation had cut off so many, that the remainder were too few to bury the dead. The corpses we saw floating down the river were only a remnant of those that had perished, whom their friends, from weakness, could not bury, nor over- gorged crocodiles devour. It is true that famine caused a great portion of this waste of human life: but the slave-trade must be deemed the chief agent in the ruin, because, as we were informed, in former droughts all the people flocked from the hills down to the marshes, which are capable of yielding crops of maize in less than three months, at any time of the year, and now they were afraid to do so. A few, encouraged by the Mission in the attempt to cultivate, had their little patches robbed as successive swarms of fugitives came from the hills. Who can blame these outcasts from house and home for stealing to save their wretched lives, or wonder that the owners protected the little all, on which their own lives depended, with club and spear? We were informed by Mr. Waller of the dreadful blight which had befallen the once smiling Shire Valley. His words, though strong, failed to impress us with the reality. In fact, they were received, as some may accept our own, as tinged with exaggeration; but when our eyes beheld the last mere driblets of this cup of woe, we for the first time felt that the enormous wrongs inflicted on our fellow-men by slaving are beyond exaggeration.

Wherever we took a walk, human skeletons were seen in every direction, and it was painfully interesting to observe the different postures in which the poor wretches had breathed their last. A whole heap had been thrown down a slope behind a village, where the fugitives often crossed the river from the east; and in one hut of the same village no fewer than twenty drums had been collected, probably the ferryman's fees. Many had ended their misery under shady trees--others under projecting crags in the hills--while others lay in their huts, with closed doors, which when opened disclosed the mouldering corpse with the poor rags round the loins--the skull fallen off the pillow--the little skeleton of the child, that had perished first, rolled up in a mat between two large skeletons. The sight of this desert, but eighteen months ago a well peopled valley, now literally strewn with human bones, forced the conviction upon us, that the destruction of human life in the middle passage, however great, constitutes but a small portion of the waste, and made us feel that unless the slave-trade--that monster iniquity, which has so long brooded over Africa--is put down, lawful commerce cannot be established.

We believed that, if it were possible to get a steamer upon the Lake, we could by her means put a check on the slavers from the East Coast; and aid more effectually still in the suppression of the slave-trade, by introducing, by way of the Rovuma, a lawful traffic in ivory. We therefore unscrewed the "Lady Nyassa" at a rivulet about five hundred yards below the first cataract, and began to make a road over the thirty- five or forty miles of land portage, by which to carry her up piecemeal. After mature consideration, we could not imagine a more noble work of benevolence, than thus to introduce light and liberty into a quarter of this fair earth, which human lust has converted into the nearest possible resemblance of what we conceive the infernal regions to be--and we sacrificed much of our private resources as an offering for the promotion of so good a cause.

The chief part of the labour of road-making consisted in cutting down trees and removing stones. The country being covered with open forest, a small tree had to be cut about every fifty or sixty yards. The land near the river was so very much intersected by ravines, that search had to be made, a mile from its banks, for more level ground. Experienced Hottentot drivers would have taken Cape wagons without any other trouble than that of occasionally cutting down a tree. No tsetse infested this district, and the cattle brought from Johanna flourished on the abundant pasture. The first half-mile of road led up, by a gradual slope, to an altitude of two hundred feet above the ship, and a sensible difference of climate was felt even there. For the remainder of the distance the height increased,--till, at the uppermost cataract, we were more than 1200 feet above the sea. The country here, having recovered from the effects of the drought, was bright with young green woodland, and mountains of the same refreshing hue. But the absence of the crowds, which had attended us as we carried up the boat, when the women followed us for miles with fine meal, vegetables, and fat fowls for sale, and the boys were ever ready for a little job--and the oppressive stillness bore heavily on our spirits. The Portuguese of Tette had very effectually removed our labourers. Not an ounce of fresh provisions could be obtained, except what could be shot, and even the food for our native crew had to be brought one hundred and fifty miles from the Zambesi.

The diet of salt provisions and preserved meats without vegetables, with the depression of spirits caused by seeing how effectually a few wretched convicts, aided by the connivance of officials, of whom better might have been hoped, could counteract our best efforts, and turn intended good to certain evil, brought on attacks of dysentery, which went the round of the Expedition--and, Dr. Kirk and Charles Livingstone having suffered most severely, it was deemed advisable that they should go home. This measure was necessary, though much to the regret of all--for having done so much, they were naturally anxious to be present, when, by the establishing ourselves on the Lake, all our efforts should be crowned with success. After it had been decided that these two officers, and all the whites who could be spared, should be sent down to the sea for a passage to England, Dr. Livingstone was seized in May with a severe attack of dysentery, which continued for a month, and reduced him to a shadow. Dr. Kirk kindly remained in attendance till the worst was passed. The parting took place on the 19th of May.

After a few miles of road were completed, and the oxen broken in, we resolved to try and render ourselves independent of the south for fresh provisions, by going in a boat up the Shire, above the Cataracts, to the tribes at the foot of Lake Nyassa, who were still untouched by the Ajawa invasion. In furtherance of this plan Dr. Livingstone and Mr. Rae determined to walk up to examine, and, if need be, mend the boat which had been left two seasons previously hung up to the limb of a large shady tree, before attempting to carry another past the Cataracts. The "Pioneer," which was to be left in charge of our active and most trustworthy gunner, Mr. Edward D. Young, R.N., was thoroughly roofed over with euphorbia branches and grass, so as completely to protect her decks from the sun: she also received daily a due amount of man-of-war scrubbing and washing; and, besides having everything put in shipshape fashion, was every evening swung out into the middle of the river, for the sake of the greater amount of air which circulated there. In addition to their daily routine work of the ship, the three stokers, one sailor, and one carpenter--now our complement--were encouraged to hunt for guinea-fowl, which in June, when the water inland is dried up, come in large flocks to the river's banks, and roost on the trees at night. Everything that can be done to keep mind and body employed tends to prevent fever.

While we were employed in these operations, some of the poor starved people about had been in the habit of crossing the river, and reaping the self-sown mapira, in the old gardens of their countrymen. In the afternoon of the 9th, a canoe came floating down empty, and shortly after a woman was seen swimming near the other side, which was about two hundred yards distant from us. Our native crew manned the boat, and rescued her; when brought on board, she was found to have an arrow-head, eight or ten inches long, in her back, below the ribs, and slanting up through the diaphragm and left lung, towards the heart--she had been shot from behind when stooping. Air was coming out of the wound, and, there being but an inch of the barbed arrow-head visible, it was thought better not to run the risk of her dying under the operation necessary for its removal; so we carried her up to her own hut. One of her relatives was less scrupulous, for he cut out the arrow and part of the lung. Mr. Young sent her occasionally portions of native corn, and strange to say found that she not only became well, but stout. The constitution of these people seems to have a wonderful power of self-repair--and it could be no slight privation which had cut off the many thousands that we saw dead around us.

We regretted that, in consequence of Dr. Meller having now sole medical charge, we could not have his company in our projected trip; but he found employment in botany and natural history, after the annual sickly season of March, April, and May was over; and his constant presence was not so much required at the ship. Later in the year, when he could be well spared, he went down the river to take up an appointment he had been offered in Madagascar; but unfortunately was so severely tried by illness while detained at the coast, that for nearly two years he was not able to turn his abilities as a naturalist to account by proceeding to that island. We have no doubt but he will yet distinguish himself in that untrodden field.

On the 16th of June we started for the Upper Cataracts, with a mule-cart, our road lying a distance of a mile west from the river. We saw many of the deserted dwellings of the people who formerly came to us; and were very much struck by the extent of land under cultivation, though that, compared with the whole country, is very small. Large patches of mapira continued to grow,--as it is said it does from the roots for three years. The mapira was mixed with tall bushes of the Congo-bean, castor-oil plants, and cotton. The largest patch of this kind we paced, and found it to be six hundred and thirty paces on one side--the rest were from one acre to three, and many not more than one-third of an acre. The cotton--of very superior quality--was now dropping off the bushes, to be left to rot--there was no one to gather what would have been of so much value in Lancashire. The huts, in the different villages we entered, were standing quite perfect. The mortars for pounding corn--the stones for grinding it--the water and beer pots--the empty corn-safes and kitchen utensils, were all untouched; and most of the doors were shut, as if the starving owners had gone out to wander in search of roots or fruits in the forest, and had never returned. When opened, several huts revealed a ghastly sight of human skeletons. Some were seen in such unnatural positions, as to give the idea that they had expired in a faint, when trying to reach something to allay the gnawings of hunger.

We took several of the men as far as the Mukuru-Madse for the sake of the change of air and for occupation, and also to secure for the ships a supply of buffalo meat--as those animals were reported to be in abundance on that stream. But though it was evident from the tracks that the report was true, it was impossible to get a glimpse of them. The grass being taller than we were, and pretty thickly planted, they always knew of our approach before we saw them. And the first intimation we had of their being near was the sound they made in rushing over the stones, breaking the branches, and knocking their horns against each other. Once, when seeking a ford for the cart, at sunrise, we saw a herd slowly wending up the hill-side from the water. Sending for a rifle, and stalking with intense eagerness for a fat beefsteak, instead of our usual fare of salted provisions, we got so near that we could hear the bulls uttering their hoarse deep low, but could see nothing except the mass of yellow grass in front; suddenly the buffalo-birds sounded their alarm-whistle, and away dashed the troop, and we got sight of neither birds nor beasts. This would be no country for a sportsman except when the grass is short. The animals are wary, from the dread they have of the poisoned arrows. Those of the natives who do hunt are deeply imbued with the hunting spirit, and follow the game with a stealthy perseverance and cunning, quite extraordinary. The arrow making no noise, the herd is followed up until the poison takes effect, and the wounded animal falls out. It is then patiently watched till it drops--a portion of meat round the wound is cut away, and all the rest eaten.

    Poisoned arrows are made in two pieces. An iron barb is firmly fastened to one end of a small wand of wood, ten inches or a foot long, the other end of which, fined down to a long point, is nicely fitted, though not otherwise secured, in the hollow of the reed, which forms the arrow shaft. The wood immediately below the iron head is smeared with the poison. When the arrow is shot into an animal, the reed either falls to the ground at once, or is very soon brushed off by the bushes; but the iron barb and poisoned upper part of the wood remain in the wound. If made in one piece, the arrow would often be torn out, head and all, by the long shaft catching in the underwood, or striking against trees. The poison used here, and called **kombi**, is obtained from a species of **strophanthus**, and is very virulent. Dr. Kirk found by an accidental experiment on himself that it acts by lowering the pulse. In using his tooth-brush, which had been in a pocket containing a little of the poison, he noticed a bitter taste, but attributed it to his having sometimes used, the handle in taking quinine. Though the quantity was small, it immediately showed its power by lowering his pulse which at the time had been raised by a cold, and next day he was perfectly restored. Not much can be inferred from a single case of this kind, but it is possible that the kombi may turn out a valuable remedy; and as Professor

Sharpey has conducted a series of experiments with this substance, we look with interest for the results. An alkaloid has been obtained from it similar to strychnine. There is no doubt that all kinds of wild animals die from the effects of poisoned arrows, except the elephant and hippopotamus. The amount of poison that this little weapon can convey into their systems being too small to kill those huge beasts, the hunters resort to the beam trap instead.

Another kind of poison was met with on Lake Nyassa, which was said to be used exclusively for killing men. It was put on small wooden arrow-heads, and carefully protected by a piece of maize-leaf tied round it. It caused numbness of the tongue when the smallest particle was tasted. The Bushmen of the northern part of the Kalahari were seen applying the entrails of a small caterpillar which they termed 'Nga to their arrows. This venom was declared to be so powerful in producing delirium, that a man in dying returned in imagination to a state of infancy, and would call for his mother's breast. Lions when shot with it are said to perish in agonies. The poisonous ingredient in this case may be derived from the plant on which the caterpillar feeds. It is difficult to conceive by what sort of experiments the properties of these poisons, known for generations, were proved. Probably the animal instincts, which have become so obtuse by civilization, that children in England eat the berries of the deadly nightshade (**Atropa belladonna**) without suspicion, were in the early uncivilized state much more keen. In some points instinct is still retained among savages. It is related that in the celebrated voyage of the French navigator, Bougainville, a young lady, who had assumed the male attire, performed all the hard duties incident to the calling of a common sailor; and, even as servant to the geologist, carried a bag of stones and specimens over hills and dales without a complaint, and without having her sex suspected by her associates; but on landing among the savages of one of the South Sea Islands, she was instantly recognized as a female. They began to show their impressions in a way that compelled her to confess her sex, and throw herself on the protection of the commander, which of course was granted. In like manner, the earlier portions of the human family may have had their instincts as to plants more highly developed than any of their descendants--if indeed much more knowledge than we usually suppose be not the effect of direct revelation from above.

The Mukuru-Madse has a deep rocky bed. The water is generally about four feet deep, and fifteen or twenty yards broad. Before reaching it, we passed five or six gullies; but beyond it the country, for two or three miles from the river, was comparatively smooth. The long grass was overrunning all the native paths, and one species (*sanu*), which has a sharp barbed seed a quarter of an inch in length, enters every pore of woollen clothing and highly irritates the skin. From its hard, sharp point a series of minute barbs are laid back, and give the seed a hold wherever it enters: the slightest touch gives it an entering motion, and the little hooks prevent its working out. These seeds are so abundant in some spots, that the inside of the stocking becomes worse than the roughest hair shirt. It is, however, an excellent self-sower, and fine fodder; it rises to the height of common meadow-grass in England, and would be a capital plant for spreading over a new country not so abundantly supplied with grasses as this is.

We have sometimes noticed two or three leaves together pierced through by these seeds, and thus made, as it were, into wings to carry them to any soil suited to their growth.

We always follow the native paths, though they are generally not more than fifteen inches broad, and so often have deep little holes in them, made for the purpose of setting traps for small animals, and are so much obscured by the long grass, that one has to keep one's eyes on the ground more than is pleasant. In spite, however, of all drawbacks, it is vastly more easy to travel on these tracks than to go straight over uncultivated ground, or virgin forest. A path usually leads to some village, though sometimes it turns out to be a mere game track leading nowhere.

In going north, we came into a part called Mpemba where Chibisa was owned as chief, but the people did not know that he had been assassinated by the Portuguese Terera. A great deal of grain was lying round the hut, where we spent the night. Very large numbers of turtledoves feasted undisturbed on the tall stalked mapira ears, and we easily secured plenty of fine fat guinea-fowls--now allowed to feed leisurely in the deserted gardens. The reason assigned for all this listless improvidence was "There are no women to grind the corn--all are dead."

The cotton patches in all cases seemed to have been so well cared for, and kept so free of weeds formerly, that, though now untended, but few weeds had sprung up; and the bushes were thus preserved in the annual grass burnings. Many baobab-trees grow in different spots, and the few people seen were using the white pulp found between the seeds to make a pleasant subacid drink.

On passing Malango, near the uppermost cataract, not a soul was to be seen; but, as we rested opposite a beautiful tree-covered island, the merry voices of children at play fell on our ears--the parents had fled thither for protection from the slave-hunting Ajawa, still urged on by the occasional visits of the Portuguese agents from Tette. The Ajawa, instead of passing below the Cataracts, now avoided us, and crossed over to the east side near to the tree on which we had hung the boat. Those of the Manganja, to whom we could make ourselves known, readily came to us; but the majority had lost all confidence in themselves, in each other, and in every one else. The boat had been burned about three months previously, and the Manganja were very anxious that we should believe that this had been the act of the Ajawa; but on scanning the spot we saw that it was more likely to have caught fire in the grass-burning of the country. Had we intended to be so long in returning to it, we should have hoisted it bottom upwards; for, as it was, it is probable that a quantity of dried leaves lay inside, and a spark ignited the whole. All the trees within fifty yards were scorched and killed, and the nails, iron, and copper sheathing, all lay undisturbed beneath. Had the Ajawa done the deed, they would have taken away the copper and iron.

Our hopes of rendering ourselves independent of the south for provisions, by means of this boat, being thus disappointed, we turned back with the intention of carrying another up to the same spot; and, in order to find level ground for this, we passed across from the Shire at Malango to the upper part of the stream Lesungwe. A fine, active, intelligent fellow, called Pekila, guided us, and was remarkable as almost the only one of the population left with any spirit in him. The depressing effect which the slave-hunting scourge has upon the native mind, though little to be wondered at, is sad, very sad to witness. Musical instruments, mats, pillows, mortars for pounding meal, were lying about unused, and becoming the prey of the white ants. With all their little comforts destroyed, the survivors were thrown still further back into barbarism.

It is of little importance perhaps to any but travellers to notice that in occupying one night a well-built hut, which had been shut up for some time, the air inside at once gave us a chill, and an attack of fever; both of which vanished when the place was well-ventilated by means of a fire. We have frequently observed that lighting a fire early in the mornings, even in the hottest time of the year, gives freshness to the whole house, and removes that feeling of closeness and langour, which a hot climate induces.

On the night of the 1st July, 1863, several loud peals of thunder awoke us; the moon was shining brightly, and not a cloud to be seen. All the natives remarked on the clearness of the sky at the time, and next morning said, "We thought it was God" (Morungo).

On arriving at the ship on the 2nd July, we found a despatch from Earl Russell, containing instructions for the withdrawal of the Expedition. The devastation caused by slave-hunting and famine lay all around. The labour had been as completely swept away from the Great Shire Valley, as it had been from the Zambesi, wherever Portuguese intrigue or power extended. The continual forays of Mariano had spread ruin and desolation on our south-east as far as Mount Clarendon.

While this was going on in our rear, the Tette slave-hunters from the West had stimulated the Ajawa to sweep all the Manganja off the hills on our East; and slaving parties for this purpose were still passing the Shire above the Cataracts. In addition to the confession of the Governor of Tette, of an intention to go on with this slaving in accordance with the counsel of his elder brother at Mosambique, we had reason to believe that slavery went on under the eye of his Excellency, the Governor-General himself; and this was subsequently corroborated by our recognizing two women at Mosambique who had lived within a hundred yards of the Mission-station at Magomero. They were well known to our attendants, and had formed a part of a gang of several hundreds taken to Mosambique by the Ajawa at the very time when his Excellency was entertaining English officers with anti-slavery palavers. To any one who understands how minute the information is, which Portuguese governors possess by means of their own slaves, and through gossiping traders who seek to curry their favour, it is idle to assert that all this slaving goes on without their approval and connivance.

If more had been wanted to prove the hopelessness of producing any change in the system which has prevailed ever since our allies, the Portuguese, entered the country, we had it in the impunity with which the freebooter, Terera, who had murdered Chibisa, was allowed to carry on his forays. Belchoir, another marauder, had been checked, but was still allowed to make war, as they term slave-hunting.

Mr. Horace Waller was living for some five months on Mount Morambala, a position from which the whole process of the slave-trade, and depopulation of the country around could be well noted. The mountain overlooks the Shire, the beautiful meanderings of which are distinctly seen, on clear days, for thirty miles. This river was for some time supposed to be closed against Mariano, who, as a mere matter of form, was declared a rebel against the Portuguese flag. When, however, it became no longer possible to keep up the sham, the river was thrown open to him; and Mr. Waller has seen in a single day from fifteen to twenty canoes of different sizes going down, laden with slaves, to the Portuguese settlements from the so-called rebel camp. These cargoes were composed entirely of women and children. For three months this traffic was incessant, and at last, so completely was the mask thrown off, that one of the officials came to pay a visit to Bishop Tozer on another part of the same mountain, and, combining business with pleasure, collected payment for some canoe work done for the Missionary party, and with this purchased slaves from the rebels, who had only to be hailed from the bank of the river. When he had concluded the bargain he trotted the slaves out for inspection in Mr. Waller's presence. This official, Senhor Mesquita, was the only officer who could be forced to live at the Kongone. From certain circumstances in his life, he had fallen under the power of the local Government; all the other Custom-house officers refused to go to Kongone, so here poor Mesquita must live on a miserable pittance--must live, and perhaps slave, sorely against his will. His name is not brought forward with a view of throwing any odium on his character. The disinterested kindness which he showed to Dr. Meller, and others, forbids that he should be mentioned by us with anything like unkindness.

Under all these considerations, with the fact that we had not found the Rovuma so favourable for navigation at the time of our visit as we expected, it was impossible not to coincide in the wisdom of our withdrawal; but we deeply regretted that we had ever given credit to the Portuguese Government for any desire to ameliorate the condition of the African race; for, with half the labour and expense anywhere else, we should have made an indelible mark of improvement on a section of the Continent. Viewing Portuguese statesmen in the light of the laws they have passed for the suppression of slavery and the slave-trade, and by the standard of the high character of our own public men, it cannot be considered weakness to have believed in the sincerity of the anxiety to aid our enterprise, professed by the Lisbon Ministry. We hoped to benefit both Portuguese and Africans by introducing free-trade and Christianity. Our allies, unfortunately, cannot see the slightest benefit in any measure that does not imply raising themselves up by thrusting others down. The official paper of the Lisbon Government has since let us know "that their policy was directed to frustrating the grasping designs of the British Government to the dominion of Eastern Africa." We, who were on the spot, and behind the scenes, knew that feelings of private benevolence had the chief share in the operations undertaken for introducing the reign of peace and good will on the Lakes and central regions, which for ages have been the abodes of violence and bloodshed. But that great change was not to be accomplished. The narrow-minded would ascribe all that was attempted to the grasping propensity of the English. But the motives that actuate many in England, both in public and private life, are much more noble than the world gives them credit for.

Seeing, then, that we were not yet arrived at "the good time coming," and that it was quite impossible to take the "Pioneer" down to the sea till the floods of December, we made arrangements to screw the "Lady Nyassa" together; and, in order to improve the time intervening, we resolved to carry a boat past the Cataracts a second time, sail along the eastern shore of the Lake, and round the northern end, and also collect data by which to verify the information collected by Colonel Rigby, that the 19,000 slaves, who go through the Custom-house of Zanzibar annually, are chiefly drawn from Lake Nyassa and the Valley of the Shire.

Our party consisted of twenty natives, some of whom were Johanna men, and were supposed to be capable of managing the six oxen which drew the small wagon with a boat on it. A team of twelve Cape oxen, with a Hottentot driver and leader, would have taken the wagon over the country we had to pass through with the greatest ease; but no sooner did we get beyond the part of the road already made, than our drivers encountered obstructions in the way of trees and gullies, which it would have been a waste of time to have overcome by felling timber and hauling out the wagon by block and tackle purchases. The Ajawa and Manganja settled at Chibisa's were therefore sent for, and they took the boat on their shoulders and carried it briskly, in a few days, past all the Cataracts except one; then coming to a comparatively still reach of the river, they took advantage of it to haul her up a couple of miles. The Makololo had her then entirely in charge; for, being accustomed to rapids in their own country, no better boatmen could be desired. The river here is very narrow, and even in what are called still places, the current is very strong, and often obliged them to haul the boat along by the reeds on the banks, or to hand a tow-rope ashore. The reeds are full of cowitch (***Dolichos pruriens***), the pods of which are covered with what looks a fine velvety down, but is in reality a multitude of fine prickles, which go in by the million, and caused an itching and stinging in the naked bodies of those who were pulling the tow-rope, that made them wriggle as if stung by a whole bed of nettles. Those on board required to be men of ready resource with oars and punting-poles, and such they were. But, nevertheless, they found, after attempting to pass by a rock, round which the water rushed in whirls, that the wiser plan would be to take the boat ashore, and carry her past the last Cataract. When this was reported, the carriers were called from the various shady trees under which they had taken refuge from the sun. This was midwinter, but the sun is always hot by day here, though the nights are cold. Five Zambesi men, who had been all their lives accustomed to great heavy canoes,--the chief recommendation of which is said to be, that they can be run against a rock with the full force of the current without injury--were very desirous to show how much better they could manage our boat than the Makololo; three jumped into her when our backs were turned, and two hauled her up a little way; the tide caught her bow, we heard a shout of distress, the rope was out of their hands in a moment, and there she was, bottom upwards; a turn or two in an eddy, and away she went, like an arrow, down the Cataracts. One of the men in swimming ashore saved a rifle. The whole party ran with all their might along the bank, but never more did we see our boat.

The five performers in this catastrophe approached with penitential looks. They had nothing to say, nor had we. They bent down slowly, and touched our feet with both hands. "Ku kuata moendo"--"to catch the foot"--is their way of asking forgiveness. It was so like what we have seen a little child do--try to bring a dish unbidden to its papa, and letting it fall, burst into a cry of distress--that they were only sentenced to go back to the ship, get provisions, and, in the ensuing journey on foot, carry as much as they could, and thus make up for the loss of the boat.

It was excessively annoying to lose all this property, and be deprived of the means of doing the work proposed, on the east and north of the Lake; but it would have been like crying over spilt milk to do otherwise now than make the best use we could of our legs. The men were sent back to the ship for provisions, cloth, and beads; and while they are gone, we may say a little of the Cataracts which proved so fatal to our boating plan.

CHAPTER XIII.

Dr. Livingstone's further explorations--Effects of slave-trade--Kirk's range--Ajawa migration--Native fishermen--Arab slave-crossing--Splendid highlands.

The Murchison Cataracts of the Shire river begin in 15 degrees 20 minutes S., and end in lat. 15 degrees 55 minutes S., the difference of latitude is therefore 35 minutes. The river runs in this space nearly north and south, till we pass Malango; so the entire distance is under 40 miles. The principal Cataracts are five in number, and are called Pamofunda or Pamozima, Morewa, Panoreba or Tedzane, Pampatamanga, and Papekira. Besides these, three or four smaller ones might be mentioned; as, for instance, Mamvira, where in our ascent we first met the broken water, and heard that gushing sound which, from the interminable windings of some 200 miles of river below, we had come to believe the tranquil Shire could never make. While these lesser cataracts descend at an angle of scarcely 20 degrees, the greater fall 100 feet in 100 yards, at an angle of about 45 degrees, and one at an angle of 70 degrees. One part of Pamozima is perpendicular, and, when the river is in flood, causes a cloud of vapour to ascend, which, in our journey to Lake Shirwa, we saw at a distance of at least eight miles. The entire descent from the Upper to the Lower Shire is 1200 feet. Only on one spot in all that distance is the current moderate--namely, above Tedzane. The rest is all rapid, and much of it being only fifty or eighty yards wide, and rushing like a mill-race, it gives the impression of water-power, sufficient to drive all the mills in Manchester, running to waste. Pamofunda, or Pamozima, has a deep shady grove on its right bank. When we were walking alone through its dark shade, we were startled by a shocking smell like that of a dissecting-room; and on looking up saw dead bodies in mats suspended from the branches of the trees, a mode of burial somewhat similar to that which we subsequently saw practised by the Parsees in their "towers of silence" at Poonah, near Bombay. The name Pamozima means, "the departed spirits or gods"--a fit name for a place over which, according to the popular belief, the disembodied souls continually hover.

The rock lowest down in the series is dark reddish-grey syenite. This seems to have been an upheaving agent, for the mica schists above it are much disturbed. Dark trappean rocks full of hornblende have in many places burst through these schists, and appear in nodules on the surface. The highest rock seen is a fine sandstone of closer grain than that at Tette, and quite metamorphosed where it comes into contact with the igneous rocks below it. It sometimes gives place to quartz and reddish clay schists, much baked by heat. This is the usual geological condition on the right bank of the Cataracts. On the other side we pass over masses of porphyritic trap, in contact with the same mica schists, and these probably give to the soil the great fertility we observed. The great body of the mountains is syenite. So much mica is washed into the river, that on looking attentively on the stream one sees myriads of particles floating and glancing in the sun; and this, too, even at low water.

It was the 15th of August before the men returned from the ship, accompanied by Mr. Rae and the steward of the "Pioneer." They brought two oxen, one of which was instantly slaughtered to put courage into all hearts, and some bottles of wine, a present from Waller and Alington. We never carried wine before, but this was precious as an expression of kindheartedness on the part of the donors. If one attempted to carry either wine or spirits, as a beverage, he would require a whole troop of followers for nothing else. Our greatest luxury in travelling was tea or coffee. We never once carried sugar enough to last a journey, but coffee is always good, while the sugarless tea is only bearable, because of the unbearable gnawing feeling of want and sinking which ensues if we begin to travel in the mornings without something warm in the stomach. Our drink generally was water, and if cool, nothing can equal it in a hot climate. We usually carried a bottle of brandy rolled up in our blankets, but that was used only as a medicine; a spoonful in hot water before going to bed, to fend off a chill and fever. Spirits always do harm, if the fever has fairly begun; and it is probable that brandy-and- water has to answer for a good many of the deaths in Africa.

Mr. Rae had made gratifying progress in screwing together the "Lady Nyassa." He had the zealous co-operation of three as fine steady workmen as ever handled tools; and, as they were noble specimens of English sailors, we would fain mention the names of men who are an honour to the British navy--John Reid, John Pennell, and Richard Wilson. The reader will excuse our doing so, but we desire to record how much they were esteemed, and how thankful we felt for their good behaviour. The weather was delightfully cool; and, with full confidence in those left behind, it was with light hearts we turned our faces north. Mr. Rae accompanied us a day in front; and, as all our party had earnestly advised that at least two Europeans should be associated together on the journey, the steward was at the last moment taken. Mr. Rae returned to get the "Lady Nyassa" ready for sea; and, as she drew less water than the "Pioneer," take her down to the ocean in October. One reason for taking the steward is worth recording. Both he and a man named King, {5} who, though only a leading stoker in the Navy, had been a promising student in the University of Aberdeen, had got into that weak bloodless-looking state which residence in the lowlands without much to do or think about often induces. The best thing for this is change and an active life. A couple of days' march only as far as the Mukuru-Madse, infused so much vigour into King that he was able to walk briskly back. Consideration for the steward's health led to his being selected for this northern journey, and the measure was so completely successful that it was often, in the hard march, a subject of regret that King had not been taken too. A removal of only a hundred yards is sometimes so beneficial that it ought in severe cases never to be omitted.

Our object now was to get away to the N.N.W., proceed parallel with Lake Nyassa, but at a considerable distance west of it, and thus pass by the Mazitu or Zulus near its northern end without contact--ascertain whether any large river flowed into the Lake from the west--visit Lake Moelo, if time permitted, and collect information about the trade on the great slave route, which crosses the Lake at its southern end, and at Tsenga and Kota-kota. The Makololo were eager to travel fast, because they wanted to be back in time to hoe their fields before the rains, and also because their wives needed looking after.

In going in the first instance N.E. from the uppermost Cataract, we followed in a measure the great bend of the river towards the foot of Mount Zomba. Here we had a view of its most imposing side, the west, with the plateau some 3000 feet high, stretching away to its south, and Mounts Chiradzuru and Mochiru towering aloft to the sky. From that goodly highland station, it was once hoped by the noble Mackenzie, who, for largeness of heart and loving disposition, really deserved to be called the "Bishop of Central Africa," that light and liberty would spread to all the interior. We still think it may be a centre for civilizing influences; for any one descending from these cool heights, and stepping into a boat on the Upper Shire, can sail three hundred miles without a check into the heart of Africa.

We passed through a tract of country covered with mopane trees, where the hard baked soil refused to let the usual thick crops of grass grow; and here we came upon very many tracks of buffaloes, elephants, antelopes, and the spoor of one lion. An ox we drove along with us, as provision for the way, was sorely bitten by the tsetse. The effect of the bite was, as usual, quite apparent two days afterwards, in the general flaccidity of the muscles, the drooping ears, and looks of illness. It always excited our wonder that we, who were frequently much bitten too by the same insects, felt no harm from their attacks. Man shares the immunity of the wild animals.

Finding a few people on the evening of the 20th of August, who were supporting a wretched existence on tamarinds and mice, we ascertained that there was no hope of our being able to buy food anywhere nearer than the Lakelet Pamalombe, where the Ajawa chief, Kainka, was now living; but that plenty could be found with the Maravi female chief, Nyango. We turned away north-westwards, and struck the stream Ribve-ribve, or Rivi- rivi, which rises in the Maravi range, and flows into the Shire.

As the Rivi-rivi came from the N.W. we continued to travel along its banks, until we came to people who had successfully defended themselves against the hordes of the Ajawa. By employing the men of one village to go forward and explain who we were to the next, we managed to prevent the frightened inhabitants from considering us a fresh party of Ajawa, or of Portuguese slaving agents. Here they had cultivated maize, and were willing to sell, but no persuasion could induce them to give us guides to the chieftainess, Nyango. They evidently felt that we were not to be trusted; though, as we had to certify to our own character, our companions did not fail "to blow our own trumpet," with blasts in which modesty was quite out of the question. To allay suspicion, we had at last to refrain from mentioning the lady's name.

It would be wearisome to repeat the names of the villages we passed on our way to the north-west. One was the largest we ever saw in Africa, and quite deserted, with the usual sad sight of many skeletons lying about. Another was called Tette. We know three places of this name, which fact shows it to be a native word; it seems to mean a place where the water rushes over rocks. A third village was called Chipanga (a great work), a name identical with the Shupanga of the Portuguese. This repetition of names may indicate that the same people first took these epithets in their traditional passage from north to south.

At this season of the year the nights are still cold, and the people, having no crops to occupy their attention, do not stir out till long after the sun is up. At other times they are off to their fields before the day dawns, and the first sound one hears is the loud talking of men and women, in which they usually indulge in the dark to scare off beasts by the sound of the human voice. When no work is to be done, the first warning of approaching day is the hemp-smoker's loud ringing cough.

Having been delayed one morning by some negotiation about guides, who were used chiefly to introduce us to other villages, we two whites walked a little way ahead, taking the direction of the stream. The men having been always able to find out our route by the prints of our shoes, we went on for a number of miles. This time, however, they lost our track, and failed to follow us. The path was well marked by elephants, hyenas, pallahs, and zebras, but for many a day no human foot had trod it. When the sun went down a deserted hamlet was reached, where we made comfortable beds for ourselves of grass. Firing muskets to attract the attention of those who have strayed is the usual resource in these cases. On this occasion the sound of firearms tended to mislead us; for, hearing shots next morning, a long weary march led us only to some native hunters, who had been shooting buffaloes. Returning to a small village, we met with some people who remembered our passing up to the Lake in the boat; they were as kind as they could be. The only food they possessed was tamarinds, prepared with ashes, and a little cowitch meal. The cowitch, as mentioned before, has a velvety brown covering of minute prickles, which, if touched, enter the pores of the skin and cause a painful tingling. The women in times of scarcity collect the pods, kindle a fire of grass over them to destroy the prickles, then steep the beans till they begin to sprout, wash them in pure water, and either boil them or pound them into meal, which resembles our bean-meal. This plant climbs up the long grass, and abounds in all reedy parts, and, though a plague to the traveller who touches its pods, it performs good service in times of famine by saving many a life from starvation. Its name here is Kitedzi.

Having travelled at least twenty miles in search of our party that day, our rest on a mat in the best hut of the village was very sweet. We had dined the evening before on a pigeon each, and had eaten only a handful of kitedzi porridge this afternoon. The good wife of the village took a little corn which she had kept for seed, ground it after dark, and made it into porridge. This, and a cup of wild vegetables of a sweetish taste for a relish, a little boy brought in and put down, with several vigorous claps of his hands, in the manner which is esteemed polite, and which is strictly enjoined on all children.

On the third day of separation, Akosanjere, the headman of this village, conducted us forward to our party who had gone on to Nseze, a district to the westward. This incident is mentioned, not for any interest it possesses, apart from the idea of the people it conveys. We were completely separated from our men for nearly three days, and had nothing wherewith to purchase food. The people were sorely pressed by famine and war, and their hospitality, poor as it was, did them great credit, and was most grateful to us. Our own men had become confused and wandered, but had done their utmost to find us; on our rejoining them, the ox was slain, and all, having been on short commons, rejoiced in this "day of slaughter." Akosanjere was, of course, rewarded to his heart's content.

As we pursued our way, we came close up to a range of mountains, the most prominent peak of which is called Mvai. This is a great, bare, rounded block of granite shooting up from the rest of the chain. It and several other masses of rock are of a light grey colour, with white patches, as if of lichens; the sides and summits are generally thinly covered with rather scraggy trees. There are several other prominent peaks--one, for instance, still further north, called Chirobve. Each has a name, but we could never ascertain that there was an appellation which applied to the whole. This fact, and our wish to commemorate the name of Dr. Kirk, induced us afterwards, when we could not discover a particular peak mentioned to us formerly as Molomo-ao-koku, or Cock's-bill, to call the whole chain from the west of the Cataracts up to the north end of the Lake, "Kirk's Range." The part we slept at opposite Mvai was named Paudio, and was evidently a continuation of the district of one of our stations on the Shire, at which observations for latitude were formerly taken.

Leaving Paudio, we had Kirk's Range close on our left and at least 3000 feet above us, and probably not less than 5000 feet above the sea. Far to our right extended a long green wooded country rising gradually up to a ridge, ornamented with several detached mountains, which bounded the Shire Valley. In front, northwards, lay a valley as rich and lovely as we ever saw anywhere, terminating at the mountains, which, stretched away some thirty miles beyond our range of vision and ended at Cape Maclear. The groups of trees had never been subjected to the landscape gardener's art; but had been cut down mercilessly, just as suited the convenience of the cultivator; yet the various combinations of open forest, sloping woodland, grassy lawns, and massive clumps of dark green foliage along the running streams, formed as beautiful a landscape as could be seen on the Thames. This valley is named Goa or Gova, and as we moved through it we found that what was smooth to the eye was very much furrowed by running streams winding round innumerable knolls. These little brooklets came down from the range on our left, and the water was deliciously cool.

When we came abreast of the peak Chirobve, the people would no longer give us guides. They were afraid of their enemies, whose dwellings we now had on our east; and, proceeding without any one to lead us, or to introduce us to the inhabitants, we were perplexed by all the paths running zigzag across instead of along the valley. They had been made by the villagers going from the hamlets on the slopes to their gardens in the meadows below. To add to our difficulties, the rivulets and mountain- torrents had worn gullies some thirty or forty feet deep, with steep sides that could not be climbed except at certain points. The remaining inhabitants on the flank of the range when they saw strangers winding from side to side, and often attempting to cross these torrent beds at impossible places, screamed out their shrill war-alarm, and made the valley ring with their wild outcries. It was war, and war alone, and we were too deep down in the valley to make our voices heard in explanation. Fortunately, they had burned off the long grass to a great extent. It only here and there hid them from us. Selecting an open spot, we spent a night regarded by all around us as slave-hunters, but were undisturbed, though the usual way of treating an enemy in this part of the country is by night attack.

The nights at the altitude of the valley were cool, the lowest temperature shown being 37 degrees; at 9 a.m. and 9 p.m. it was 58 degrees, about the average temperature of the day; at mid-day 82 degrees, and sunset 70 degrees. Our march was very much hindered by the imperfectly burned corn and grass stalks having fallen across the paths. To a reader in England this will seem a very small obstacle. But he must fancy the grass stems as thick as his little finger, and the corn-stalks like so many walkingsticks lying in one direction, and so supporting each other that one has to lift his feet up as when wading through deep high heather. The stems of grass showed the causes of certain explosions as loud as pistols, which are heard when the annual fires come roaring over the land. The heated air inside expanding bursts the stalk with a loud report, and strews the fragments on the ground.

A very great deal of native corn had been cultivated here, and we saw buffaloes feeding in the deserted gardens, and some women, who ran away very much faster than the beasts did.

On the 29th, seeing some people standing under a tree by a village, we sat down, and sent Masego, one of our party, to communicate. The headman, Matunda, came back with him, bearing a calabash with water for us. He said that all the people had fled from the Ajawa, who had only just desisted from their career of pillage on being paid five persons as a fine for some offence for which they had commenced the invasion. Matunda had plenty of grain to sell, and all the women were soon at work grinding it into meal. We secured an abundant supply, and four milk goats. The Manganja goat is of a very superior breed to the general African animal, being short in the legs and having a finely-shaped broad body. By promising the Makololo that, when we no longer needed the milk, they should have the goats to improve the breed of their own at home, they were induced to take the greatest possible care of both goats and kids in driving and pasturing.

After leaving Matunda, we came to the end of the highland valley; and, before descending a steep declivity of a thousand feet towards the part which may be called the heel of the Lake, we had the bold mountains of Cape Maclear on our right, with the blue water at their base, the hills of Tsenga in the distance in front, and Kirk's Range on our left, stretching away northwards, and apparently becoming lower. As we came down into a fine rich undulating valley, many perennial streams running to the east from the hills on our left were crossed, while all those behind us on the higher ground seemed to unite in one named Lekue, which flowed into the Lake.

After a long day's march in the valley of the Lake, where the temperature was very much higher than in that we had just left, we entered the village of Katosa, which is situated on the bank of a stream among gigantic timber trees, and found there a large party of Ajawa--Waiau, they called themselves--all armed with muskets. We sat down among them, and were soon called to the chiefs court, and presented with an ample mess of porridge, buffalo meat, and beer. Katosa was more frank than any Manganja chief we had met, and complimented us by saying that "we must be his 'Bazimo' (good spirits of his ancestors); for when he lived at Pamalombe, we lighted upon him from above--men the like of whom he had never seen before, and coming he knew not whence." He gave us one of his own large and clean huts to sleep in; and we may take this opportunity of saying that the impression we received, from our first journey on the hills among the villages of Chisunse, of the excessive dirtiness of the Manganja, was erroneous. This trait was confined to the cool highlands. Here crowds of men and women were observed to perform their ablutions daily in the stream that ran past their villages; and this we have observed elsewhere to be a common custom with both Manganja and Ajawa.

Before we started on the morning of the 1st September, Katosa sent an enormous calabash of beer, containing at least three gallons, and then came and wished us to "stop a day and eat with him." On explaining to him the reasons for our haste, he said that he was in the way by which travellers usually passed, he never stopped them in their journeys, but would like to look at us for a day. On our promising to rest a little with him on our return, he gave us about two pecks of rice, and three guides to conduct us to a subordinate female chief, Nkwinda, living on the borders of the Lake in front.

The Ajawa, from having taken slaves down to Quillimane and Mosambique, knew more of us than Katosa did. Their muskets were carefully polished, and never out of these slaver's hands for a moment, though in the chiefs presence. We naturally felt apprehensive that we should never see Katosa again. A migratory afflatus seems to have come over the Ajawa tribes. Wars among themselves, for the supply of the Coast slave-trade, are said to have first set them in motion. The usual way in which they have advanced among the Manganja has been by slave-trading in a friendly way. Then, professing to wish to live as subjects, they have been welcomed as guests, and the Manganja, being great agriculturists, have been able to support considerable bodies of these visitors for a time. When the provisions became scarce, the guests began to steal from the fields; quarrels arose in consequence, and, the Ajawa having firearms, their hosts got the worst of it, and were expelled from village after village, and out of their own country. The Manganja were quite as bad in regard to slave-trading as the Ajawa, but had less enterprise, and were much more fond of the home pursuits of spinning, weaving, smelting iron, and cultivating the soil, than of foreign travel. The Ajawa had little of a mechanical turn, and not much love for agriculture, but were very keen traders and travellers. This party seemed to us to be in the first or friendly stage of intercourse with Katosa; and, as we afterwards found, he was fully alive to the danger.

Our course was shaped towards the N.W., and we traversed a large fertile tract of rich soil extensively cultivated, but dotted with many gigantic thorny acacias which had proved too large for the little axes of the cultivators. After leaving Nkwinda, the first village we spent a night at in the district Ngabi was that of Chembi, and it had a stockade around it. The Azitu or Mazitu were said to be ravaging the country to the west of us, and no one was safe except in a stockade. We have so often, in travelling, heard of war in front, that we paid little attention to the assertion of Chembi, that the whole country to the N.W. was in flight before these Mazitu, under a chief with the rather formidable name of Mowhiriwhiri; we therefore resolved to go on to Chinsamba's, still further in the same direction, and hear what he said about it.

The only instrument of husbandry here is the short-handled hoe; and about Tette the labour of tilling the soil, as represented in the woodcut, is performed entirely by female slaves. On the West Coast a double-handled hoe is employed. Here the small hoe is seen in the hands of both men and women. In other parts of Africa a hoe with a handle four feet long is used, but the plough is quite unknown.

In illustration of the manner in which the native knowledge of agriculture strikes an honest intelligent observer, it may be mentioned that the first time good Bishop Mackenzie beheld how well the fields of the Manganja were cultivated on the hills, he remarked to Dr. Livingstone, then his fellow-traveller--"When telling the people in England what were my objects in going out to Africa, I stated that, among other things, I meant to teach these people agriculture; but I now see that they know far more about it than I do." This, we take it, was an honest straightforward testimony, and we believe that every unprejudiced witness, who has an opportunity of forming an opinion of Africans who have never been debased by slavery, will rank them very much higher in the scale of intelligence, industry, and manhood, than others who know them only in a state of degradation.

On coming near Chinsamba's two stockades, on the banks of the Lintipe, we were told that the Mazitu had been repulsed there the day before, and we had evidence of the truth of the report of the attack in the sad sight of the bodies of the slain. The Zulus had taken off large numbers of women laden with corn; and, when driven back, had cut off the ears of a male prisoner, as a sort of credential that he had been with the Mazitu, and with grim humour sent him to tell Chinsamba "to take good care of the corn in the stockades, for they meant to return for it in a month or two."

Chinsamba's people were drumming with might and main on our arrival, to express their joy at their deliverance from the Mazitu. The drum is the chief instrument of music among the Manganja, and with it they express both their joy and grief. They excel in beating time. Chinsamba called us into a very large hut, and presented us with a huge basket of beer. The glare of sunlight from which we had come enabled him, in diplomatic fashion, to have a good view of us before our eyes became enough accustomed to the dark inside to see him. He has a Jewish cast of countenance, or rather the ancient Assyrian face, as seen in the monuments brought to the British Museum by Mr. Layard. This form of face is very common in this country, and leads to the belief that the true type of the negro is not that met on the West Coast, from which most people have derived their ideas of the African.

Chinsamba had many Abisa or Babisa in his stockade, and it was chiefly by the help of their muskets that he had repulsed the Mazitu: these Babisa are great travellers and traders.

We liked Chinsamba very well, and found that he was decidedly opposed to our risking our lives by going further to the N.W. The Mazitu were believed to occupy all the hills in that direction, so we spent the 4th of September with him.

It is rather a minute thing to mention, and it will only be understood by those who have children of their own, but the cries of the little ones, in their infant sorrows, are the same in tone, at different ages, here as all over the world. We have been perpetually reminded of home and family by the wailings which were once familiar to parental ears and heart, and felt thankful that to the sorrows of childhood our children would never have superadded the heartrending woes of the slave-trade.

Taking Chinsamba's advice to avoid the Mazitu in their marauding, we started on the 5th September away to the N.E., and passed mile after mile of native corn-fields, with an occasional cotton-patch.

After a long march, we passed over a waterless plain about N.N.W. of the hills of Tsenga to a village on the Lake, and thence up its shores to Chitanda. The banks of the Lake were now crowded with fugitives, who had collected there for the poor protection which the reeds afforded. For miles along the water's edge was one continuous village of temporary huts. The people had brought a little corn with them; but they said, "What shall we eat when that is done? When we plant corn, the wild beasts (Zinyama, as they call the Mazitu) come and take it. When we plant cassava, they do the same. How are we to live?" A poor blind woman, thinking we were Mazitu, rushed off in front of us with outspread arms, lifting the feet high, in the manner peculiar to those who have lost their sight, and jumped into the reeds of a stream for safety.

In our way along the shores we crossed several running rivulets of clear cold water, which, from having reeds at their confluences, had not been noticed in our previous exploration in the boat. One of these was called Mokola, and another had a strong odour of sulphuretted hydrogen. We reached Molamba on the 8th September, and found our old acquaintance, Nkomo, there still. One of the advantages of travelling along the shores of the Lake was, that we could bathe anywhere in its clear fresh water. To us, who had been obliged so often to restrain our inclination in the Zambesi and Shire for fear of crocodiles, this was pleasant beyond measure. The water now was of the same temperature as it was on our former visit, or 72 degrees Fahr. The immense depth of the Lake prevents the rays of the sun from raising the temperature as high as that of the Shire and Zambesi; and the crocodiles, having always clear water in the Lake, and abundance of fish, rarely attack man; many of these reptiles could be seen basking on the rocks.

A day's march beyond Molamba brought us to the lakelet Chia, which lies parallel with the Lake. It is three or four miles long, by from one to one and a half broad, and communicates with the Lake by an arm of good depth, but with some rocks in it. As we passed up between the Lake and the eastern shore of this lakelet, we did not see any streams flowing into it. It is quite remarkable for the abundance of fish; and we saw upwards of fifty large canoes engaged in the fishery, which is carried on by means of hand-nets with side-frame poles about seven feet long. These nets are nearly identical with those now in use in Normandy--the difference being that the African net has a piece of stick lashed across the handle-ends of the side poles to keep them steady, which is a great improvement. The fish must be very abundant to be scooped out of the water in such quantities as we saw, and by so many canoes. There is quite a trade here in dried fish.

The country around is elevated, undulating, and very extensively planted with cassava. The hoe in use has a handle of four feet in length, and the iron part is exactly of the same form as that in the country of the Bechuanas. The baskets here, which are so closely woven together as to hold beer, are the same with those employed to hold milk in Kaffirland--a thousand miles distant.

Marching on foot is peculiarly conducive to meditation--one is glad of any subject to occupy the mind, and relieve the monotony of the weary treadmill-like trudge-trudging. This Chia net brought to our mind that the smith's bellows made here of a goatskin bag, with sticks along the open ends, are the same as those in use in the Bechuana country far to the south-west. These, with the long-handled hoe, may only show that each successive horde from north to south took inventions with it from the same original source. Where that source may have been is probably indicated by another pair of bellows, which we observed below the Victoria Falls, being found in Central India and among the Gipsies of Europe.

Men in remote times may have had more highly-developed instincts, which enabled them to avoid or use poisons; but the late Archbishop Whately has proved, that wholly untaught savages never could invent anything, or even subsist at all. Abundant corroboration of his arguments is met with in this country, where the natives require but little in the way of clothing, and have remarkably hardy stomachs. Although possessing a knowledge of all the edible roots and fruits in the country, having hoes to dig with, and spears, bows, and arrows to kill the game,-

-we have seen that, notwithstanding all these appliances and means to boot, they have perished of absolute starvation.

The art of making fire is the same in India as in Africa. The smelting furnaces, for reducing iron and copper from the ores, are also similar. Yellow haematite, which bears not the smallest resemblance either in colour or weight to the metal, is employed near Kolobeng for the production of iron. Malachite, the precious green stone used in civilized life for vases, would never be suspected by the uninstructed to be a rich ore of copper, and yet it is extensively smelted for rings and other ornaments in the heart of Africa. A copper bar of native manufacture four feet long was offered to us for sale at Chinsamba's. These arts are monuments attesting the fact, that some instruction from above must at some time or other have been supplied to mankind; and, as Archbishop Whately says, "the most probable conclusion is, that man when first created, or very shortly afterwards, was advanced, by the Creator Himself, to a state above that of a mere savage."

The argument for an original revelation to man, though quite independent of the Bible history, tends to confirm that history. It is of the same nature with this, that man could not have *made* himself, and therefore must have had a Divine *Creator*. Mankind could not, in the first instance, have *civilized* themselves, and therefore must have had a superhuman *Instructor*.

In connection with this subject, it is remarkable that throughout successive generations no change has taken place in the form of the various inventions. Hammers, tongs, hoes, axes, adzes, handles to them; needles, bows and arrows, with the mode of feathering the latter; spears, for killing game, with spear-heads having what is termed "dish" on both sides to give them, when thrown, the rotatory motion of rifle-balls; the arts of spinning and weaving, with that of pounding and steeping the inner bark of a tree till it serves as clothing; millstones for grinding corn into meal; the manufacture of the same kind of pots or *chatties* as in India; the art of cooking, of brewing beer and straining it as was done in ancient Egypt; fish-hooks, fishing and hunting nets, fish-baskets, and weirs, the same as in the Highlands of Scotland; traps for catching animals, etc., etc.,--have all been so very permanent from age to age, and some of them of identical patterns are so widely spread over the globe, as to render it probable that they were all, at least in some degree, derived from one Source. The African traditions, which seem possessed of the same unchangeability as the arts to which they relate, like those of all other nations refer their origin to a superior Being. And it is much more reasonable to receive the hints given in Genesis, concerning direct instruction from God to our first parents or their children in religious or moral duty, and probably in the knowledge of the arts of life, {6} than to give credence to the theory that untaught savage man subsisted in a state which would prove fatal to all his descendants, and that in such helpless state he made many inventions which most of his progeny retained, but never improved upon during some thirty centuries.

We crossed in canoes the arm of the Lake, which joins Chia to Nyassa, and spent the night on its northern bank. The whole country adjacent to the Lake, from this point up to Kota-kota Bay, is densely peopled by thousands who have fled from the forays of the Mazitu in hopes of protection from the Arabs who live there. In three running rivulets we saw the **Shuare** palm, and an oil palm which is much inferior to that on the West Coast. Though somewhat similar in appearance, the fruit is not much larger than hazel-nuts, and the people do not use them, on account of the small quantity of oil which they afford.

The idea of using oil for light never seems to have entered the African mind. Here a bundle of split and dried bamboo, tied together with creeping plants, as thick as a man's body, and about twenty feet in length, is employed in the canoes as a torch to attract the fish at night. It would be considered a piece of the most wasteful extravagance to burn the oil they obtain from the castor-oil bean and other seeds, and also from certain fish, or in fact to do anything with it but anoint their heads and bodies.

We arrived at Kota-kota Bay in the afternoon of the 10th September, 1863; and sat down under a magnificent wild fig-tree with leaves ten inches long, by five broad, about a quarter of a mile from the village of Juma ben Saidi, and Yakobe ben Arame, whom we had met on the River Kaombe, a little north of this, in our first exploration of the Lake. We had rested but a short time when Juma, who is evidently the chief person here, followed by about fifty people, came to salute us and to invite us to take up our quarters in his village. The hut which, by mistake, was offered, was so small and dirty, that we preferred sleeping in an open space a few hundred yards off.

Juma afterwards apologized for the mistake, and presented us with rice, meal, sugar-cane, and a piece of malachite. We returned his visit on the following day, and found him engaged in building a dhow or Arab vessel, to replace one which he said had been wrecked. This new one was fifty feet long, twelve feet broad, and five feet deep. The planks were of a wood like teak, here called Timbati, and the timbers of a closer grained wood called Msoro. The sight of this dhow gave us a hint which, had we previously received it, would have prevented our attempting to carry a vessel of iron past the Cataracts. The trees around Katosa's village were Timbati, and they would have yielded planks fifty feet long and thirty inches broad. With a few native carpenters a good vessel could be built on the Lake nearly as quickly as one could be carried past the Cataracts, and at a vastly less cost. Juma said that no money would induce him to part with this dhow. He was very busy in transporting slaves across the Lake by means of two boats, which we saw returning from a trip in the afternoon. As he did not know of our intention to visit him, we came upon several gangs of stout young men slaves, each secured by the neck to one common chain, waiting for exportation, and several more in slave-sticks. These were all civilly removed before our interview was over, because Juma knew that we did not relish the sight.

When we met the same Arabs in 1861, they had but few attendants: according to their own account, they had now, in the village and adjacent country, 1500 souls. It is certain that tens of thousands had flocked to them for protection, and all their power and influence must be attributed to the possession of guns and gunpowder. This crowding of refugees to any point where there is a hope for security for life and property is very common in this region, and the knowledge of it made our hopes beat high for the success of a peaceful Mission on the shores of the Lake. The rate, however, in which the people here will perish by the next famine, or be exported by Juma and others, will, we fear, depopulate those parts which we have just described as crowded with people. Hunger will ere long compel them to sell each other. An intelligent man complained to us of the Arabs often seizing slaves, to whom they took a fancy, without the formality of purchase; but the price is so low--from two to four yards of calico--that one can scarcely think this seizure and exportation without payment worth their while. The boats were in constant employment, and, curiously enough, Ben Habib, whom we met at Linyanti in 1855, had been taken across the Lake, the day before our arrival at this Bay, on his way from Sesheke to Kilwa, and we became acquainted with a native servant of the Arabs, called Selele Saidallah, who could speak the Makololo language pretty fairly from having once spent some months in the Barotse Valley.

From boyhood upwards we have been accustomed, from time to time, to read in books of travels about the great advances annually made by Mohammedanism in Africa. The rate at which this religion spreads was said to be so rapid, that in after days, in our own pretty extensive travels, we have constantly been on the look out for the advancing wave from North to South, which, it was prophesied, would soon reduce the entire continent to the faith of the false prophet. The only foundation that we can discover for the assertions referred to, and for others of more recent date, is the fact that in a remote corner of North-Western Africa the Fulahs, and Mandingoes, and some others in Northern Africa, as mentioned by Dr. Barth, have made conquests of territory; but even they care so very little for the extension of their faith, that after the conquest no pains whatever are taken to indoctrinate the adults of the tribe. This is in exact accordance with the impression we have received from our intercourse with Mohammedans and Christians. The followers of Christ alone are anxious to propagate their faith. A *quasi* philanthropist would certainly never need to recommend the followers of Islam, whom we have met, to restrain their benevolence by preaching that "Charity should begin at home."

Though Selele and his companions were bound to their masters by domestic ties, the only new idea they had imbibed from Mohammedanism was, that it would be wrong to eat meat killed by other people. They thought it would be "unlucky." Just as the inhabitants of Kolobeng, before being taught the requirements of Christianity, refrained from hoeing their gardens on Sundays, lest they should reap an unlucky crop. So far as we could learn, no efforts had been made to convert the natives, though these two Arabs, and about a dozen half-castes, had been in the country for many years; and judging from our experience with a dozen Mohammedans in our employ at high wages for sixteen months, the Africans would be the better men in proportion as they retained their native faith. This may appear only a harsh judgment from a mind imbued with Christian prejudices; but without any pretention to that impartiality, which leaves it doubtful to which side the affections lean, the truth may be fairly stated by one who viewed all Mohammedans and Africans with the sincerest good will.

Our twelve Mohammedans from Johanna were the least open of any of our party to impression from kindness. A marked difference in general conduct was apparent. The Makololo, and other natives of the country, whom we had with us, invariably shared with each other the food they had cooked, but the Johanna men partook of their meals at a distance. This, at first, we attributed to their Moslem prejudices; but when they saw the cooking process of the others nearly complete, they came, sat beside them, and ate the portion offered without ever remembering to return the compliment when their own turn came to be generous. The Makololo and the others grumbled at their greediness, yet always followed the common custom of Africans of sharing their food with all who sit around them. What vexed us most in the Johanna men was their indifference to the welfare of each other. Once, when they were all coming to the ship after sleeping ashore, one of them walked into the water with the intention of swimming off to the boat, and while yet hardly up to his knees was seized by a horrid crocodile and dragged under; the poor fellow gave a shriek, and held up his hand for aid, but none of his countrymen stirred to his assistance, and he was never seen again. On asking his brother-in-law why he did not help him, he replied, "Well, no one told him to go into the water. It was his own fault that he was killed." The Makololo on the other hand rescued a woman at Senna by entering the water, and taking her out of the crocodile's mouth.

It is not assumed that their religion had much to do in the matter. Many Mohammedans might contrast favourably with indifferent Christians; but, so far as our experience in East Africa goes, the moral tone of the follower of Mahomed is pitched at a lower key than that of the untutored African. The ancient zeal for propagating the tenets of the Koran has evaporated, and been replaced by the most intense selfishness and grossest sensuality. The only known efforts made by Mohammedans, namely, those in the North-West and North of the continent, are so linked with the acquisition of power and plunder, as not to deserve the name of religious propagandism; and the only religion that now makes proselytes is that of Jesus Christ. To those who are capable of taking a comprehensive view of this subject, nothing can be adduced of more telling significance than the well-attested fact, that while the Mohammedans, Fulahs, and others towards Central Africa, make a few proselytes by a process which gratifies their own covetousness, three small sections of the Christian converts, the Africans in the South, in the West Indies, and on the

West Coast of Africa actually contribute for the support and spread of their religion upwards of 15,000 pounds annually. {7} That religion which so far overcomes the selfishness of the human heart must be Divine.

Leaving Kota-kota Bay, we turned away due West on the great slave route to Katanga's and Cazembe's country in Londa. Juma lent us his servant, Selele, to lead us the first day's march. He said that the traders from Kilwa and Iboe cross the Lake either at this bay, or at Tsenga, or at the southern end of the Lake; and that wherever they may cross they all go by this path to the interior. They have slaves with them to carry their goods, and when they reach a spot where they can easily buy others, they settle down and begin the traffic, and at once cultivate grain. So much of the land lies waste, that no objection is ever made to any one taking possession of as much as he needs; they can purchase a field of cassava for their present wants for very little, and they continue trading in the country for two or three years, and giving what weight their muskets possess to the chief who is most liberal to them.

The first day's march led us over a rich, well-cultivated plain. This was succeeded by highlands, undulating, stony, and covered with scraggy trees. Many banks of well rounded shingle appear. The disintegration of the rocks, now going on, does not round off the angles; they are split up by the heat and cold into angular fragments. On these high downs we crossed the River Kaombe. Beyond it we came among the upland vegetation--rhododendrons, proteas, the masuko, and molompi. At the foot of the hill, Kasuko-suko, we found the River Bua running north to join the Kaombe. We had to go a mile out of our way for a ford; the stream is deep enough in parts for hippopotami. The various streams not previously noticed, crossed in this journey, had before this led us to the conclusion, independently of the testimony of the natives, that no large river ran into the north end of the Lake. No such affluent was needed to account for the Shire's perennial flow.

On September 15th we reached the top of the ascent which, from its many ups and downs, had often made us puff and blow as if broken-winded. The water of the streams we crossed was deliciously cold, and now that we had gained the summit at Ndonda, where the boiling-point of water showed an altitude of 3440 feet above the sea, the air was delightful. Looking back we had a magnificent view of the Lake, but the haze prevented our seeing beyond the sea horizon. The scene was beautiful, but it was impossible to dissociate the lovely landscape whose hills and dales had so sorely tried our legs and lungs, from the sad fact that this was part of the great slave route now actually in use. By this road many "Ten thousands" have here seen "the Sea," "the Sea," but with sinking hearts; for the universal idea among the captive gangs is, that they are going to be fattened and eaten by the whites. They cannot of course be so much shocked as we should be--their sensibilities are far from fine, their feelings are more obtuse than ours--in fact, "the live eels are used to being skinned," perhaps they rather like it. We who are not philosophic, blessed the Providence which at Thermopylae in ancient days rolled back the tide of Eastern conquest from the West, and so guided the course of events that light and liberty and gospel truth spread to our distant isle, and emancipating our race freed them from the fear of ever again having to climb fatiguing heights and descend wearisome hollows in a slave-gang, as we suppose they did when the fair English youths were exposed for sale at Rome.

Looking westwards we perceived that, what from below had the appearance of mountains, was only the edge of a table-land which, though at first undulating, soon became smooth, and sloped towards the centre of the country. To the south a prominent mountain called Chipata, and to the south-west another named Ngalla, by which the Bua is said to rise, gave character to the landscape. In the north, masses of hills prevented our seeing more than eight or ten miles.

The air which was so exhilarating to Europeans had an opposite effect on five men who had been born and reared in the malaria of the Delta of the Zambesi. No sooner did they reach the edge of the plateau at Ndonda, than they lay down prostrate, and complained of pains all over them. The temperature was not much lower than that on the shores of the Lake below, 76 degrees being the mean temperature of the day, 52 degrees the lowest, and 82 degrees the highest during the twenty-four hours; at the Lake it was about 10 degrees higher. Of the symptoms they complained of--pains everywhere--nothing could be made. And yet it was evident that they had good reason for saying that they were ill. They scarified almost every part of their bodies as a remedial measure; medicines, administered on the supposition that their malady was the effect of a sudden chill, had no effect, and in two days one of them actually died in consequence of, as far as we could judge, a change from a malarious to a purer and more rarefied atmosphere.

As we were on the slave route, we found the people more churlish than usual.

On being expostulated with about it, they replied, "We have been made wary by those who come to buy slaves." The calamity of death having befallen our party, seemed, however, to awaken their sympathies. They pointed out their usual burying-place, lent us hoes, and helped to make the grave. When we offered to pay all expenses, they showed that they had not done these friendly offices without fully appreciating their value; for they enumerated the use of the hut, the mat on which the deceased had lain, the hoes, the labour, and the medicine which they had scattered over the place to make him rest in peace.

The primitive African faith seems to be that there is one Almighty Maker of heaven and earth; that he has given the various plants of earth to man to be employed as mediators between him and the spirit world, where all who have ever been born and died continue to live; that sin consists in offences against their fellow-men, either here or among the departed, and that death is often a punishment of guilt, such as witchcraft. Their idea of moral evil differs in no respect from ours, but they consider themselves amenable only to inferior beings, not to the Supreme. Evil- speaking--lying--hatred--disobedience to parents--neglect of them--are said by the intelligent to have been all known to be sin, as well as theft, murder, or adultery, before they knew aught of Europeans or their teaching. The only new addition to their moral code is, that it is wrong to have more wives than one. This, until the arrival of Europeans, never entered into their minds even as a doubt.

Everything not to be accounted for by common causes, whether of good or evil, is ascribed to the Deity. Men are inseparably connected with the spirits of the departed, and when one dies he is believed to have joined the hosts of his ancestors. All the Africans we have met with are as firmly persuaded of their future existence as of their present life. And we have found none in whom the belief in the Supreme Being was not rooted. He is so invariably referred to as the Author of everything supernatural, that, unless one is ignorant of their language, he cannot fail to notice this prominent feature of their faith. When they pass into the unseen world, they do not seem to be possessed with the fear of punishment. The utensils placed upon the grave are all broken as if to indicate that they will never be used by the departed again. The body is put into the grave in a sitting posture, and the hands are folded in front. In some parts of the country there are tales which we could translate into faint glimmerings of a resurrection; but whether these fables, handed down from age to age, convey that meaning to the natives themselves we cannot tell. The true tradition of faith is asserted to be "though a man die he will live again;" the false that when he dies he is dead for ever.

CHAPTER XIV.

Important geographical discoveries in the Wabisa countries--Cruelty of the slave-trade--The Mazitu--Serious illness of Dr. Livingstone--Return to the ship.

In our course westwards, we at first passed over a gently undulating country, with a reddish clayey soil, which, from the heavy crops, appeared to be very fertile. Many rivulets were crossed, some running southwards into the Bua, and others northwards into the Loangwa, a river which we formerly saw flowing into the Lake. Further on, the water was chiefly found in pools and wells. Then still further, in the same direction, some watercourses were said to flow into that same "Loangwa of the Lake," and others into the Loangwa, which flows to the south-west, and enters the Zambesi at Zumbo, and is here called the "Loangwa of the Maravi." The trees were in general scraggy, and covered, exactly as they are in the damp climate of the Coast, with lichens, resembling orchilla- weed. The maize, which loves rather a damp soil, had been planted on ridges to allow the superfluous moisture to run off. Everything indicated a very humid climate, and the people warned us that, as the rains were near, we were likely to be prevented from returning by the country becoming flooded and impassable.

Villages, as usual encircled by euphorbia hedges, were numerous, and a great deal of grain had been cultivated around them. Domestic fowls, in plenty, and pigeons with dovecots like those in Egypt were seen. The people call themselves Matumboka, but the only difference between them and the rest of the Manganja is in the mode of tattooing the face. Their language is the same. Their distinctive mark consists of four tattooed lines diverging from the point between the eyebrows, which, in frowning, the muscles form into a furrow. The other lines of tattooing, as in all Manganja, run in long seams, which crossing each other at certain angles form a great number of triangular spaces on the breast, back, arms, and thighs. The cuticle is divided by a knife, and the edges of the incision are drawn apart till the true skin appears. By a repetition of this process, lines of raised cicatrices are formed, which are thought to give beauty, no matter how much pain the fashion gives.

It would not be worth while to advert for a moment to the routine of travelling, or the little difficulties that beset every one who attempts to penetrate into a new country, were it not to show the great source of the power here possessed by slave-traders. We needed help in carrying our goods, while our men were ill, though still able to march. When we had settled with others for hire, we were often told, that the dealers in men had taken possession of some, and had taken them away altogether. Other things led us to believe that the slave-traders carry matters with a high hand; and no wonder, for the possession of gunpowder gives them almost absolute power. The mode by which tribes armed with bows and arrows carry on warfare, or defend themselves, is by ambuscade. They never come out in open fight, but wait for the enemy ensconced behind trees, or in the long grass of the country, and shoot at him unawares. Consequently, if men come against them with firearms, when, as is usually the case, the long grass is all burned off, the tribe attacked are as helpless as a wooden ship, possessing only signal guns, would be before an iron-clad steamer. The time of year selected for this kind of warfare is nearly always that in which the grass is actually burnt off, or is so dry as readily to take fire. The dry grass in Africa looks more like ripe English wheat late in the autumn, than anything else we can compare it to. Let us imagine an English village standing in a field of this sort, bounded only by the horizon, and enemies setting fire to a line of a mile or two, by running along with bunches of burning straw in their hands, touching here and there the inflammable material,--the wind blowing towards the doomed village--the inhabitants with only one or two old muskets, but ten to one no powder,--the long line of flames, leaping thirty feet into the air with dense masses of black smoke--and pieces of charred grass falling down in showers. Would not the stoutest English villager, armed only with the bow and arrow against the enemy's musket, quail at the idea of breaking through that wall of fire? When at a distance, we once saw a scene like this, and had the charred grass, literally as thick as flakes of black snow, falling around us, there was no difficulty in understanding the secret of the slave-trader's power.

On the 21st of September, we arrived at the village of the chief Muasi, or Muazi; it is surrounded by a stockade, and embowered in very tall euphorbia-trees; their height, thirty or forty feet, shows that it has been inhabited for at least one generation. A visitation of disease or death causes the headmen to change the site of their villages, and plant new hedges; but, though Muazi has suffered from the attacks of the Mazitu, he has evidently clung to his birthplace. The village is situated about two miles south-west of a high hill called Kasungu, which gives the name to a district extending to the Loangwa of the Maravi. Several other detached granite hills have been shot up on the plain, and many stockaded villages, all owing allegiance to Muazi, are scattered over it.

On our arrival, the chief was sitting in the smooth shady place, called Boalo, where all public business is transacted, with about two hundred men and boys around him. We paid our guides with due ostentation. Masiko, the tallest of our party, measured off the fathom of cloth agreed upon, and made it appear as long as possible, by facing round to the crowd, and cutting a few inches beyond what his outstretched arms could reach, to show that there was no deception. This was by way of advertisement. The people are mightily gratified at having a tall fellow to measure the cloth for them. It pleases them even better than cutting it by a tape-line--though very few men of six feet high can measure off their own length with their outstretched arms. Here, where Arab traders have been, the cubit called **mokono**, or elbow, begins to take the place of the fathom in use further south. The measure is taken from the point of the bent elbow to the end of the middle finger.

We found, on visiting Muazi on the following day, that he was as frank and straightforward as could reasonably be expected. He did not wish us to go to the N.N.W., because he carries on a considerable trade in ivory there. We were anxious to get off the slave route, to people not visited before by traders; but Muazi naturally feared, that if we went to what is said to be a well-watered country, abounding in elephants, we might relieve him of the ivory which he now obtains at a cheap rate, and sells to the slave-traders as they pass Kasungu to the east; but at last he consented, warning us that "great difficulty would be experienced in obtaining food--a district had been depopulated by slave wars--and a night or two must be spent in it; but he would give us good guides, who would go three days with us, before turning, and then further progress must depend on ourselves." Some of our men having been ill ever since we mounted this highland plain, we remained two days with Muazi.

A herd of fine cattle showed that no tsetse existed in the district. They had the Indian hump, and were very fat, and very tame. The boys rode on both cows and bulls without fear, and the animals were so fat and lazy, that the old ones only made a feeble attempt to kick their young tormentors. Muazi never milks the cows; he complained that, but for the Mazitu having formerly captured some, he should now have had very many. They wander over the country at large, and certainly thrive.

After leaving Muazi's, we passed over a flat country sparsely covered with the scraggy upland trees, but brightened with many fine flowers. The grass was short, reaching no higher than the knee, and growing in tufts with bare spaces between, though the trees were draped with many various lichens, and showed a moist climate. A high and very sharp wind blew over the flats; its piercing keenness was not caused by low temperature, for the thermometer stood at 80 degrees.

We were now on the sources of the Loangwa of the Maravi, which enters the Zambesi at Zumbo, and were struck by the great resemblance which the boggy and sedgy streams here presented to the sources of the Leeba, an affluent of the Zambesi formerly observed in Londa, and of the Kasai, which some believe to be the principal branch of the Congo or Zaire.

We had taken pains to ascertain from the travelled Babisa and Arabs as much as possible about the country in front, which, from the lessening time we had at our disposal, we feared we could scarcely reach, and had heard a good deal of a small lake called Bemba. As we proceeded west, we passed over the sources not only of the Loangwa, but of another stream, called Moitawa or Moitala, which was represented to be the main feeder of Lake Bemba. This would be of little importance, but for the fact that the considerable river Luapula, or Loapula is said to flow out of Bemba to the westward, and then to spread out into another and much larger lake, named Moero, or Moelo. Flowing still further in the same direction, the Loapula forms Lake Mofue, or Mofu, and after this it is said to pass the town of Cazembe, bend to the north, and enter Lake Tanganyika. Whither the water went after it entered the last lake, no one would venture an assertion. But that the course indicated is the true watershed of that part of the country, we believe from the unvarying opinion of native travellers. There could be no doubt that our informants had been in the country beyond Cazembe's, for they knew and described chiefs whom we afterwards met about thirty-five or forty miles west of his town. The Lualaba is said to flow into the Loapula--and when, for the sake of testing the accuracy of the travelled, it was asserted that all the water of the region round the town of Cazembe flowed into the Luambadzi, or Luambezi (Zambesi), they remarked with a smile, "He says, that the Loapula flows into the Zambesi--did you ever hear such nonsense?" or words to that effect. We were forced to admit, that according to native accounts, our previous impression of the Zambesi's draining the country about Cazembe's had been a mistake. Their geographical opinions are now only stated, without any further comment than that the itinerary given by the Arabs and others shows that the Loapula is twice crossed on the way to Cazembe's; and we may add that we have never found any difficulty from the alleged incapacity of the negro to tell which way a river flows.

The boiling-point of water showed a descent, from the edge of the plateau to our furthest point west, of 170 feet; but this can only be considered as an approximation, and no dependence could have been placed on it, had we not had the courses of the streams to confirm this rather rough mode of ascertaining altitudes. The slope, as shown by the watershed, was to the "Loangwa of the Maravi," and towards the Moitala, or south-west, west, and north-west. After we leave the feeders of Lake Nyassa, the water drains towards the centre of the continent. The course of the Kasai, a river seen during Dr. Livingstone's journey to the West Coast, and its feeders was to the north-east, or somewhat in the same direction. Whether the water thus drained off finds its way out by the Congo, or by the Nile, has not yet been ascertained. Some parts of the continent have been said to resemble an inverted dinner-plate. This portion seems more of the shape, if shape it has, of a wide-awake hat, with the crown a little depressed. The altitude of the brim in some parts is considerable; in others, as at Tette and the bottom of Murchison's Cataracts, it is so small that it could be ascertained only by eliminating the daily variations of the barometer, by simultaneous observations on the Coast, and at points some two or three hundred miles inland. So long as African rivers remain in what we may call the brim, they present no obstructions; but no sooner do they emerge from the higher lands than their utility is impaired by cataracts. The low lying belt is very irregular. At times sloping up in the manner of the rim of an inverted dinner-plate-

-while in other cases, a high ridge rises near the sea, to be succeeded by a lower district inland before we reach the central plateau. The breadth of the low lands is sometimes as much as three hundred miles, and that breadth determines the limits of navigation from the seaward.

We made three long marches beyond Muazi's in a north-westerly direction; the people were civil enough, but refused to sell us any food. We were travelling too fast, they said; in fact, they were startled, and before they recovered their surprise, we were obliged to depart. We suspected that Muazi had sent them orders to refuse us food, that we might thus be prevented from going into the depopulated district; but this may have been mere suspicion, the result of our own uncharitable feelings.

We spent one night at Machambwe's village, and another at Chimbuzi's. It is seldom that we can find the headman on first entering a village. He gets out of the way till he has heard all about the strangers, or he is actually out in the fields looking after his farms. We once thought that when the headman came in from a visit of inspection, with his spear, bow and arrows, they had been all taken up for the occasion, and that he had all the while been hidden in some hut slily watching till he heard that the strangers might be trusted; but on listening to the details given by these men of the appearances of the crops at different parts, and the astonishing minuteness of the speakers' topography, we were persuaded that in some cases we were wrong, and felt rather humiliated. Every knoll, hill, mountain, and every peak on a range has a name; and so has every watercourse, dell, and plain. In fact, every feature and portion of the country is so minutely distinguished by appropriate names, that it would take a lifetime to decipher their meaning. It is not the want, but the superabundance of names that misleads travellers, and the terms used are so multifarious that good scholars will at times scarcely know more than the subject of conversation. Though it is a little apart from the topic of the attention which the headmen pay to agriculture, yet it may be here mentioned, while speaking of the fulness of the language, that we have heard about a score of words to indicate different varieties of gait--one walks leaning forward, or backward, swaying from side to side, loungingly, or smartly, swaggeringly, swinging the arms, or only one arm, head down or up, or otherwise; each of these modes of walking was expressed by a particular verb; and more words were used to designate the different varieties of fools than we ever tried to count.

Mr. Moffat has translated the whole Bible into the language of the Bechuana, and has diligently studied this tongue for the last forty-four- years; and, though knowing far more of the language than any of the natives who have been reared on the Mission-station of Kuruman, he does not pretend to have mastered it fully even yet. However copious it may be in terms of which we do not feel the necessity, it is poor in others, as in abstract terms, and words used to describe mental operations.

Our third day's march ended in the afternoon of the 27th September, 1863, at the village of Chinanga on the banks of a branch of the Loangwa. A large, rounded mass of granite, a thousand feet high, called **Nombe rume**, stand on the plain a few miles off. It is quite remarkable, because it has so little vegetation on it. Several other granitic hills stand near it, ornamented with trees, like most heights of this country, and a heap of blue mountains appears away in the north.

The effect of the piercing winds upon the men had never been got rid of. Several had been unable to carry a load ever since we ascended to the highlands; we had lost one, and another poor lad was so ill as to cause us great anxiety. By waiting in this village, which was so old that it was full of vermin, all became worse. Our European food was entirely expended, and native meal, though finely ground, has so many sharp angular particles in it, that it brought back dysentery, from which we had suffered so much in May. We could scarcely obtain food for the men. The headman of this village of Chinanga was off in a foray against some people further north to supply slaves to the traders expected along the slave route we had just left; and was said, after having expelled the inhabitants, to be living in their stockade, and devouring their corn. The conquered tribe had purchased what was called a peace by presenting the conqueror with three women.

This state of matters afforded us but a poor prospect of finding more provisions in that direction than we could with great difficulty and at enormous prices obtain here. But neither want of food, dysentery, nor slave wars would have prevented our working our way round the Lake in some other direction, had we had time; but we had received orders from the Foreign Office to take the "Pioneer" down to the sea in the previous April. The salaries of all the men in her were positively "in any case to cease by the 31st of December."

We were said to be only ten days' distant from Lake Bemba. We might speculate on a late rise of the river. A month or six weeks would secure a geographical feat, but the rains were near. We had been warned by different people that the rains were close at hand, and that we should then be bogged and unable to travel. The flood in the river might be an early one, or so small in volume as to give but one chance of the "Pioneer" descending to the ocean. The Makololo too were becoming dispirited by sickness and want of food, and were naturally anxious to be back to their fields in time for sowing. But in addition to all this and more, it was felt that it would not be dealing honestly with the Government, were we, for the sake of a little eclat, to risk the detention of the "Pioneer" up the river during another year; so we decided to return; and though we had afterwards the mortification to find that we were detained two full months at the ship waiting for the flood which we expected immediately after our arrival there, the chagrin was lessened by a consciousness of having acted in a fair, honest, above-board manner throughout.

On the night of the 29th of September a thief came to the sleeping-place of our men and stole a leg of a goat. On complaining to the deputy headman, he said that the thief had fled, but would be caught. He suggested a fine, and offered a fowl and her eggs; but wishing that the thief alone should be punished, it was advised that *he* should be found and fined. The Makololo thought it best to take the fowl as a means of making the punishment certain. After settling this matter on the last day of September, we commenced our return journey. We had just the same time to go back to the ship, that we had spent in coming to this point, and there is not much to interest one in marching over the same ground a second time.

While on our journey north-west, a cheery old woman, who had once been beautiful, but whose white hair now contrasted strongly with her dark complexion, was working briskly in her garden as we passed. She seemed to enjoy a hale, hearty old age. She saluted us with what elsewhere would be called a good address; and, evidently conscious that she deserved the epithet, "dark but comely," answered each of us with a frank "Yes, my child." Another motherly-looking woman, sitting by a well, began the conversation by "You are going to visit Muazi, and you have come from afar, have you not?" But in general women never speak to strangers unless spoken to, so anything said by them attracts attention. Muazi once presented us with a basket of corn. On hinting that we had no wife to grind our corn, his buxom spouse struck in with roguish glee, and said, "I will grind it for you; and leave

Muazi, to accompany and cook for you in the land of the setting sun." As a rule the women are modest and retiring in their demeanour, and, without being oppressed with toil, show a great deal of industry. The crops need about eight months' attention. Then when the harvest is home, much labour is required to convert it into food as porridge, or beer. The corn is pounded in a large wooden mortar, like the ancient Egyptian one, with a pestle six feet long and about four inches thick. The pounding is performed by two or even three women at one mortar. Each, before delivering a blow with her pestle, gives an upward jerk of the body, so as to put strength into the stroke, and they keep exact time, so that two pestles are never in the mortar at the same moment. The measured thud, thud, thud, and the women standing at their vigorous work, are associations inseparable from a prosperous African village. By the operation of pounding, with the aid of a little water, the hard outside scale or husk of the grain is removed, and the corn is made fit for the millstone. The meal irritates the stomach unless cleared from the husk; without considerable energy in the operator, the husk sticks fast to the corn. Solomon thought that still more vigour than is required to separate the hard husk or bran from wheat would fail to separate "a fool from his folly." "Though thou shouldst bray a fool in a mortar among wheat with a pestle, *yet* will not his foolishness depart from him." The rainbow, in some parts, is called the "pestle of the Barimo," or gods. Boys and girls, by constant practice with the pestle, are able to plant stakes in the ground by a somewhat similar action, in erecting a hut, so deftly that they never miss the first hole made.

Let any one try by repeatedly jobbing a pole with all his force to make a deep hole in the ground, and he will understand how difficult it is always to strike it into the same spot.

As we were sleeping one night outside a hut, but near enough to hear what was going on within, an anxious mother began to grind her corn about two o'clock in the morning. "Ma," inquired a little girl, "why grind in the dark?" Mamma advised sleep, and administered material for a sweet dream to her darling, by saying, "I grind meal to buy a cloth from the strangers, which will make you look a little lady." An observer of these primitive races is struck continually with such little trivial touches of genuine human nature.

The mill consists of a block of granite, syenite, or even mica schist, fifteen or eighteen inches square and five or six thick, with a piece of quartz or other hard rock about the size of a half brick, one side of which has a convex surface, and fits into a concave hollow in the larger and stationary stone. The workwoman kneeling, grasps this upper millstone with both hands, and works it backwards and forwards in the hollow of the lower millstone, in the same way that a baker works his dough, when pressing it and pushing from him. The weight of the person is brought to bear on the movable stone, and while it is pressed and pushed forwards and backwards, one hand supplies every now and then a little grain to be thus at first bruised and then ground on the lower stone, which is placed on the slope so that the meal when ground falls on to a skin or mat spread for the purpose. This is perhaps the most primitive form of mill, and anterior to that in oriental countries, where two women grind at one mill, and may have been that used by Sarah of old when she entertained the Angels.

On 2nd October we applied to Muazi for guides to take us straight down to Chinsamba's at Mosapo, and thus cut off an angle, which we should otherwise make, by going back to Kota-kota Bay. He replied that his people knew the short way to Chinsamba's that we desired to go, but that they all were afraid to venture there, on account of the Zulus, or Mazitu. We therefore started back on our old route, and, after three hours' march, found some Babisa in a village who promised to lead us to Chinsamba.

We meet with these keen traders everywhere. They are easily known by a line of horizontal cicatrices, each half an inch long, down the middle of the forehead and chin. They often wear the hair collected in a mass on the upper and back part of the head, while it is all shaven off the forehead and temples. The Babisa and Waiau or Ajawa heads have more of the round bullet-shape than those of the Manganja, indicating a marked difference in character; the former people being great traders and travellers, the latter being attached to home and agriculture. The Manganja usually intrust their ivory to the Babisa to be sold at the Coast, and complain that the returns made never come up to the high prices which they hear so much about before it is sent. In fact, by the time the Babisa return, the expenses of the journey, in which they often spend a month or two at a place where food abounds, usually eat up all the profits.

Our new companions were trading in tobacco, and had collected quantities of the round balls, about the size of nine pounder shot, into which it is formed. One of them owned a woman, whose child had been sold that morning for tobacco. The mother followed him, weeping silently, for hours along the way we went; she seemed to be well known, for at several hamlets, the women spoke to her with evident sympathy; we could do nothing to alleviate her sorrow--the child would be kept until some slave- trader passed, and then sold for calico. The different cases of slave- trading observed by us are mentioned, in order to give a fair idea of its details.

We spent the first night, after leaving the slave route, at the village of Nkoma, among a section of Manganja, called Machewa, or Macheba, whose district extends to the Bua.

The next village at which we slept was also that of a Manganja smith. It was a beautiful spot, shaded with tall euphorbia-trees. The people at first fled, but after a short time returned, and ordered us off to a stockade of Babisa, about a mile distant. We preferred to remain in the smooth shady spot outside the hamlet, to being pent up in a treeless stockade. Twenty or thirty men came dropping in, all fully armed with bows and arrows, some of them were at least six feet four in height, yet these giants were not ashamed to say, "We thought that you were Mazitu, and, being afraid, ran away." Their orders to us were evidently inspired by terror, and so must the refusal of the headman to receive a cloth, or lend us a hut have been; but as we never had the opportunity of realizing what feelings a successful invasion would produce, we did not know whether to blame them or not. The headman, a tall old smith, with an enormous, well-made knife of his own workmanship, came quietly round, and, inspecting the shelter, which, from there being abundance of long grass and bushes near, our men put up for us in half an hour, gradually changed his tactics, and, in the evening, presented us with a huge pot of porridge and a deliciously well-cooked fowl, and made an apology for having been so rude to strangers, and a lamentation that he had been so foolish as to refuse the fine cloth we had offered. Another cloth was of course presented, and we had the pleasure of parting good friends next day.

Our guide, who belonged to the stockade near to which we had slept, declined to risk himself further than his home. While waiting to hire another, Masiko attempted to purchase a goat, and had nearly concluded the bargain, when the wife of the would-be seller came forward, and said to her husband, "You appear as if you were unmarried; selling a goat without consulting your wife; what an insult to a woman! What sort of man are you?" Masiko urged the man, saying, "Let us conclude the bargain, and never mind her;" but he being better instructed, replied, "No, I have raised a host against myself already," and refused.

We now pushed on to the east, so as to get down to the shores of the Lake, and into the parts where we were known. The country was beautiful, well wooded, and undulating, but the villages were all deserted; and the flight of the people seemed to have been quite recent, for the grain was standing in the corn-safes untouched. The tobacco, though ripe, remained uncut in the gardens, and the whole country was painfully quiet: the oppressive stillness quite unbroken by the singing of birds, or the shrill calls of women watching their corn.

On passing a beautiful village, called Bangwe, surrounded by shady trees, and placed in a valley among mountains, we were admiring the beauty of the situation, when some of the much dreaded Mazitu, with their shields, ran out of the hamlet, from which we were a mile distant. They began to scream to their companions to give us chase. Without quickening our pace we walked on, and soon were in a wood, through which the footpath we were following led. The first intimation we had of the approaching Mazitu was given by the Johanna man, Zachariah, who always lagged behind, running up, screaming as if for his life. The bundles were all put in one place to be defended; and Masiko and Dr. Livingstone walked a few paces back to meet the coming foe. Masiko knelt down anxious to fire, but was ordered not to do so. For a second or two dusky forms appeared among the trees, and the Mazitu were asked, in their own tongue, "What do you want?" Masiko adding, "What do you say?" No answer was given, but the dark shade in the forest vanished. They had evidently taken us for natives, and the sight of a white man was sufficient to put them to flight. Had we been nearer the Coast, where the people are accustomed to the slave-trade, we should have found this affair a more difficult one to deal with; but, as a rule, the people of the interior are much more mild in character than those on the confines of civilization.

The above very small adventure was all the danger we were aware of in this journey; but a report was spread from the Portuguese villages on the Zambesi, similar to several rumours that had been raised before, that Dr. Livingstone had been murdered by the Makololo; and very unfortunately the report reached England before it could be contradicted.

One benefit arose from the Mazitu adventure. Zachariah, and others who had too often to be reproved for lagging behind, now took their places in the front rank; and we had no difficulty in making very long marches for several days, for all believed that the Mazitu would follow our footsteps, and attack us while we slept.

A party of Babisa tobacco-traders came from the N.W. to Molamba, while we were there; and one of them asserted several times that the Loapula, after emerging from Moelo, received the Lulua, and then flowed into Lake Mofu, and thence into Tanganyika; and from the last-named Lake into the sea. This is the native idea of the geography of the interior; and, to test the general knowledge of our informant, we asked him about our acquaintances in Londa; as Moene, Katema, Shinde or Shinte, who live south-west of the rivers mentioned, and found that our friends there were perfectly well-known to him and to others of these travelled natives. In the evening two of the Babisa came in, and reported that the Mazitu had followed us to the village called Chigaragara, at which we slept at the bottom of the descent. The whole party of traders set off at once, though the sun had set. We ourselves had given rise to the report, for the women of Chigaragara, supposing us in the distance to be Mazitu, fled, with all their household utensils on their heads, and had no opportunity afterwards of finding out their mistake. We spent the night where we were, and next morning, declining Nkomo's entreaty to go and kill elephants, took our course along the shores of the Lake southwards.

We have only been at the Lake at one season of the year: then the wind blows strongly from the east, and indeed this is its prevailing direction hence to the Orange River; a north or a south wind is rare, and seldom lasts more than three days. As the breeze now blew over a large body of water, towards us, it was delightful; but when facing it on the table- land it was so strong as materially to impede our progress, and added considerably to the labour of travelling. Here it brought large quantities of the plant (***Vallisneriae***), from which the natives extract salt by burning, and which, if chewed, at once shows its saline properties by the taste. Clouds of the kungo, or edible midges, floated on the Lake, and many rested on the bushes on land.

The reeds along the shores of the Lake were still crowded with fugitives, and a great loss of life must since have taken place; for, after the corn they had brought with them was expended, famine would ensue. Even now we passed many women and children digging up the roots, about the size of peas, of an aromatic grass; and their wasted forms showed that this poor hard fare was to allay, if possible, the pangs of hunger. The babies at the breast crowed to us as we passed, their mothers kneeling and grubbing for the roots; the poor little things still drawing nourishment from the natural fountain were unconscious of that sinking of heart which their parents must have felt in knowing that the supply for the little ones must soon fail. No one would sell a bit of food to us: fishermen, even, would not part with the produce of their nets, except in exchange for some other kind of food. Numbers of newly-made graves showed that many had already perished, and hundreds were so emaciated that they had the appearance of human skeletons swathed in brown and wrinkled leather. In passing mile after mile, marked with these sad proofs that "man's inhumanity to man makes countless thousands mourn," one experiences an overpowering sense of helplessness to alleviate human woe, and breathes a silent prayer to the Almighty to hasten the good time coming when "man and man the world o'er, shall brothers be for all that." One small redeeming consideration in all this misery could not but be felt; these ills were inflicted by heathen Mazitu, and not by, or for, those who say to Him who is higher than the highest, "We believe that thou shalt come to be our Judge."

We crossed the Mokole, rested at Chitanda, and then left the Lake, and struck away N.W. to Chinsamba's. Our companions, who were so much oppressed by the rarefied air of the plateau, still showed signs of exhaustion, though now only 1300 feet above the sea, and did not recover flesh and spirits till we again entered the Lower Shire Valley, which is of so small an altitude, that, without simultaneous observations with the barometer there and on the sea-coast, the difference would not be appreciable.

On a large plain on which we spent one night, we had the company of eighty tobacco traders on their way from Kasungu to Chinsamba's. The Mazitu had attacked and killed two of them, near the spot where the Zulus fled from us without answering our questions. The traders were now so frightened that, instead of making a straight course with us, they set off by night to follow the shores of the Lake to Tsenga, and then turn west. It is the sight of shields, or guns that inspires terror.

The bowmen feel perfectly helpless when the enemy comes with even the small protection the skin shield affords, or attacks them in the open field with guns. They may shoot a few arrows, but they are such poor shots that ten to one if they hit. The only thing that makes the arrow formidable is the poison; for if the poisoned barb goes in nothing can save the wounded. A bow is in use in the lower end of Lake Nyassa, but is more common in the Maravi country, from six to eight inches broad, which is intended to be used as a shield as well as a bow; but we never saw one with the mark on it of an enemy's arrow. It certainly is no match for the Zulu shield, which is between four and five feet long, of an oval shape, and about two feet broad. So great is the terror this shield inspires that we sometimes doubted whether the Mazitu here were Zulus at all, and suspected that the people of the country took advantage of that fear, and, assuming shields, pretended to belong to that nation.

On the 11th October we arrived at the stockade of Chinsamba in Mosapo, and had reason to be very well satisfied with his kindness. A paraffin candle was in his eyes the height of luxury, and the ability to make a light instantaneously by a lucifer match, a marvel that struck him with wonder. He brought all his relatives in different groups to see the strange sights,--instantaneous fire-making, and a light, without the annoyance of having fire and smoke in the middle of the floor. When they wish to look for anything in the dark, a wisp of dried grass is lighted.

Chinsamba gave us a great deal of his company during our visits. As we have often remarked in other cases, a chief has a great deal to attend to in guiding the affairs of his people. He is consulted on all occasions, and gives his advice in a stream of words, which show a very intimate acquaintance with the topography of his district; he knows every rood cultivated, every weir put in the river, every hunting-net, loom, gorge, and every child of his tribe. Any addition made to the number of these latter is notified to him; and he sends thanks and compliments to the parents.

The presents which, following the custom of the country, we gave to every headman, where we either spent a night or a longer period, varied from four to eight yards of calico. We had some Manchester cloths made in imitation of the native manufactured robes of the West Coast, each worth five or six shillings. To the more important of the chiefs, for calico we substituted one of these strong gaudy dresses, iron spoons, a knife, needles, a tin dish, or pannikin, and found these presents to be valued more than three times their value in cloth would have been. Eight or ten shillings' worth gave abundant satisfaction to the greediest; but this is to be understood as the prime cost of the articles, and a trader would sometimes have estimated similar generosity as equal to from 30 to 50 pounds. In some cases the presents we gave exceeded the value of what was received in return; in others the excess of generosity was on the native side.

We never asked for leave to pass through the country; we simply told where we were going, and asked for guides; if they were refused, or if they demanded payment beforehand, we requested to be put into the beginning of the path, and said that we were sorry we could not agree about the guides, and usually they and we started together. Greater care would be required on entering the Mazitu or Zulu country, for there the Government extends over very large districts, while among the Manganja each little district is independent of every other. The people here have not adopted the exacting system of the Banyai, or of the people whose country was traversed by Speke and Grant.

In our way back from Chinsamba's to Chembi's and from his village to Nkwinda's, and thence to Katosa's, we only saw the people working in their gardens, near to the stockades. These strongholds were strengthened with branches of acacias, covered with strong hooked thorns; and were all crowded with people. The air was now clearer than when we went north, and we could see the hills of Kirk's Range five or six miles to the west of our path. The sun struck very hot, and the men felt it most in their feet. Every one who could get a bit of goatskin made it into a pair of sandals.

While sitting at Nkwinda's, a man behind the court hedge-wall said, with great apparent glee, that an Arab slaving party on the other side of the confluence of the Shire and Lake were "giving readily two fathoms of calico for a boy, and two and a half for a girl; never saw trade so brisk, no haggling at all." This party was purchasing for the supply of the ocean slave-trade. One of the evils of this traffic is that it profits by every calamity that happens in a country. The slave-trader naturally reaps advantage from every disorder, and though in the present case some lives may have been saved that otherwise would have perished, as a rule he intensifies hatreds, and aggravates wars between the tribes, because the more they fight and vanquish each other the richer his harvest becomes. Where slaving and cattle are unknown the people live in peace. As we sat leaning against that hedge, and listened to the harangue of the slave-trader's agent, it glanced across our mind that this was a terrible world; the best in it unable, from conscious imperfections, to say to the worst "Stand by! for I am holier than thou." The slave-trader, imbued no doubt with certain kindly feelings, yet pursuing a calling which makes him a fair specimen of a human fiend, stands grouped with those by whom the slave-traders are employed, and with all the workers of sin and misery in more highly-favoured lands, an awful picture to the All-seeing Eye.

We arrived at Katosa's village on the 15th October, and found about thirty young men and boys in slave-sticks. They had been bought by other agents of the Arab slavers, still on the east side of the Shire. They were resting in the village, and their owners soon removed them. The weight of the goree seemed very annoying when they tried to sleep. This taming instrument is kept on, until the party has crossed several rivers and all hope of escape has vanished from the captive's mind.

On explaining to Katosa the injury he was doing in selling his people as slaves, he assured us that those whom we had seen belonged to the Arabs, and added that he had far too few people already. He said he had been living in peace at the lakelet Pamalombe; that the Ajawa, or Machinga, under Kainka and Karamba, and a body of Babisa, under Maonga, had induced him to ferry them over the Shire; that they had lived for a considerable time at his expense, and at last stole his sheep, which induced him to make his escape to the place where he now dwelt, and in this flight he had lost many of his people. His account of the usual conduct of the Ajawa quite agrees with what these people have narrated themselves, and gives but a low idea of their moral tone. They have repeatedly broken all the laws of hospitality by living for months on the bounty of the Manganja, and then, by a sudden uprising, overcoming their hosts, and killing or chasing them out of their inheritances. The secret of their success is the possession of firearms. There were several of these Ajawa here again, and on our arrival they proposed to Katosa that they should leave; but he replied that they need not be afraid of us. They had red beads strung so thickly on their hair that at a little distance they appeared to have on red caps. It is curious that the taste for red hair should be so general among the Africans here and further north; in the south black mica, called *Sebilo*, and even soot are used to deepen the colour of the hair; here many smear the head with red-ochre, others plait the inner bark of a tree stained red into it; and a red powder called **Mukuru** is employed, which some say is obtained from the ground, and others from the roots of a tree.

It having been doubted whether sugar-cane is indigenous to this country or not, we employed Katosa to procure the two varieties commonly cultivated, with the intention of conveying them to Johanna. One is yellow, and the other, like what we observed in the Barotse Valley, is variegated with dark red and yellow patches, or all red. We have seen it "arrow," or blossom. Bamboos also run to seed, and the people are said to use the seed as food. The sugar-cane has native names, which would lead us to believe it to be indigenous. Here it is called **Zimbi**, further south **Mesari**, and in the centre of the country **Meshuati**. Anything introduced in recent times, as maize, superior cotton, or cassava, has a name implying its foreign origin.

Katosa's village was embowered among gigantic trees of fine timber: several caffiaceous bushes, with berries closely resembling those of the common coffee, grew near, but no use had ever been made of them. There are several cinchonaceous trees also in the country; and some of the wild fruits are so good as to cause a feeling of regret that they have not been improved by cultivation, or whatever else brought ours to their present perfection. Katosa lamented that this locality was so inferior to his former place at Pamalombe; there he had maize at the different stages of growth throughout the year. To us, however, he seemed, by digging holes, and taking advantage of the moisture beneath, to have succeeded pretty well in raising crops at this the driest time. The Makololo remarked that "here the maize had no season,"--meaning that the whole year was proper for its growth and ripening. By irrigation a succession of crops of grain might be raised anywhere within the south intertropical region of Africa.

When we were with Motunda, on the 20th October, he told us frankly that all the native provisions were hidden in Kirk's Range, and his village being the last place where a supply of grain could be purchased before we reached the ship, we waited till he had sent to his hidden stores. The upland country, beyond the mountains now on our right, is called Deza, and is inhabited by Maravi, who are only another tribe of Manganja. The paramount chief is called Kabambe, and he, having never been visited by war, lives in peace and plenty. Goats and sheep thrive; and Nyango, the chieftainess further to the south, has herds of horned cattle. The country being elevated is said to be cold, and there are large grassy plains on it which are destitute of trees. The Maravi are reported to be brave, and good marksmen with the bow; but, throughout all the country we have traversed, guns are enabling the trading tribes to overcome the agricultural and manufacturing classes.

On the ascent at the end of the valley just opposite Mount Mvai, we looked back for a moment to impress the beauties of the grand vale on our memory. The heat of the sun was now excessive, and Masiko, thinking that it was overpowering, proposed to send forward to the ship and get a hammock, in which to carry any one who might knock up. He was truly kind and considerate. Dr. Livingstone having fallen asleep after a fatiguing march, a hole in the roof of the hut he was in allowed the sun to beat on his head, and caused a splitting headache and deafness: while he was nearly insensible, he felt Masiko repeatedly lift him back to the bed off which he had rolled, and cover him up.

On the 24th we were again in Banda, at the village of Chasundu, and could now see clearly the hot valley in which the Shire flows, and the mountains of the Manganja beyond to our south-east. Instead of following the road by which we had come, we resolved to go south along the Lesungwe, which rises at Zunje, a peak on the same ridge as Mvai, and a part of Kirk's Range, which bounds the country of the Maravi on our west. This is about the limit of the beat of the Portuguese native traders, and it is but recently that, following our footsteps, they have come so far. It is not likely that their enterprise will lead them further north, for Chasundu informed us that the Babisa under-sell the agents from Tette. He had tried to deal with the latter when they first came; but they offered only ten fathoms of calico for a tusk, for which the Babisa gave him twenty fathoms and a little powder. Ivory was brought to us for sale again and again, and, as far as we could judge, the price expected would be about one yard of calico per pound, or possibly more, for there is no scale of prices known. The rule seems to be that buyer and seller shall spend a good deal of time in trying to cheat each other before coming to any conclusion over a bargain.

We found the Lesungwe a fine stream near its source, and about forty feet wide and knee-deep, when joined by the Lekudzi, which comes down from the Maravi country.

Guinea-fowl abounded, but no grain could be purchased, for the people had cultivated only the holmes along the banks with maize and pumpkins. Time enough had not elapsed since the slave-trader's invasion, and destruction of their stores, for them to raise crops of grain on the adjacent lands. To deal with them for a few heads of maize was the hungry bargaining with the famished, so we hastened on southwards as fast as the excessive heat would allow us. It was impossible to march in the middle of the day, the heat was so intolerable; and we could not go on at night, because, if we had chanced to meet any of the inhabitants, we should have been taken for marauders.

We had now thunder every afternoon; but while occasional showers seemed to fall at different parts, none fell on us. The air was deliciously clear, and revealed all the landscape covered everywhere with forest, and bounded by beautiful mountains. On the 31st October we reached the Mukuru-Madse, after having travelled 660 geographical miles, or 760 English miles in a straight line. This was accomplished in fifty-five travelling days, twelve miles per diem on an average. If the numerous bendings and windings, and ups and downs of the paths could have been measured too, the distance would have been found at least fifteen miles a day.

The night we slept at the Mukuru-Madse it thundered heavily, but, as this had been the case every afternoon, and no rain had followed, we erected no shelter, but during this night a pouring rain came on. When very tired a man feels determined to sleep in spite of everything, and the sound of dropping water is said to be conducive to slumber, but that does not refer to an African storm. If, when half asleep in spite of a heavy shower on the back of the head, he unconsciously turns on his side, the drops from the branches make such capital shots into his ear, that the brain rings again.

We were off next morning, the 1st of November, as soon as the day dawned. In walking about seven miles to the ship, our clothes were thoroughly dried by the hot sun, and an attack of fever followed. We relate this little incident to point out the almost certain consequence of getting wet in this climate, and allowing the clothes to dry on the person. Even if we walk in the mornings when the dew is on the grass, and only get our feet and legs wet, a very uneasy feeling and partial fever with pains in the limbs ensue, and continue till the march onwards bathes them in perspiration. Had Bishop Mackenzie been aware of this, which, before experience alone had taught us, entailed many a severe lesson, we know no earthly reason why his valuable life might not have been spared. The difference between getting the clothes soaked in England and in Africa is this: in the cold climate the patient is compelled, or, at any rate, warned, by discomfort to resort at once to a change of raiment; while in Africa it is cooling and rather pleasant to allow the clothes to dry on the person. A Missionary in proportion as he possesses an athletic frame, hardened by manly exercises, in addition to his other qualifications, will excel him who is not favoured with such bodily endowments; but in a hot climate efficiency mainly depends on husbanding the resources. He must never forget that, in the tropics, he is an exotic plant.

CHAPTER XV.

Confidence of natives--Bishop Tozer--Withdrawal of the Mission party--The English leave--Hazardous voyage to Mosambique--Dr. Livingstone's voyage to Bombay--Return to England.

We were delighted and thankful to find all those left at the ship in good health, and that from the employments in which they had been occupied they had suffered less from fever than usual during our absence. My companion, Thomas Ward, the steward, after having performed his part in the march right bravely, rejoined his comrades stronger than he had ever been before.

An Ajawa chief, named Kapeni, had so much confidence in the English name that he, with most of his people, visited the ship; and asserted that nothing would give his countrymen greater pleasure than to receive the associates of Bishop Mackenzie as their teachers. This declaration, coupled with the subsequent conduct of the Ajawa, was very gratifying, inasmuch as it was clear that no umbrage had been taken at the check which the Bishop had given to their slaving; their consciences had told them that the course he had pursued was right.

When we returned, the contrast between the vegetation about Muazi's and that near the ship was very striking. We had come so quickly down, that while on the plateau in latitude 12 degrees S., the young leaves had in many cases passed from the pink or other colour they have on first coming out to the light fresh green which succeeds it, here, on the borders of 16 degrees S., or from 150 to 180 miles distant, the trees were still bare, the grey colour of the bark predominating over every other hue. The trees in the tropics here have a very well-marked annual rest. On the Rovuma even, which is only about ten degrees from the equator, in September the slopes up from the river some sixty miles inland were of a light ashy-grey colour; and on ascending them, we found that the majority of the trees were without leaves; those of the bamboo even lay crisp and crumpled on the ground. As the sun is usually hot by day, even in the winter, this withering process may be owing to the cool nights; Africa differing so much from Central India in the fact that, in Africa, however hot the day may be, the air generally cools down sufficiently by the early morning watches to render a covering or even a blanket agreeable.

The first fortnight after our return to the ship was employed in the delightful process of resting, to appreciate which a man must have gone through great exertions. In our case the muscles of the limbs were as hard as boards, and not an ounce of fat existed on any part of the body. We now had frequent showers; but, these being only the earlier rains, the result on the rise of the river was but a few inches. The effect of these rains on the surrounding scenery was beautiful in the extreme. All trace of the dry season was soon obliterated, and hills and mountains from base to summit were covered with a mantle of living green. The sun passed us on his way south without causing a flood, so all our hopes of a release were centred on his return towards the Equator, when, as a rule, the waters of inundation are made to flow. Up to this time the rains descended simply to water the earth, fill the pools, and make ready for the grand overflow for which we had still to wait six weeks. It is of no use to conceal that we waited with much chagrin; for had we not been forced to return from the highlands west of Nyassa we might have visited Lake Bemba; but unavailing regrets are poor employment for the mind; so we banished them to the best of our power.

About the middle of December, 1863, we were informed that Bishop Mackenzie's successor, after spending a few months on the top of a mountain about as high as Ben Nevis in Scotland, at the mouth of the Shire, where there were few or no people to be taught, had determined to leave the country. This unfortunate decision was communicated to us at the same time that six of the boys reared by Bishop Mackenzie were sent back into heathenism. The boys were taken to a place about seven miles from the ship, but immediately found their way up to us. We told them that if they wished to remain in the country they had better so arrange at once, for we were soon to leave. The sequel will show their choice.

As soon as the death of Bishop Mackenzie was known at the Cape, Dr. Gray, the excellent Bishop there, proceeded at once to England, with a view of securing an early appointment of another head to the Mission, which in its origin owed so much to his zeal for the spread of the gospel among the heathen, and whose interests he had continually at heart. About the middle of 1862 we heard that Dr. Gray's efforts had been successful, and that another clergyman would soon take the place of our departed friend. This pleasing intelligence was exceedingly cheering to the Missionaries, and gratifying also to the members of the Expedition. About the beginning of 1863 the new Bishop arrived at the mouth of the river in a man-of-war, and after some delay proceeded inland. The Bishop of the Cape had taken a voyage home at considerable inconvenience to himself, for the sole object of promoting this Mission to the heathen; and it was somehow expected that the man he would secure would be an image of himself; and we must say, that whatever others, from the representations that have gone abroad, may think of his character, we invariably found Dr. Gray to be a true, warm-hearted promoter of the welfare of his fellow- men; a man whose courage and zeal have provoked very many to good works.

It was hoped that the presence of a new head to the Mission would infuse new energy and life into the small band of Missionaries, whose ranks had been thinned by death; and who, though discouraged by the disasters which the slave war and famine had induced, and also dispirited by the depressing influences of a low and unhealthy position in the swampy Shire Valley, were yet bravely holding out till the much-needed moral and material aid should arrive.

We believe that we are uttering the sentiments of many devout members of different sections of Christians, when we say, it was a pity that the Mission of the Universities was abandoned. The ground had been consecrated in the truest sense by the lives of those brave men who first occupied it. In bare justice to Bishop Mackenzie, who was the first to fall, it must be said, that the repudiation of all he had done, and the sudden abandonment of all that had cost so much life and money to secure, was a serious line of conduct for one so unversed in Missionary operations as his successor, to inaugurate. It would have been no more than fair that Bishop Tozer, before winding up the affairs of the Mission, should actually have examined the highlands of the Upper Shire; he would thus have gratified the associates of his predecessor, who believed that the highlands had never had a fair trial, and he would have gained from personal observation a more accurate knowledge of the country and the people than he could possibly have become possessed of by information gathered chiefly on the coast. With this examination, rather than with a stay of a few months on the humid, dripping top of misty Morambala, we should have felt much more satisfied.

In January, 1864, the natives all confidently asserted that at next full moon the river would have its great and permanent flood. It had several times risen as much as a foot, but fell again as suddenly. It was curious that their observation coincided exactly with ours, that the flood of inundation happens when the sun comes overhead on his way back to the Equator. We mention this more minutely because, from the observation of several years, we believe that in this way the inundation of the Nile is to be explained. On the 19th the Shire suddenly rose several feet, and we started at once; and stopping only for a short time at Chibisa's to bid adieu to the Ajawa and Makololo, who had been extremely useful to us of late in supplying maize and fresh provisions, we hastened on our way to the ocean. In order to keep a steerage way on the "Pioneer," we had to go quicker than the stream, and unfortunately carried away her rudder in passing suddenly round a bank. The delay required for the repairs prevented our reaching Morambala till the 2nd of February.

The flood-water ran into a marsh some miles above the mountain, and became as black as ink; and when it returned again to the river emitted so strong an effluvium of sulphuretted hydrogen, that one could not forget for an instant that the air was most offensive. The natives said this stench did not produce disease. We spent one night in it, and suffered no ill effects, though we fully expected an attack of fever. Next morning every particle of white paint on both ships was so deeply blackened, that it could not be cleaned by scrubbing with soap and water. The brass was all turned to a bronze colour, and even the iron and ropes had taken a new tint. This is an additional proof that malaria and offensive effluvia are not always companions. We did not suffer more from fever in the mangrove swamps, where we inhaled so much of the heavy mousey smell that it was distinguishable in the odour of our shirts and flannels, than we did elsewhere.

We tarried in the foul and blackening emanations from the marsh because we had agreed to receive on board about thirty poor orphan boys and girls, and a few helpless widows whom Bishop Mackenzie had attached to his Mission. All who were able to support themselves had been encouraged by the Missionaries to do so by cultivating the ground, and they now formed a little free community. But the boys and girls who were only from seven to twelve years of age, and orphans without any one to help them, could not be abandoned without bringing odium on the English name. The effect of an outcry by some persons in England, who knew nothing of the circumstances in which Bishop Mackenzie was placed, and who certainly had not given up their own right of appeal to the sword of the magistrate, was, that the new head of the Mission had gone to extremes in the opposite direction from his predecessor; not even protesting against the one monstrous evil of the country, the slave-trade. We believed that we ought to leave the English name in the same good repute among the natives that we had found it; and in removing the poor creatures, who had lived with Mackenzie as children with a father, to a land where the education he began would be completed, we had the aid and sympathy of the best of the Portuguese, and of the whole population. The difference between shipping slaves and receiving these free orphans struck us as they came on board. As soon as permission to embark was given, the rush into the boat nearly swamped her--their eagerness to be safe on the "Pioneer's" deck had to be repressed.

Bishop Tozer had already left for Quillimane when we took these people and the last of the Universities' Missionaries on board and proceeded to the Zambesi. It was in high flood. We have always spoken of this river as if at its lowest, for fear lest we should convey an exaggerated impression of its capabilities for navigation. Instead of from five to fifteen feet, it was now from fifteen to thirty feet, or more, deep. All the sandbanks and many of the islands had disappeared, and before us rolled a river capable, as one of our naval friends thought, of carrying a gunboat. Some of the sandy islands are annually swept away, and the quantities of sand carried down are prodigious.

The process by which a delta, extending eighty or one hundred miles from the sea, has been formed may be seen going on at the present day--the coarser particles of sand are driven out into the ocean, just in the same way as we see they are over banks in the beds of torrents. The finer portions are caught by the returning tide, and, accumulating by successive ebbs and flows, become, with the decaying vegetation, arrested by the mangrove roots. The influence of the tide in bringing back the finer particles gives the sea near the mouth of the Zambesi a clean and sandy bottom. This process has been going on for ages, and as the delta has enlarged eastwards, the river has always kept a channel for itself behind. Wherever we see an island all sand, or with only one layer of mud in it, we know it is one of recent formation, and that it may be swept away at any time by a flood; while those islands which are all of mud are the more ancient, having in fact existed ever since the time when the ebbing and flowing tides originally formed them as parts of the delta. This mud resists the action of the river wonderfully. It is a kind of clay on which the eroding power of water has little effect. Were maps made, showing which banks and which islands are liable to erosion, it would go far to settle where the annual change of the channel would take place; and, were a few stakes driven in year by year to guide the water in its course, the river might be made of considerable commercial value in the hands of any energetic European nation. No canal or railway would ever be thought of for this part of Africa. A few improvements would make the Zambesi a ready means of transit for all the trade that, with a population thinned by Portuguese slaving, will ever be developed in our day. Here there is no instance on record of the natives flocking in thousands to the colony, as they did at Natal, and even to the Arabs on Lake Nyassa. This keeping aloof renders it unlikely that in Portuguese hands the Zambesi will ever be of any more value to the world than it has been.

After a hurried visit to Senna, in order to settle with Major Sicard and Senhor Ferrao for supplies we had drawn thence after the depopulation of the Shire, we proceeded down to the Zambesi's mouth, and were fortunate in meeting, on the 13th February, with H.M.S. "Orestes." She was joined next day by H.M.S. "Ariel." The "Orestes" took the "Pioneer," and the "Ariel" the "Lady Nyassa" in tow, for Mosambique. On the 16th a circular storm proved the sea-going qualities of the "Lady of the Lake;" for on this day a hurricane struck the "Ariel," and drove her nearly backwards at a rate of six knots. The towing hawser wound round her screw and stopped her engines. No sooner had she recovered from this shock than she was again taken aback on the other tack, and driven stem on towards the "Lady Nyassa's" broadside. We who were on board the little vessel saw no chance of escape unless the crew of the "Ariel" should think of heaving ropes when the big ship went over us; but she glided past our bow, and we breathed freely again. We had now an opportunity of witnessing man-of-war seamanship. Captain Chapman, though his engines were disabled, did not think of abandoning us in the heavy gale, but crossed the bows of the "Lady Nyassa" again and again, dropping a cask with a line by which to give us another hawser. We might never have picked it up, had not a Krooman jumped overboard and fastened a second line to the cask; and then we drew the hawser on board, and were again in tow. During the whole time of the hurricane the little vessel behaved admirably, and never shipped a single green sea. When the "Ariel" pitched forwards we could see a large part of her bottom, and when her stern went down we could see all her deck. A boat, hung at her stern davits, was stove in by the waves. The officers on board the "Ariel" thought that it was all over with us: we imagined that they were suffering more than we were. Nautical men may suppose that this was a serious storm only to landsmen; but the "Orestes," which was once in sight, and at another time forty miles off during the same gale, split eighteen sails; and the "Pioneer" had to be lightened of parts of a sugar-mill she was carrying; her round-house was washed away, and the cabin was frequently knee-deep in water. When the "Orestes" came into Mosambique harbour nine days after our arrival there, our vessel, not being anchored close to the "Ariel," for we had run in under the lee of the fort, led to the surmise on board the "Orestes" that we had gone to the bottom. Captain Chapman and his officers pronounced the "Lady Nyassa" to be the finest little sea-boat they had ever seen. She certainly was a contrast to the "Ma-Robert," and did great credit to her builders, Ted and Macgregor of Glasgow. We can but regret that she was not employed on the Lake after which she was named, and for which she was intended and was so well adapted.

What struck us most, during the trip from the Zambesi to Mosambique, was the admirable way in which Captain Chapman handled the "Ariel" in the heavy sea of the hurricane; the promptitude and skill with which, when we had broken three hawsers, others were passed to us by the rapid evolutions of a big ship round a little one; and the ready appliance of means shown in cutting the hawser off the screw nine feet under water with long chisels made for the occasion; a task which it took three days to accomplish. Captain Chapman very kindly invited us on board the "Ariel," and we accepted his hospitality after the weather had moderated.

The little vessel was hauled through and against the huge seas with such force that two hawsers measuring eleven inches each in circumference parted. Many of the blows we received from the billows made every plate quiver from stem to stern, and the motion was so quick that we had to hold on continually to avoid being tossed from one side to the other or into the sea. Ten of the late Bishop's flock whom we had on board became so sick and helpless that do what we could to aid them they were so very much in the way that the idea broke in upon us, that the close packing resorted to by slavers is one of the necessities of the traffic. If this is so, it would account for the fact that even when the trade was legal the same injurious custom was common, if not universal. If, instead of ten such passengers, we had been carrying two hundred, with the wind driving the rain and spray, as by night it did, nearly as hard as hail against our faces, and nothing whatever to be seen to windward but the occasional gleam of the crest of a wave, and no sound heard save the whistling of the storm through the rigging, it would have been absolutely necessary for the working of the ship and safety of the whole that the live cargo should all have been stowed down below, whatever might have been the consequences.

Having delivered the "Pioneer" over to the Navy, she was towed down to the Cape by Captain Forsyth of the "Valorous," and after examination it was declared that with repairs to the amount of 300 pounds she would be as serviceable as ever. Those of the Bishop's flock whom we had on board were kindly allowed a passage to the Cape. The boys went in the "Orestes," and we are glad of the opportunity to record our heartfelt thanks to Captains Forsyth, Gardner, and Chapman for rendering us, at various times, every aid in their power. Mr. Waller went in the "Pioneer," and continued his generous services to all connected with the Mission, whether white or black, till they were no longer needed; and we must say that his conduct to them throughout was truly noble, and worthy of the highest praise.

After beaching the "Lady Nyassa" at Caboceira, opposite the house of a Portuguese gentleman well known to all Englishmen, Joao da Costa Soares, we put in brine cocks, and cleaned and painted her bottom. Mr. Soares appeared to us to have been very much vilified in a publication in England a few years ago; our experience proved him to be extremely kind and obliging. All the members of the Expedition who passed Mosambique were unanimous in extolling his generosity and, from the general testimony of English visitors in his favour, we very much regret that his character was so grievously misrepresented. To the authorities at Mosambique our thanks are also due for obliging accommodation; and though we differ entirely from the Portuguese officials as to the light in which we regard the slave-trade, we trust our exposure of the system, in which unfortunately they are engaged, will not be understood as indicating any want of kindly feeling and good will to them personally. Senhor Canto e Castro, who arrived at Mosambique two days after our departure to take the office of Governor-General, was well known to us in Angola. We lived two months in his house when he was Commandant of Golungo Alto; and, knowing him thoroughly, believe that no better man could have been selected for the office. We trust that his good principles may enable him to withstand the temptations of his position; but we should be sorry to have ours tried in a den of slave-traders with the miserable pittance he receives for his support.

While at Mosambique, a species of Pedalia called by Mr. Soares Dadeleira, and by the natives--from its resemblance to Gerzilin, or sesamum--"wild sesamum," was shown to us, and is said to be well known among native nurses as a very gentle and tasteless aperient for children. A few leaves of it are stirred in a cup of cold water for eight or nine seconds, and a couple of teaspoonfuls of the liquid given as a dose. The leaves form a sort of mucilage in the water by longer stirring, which is said to have diuretic properties besides.

On the 16th April we steamed out from Mosambique; and, the currents being in our favour, in a week reached Zanzibar. Here we experienced much hospitality from our countrymen, and especially from Dr. Seward, then acting consul and political agent for Colonel Playfair.

Dr. Seward was very doubtful if we could reach Bombay before what is called the break of the monsoon took place. This break occurs usually between the end of May and the 12th of June. The wind still blows from Africa to India, but with so much violence, and with such a murky atmosphere, that few or no observations for position can be taken. We were, however, at the time very anxious to dispose of the "Lady Nyassa," and, the only market we could reach being Bombay, we resolved to run the risk of getting there before the stormy period commenced; and, after taking fourteen tons of coal on board, we started on the 30th April from Zanzibar.

Our complement consisted of seven native Zambesians, two boys, and four Europeans; namely, one stoker, one sailor, one carpenter, whose names have been already mentioned, and Dr. Livingstone, as navigator. The "Lady Nyassa" had shown herself to be a good sea-boat. The natives had proved themselves capital sailors, though before volunteering not one of them had ever seen the sea. They were not picked men, but, on paying a dozen whom we had in our employment for fifteen months, they were taken at random from several hundreds who offered to accompany us. Their wages were ten shillings per mensem, and it was curious to observe, that so eager were they to do their duty, that only one of them lay down from sea-sickness during the whole voyage. They took in and set sail very cleverly in a short time, and would climb out along a boom, reeve a rope through the block, and come back with the rope in their teeth, though at each lurch the performer was dipped in the sea. The sailor and carpenter, though anxious to do their utmost, had a week's severe illness each, and were unfit for duty.

It is pleasant enough to take the wheel for an hour or two, or even for a watch, but when it comes to be for every alternate four hours, it is utterly wearisome. We set our black men to steer, showing them which arm of the compass needle was to be kept towards the vessel's head, and soon three of them could manage very well, and they only needed watching. In going up the East Coast to take advantage of the current of one hundred miles a day, we would fain have gone into the Juba or Webbe River, the mouth of which is only 15 minutes south of the line, but we were too shorthanded. We passed up to about ten degrees north of the Equator, and then steamed out from the coast. Here Maury's wind chart showed that the calm-belt had long been passed, but we were in it still; and, instead of a current carrying us north, we had a contrary current which bore us every day four miles to the south. We steamed as long as we dared, knowing as we did that we must use the engines on the coast of India.

After losing many days tossing on the silent sea, with innumerable dolphins, flying-fish, and sharks around us, we had six days of strong breezes, then calms again tried our patience; and the near approach of that period, "the break of the monsoon," in which it was believed no boat could live, made us sometimes think our epitaph would be "Left Zanzibar on 30th April, 1864, and never more heard of." At last, in the beginning of June, the chronometers showed that we were near the Indian coast. The black men believed it was true because we told them it was so, but only began to dance with joy when they saw sea-weed and serpents floating past. These serpents are peculiar to these parts, and are mentioned as poisonous in the sailing directions. We ventured to predict that we should see land next morning, and at midday the high coast hove in sight, wonderfully like Africa before the rains begin. Then a haze covered all the land, and a heavy swell beat towards it. A rock was seen, and a latitude showed it to be the Choule rock. Making that a fresh starting- point, we soon found the light-ship, and then the forest of masts loomed through the haze in Bombay harbour. We had sailed over 2500 miles.

NOTES

{1} A remedy composed of from six to eight grains of resin of jalap, the same of rhubarb, and three each of calomel and quinine, made up into four pills, with tincture of cardamoms, usually relieved all the symptoms in five or six hours. Four pills are a full dose for a man--one will suffice for a woman. They received from our men the name of "rousers," from their efficacy in rousing up even those most prostrated. When their operation is delayed, a dessert-spoonful of Epsom salts should be given. Quinine after or during the operation of the pills, in large doses every two or three hours, until deafness or cinchonism ensued, completed the cure. The only cases in which, we found ourselves completely helpless, were those in which obstinate vomiting ensued.

{2} The late Mr. Robson.

{3} In 1865, four years after these forebodings were penned, we received intelligence that they had all come to pass. Sekeletu died in the beginning of 1864--a civil war broke out about the succession to the chieftainship; a large body of those opposed to the late chief's uncle, Impololo, being regent, departed with their cattle to Lake Ngami; an insurrection by the black tribes followed; Impololo was slain, and the kingdom, of which, under an able sagacious mission, a vast deal might have been made, has suffered the usual fate of African conquests. That fate we deeply deplore; for, whatever other faults the Makololo might justly be charged with, they did not belong to the class who buy and sell each other, and the tribes who have succeeded them do.

{4} It was with sorrow that we learned by a letter from Mr. Moffat, in 1864, that poor Sekeletu was dead. As will be mentioned further on, men were sent with us to bring up more medicine. They preferred to remain on the Shire, and, as they were free men, we could do no more than try and persuade them to hasten back to their chief with iodine and other remedies. They took the parcel, but there being only two real Makololo among them, these could neither return themselves alone or force their attendants to leave a part of the country where they were independent, and could support themselves with ease. Sekeletu, however, lived long enough to receive and acknowledge goods to the value of 50 pounds, sent, in lieu of those which remained in Tette, by Robert Moffat, jun., since dead.

{5} A brother, we believe, of one who accompanied Burke and Willis in the famous but unfortunate Australian Expedition.

{6} Genesis, chap. iii., verses 21 and 23, "make coats of skins, and clothed them"--"sent him forth from the garden of Eden to till the ground" imply teaching. Vide Archbishop Whately's "History of Religious Worship." John W. Parker, West Strand, London, 1849.

{7} "In 1854 the native church at Sierra-Leone undertook to pay for their primary schools, and thereby effected a saving to the Church Missionary Society of 800 pounds per annum. In 1861 the contributions of this one section of native Christians had amounted to upwards of 10,000 pounds."--"Manual of Church Missionary Society's African Missions."

www.bookjungle.com *email: sales@bookjungle.com fax: 630-214-0564 mail: Book Jungle PO Box 2226 Champaign, IL 61825*

The Codes Of Hammurabi And Moses
W. W. Davies

QTY

The discovery of the Hammurabi Code is one of the greatest achievements of archaeology, and is of paramount interest, not only to the student of the Bible, but also to all those interested in ancient history...

Religion **ISBN:** *1-59462-338-4* Pages:132 *MSRP $12.95*

The Theory of Moral Sentiments
Adam Smith

QTY

This work from 1749. contains original theories of conscience amd moral judgment and it is the foundation for systemof morals.

Philosophy **ISBN:** *1-59462-777-0* Pages:536 *MSRP $19.95*

Jessica's First Prayer
Hesba Stretton

QTY

In a screened and secluded corner of one of the many railway-bridges which span the streets of London there could be seen a few years ago, from five o'clock every morning until half past eight, a tidily set-out coffee-stall, consisting of a trestle and board, upon which stood two large tin cans, with a small fire of charcoal burning under each so as to keep the coffee boiling during the early hours of the morning when the work-people were thronging into the city on their way to their daily toil...

Childrens **ISBN:** *1-59462-373-2* Pages:84 *MSRP $9.95*

My Life and Work
Henry Ford

QTY

Henry Ford revolutionized the world with his implementation of mass production for the Model T automobile. Gain valuable business insight into his life and work with his own auto-biography... "We have only started on our development of our country we have not as yet, with all our talk of wonderful progress, done more than scratch the surface. The progress has been wonderful enough but..."

Biographies/ **ISBN:** *1-59462-198-5* Pages:300 *MSRP $21.95*

www.bookjungle.com *email: sales@bookjungle.com fax: 630-214-0564 mail: Book Jungle PO Box 2226 Champaign, IL 61825*

The Art of Cross-Examination
Francis Wellman

QTY

I presume it is the experience of every author, after his first book is published upon an important subject, to be almost overwhelmed with a wealth of ideas and illustrations which could readily have been included in his book, and which to his own mind, at least, seem to make a second edition inevitable. Such certainly was the case with me; and when the first edition had reached its sixth impression in five months, I rejoiced to learn that it seemed to my publishers that the book had met with a sufficiently favorable reception to justify a second and considerably enlarged edition. ..

Reference   ISBN: *1-59462-647-2*   Pages:412   MSRP *$19.95*

On the Duty of Civil Disobedience
Henry David Thoreau

QTY

Thoreau wrote his famous essay, On the Duty of Civil Disobedience, as a protest against an unjust but popular war and the immoral but popular institution of slave-owning. He did more than write—he declined to pay his taxes, and was hauled off to gaol in consequence. Who can say how much this refusal of his hastened the end of the war and of slavery ?

Law   ISBN: *1-59462-747-9*   Pages:48   MSRP *$7.45*

Dream Psychology Psychoanalysis for Beginners
Sigmund Freud

QTY

Sigmund Freud, born Sigismund Schlomo Freud (May 6, 1856 - September 23, 1939), was a Jewish-Austrian neurologist and psychiatrist who co-founded the psychoanalytic school of psychology. Freud is best known for his theories of the unconscious mind, especially involving the mechanism of repression; his redefinition of sexual desire as mobile and directed towards a wide variety of objects; and his therapeutic techniques, especially his understanding of transference in the therapeutic relationship and the presumed value of dreams as sources of insight into unconscious desires.

Psychology   ISBN: *1-59462-905-6*   Pages:196   MSRP *$15.45*

The Miracle of Right Thought
Orison Swett Marden

QTY

Believe with all of your heart that you will do what you were made to do. When the mind has once formed the habit of holding cheerful, happy, prosperous pictures, it will not be easy to form the opposite habit. It does not matter how improbable or how far away this realization may see, or how dark the prospects may be, if we visualize them as best we can, as vividly as possible, hold tenaciously to them and vigorously struggle to attain them, they will gradually become actualized, realized in the life. But a desire, a longing without endeavor, a yearning abandoned or held indifferently will vanish without realization.

Self Help   ISBN: *1-59462-644-8*   Pages:360   MSRP *$25.45*

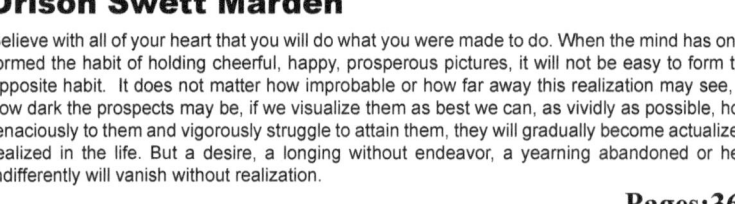
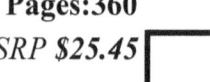

www.bookjungle.com *email: sales@bookjungle.com fax: 630-214-0564 mail: Book Jungle PO Box 2226 Champaign, IL 61825*

QTY

	Title	ISBN	Price
☐	**The Rosicrucian Cosmo-Conception Mystic Christianity** by *Max Heindel*	ISBN: *1-59462-188-8*	**$38.95**

The Rosicrucian Cosmo-conception is not dogmatic, neither does it appeal to any other authority than the reason of the student. It is: not controversial, but is: sent forth in the, hope that it may help to clear...
New Age/Religion Pages 646

☐ **Abandonment To Divine Providence** by *Jean-Pierre de Caussade* ISBN: *1-59462-228-0* **$25.95**
"The Rev. Jean Pierre de Caussade was one of the most remarkable spiritual writers of the Society of Jesus in France in the 18th Century. His death took place at Toulouse in 1751. His works have gone through many editions and have been republished...
Inspirational/Religion Pages 400

☐ **Mental Chemistry** by *Charles Haanel* ISBN: *1-59462-192-6* **$23.95**
Mental Chemistry allows the change of material conditions by combining and appropriately utilizing the power of the mind. Much like applied chemistry creates something new and unique out of careful combinations of chemicals the mastery of mental chemistry...
New Age Pages 354

☐ **The Letters of Robert Browning and Elizabeth Barret Barrett 1845-1846 vol II** ISBN: *1-59462-193-4* **$35.95**
by *Robert Browning* and *Elizabeth Barrett*
Biographies Pages 596

☐ **Gleanings In Genesis (volume I)** by *Arthur W. Pink* ISBN: *1-59462-130-6* **$27.45**
Appropriately has Genesis been termed "the seed plot of the Bible" for in it we have, in germ form, almost all of the great doctrines which are afterwards fully developed in the books of Scripture which follow...
Religion/Inspirational Pages 420

☐ **The Master Key** by *L. W. de Laurence* ISBN: *1-59462-001-6* **$30.95**
In no branch of human knowledge has there been a more lively increase of the spirit of research during the past few years than in the study of Psychology, Concentration and Mental Discipline. The requests for authentic lessons in Thought Control, Mental Discipline and... New Age/Business Pages 422

☐ **The Lesser Key Of Solomon Goetia** by *L. W. de Laurence* ISBN: *1-59462-092-X* **$9.95**
This translation of the first book of the "Lernegton" which is now for the first time made accessible to students of Talismanic Magic was done, after careful collation and edition, from numerous Ancient Manuscripts in Hebrew, Latin, and French...
New Age/Occult Pages 92

☐ **Rubaiyat Of Omar Khayyam** by *Edward Fitzgerald* ISBN:*1-59462-332-5* **$13.95**
Edward Fitzgerald, whom the world has already learned, in spite of his own efforts to remain within the shadow of anonymity, to look upon as one of the rarest poets of the century, was born at Bredfield, in Suffolk, on the 31st of March, 1809. He was the third son of John Purcell... Music Pages 172

☐ **Ancient Law** by *Henry Maine* ISBN: *1-59462-128-4* **$29.95**
The chief object of the following pages is to indicate some of the earliest ideas of mankind, as they are reflected in Ancient Law, and to point out the relation of those ideas to modern thought.
Religiom/History Pages 452

☐ **Far-Away Stories** by *William J. Locke* ISBN: *1-59462-129-2* **$19.45**
"Good wine needs no bush, but a collection of mixed vintages does. And this book is just such a collection. Some of the stories I do not want to remain buried for ever in the museum files of dead magazine-numbers an author's not unpardonable vanity..."
Fiction Pages 272

☐ **Life of David Crockett** by *David Crockett* ISBN: *1-59462-250-7* **$27.45**
"Colonel David Crockett was one of the most remarkable men of the times in which he lived. Born in humble life, but gifted with a strong will, an indomitable courage, and unremitting perseverance...
Biographies/New Age Pages 424

☐ **Lip-Reading** by *Edward Nitchie* ISBN: *1-59462-206-X* **$25.95**
Edward B. Nitchie, founder of the New York School for the Hard of Hearing, now the Nitchie School of Lip-Reading, Inc, wrote "LIP-READING Principles and Practice". The development and perfecting of this meritorious work on lip-reading was an undertaking...
How-to Pages 400

☐ **A Handbook of Suggestive Therapeutics, Applied Hypnotism, Psychic Science** ISBN: *1-59462-214-0* **$24.95**
by *Henry Munro*
Health/New Age/Health/Self-help Pages 376

☐ **A Doll's House: and Two Other Plays** by *Henrik Ibsen* ISBN: *1-59462-112-8* **$19.95**
Henrik Ibsen created this classic when in revolutionary 1848 Rome. Introducing some striking concepts in playwriting for the realist genre, this play has been studied the world over.
Fiction/Classics/Plays 308

☐ **The Light of Asia** by *sir Edwin Arnold* ISBN: *1-59462-204-3* **$13.95**
In this poetic masterpiece, Edwin Arnold describes the life and teachings of Buddha. The man who was to become known as Buddha to the world was born as Prince Gautama of India but he rejected the worldly riches and abandoned the reigns of power when... Religion/History/Biographies Pages 170

☐ **The Complete Works of Guy de Maupassant** by *Guy de Maupassant* ISBN: *1-59462-157-8* **$16.95**
"For days and days, nights and nights, I had dreamed of that first kiss which was to consecrate our engagement, and I knew not on what spot I should put my lips..."
Fiction/Classics Pages 240

☐ **The Art of Cross-Examination** by *Francis L. Wellman* ISBN: *1-59462-309-0* **$26.95**
Written by a renowned trial lawyer, Wellman imparts his experience and uses case studies to explain how to use psychology to extract desired information through questioning.
How-to/Science/Reference Pages 408

☐ **Answered or Unanswered?** by *Louisa Vaughan* ISBN: *1-59462-248-5* **$10.95**
Miracles of Faith in China
Religion Pages 112

☐ **The Edinburgh Lectures on Mental Science (1909)** by *Thomas* ISBN: *1-59462-008-3* **$11.95**
This book contains the substance of a course of lectures recently given by the writer in the Queen Street Hail, Edinburgh. Its purpose is to indicate the Natural Principles governing the relation between Mental Action and Material Conditions...
New Age/Psychology Pages 148

☐ **Ayesha** by *H. Rider Haggard* ISBN: *1-59462-301-5* **$24.95**
Verily and indeed it is the unexpected that happens! Probably if there was one person upon the earth from whom the Editor of this, and of a certain previous history, did not expect to hear again...
Classics Pages 380

☐ **Ayala's Angel** by *Anthony Trollope* ISBN: *1-59462-352-X* **$29.95**
The two girls were both pretty, but Lucy who was twenty-one who supposed to be simple and comparatively unattractive, whereas Ayala was credited, as her Bombwhat romantic name might show, with poetic charm and a taste for romance. Ayala when her father died was nineteen... Fiction Pages 484

☐ **The American Commonwealth** by *James Bryce* ISBN: *1-59462-286-8* **$34.45**
An interpretation of American democratic political theory. It examines political mechanics and society from the perspective of Scotsman James Bryce
Politics Pages 572

☐ **Stories of the Pilgrims** by *Margaret P. Pumphrey* ISBN: *1-59462-116-0* **$17.95**
This book explores pilgrims religious oppression in England as well as their escape to Holland and eventual crossing to America on the Mayflower, and their early days in New England...
History Pages 268

www.bookjungle.com *email: sales@bookjungle.com fax:* 630-214-0564 *mail:* Book Jungle PO Box 2226 Champaign, IL 61825

Book	ISBN	Price	QTY
The Fasting Cure by *Sinclair Upton* In the Cosmopolitan Magazine for May, 1910, and in the Contemporary Review (London) for April, 1910, I published an article dealing with my experiences in fasting. I have written a great many magazine articles, but never one which attracted so much attention... *New Age/Self Help/Health Pages 164*	**ISBN:** *1-59462-222-1*	**$13.95**	
Hebrew Astrology by *Sepharial* In these days of advanced thinking it is a matter of common observation that we have left many of the old landmarks behind and that we are now pressing forward to greater heights and to a wider horizon than that which represented the mind-content of our progenitors... *Astrology Pages 144*	**ISBN:** *1-59462-308-2*	**$13.45**	
Thought Vibration or The Law of Attraction in the Thought World by *William Walker Atkinson* *Psychology/Religion Pages 144*	**ISBN:** *1-59462-127-6*	**$12.95**	
Optimism by *Helen Keller* Helen Keller was blind, deaf, and mute since 19 months old, yet famously learned how to overcome these handicaps, communicate with the world, and spread her lectures promoting optimism. An inspiring read for everyone... *Biographies/Inspirational Pages 84*	**ISBN:** *1-59462-108-X*	**$15.95**	
Sara Crewe by *Frances Burnett* In the first place, Miss Minchin lived in London. Her home was a large, dull, tall one, in a large, dull square, where all the houses were alike, and all the sparrows were alike, and where all the door-knockers made the same heavy sound... *Childrens/Classic Pages 88*	**ISBN:** *1-59462-360-0*	**$9.45**	
The Autobiography of Benjamin Franklin by *Benjamin Franklin* The Autobiography of Benjamin Franklin has probably been more extensively read than any other American historical work, and no other book of its kind has had such ups and downs of fortune. Franklin lived for many years in England, where he was agent... *Biographies/History Pages 332*	**ISBN:** *1-59462-135-7*	**$24.95**	

Name	
Email	
Telephone	
Address	
City, State ZIP	

☐ Credit Card   ☐ Check / Money Order

Credit Card Number	
Expiration Date	
Signature	

Please Mail to: Book Jungle
　　　　　　　　　PO Box 2226
　　　　　　　　　Champaign, IL 61825
or Fax to:　　　　630-214-0564

ORDERING INFORMATION

web: *www.bookjungle.com*
email: *sales@bookjungle.com*
fax: *630-214-0564*
mail: *Book Jungle PO Box 2226 Champaign, IL 61825*
or PayPal *to sales@bookjungle.com*

Please contact us for bulk discounts

DIRECT-ORDER TERMS

20% Discount if You Order Two or More Books
Free Domestic Shipping!
Accepted: Master Card, Visa, Discover, American Express

www.ingramcontent.com/pod-product-compliance
Lightning Source LLC
Chambersburg PA
CBHW081209230426
43666CB00015B/2689